Mike McClintock's

Home Sense

Care & Repair
A·L·M·A·N·A·C

No. 3149
$29.95

Mike McClintock's

Home Sense

Care & Repair
A·L·M·A·N·A·C

TAB BOOKS Inc.
Blue Ridge Summit, PA

FIRST EDITION
THIRD PRINTING

Library of Congress Cataloging in Publication Data

McClintock, Michael, 1945-
    Mike McClintock's home sense care and repair almanac / by Mike
McClintock.
        p.   cm.
    Includes index.
    ISBN 0-8306-0449-9   ISBN 0-8306-0349-2 (pbk.)
    1. Dwellings—Maintenance and repair—Amateurs' manuals. 2. Home
ownership. I. Title. II. Title: Home sense care and repair
almanac.
TH4817.3.M343   1989
643'.7—dc19   88-37564
                                                          CIP

TAB BOOKS Inc. offers software for sale. For information and a catalog,
please contact TAB Software Department, Blue Ridge Summit, PA 17294-0850.

Questions regarding the content of this book
should be addressed to:

    Reader Inquiry Branch
    TAB BOOKS Inc.
    Blue Ridge Summit, PA 17294-0214

Acquisitions Editor: Kim Tabor
Technical Editor: Joanne M. Slike
Katherine Brown: Production
Book Design: Jaclyn B. Saunders

Cover photograph by George Ancona, Inc.

Contents

TOOLS AND MATERIALS

CONTRACTS AND CONTRACTORS

NEW CONSTRUCTION

HOME IMPROVEMENT PRIMER

IMPROVEMENTS AND REPAIRS INSIDE

IMPROVEMENTS AND REPAIRS OUTSIDE

Preface

FINDING, FINANCING, FIXING, IMPROVING, AND MANAGING A PLACE TO live—safely and without undue risk from environmental hazards, or financial loss—is not something you do very often. If you did, you would learn by experience, and get pretty good at it.

That might be a painful way to learn. But eventually you would know what to look for when buying a house, recognize the real estate deals that are, in fact, too good to be true, deal successfully with contractors, select energy efficient appliances, write your own home improvement contracts, and a lot more.

You would know from your own records that all those service contracts to cover repairs on washers, dryers, and lawn mowers turned out to be money-makers for the manufacturers, and rotten deals for you. You would be able to save a bundle making some repairs and improvements yourself, install your own phone system, improve your home security without buying expensive electronic systems, keep costs and schedules under control on larger projects you paid professionals to handle. You would be aware of housing and home improvement trends, innovate insulation systems, the newest building materials, the most recent information on radon, and water quality.

After a while you would have a lot of the answers, and you wouldn't need a book like this. But you probably have a few other things to occupy your time—like a job, for instance.

The Home Sense Almanac certainly doesn't have all the answers. No book, person, trade group, or professional society does. But *Home Sense* covers a lot of ground for consumers who need unbiased, straightforward information—workable advice based on experience.

That's what the *Home Sense Almanac* is about—covering design and construction, repairs and improvements, real estate, and all kinds of consumer information that can save you time and money, and make life at the place where you live more enjoyable and rewarding.

And since life at your home, like life at my house, might not be 100 percent business (when a family of raccoons climbs through the screen door on the porch and tosses the wicker couch cushions in search of a pizza crust one of the boys parked there, for instance), *Home Sense* includes some of the real-life craziness all of us have to cope with—and some of the magic moments that become more amusing in hindsight.

The *Home Sense Almanac* won't swamp you with statistics, technical formulas, and incomprehensible trade talk. It doesn't assume that you are a perfect computer, a master builder, or even a do-it-yourselfer. It assumes that you are a person who could use some sensible, straightforward, and most importantly, usable information.

To that end, the information in *Home Sense* is compartmentalized—set out in readable, bite-size pieces that don't try to tell you everything there is to know about a particular subject. But they do include the key points, the most important information you need to make decisions, and perspective on important issues. And you'll find the crucial, and sometimes surprising, details that can push a close call one way or the other, backed up with a particular kind of common sense: Home Sense.

Planning *and* Design Options

CONSTRUCTION METHODS AND HOME STYLES

Government Blueprints
Energy-Efficient House Plans from Uncle Sam

House plans are available from many sources. Architects, the most obvious source, provide plans that combine their professional preferences for materials and designs, your particular needs, and constraints imposed by the building site. This service can cost several thousand dollars.

Less expensive blueprints (in the $50 to $100 range) are available from plan companies. Such firms do not construct a one-of-a-kind design for their clients. Instead, they take the scattershot approach and offer hundreds of different styles and sizes, and sometimes hundreds more with only slight variations from a basic model.

Between these two options is a lesser-known source of modestly priced, well-thought-out house plans—the Department of Housing and Urban Development (HUD). In 1980, HUD started a project called the "Building Value Into Housing Program." Initially, 19 individuals and organizations were asked to design homes and provide plans—a complete set of construction blueprints—based on a concept known as value engineering.

The premise is to increase construction quality without increasing cost—a difficult task. But some of the, by now, over 50 plans in the program, have met the goals of value engineering by following some very level-headed guidelines.

The most successful plan, accounting for 15 percent of HUD plan sales, is the Brookhaven House. Ralph Jones, an architect and researcher at Brookhaven National Laboratory who participated in the Department of Energy funded design process, describes it as "a house that successfully combines traditional appearance and modern energy-efficiency."

The Brookhaven House looks like many homes in the Northeast, and has been built in about 15 states so far. It has a 45-degree roof pitch and clapboard siding—"the kind of house you see when driving through Vermont and New Hampshire," says Jones. But the house also incorporates passive solar features including a greenhouse, and materials such as brick walls and quarry tile floors that store heat during the day, then radiate it into the living space at night.

Opposite: This unusual view (looking straight up) into a custom-built timber frame shows how the web of beefy oak beams can create an elegant, soaring, open space. This hall is the work of Ed Levin, a premier timber-framer from Canaan, New Hampshire who makes curved railings, beams, and an entire house frame like a piece of fine furniture.

BROOKHAVEN HOUSE

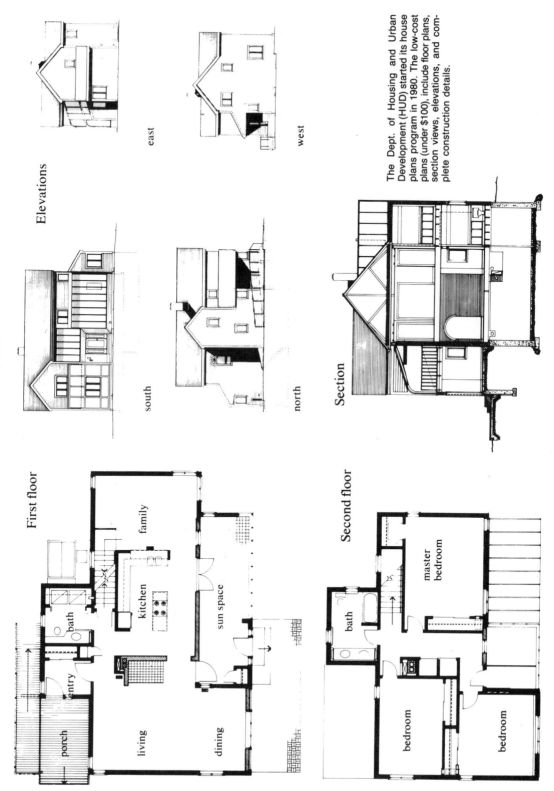

Elevations

east

west

south

north

First floor

porch

entry

bath

living

kitchen

family

dining

sun space

Second floor

bath

bedroom

master bedroom

bedroom

Section

The Dept. of Housing and Urban Development (HUD) started its house plans program in 1980. The low-cost plans (under $100), include floor plans, section views, elevations, and complete construction details.

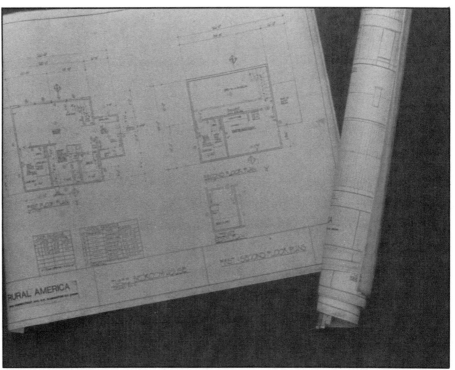

The most successful HUD plan by far is the Brookhaven House, named by its designers at the Brookhaven National Laboratory.

The 2,000-square-foot house uses about 200 gallons of heating oil a year, although other fuel sources can be used, too. That translates to annual, northeast-region heating costs of about $200 a year. In fact, one of the design problems was locating a heating system small enough to do the job efficiently.

At the heart of the building's energy efficiency is the principle of mass gain. This is a natural process in which certain building materials absorb, temporarily store, and then give off heat. Some materials do this more efficiently than others. Generally, thermal storage efficiency increases with material density. In other words, a sack of cement works better than a sack of feathers.

Mass-gain systems have spawned some exotic and downright peculiar-looking homes in which 50 gallon oil drums filled with water (the heat storage medium) line the walls, or gas-loaded cylinders hang in the greenhouse. These configurations can make a home look suspiciously like a chemical factory.

While some of the innovative storage systems are efficient, they remain architectural gadgets, difficult to build in, much less integrate, with a human-scale, residential house design. Such thermal tricks, no matter how technically successful, were screened out by three of the design premises used for the Brookhaven plan.

First, the overall design had to be aesthetically acceptable to a broad spectrum of potential owners, which rules out oil drums. Second, the building technology had to be widely understood and code-approved. Third, all building materials, including mechanical equipment used in plumbing, heating, and electrical systems, had to be widely available, "off the shelf" goods.

In the Brookhaven plan energy-efficient features are built in because they are part of the house, (really, the house itself). For example, heat from the sun is captured in the greenhouse and stored in the surrounding masonry. The system works on a natural, 5-hour cycle, without huge beds of gravel or tubs of water that use potential living space for heat storage space.

In the evening, when the furnace in a typical house would begin its most active cycle, the masonry begins to release stored heat into the living area. This continues for about 5 hours in the Brookhaven House—enough time to get into bed, under the covers, and fall asleep. The system works so well that no mechanically made heat (in other words, from a furnace) is ducted or piped to the second floor. Instead, fans circulate warm air through the house.

The advantages of mass-gain work in conjunction with other passive, or built-in features. For instance, this plan incorporates 2-by-6-inch wall studs set 24 inches on center, instead of more conventional 2-by-4-inch studs 16 inches on center. The structural change is an even trade financially, but makes room for more insulation in the walls. The hefty "thermal envelope" helps to conserve the solar gain.

The Brookhaven House plan is now in the public domain. Plans are sold through several magazines, and through HUD. Other plans in the HUD catalog include earth-sheltered designs, steel-frame structures, on-site precast concrete buildings, poured adobe construction, flexible truss frames, and other interesting types of building systems. Sizes range from small starter homes under 1,000 square feet to homes over 2,000 square feet. At least some are suitable for any region in the country.

All of the plans are outlined briefly in the Blueprint Catalog, available free from HUD USER.[1] The catalog includes ordering information for blueprints, which range from $15 for small, simple homes, to $55 for large homes.

The plans qualify as working drawings. That means they are detailed enough to submit to contractors for bids, and to building departments for a building permit. The blueprints are comprehensive, running 12 to 15, 24-by-36-inch sheets for larger homes.

One drawback is that material specifications—a precise listing of materials including manufacturer, model number, and such—is not included. Brookhaven designers, working on a government-subsidized program, thought it inadvisable to single out one firm over another, since, in many cases, several firms can supply materials of approximately the same quality and price. And even on a private architect's plans, it is common to reflect this condition by listing a specific product followed by the phrase "or equal."

Plans for the "Brookhaven House," designed at the Brookhaven National Laboratory[2] are the same ones drawn up for the original demonstration house, formerly open to the public, which still stands on the Brookhaven grounds. Visitors can still make an appointment to view it, and check on some of the construction details, but only from the outside. It is currently occupied by a Brookhaven scientist and family who have very low heating bills.

---

[1]HUD USER, P.O. Box 280, Germantown, MD 20874
[2]Brookhaven Ntl. Laboratory, Public Relations Dept., Upton, NY 11973

Timber-Frame Houses
Solid Houses Built the Old-Fashioned Way

Many lumber company brochures stress the efficient use of wood in modern construction. Illustrations show how a tree is sawn into many small pieces that are engineered—a key word in modern house building—into a structure. "Engineered" is a reassuring word, as though you're getting a suspension bridge instead of a simple house frame.

Proponents of this kind of minimal framing say it is efficient and economical. But more and more home buyers are choosing houses built the old-fashioned way: with fewer, much larger pieces of wood. Instead of 2 by 4s and 2 by 6s, timber-frame buildings use mammoth beams on the scale of 8 by 8 and 8 by 12 inches.

Timber framing is a very old building system. Trees hewn to specific shapes were used in construction 2,000 years ago. The buildings are durable, too. Some European timber frames, built in the fourteenth century, still stand.

Action on this timber-frame job site is about the same as it might have been centuries ago. Completely framed sections of the house, called bents, are laid on the deck, then tipped into place. A walkway suspended under a bent design called a "hammer-beam truss" will connect loft spaces at each end of the house.

Timber frames began as modifications of very basic, hut-type shelters. The structural heart of many primitive systems was called a *cruck*—a curving tree trunk split in half and turned upside down to form an inverted V-shape structure.

Over several centuries, this basic frame was refined. Slightly curved walls were straightened. Separate roof rafters were joined to the walls and to each other at the roof ridge with interlocking joints secured by large wooden pegs. Beams set parallel to the floor between angled roof rafters, called *collar ties*, were added to strengthen the structure. Smaller timbers were added within the overall frame to reinforce the building, permitting large, uninterrupted spans.

Early American timber frames reflected traditional construction techniques used in England. Some precut frames were even imported from England, foreshadowing the ready-to-assemble house kits offered by several firms today.

Initially, American colonists filled the spaces between timbers with wattle and daub, a basket weave of sticks coated with different combinations of mud and straw. But cold, wet, and windy New England winters proved too severe for this building skin, which was soon replaced by wooden clapboards.

Looking more closely, you can see how weight from the roof "steps" down this frame of interconnected A-shapes. This work, mortise-and-tenon beams and braces pinned together with wooden pegs, belongs to another one of the consummate New England timber framers—Tedd Benson, of Alstead Center, New Hampshire.

Eyeball to eyeball with a hammer-beam truss, you can see how joining beams are shaped to fit into each other. The dark spots are wooden pegs driven through the beams, then cut and sanded flush. In this kind of fine carpentry, time and care is taken to add chamfered edges, and carve classic colonial end caps on exposed beams.

Now, many custom builders and house kit companies have combined the simple, rugged, timber frame and clapboard siding with energy-efficient skins. But instead of opting for modern, low-maintenance materials such as aluminum and vinyl siding on the exterior, these high-efficiency wall panels are integrated into the traditional timber framing system.

Large panels, assembled in the shop under controlled conditions, are composed of wallboard, layers of foam insulation, vapor barriers, air-infiltration barriers, and other energy-conserving features. The panels are applied from the outside, after the structural frame is erected, and then covered with clapboards or other siding. This leaves exposed both the traditional clapboards, from the outside, and the elegant structural frame, from the inside.

Timber-frame houses are available from several sources: in some beautiful old houses that come up for sale, from small, custom-building firms, and from a variety of prefab or kit home companies. Some provide an entire, completed house. Others can provide frame-only packages, leaving everything but the heavy-duty structural work up to you and your contractor.

The key difference in timber frames available today is the joinery: the crucial, and often very intricate connections between beams. Some firms use large timbers, but connect them with nails and beam hardware, which are preformed metal plates fastened between beams. Such hardware horrifies purists.

Other builders go a big step further by using simple mortise-and-tenon connections throughout the building, pinned with one or more wooden dowels. In this method, the end of one beam capping a series of wall studs, for example, is cut to fit into a hole in the corner post. Stresses at the resulting joint do not have to depend only on nails or other fasteners.

At the upper end of the spectrum, in both cost and quality, are custom builders who use the extensive catalog of timber frame joints. Many are dazzling masterpieces of creative carpentry. One connection can include an array of angles and shapes that dovetail one piece of wood into another so that, when pinned together with oak pegs, the joint is as strong or stronger than the massive timbers adjacent to it.

In his book, *Building the Timber-Frame House* (and a follow-up, *Building the Timber-Frame Home*), Tedd Benson describes one of his first encounters with timber frames—a case of meeting the immovable object—during a job that called for tearing down part of a frame. It hung together so tenaciously that he wound up dismantling it one piece at a time.

While current trends in architectural style seem to favor twists and turns, nooks and crannies, and decorative details, timber frames revert to building basics: an elegantly simple system of massive timbers, obviously strong enough to form a safe and extremely durable living space.

Manufactured Houses

Affordable Homes for the "Puppies" of "Yuppies"

You won't find them on the cover of *Metropolitan Home* or *House and Garden*. Some say they're not very attractive. They don't come close to the cost of houses in *Architectural Digest*. (Some say that makes them very attractive.) At an average price of about $20 per square foot, less than half that of typical site-built houses, manufactured homes offer a realistic, reasonably-priced alternative for home buyers.

They used to be called "mobile homes" because the floor rested on a chassis, and the buildings were transported from factory to home site on wheels. That history is one reason these low-cost houses are not particularly upscale or trendy, despite the name change to "manufactured."

But unless housing costs stabilize in the future, which isn't about to happen, these low-cost homes are likely to provide an ever increasing share of the nation's housing, particularly for young, first-time buyers with modest incomes—houses of the future for the "puppies" of "yuppies."

Most new manufactured homes, about 70 percent, are sold to buyers under 40 with median household incomes of $20,000. Approximately 300,000 are sold each year.

What these mass-produced homes may lack in style and architectural variation, they make up for in affordability—the operative word in housing over the last decade. As interest rates, and the costs of labor, material, and land rose, the building industry suffered. Fewer and fewer potential buyers could qualify financially to buy new homes.

The industry responded with a number of measures designed to make increasingly expensive housing more affordable. Some attempts, such as "no-frills" homes stripped of appliances, trim, and other amenities, never caught on. Building smaller homes did help. The general trend of shaving room sizes didn't seem to dampen buyer enthusiasm.

But housing costs have been reduced most dramatically and consistently by factory building. Construction in a controlled factory environment free from stoppages caused by bad weather and other on-site problems, has proven to be very economical. In the last few years, in fact, while the cost per square foot of conventionally built homes continued to rise, the cost of manufactured homes decreased slightly.

Many consumers are not quite sure what makes a manufactured home different from a factory-built or prefab or modular or mobile home. The housing industry has had some difficulty sorting out the names as well. One reason is that "mobile" homes no longer exist. That term, tarnished in some minds by the image of temporary trailer parks, has been replaced by "manufactured."

Manufactured homes, complete with chassis and wheels, are transported to a building site by towing. Modular, or prefabricated, homes without wheels are carried on a truck to the building site and fixed to foundations. The distinction is a small one, however, since the Manufactured Housing Institute reports that 95 percent of manufactured homes are not moved once transported to a home site.

Also, all types of conventional and government-backed home financing programs, including Veterans Administration (VA) and Federal Housing Administration (FHA) loans, for instance, are available for manufactured homes.

Most homes do not come with tires. But, by now, almost all have at least some factory-built components, just like manufactured homes. For instance, 80 percent of new single-family construction, including many unique, custom-built homes, have *prefab roof trusses*, which are series of small boards fastened together at a factory into a low-slope triangle that frames roof and ceiling at once.

Since manufactured homes are "vehicles," if only for one trip, their shape is influenced by state highway regulations. Manufactured homes, already somewhat standardized by the constraints of factory mass production, become even more homogeneous in appearance by highway limits on length, width, and height. These conditions produce homes that are long rectangles with low-slope roofs.

A compact but open space like this could make a nice vacation home, or certainly a more than adequate starter home. But would you be as interested if the salesperson said it's a "mobile" home? These factory-built, double-wide units are still a good deal, averaging about $20 a square foot. But now they're called "manufactured" homes.

Highway regulations vary from state to state. But most manufactured homes are built in 14-foot-wide sections in lengths up to 80 feet. Actually, about 4 feet are used for the towing rig so that the living space in a so-called 80-footer is 76 feet. In some western states 16-foot-wide sections can be transported. To be certain, check with the retailer and state highway department.

While 14 feet might seem more like an apartment than house width, single units can be combined to form multi-section manufactured homes 28 by 76 feet with 2,128 square feet. By mixing and matching basic components, a great variety of floor plans are possible. And, as is the case with other types of homes, construction quality and the number of amenities also vary greatly. Stated simply, you get what you pay for, starting from about $12,000, to $14,000, on up to $50,000 and more for the home alone, without land.

Since manufactured homes are built in a factory and trucked to the site, their width is limited by laws governing vehicle size on highways. But by building individual units with low-slope roofs, joining them at the ridge and removing the common wall, manufactured spaces rival the open feeling of site-built homes.

While chic upscale houses and apartments win most of the awards, manufactured homes come in last in price—an appealing position for many buyers.

◆

Cordwood Masonry Construction
Building Houses from Firewood

Building homes out of logs is an old idea that has become increasingly popular. Building homes out of short lengths of logs stacked up like long rows of firewood and held together with mortar is also an old idea. But not many people have found out about this other form of log home building called cordwood construction.

The unusual, practical, low-cost and traditional building system—it probably was first brought to North America by the Vikings—consists of short lengths (about 16 inches) of dry, hardwood logs stacked more loosely than they would settle naturally in a pile

This partially earth-sheltered home near the Canadian border combines timber frames and walls of cordwood masonry. Random widths of hardwood logs about 10 inches long are mortared together. The dark circles are bottle ends placed in the wall for decoration and added light.

of firewood, and tied together into a very solid wall like bricks or concrete blocks with mortar mix. The short logs are stacked with the ends forming the inside and outside wall surfaces.

Cordwood construction, also called stackwall, probably grew out of the very basic shelter offered by a large stack of firewood. That theory is subscribed to by several cordwood builders, including Jack Henstridge, an experienced Canadian cordwood designer and builder.

Henstridge, who has built many cordwood homes, a restaurant for $16 a square foot, and other buildings in a rugged, rural section of New Brunswick, is also one of the few chroniclers of cordwood history. He thinks the system may be about 1,000 years old, and that it started as a commonsense extension of the shelter provided by a large stack of logs waiting to be fed into an open fire. He says it would have been a logical next step for primitive man to stuff mud and clay between the gaps in the stack of logs to keep out the wind, and, at some point, to lay branches from one stack to another to protect themselves and the precious fire that kept them warm.

But Henstridge has done more than imagine the thoughts in some Viking's head. He examined structures at a Viking base called L'Anse de Mere Meadows in northern Newfoundland. He says the remains of rounded shelters there appear to be made from stacked logs that were packed with clay and then fired into a hard, weather-resistant material by lighting a bonfire inside the structure.

Construction methods are no longer this drastic. But cordwood is still predominantly a rural building method—even though it is just as practical a choice as a more recognizable log cabin for a vacation home. But there are a few monumental cordwood homes on the scale of an estate in Westchester County, New York that includes a cordwood "guest house" complete with several bedrooms, baths, a theater, and other rooms. This elegant, 1929 building is still structurally solid as a rock. In fact, it's exterior walls look from a distance like mortared stone since many of the logs used in its walls were squared off like railroad ties.

Several characteristics of cordwood construction have made it particularly attractive to owner-builders. It's not a difficult craft to learn, for one thing. It makes sense, and follows the laws of gravity, balance, and symmetry that are obvious to almost everyone regardless of construction experience. For another, it is a very low-cost and energy-efficient building system. Cost per square foot is frequently in the range of $15 to $25 and can be reduced even further if builders use some of the timber on their site to make the house.

Without a doubt, there is a beautiful, economical logic to the idea of felling trees to make a clearing for your house, and then using the trees to build it.

The thick walls of a cordwood house are strong enough to support large ceiling joist and rafters—big enough to create dramatic spans of 20 feet or more. And they are energy efficient. Rob Roy, a cordwood builder who also teaches the trade in upstate New York, heated his first cordwood home near the Canadian border with three cords of firewood a year.

This economy is due in large part to massive cordwood walls, which have the capacity to store heat during the day and radiate much of it back into the living space at night. In such cold climates modern cordwood construction includes a center strip of insulation laid in a center cavity between a two-part mortar bed, one facing inside and one outside. This greatly reduces temperature transfer in the masonry part of the wall.

There are several basic ways to build with cordwood. The three most common are: conventional, square-cornered buildings with interlaced cordwood corners; unconventional, round-walled buildings; and a combination of cordwood and traditional

Cordwood walls can be built in many ways. Rob Roy, who teaches the system in the small town of West Chazy in northern New York State, heats his cordwood house with only three cords of firewood. The massive walls soak up heat from the stove (and the sun) during the day, then radiate it back into the living space at night.

timber-frame construction in which the building skeleton is made of large, widely-spaced timbers (typical barn construction). The spaces between the timbers are filled in with cordwood masonry.

The overall texture of a cordwood building is as variable as the shape, color, and texture of the logs you use. Some cordwood builders create fantastic patterns mounting huge 16-inch-diameter log sections in combinations with 2- and 3-inch logs. Some like square ends, or a pattern created by using round logs and milled logs together.

In a typical project, dried hardwood logs are laid in a bed of mortar over a concrete foundation. After adding more mortar to fill up the voids between the logs, a second log layer is positioned offset from the first row in the same way that bricks are offset to span joints in the previous layer. In cold climates two narrower mortar beds are laid—one several inches wide up to the exterior face of the wall and another along the interior. The cavity between the two beds is normally filled with strips of fiberglass insulation laid over the logs in each course.

The logs themselves offer good thermal protection—about an R-20 insulation value in a 16-inch-thick cordwood wall, compared to an R-12 or R-13 with 3½ inches of fiberglass insulation in a conventional frame wall. This, plus the storage and radiating capacity, a phenomenon called *mass gain* that is starting to be recognized by some state building codes, makes living space in a cordwood home energy-efficient year round, and surprisingly snug in even the coldest winter weather.

Information on cordwood can be difficult to locate. But one good source is the Earthwood Building School,[3] Rob Roy's workshop, home and teaching center.

Affordable Kit Homes
Some of the Best Buys Come in a Box

Young homebuyers today can dream that they will have a house like the Keatons' on ''Family Ties'' or the Huxtables' on ''The Cosby Show''—if they ever could afford it. Fifty years ago, young homebuyers could dream of a house like the one where Andy Hardy lived in a popular series of films. But when the people who watched those movies went house hunting, a lot of them could afford their picture of the American home.

Back then, some of the best deals could be found in the Sears Book of Modern Homes, which advertised completely precut kit houses. Over 100,000 were sold between 1908 and 1940, thanks to a businessman who didn't do what he was supposed to do.

Frank W. Kushel, the manager of Sears' china department, was assigned to close down Sears' unprofitable building materials mail-order division. Instead, he produced a catalog of 22 precut houses priced from $650 to $2,500. The price included all materials aside from the foundation—right down to the nails.

Many still exist today when there are hundreds of kit home manufacturers, and the idea of buying a home in precut pieces is no longer novel. Prior to World War

---

[3]Earthwood Building School, RR1, Box 105, West Chazy, NY 12992

$1,400.00 Builds This Modern Eight-Room House

OUR FREE BUILDING PLANS, SPECIFICATIONS AND BILL OF MATERIALS MAKE THIS LOW COST POSSIBLE.

OUR WAY OF GIVING THESE PLANS FREE IS EXPLAINED ON PAGE 2.

MODERN HOME No. 24

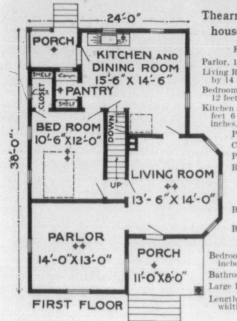

FIRST FLOOR

The arrangement of this house is as follows:

FIRST FLOOR.

Parlor, 14 feet by 13 feet.

Living Room, 13 feet 6 inches by 14 feet.

Bedroom, 10 feet 6 inches by 12 feet.

Kitchen and Dining Room, 15 feet 6 inches by 14 feet 6 inches.

Pantry.

Closet.

Porch, 11 feet by 8 feet.

Rear Porch, 8 feet by 7 feet.

SECOND FLOOR.

Bedroom, 14 feet by 13 feet.

Bedroom, 13 feet 6 inches by 11 feet 6 inches.

Bedroom, 7 feet by 8 feet 6 inches.

Bathroom.

Large Hall.

Length of building, 38 feet; width of building, 29 feet.

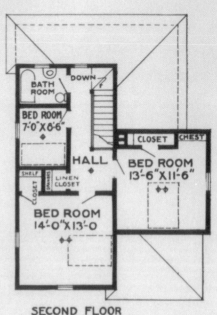

SECOND FLOOR

II however, Sears had what people wanted—homes where good things happened, where kids as bright-eyed and happily hyperactive as Andy (played by Mickey Rooney) lived, supervised by parents like white-haired Judge James Hardy who was stern but fair.

At first, the houses were differentiated with impersonal, utilitarian tags: Modern Home No. 24, Modern Home No. 259. But number gave way to names: The Melrose, The Brookside, The Kismet, The Washington (and The Martha Washington), The Brookwood, The Ferndale, and dozens of others with porches and pantries and lots of detailing. All told there were over 450 models to choose from, representing every twist on mainstream American architecture.

The complete collection of precut Sears homes is recorded in a fascinating book called *Houses By Mail,* by Katherine Cole Stevenson and H. Ward Jandl (The Preservation Press). It reproduces many original catalog pages and provides an illustration and floor plan of every model.

The variety was one reason for Sears' success with kit homes. Affordability was another. In 1918, Modern Home No. 102, The Magnolia, sold for $5,140. It was the most elaborate model ever offered—a mini Mount Vernon with eight rooms, two-and-a-half baths, second floor roof terraces, a side porte-cochere and about 3,000 interior square feet tucked behind a massive, two-story, entrance portico. It was grand. And it was a steal.

But in the early 1900s, before the widespread use of power tools, houses that arrived on site in premeasured, precut pieces also saved a lot of construction time, particularly time with a handsaw. Many buyers subcontracted the excavation and masonry work, then started picking through the 25 to 30 tons of materials that were shipped nationwide in one or two railroad boxcars and trucked to the building site.

Although business wasn't always booming, by 1930 Sears had 48 sales offices east of the Mississippi and a new plant in Newark, NJ. However, only a few years after the stock market crash (the first one—in 1929), Sears closed down the department.

In 1935 Sears tried a pared-down version of the operation, farming out the fabrication business to a Chicago building firm, and foregoing auxiliary services such as financing and construction supervision. The new homes had plywood walls over steel frames. But despite some success initially, Sears closed its precut home business for good 4 years later.

Sears may have been ahead of its time with precut houses, or just unlucky to have over $10 million in mortgages outstanding during the depression when many debts went unpaid. In any case, the precut home field today is filled with firms making every conceivable type of house from tiny vacation cabins to palatial estates.

Precut kit homes are still a good deal compared to typical, conventionally built houses, which hover around $100,000 nationally, and considerably higher within commuting distance of many major cities. No one is making a house like The Magnolia for $5,000. But some basic shell kits cost only $10 a square foot, while more complete

Opposite: Today, Sears sells just about everything you can put inside a home. But they used to sell homes as well—all in kit form. Their catalog included many styles of precut kit houses at very reasonable prices. Over 100,000 were sold between 1908 and 1940. As an incentive, blueprints, specifications, and a bill of materials were offered free.

packages including the structural frame plus sheathing, windows, and doors are $15 to $25 per foot.

At the upscale end of the spectrum there are expansive homes with imported cabinetry, select cedar decking, and other pricey details. They may cost $100 a foot— that's $200,000 to $250,000 without land or excavation or foundation or utility connections or mechanical systems.

A good way to preview these homes is to look at ads in shelter magazines or a book that describes a lot of homes from many manufacturers, such as *The Best Kit Homes* by Joanna Wissinger (Rodale Press). Once you narrow your choices you can spend the $5 or $10 for a more detailed picture in a presentation portfolio offered by most firms.

Many companies offer dozens of models, and allow you to tinker with the basic floor plan. But the biggest advantage of a kit home may be that it reduces the number of surprises that are part of building a house from scratch. This makes them a good choice for first-time buyers.

There are hundreds of log home companies making everything from vacation cabins to mansions. Like Timber Log Homes, a Connecticut company, most firms machine their raw logs into standard sizes, usually with some interlocking feature such as a sealed tongue-and-groove. This eliminates the need for chinking between seams, and still keeps out the weather.

In most cases, you can nail down a delivery date and estimate very accurately when the house will be ready for occupancy. Since the pieces are cut indoors in a factory, weather is less of a factor, and it is somewhat easier to ensure consistency than it is putting the house together one stick at a time out in the field.

The Bungalow
America's Classic Cottage Architecture

Some look like small summer cabins painted white with aquamarine or robin's-egg-blue trim. Others are larger, year-round homes in sedate brown shakes with two or three bedrooms upstairs, deep overhangs, and an inviting front porch—a fine spot to watch a high school band in the July 4th parade down Main Street. Most look like a friendly and comfortable place for a family. Many are at least 40 years old, or twice that, and may be seedy around the edges now, but surprisingly solid.

Components of the bungalow style are carried on in many modern designs. This Pole House Kit of California home includes several bungalow basics: functional design, harmony with nature, extensive use of wood, and fully extended porch roofs. Ample, low-slope overhangs around the house display exposed rafter tails, showing the structure.

The style flourished first in sunny, simple, modest, middle-class, pre-glitzy California—a perfect house for Peg and Babs and Junior on "The Life of Riley"—then swept the country. The theme was functionalism and harmony with nature, executed in wood shakes, stucco, and field stone. The roof extended fully over the front porch, and often was supported by distinctive trapezoidal columns, which were thick on the bottom, square, and thinner toward the top. Heavy, comfortable, low-slope overhangs around the house featured exposed rafter tails, sometimes extended into a vine-covered pergola.

Designed by a team for the Dallas Exposition of the National Association of Home Builders, this "show" house displays how other bungalow details can be updated. Here, wide steps and heavy columns lead to a "porch" that is airlocked for energy efficiency with a sunspace. Its thin frame mirrors the traditional bungalow "pergola"—a shaded veranda.

Let's hear it for one of the most common and most popular old house styles in America, the epitome of Craftsman architecture and Arts and Crafts detailing, the staple of Maple Avenue, Elm Street, and all the other residential streets a block off the main drag of stores and theaters and churches, glorified in some 22 songs and even a poem in *Good Housekeeping*--the bungalow.

The Craftsman bungalow was architecture almost everyone understood. With minor modifications that, except to purists, made as much sense as the original lines, bungalows were easily transplanted. More delicate and restrained lines with narrower fascia boards and shutters became colonial bungalows. Low-slope, heavier, hunkered-down versions with deep overhangs became prairie bungalows. The style made room for customized special cases with carved rafter tails, and for mass-produced yet classic craftsman-style homes sold out of the Sears Catalog.

The word "bungalow" seems to have stemmed from "bunguloues," the name given by the English to dwellings built for them in India with the deep eaves and protected porch characteristic of American bungalow style. The word was used to describe small, fashionable vacation houses on the English coast, and by the late 1800s, was firmly transplanted in America.

Closer to the climate of India than the New England states, California became the center of bungalow building. At the turn of the century Los Angeles was a city of low buildings filling up with single-family homes, executing the ultimate suburban sprawl over the next 3 decades in which the modest, affordable, comfortable California bungalow became the centerpiece of construction that put 9 out of 10 Los Angeles families in their own houses.

The functional, natural architecture complemented a climate suited for outdoor living. Conventional barriers between inside and outside space were reduced by using stone (a large rubble-stone hearth), wood (exposed, box-pattern ceiling beams), and other typically exterior materials inside the house, too. Living spaces opened up to large porches, closed in by many owners as families grew to make one or two extra bedrooms, and to patios shaded by exposed framing and trellis work.

The bungalow bible was Gustav Stickley's *The Craftsman* magazine, which regularly featured the latest houses and detailed interior woodwork of Greene & Greene, a Pasadena architectural firm of two brothers generally credited with establishing the bungalow on the West Coast, and propelling it with the Arts and Crafts Movement to widespread popularity.

The exceptional woodwork of Greene & Greene houses was a highly developed version of joinery and careful wood finishing at least theoretically within the reach of many carpenters and a growing number of do-it-yourselfers.

Two of the best known Greene & Greene bungalows, the Blacker House (1907) and the Gamble House (1908), both in Pasadena, are masterpieces of interior woodwork. Charles Greene in particular saw designs through to the end, working closely with contractors in the shop and on-site, coordinating the design of furniture, parquet patterns, carpeting, lighting fixtures—a complete environment. The most elaborate example, the Blacker House, cost $100,000 to build in 1907, which is a number with too many zeros in current dollars.

While the extravagant, exceptional bungalows served as working models to thousands of amateur arts and crafts homeowners, the Greenes built some 540 other bungalows in Pasadena alone, and practiced together for 21 years before parting company. After World War II, new interest in wooden architecture and preservation led to a rediscovery of the Greene brothers pioneering work, and numerous, if belated, awards.

What most people visualize as a bungalow is a far cry from the spacious, rambling prototypes—Greene & Greene designs with 20-by-25-foot living rooms, which seemed even larger due to oversize passageways to connecting rooms and halls. Many of those buildings evoked the same feelings as prairie architecture. Frank Lloyd Wright's horizontal, hunkered-down homes with overhanging roof lines and intricately detailed woodwork regularly shared pages of *The Craftsman* with California bungalows.

Stickley devoted a lot of space to bungalows, and much ink to their description, trying to reduce in words the synthesis of practical bungalow construction: "A house reduced to its simplest form where life can be carried on with the greatest amount of freedom; it never fails to harmonize with its surroundings."

A more carefree description was offered in a poem, composed by Burgess Johnson in 1909 and published in *Good Housekeeping*. One stanza will give you the idea (no groaning, please).

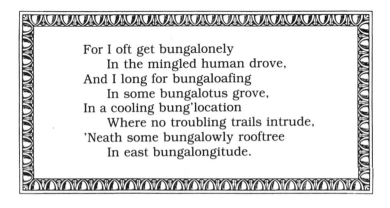

> For I oft get bungalonely
>   In the mingled human drove,
> And I long for bungaloafing
>   In some bungalotus grove,
> In a cooling bung'location
>   Where no troubling trails intrude,
> 'Neath some bungalowly rooftree
>   In east bungalongitude.

Prefab Houses
An Alternative to Expensive Custom Building

Aside from log cabins or stone huts built with materials found on the site and used in their natural states, all buildings are partially prefabricated. In the broadest sense, this means that pieces of the building, 2-by-4 wall studs, for example, are made somewhere else, then shipped to the building site for final assembly.

Gradually, larger and larger pieces of houses have been prefabricated to the point where many firms construct most of the building inside at their factory and minimize the work on-site. This makes it easier and less expensive to build. But until recently prefabrication also limited architectural variation.

When building materials and labor were cheap, it was relatively easy to custom build a house, cutting every stick of lumber to fit unique nooks and crannies. But when the postwar demand for housing made leisurely, one-of-a-kind construction impractical, mass-production techniques were used to speed production and increase the supply of housing.

The assembly-line approach reduced architectural variety but also reduced housing costs. Veterans were able to buy a small Cape or Ranch house in Levittown, New York, for instance, for about $10,000. In 1948, Levitt's crews were finishing 150 houses a week. Even though the homes were constructed with many precut, prefabricated pieces, the pieces were put together one at a time. And the homes included such labor-intensive features as plaster walls.

Today, that mass production has evolved into prefabrication. Building houses in prefabricated pieces considerably larger than individual studs, joists and rafters saves even more time and money.

Prefab roof trusses are now used in four out of five new homes. Some designs take prefabrication a step further by connecting a roof truss and floor truss with wall studs, making complete one-piece cross sections of the building frame. This system, called truss framing, saves up to 30 percent of the lumber used in conventional framing, and offers a 5-to-1 advantage in construction time over stick-built homes.

But even the word "prefabrication" evokes images of Quonset huts popping off an assembly line and raises questions for many buyers. Are prefabs too much alike, too expensive to ship from factory to site, too flimsy?

Prefab homes now come in all shapes and sizes. Some factory-built models are as elaborate and pricey as custom-built houses. But many retain factory-built economy with some added detail and style. The Regency, a quasi-Victorian prefab made by Marley Continental Homes in Roanoke, provides just over 1,400 square feet of space on two stories.

Prefabricated homes now come in all shapes and sizes. Also, many homes have only a few prefab parts, while others have only a few that are not factory assembled. Homes with different degrees of prefabrication now present consumers with a variety of alternatives to expensive, custom building, and to less expensive suburban development building that can produce rows of homes with only slight variations in floor plans and facades.

Prefabs also vary in quality and cost just like their stick-built counterparts. While they may lack the individual attention to detail of a master carpenter working under the direction of an architect, quality control is easier to handle and somewhat more reliable in the factory than on-site. For one thing, it doesn't rain or snow in factories.

Many prefab firms concentrate on "starter" homes, so called because their relatively low cost due to prefabrication and size (in the 1,000- to 2,000-square-foot range) make them ideal first homes for young, first-time buyers. Many firms also offer small vacation or second-home prefabs, even very small-scale, one-room timber-frame and log cabins with a counter for a kitchen, a closet-sized bath and a loft for sleeping.

However, there are also many firms making everything from prefab Victorian-style townhouses and huge rambling Colonials, to huge domes and completely precut pole houses that can be built on steep, rugged sites unsuitable for most housing. Costs range from close to $10 per foot for the most basic shell kits (they include only the basic structural components and exterior building skin) to well over $100 per square foot for large prefabs with every conceivable amenity.

Some prefab firms also make their homes available in different stages of completion. For instance, a timber-frame firm may offer a model three ways:
- the frame only
- the frame including set up by a factory crew
- the frame set up and closed in, including the building skin, windows, doors, and roofing, leaving all interior finishing to the owners.

This variety offers buyers who might not qualify for a mortgage on a finished house, a chance to reduce costs by contributing their sweat equity to the project.

To overcome consumer resistance to buying a house out of a plan book—like buying clothes without alterations straight off the rack—most prefab firms also allow some modifications to their basic plans. For example, to suit your building site the garage may be relocated on the opposite side of the house, or a first floor lavatory can be converted to a kitchen pantry. For many buyers starting with a complete plan that can be altered somewhat is a lot easier than starting from scratch with empty space and no floor plan at all.

Shipping still poses a problem for the industry. Houses are heavy. It costs a lot to move them, even in pieces. Large national firms usually can offer the best deals to consumers since they are likely to have three or four regional plants to reduce transportation costs. These companies often sell through dealer networks and local builders who are familiar with the prefab systems.

If you find the right house at a local prefab firm—at least in the same state as your building site—final building costs may be 15 or 20 percent below costs for the same house built one stick at a time on-site.

Marley Continental Homes

Modular sections of Marley's factory-built prefabs are trucked to site, then hoisted onto the foundation. Architectural elements, such as the front porch, are built as a unit, then fastened to the building frame. Fancy shakes and decorative moldings are new trends in formerly drab factory-built design.

Two

ADDITIONS AND REMODELING

Remodeling Trends
Projects That Pay Off

There are over 80 million single family homes in the United States. Approximately 60 percent are 15 years old or older—good candidates for a variety of remodeling and improvement projects that can make them more spacious, stylish and efficient.

According to the National Association of the Remodeling Industry (NARI), a Washington-based trade group representing approximately 4,000 remodeling companies and related groups, an aging housing stock will inevitably help the remodeling business continue to grow. Some estimate that it is already a $70 billion industry.

Increases in remodeling of 10 to 12 percent per year are due in large part to relatively moderate interest rates, and accessible financing—often through home equity loans—in amounts large enough to pay for substantial projects.

Surveys by NARI, and statistics gathered by the U.S. Department of Commerce, the Council of Better Business Bureaus, *Qualified Remodeler* magazine, and other sources, show a variety of trends in the remodeling industry, including where consumers will be spending their money, and some of the most and least popular home remodeling and improvement projects and materials.

Although many consumers are do-it-yourselfers, most remodeling money is paid to professionals. NARI estimates that there are 45,000 full-time, professional remodeling firms nationwide, which handle jobs such as re-siding, replacing windows, painting, and many other tasks on existing homes. About 60 percent are small- or medium-sized businesses, with annual sales under $500,000. There are about 10,000 large firms that handle more than a million dollars worth of remodeling business a year.

Approximately two-thirds of all professional remodelers have been in business more than 10 years; almost half have been in business 15 years or more. When you're in the market for a remodeling contractor, pay attention to age of business. Longevity is usually a positive indicator. After all, if the firm's work were shabby or their business practices less than forthright, how could they stay in business a decade or more?

On the other hand, remodeling companies as a group ranked No. 2 on the Council of Better Business Bureaus (BBB) top-ten complaint list in 1984 and 1985. However, records published in 1988 show that remodeling firms have improved in this regard. The 177 Better Business Bureaus across the country now receive more prepurchase inquiries about remodelers than any other group. But the number of complaints is falling. Remodeling firms now rank fourth on the complaint list.

BEFORE: a typical, post-war ranch-style house outside Dallas, ready for an updating renovation. The 1,650 square foot, two-bedroom, brick-facade home had been altered only once before, to convert a garage into a third bedroom. Then, Metropolitan Home and Remodeling Magazine designers joined forces to create a new space and a new look.

ALMOST AFTER: shows work in progress: two columned porticos with lattice pediments; a reoriented, more formal, and more inviting entrance; unifying, cream-color paint over the dark, multi-color brick; and a more streamlined arrangement of windows. The new raised entry patio was covered in blue tile.

Remodeling companies generated 9 percent of all BBB complaints in 1985, and 17 percent of all consumer inquiries, when over 750,000 consumers called local Better Business Bureaus to ask about a remodeling firm's reputation. Figures for 1988 from the Council of Better Business Bureaus[1] show that almost 900,000 inquiries were received.

The industry continues to combat this dubious record by instituting programs such as Remodelcare, a dispute-settling program sponsored jointly by NARI and the Council of Better Business Bureaus. Since contractors in this program agree in advance to binding arbitration of disputes, consumers are at least assured that their projects will be brought to a conclusion, and that problems will be resolved one way or another.

In 1983, NARI started a certification program for its members that may help consumers in selecting a remodeler. Certified firms have the right to display a C.R. (for Certified Remodeler) after their names. The designation, which must be reconfirmed annually, is given to NARI members who have been in business continously for at least 10 years and meet a variety of other tests. For instance, they must pass examinations, and demonstrate a history of providing accurate estimates, and writing detailed job specifications.

NARI-certified and many other remodelers will continue to do a banner business unless interest rates balloon. According to NARI, the top remodeling job categories will continue to be windows and doors, kitchens, additions and dormers, roofing, siding, and bathrooms.

Almost 25 million windows and doors will be used annually in remodeling projects, room additions, and to replace older units. Although NARI surveys steer clear of brand names, its most recent statistics show that consumers are almost equally split on the preferences for doors. Fifty-one percent prefer steel-clad doors, which tend to be more stable and, with a foam core, more energy efficient than wood doors, which are preferred by 49 percent.

Wood is the material of choice for windows, preferred by 45 percent, compared to 35 percent for aluminum, 18 percent for vinyl, and 2 percent for steel. *Practical Homeowner* magazine, which studied the costs of various remodeling projects and their return on investment, reported that the average door and replacement window project costs $9,000, and, over the long term, recovers only 43 percent of job costs.

In kitchens, the second-hottest category according to NARI, almost $8 billion will be spent annually in close to 3 million kitchen remodeling projects—half of that amount on cabinets alone. Average job cost is estimated to be $11,000, and to yield a 74-percent recovery of investment long-term. Aside from cabinets, consumers will spend the most for countertops and built-in ranges. Stainless steel sinks are favored three to one over cast porcelain.

Over $6 billion each year will go for room additions and building dormers to make attic storage space into living space. A similar amount will be spent on roofing projects, normally dictated by deterioration after anywhere from 5 to 20 years of life on an existing roof.

---

[1]Council of Better Business Bureaus, 1515 Wilson Blvd., Arlington, VA 22209

The average re-siding job, the fifth most popular remodeling project, will cost about $6,000. On homes where existing siding would be a deterrent to sale—a nice way of saying the walls are an eyesore—a re-siding job is estimated to return 100 percent of the investment in resale value; in other cases, a 61-percent return is predicted. Vinyl siding is preferred by 31 percent of consumers (in part because it is the least expensive), aluminum by 27 percent, wood by 24 percent, hardboard by 11 percent and steel by 7 percent.

NARI estimates that about $4 billion will be spent on over 4 million bathroom remodeling projects every year. About 25 percent of the jobs will be for additions, the rest for changes in existing baths. On average, a standard-size bath remodeling project will cost $3,500, and recover 71 percent of the investment long-term. Most of the money will be spent on vanities, followed by new ceramic tile installations and whirlpools. Traditional cast iron tubs still out pace their modern, one-piece acrylic and fiberglass counterparts.

The inverted U-shape of square vent windows on the exterior creates a unique headboard in the bedroom—an architectural niche. Many modern designers are adding detail, moldings, color, and character that make individual, unique spaces within a room. Translucent shades can be lowered for privacy at night.

Remodeling Traps and Solutions
Clearing the Roadblocks to Renovation

Despite the rewards of increased or improved space, less maintenance, higher resale value, and a sense of accomplishment, most people are not prepared for the inevitable trials and tribulations of renovation. Peeling away successive layers of paint, wallpaper, paneling, and molding can seem like an archaeological dig. Artifacts appear such as rusted electrical cables that don't seem to lead anywhere and densely packed bundles of fibers that could be old insulation or an animal's nest. Who knows. The overriding rule is to expect the unexpected. Pessimists may substitute Murphy's Law (if something can go wrong it will). But often what seems "wrong" is just another part of the job—something unexpected to fix or change.

For instance, while repapering a wall you discover that one area seems damp and spongy, which means removing a section of paper to discover stained plaster, which, in turn, means removing a section of plaster to discover a pinhole leak in a water supply pipe. What may start as a weekend do-it-yourself project, can mushroom to include a plasterer and a plumber, and an unexpected amount of time and money.

Here are some of the most common unexpected events that can complicate a renovation project, add to its cost, and take away from its enjoyment. Knowing what might happen physically and financially gives you a much better chance to enjoy the renovation process as well as the finished product.

▸ *The job takes longer and costs more than planned.* Unfortunately, the discouraging advice to figure twice the initial estimate for job duration is often accurate. The more complex the job, the more realistic the advice. Once work has begun, renovation projects take on an open-ended quality that should be counterbalanced with a detailed job schedule. Working with a contractor or on your own, try to divide the project into phases, each with its own time frame. Keep a running account of expenses, too—to track how much and how fast you're spending. What may seem like a dry, statistical approach to nitty-gritty construction before you start can provide valuable parameters—something you can hang your hat on—as the work progresses.

▸ *The work cannot be neatly contained in one area.* Damage control plans usually are not effective unless they are a prominent feature of the contract. Sawdust, noise, the smell of paint thinner, and the general commotion of workers coming in and out all seem to escape the immediate work area to permeate a house or apartment. To make particular places or things off-limits—a home office with sensitive computer equipment, for instance—specify them as such in the contract. This may drive the estimate up a bit, as a contractor becomes wary of spending as much time sweeping up as building.

▸ *New materials don't always work on old buildings.* Over many decades the basic 2 by 4 has been trimmed from 2 by 4 inches, called the "nominal" dimension, to $1\frac{1}{2}$ by $3\frac{1}{2}$ inches, called the "actual" dimension. For many years this shrinking stabilized at $1\frac{5}{8}$ by $3\frac{5}{8}$ inches. Obviously, adding a skinny new stud to a wall of beefy old studs can cause some trouble—maybe only a slight depression or ridge, but enough to leave open joints between molding and wallboard and paneling. Such mismatches in structural timbers can cause trouble throughout the house.

On hidden structural members these discrepancies can be "packed out." A new 2 by 4, for example, framing a new doorway in an old wall, can be thickened by nailing on a piece of ½-inch plywood so it equals the old, full-thickness 2 by 4s next to it. Obviously, this procedure is too unsightly to use on visible woodwork, such as an extension of old baseboard molding into a new addition.

To match new materials to old buildings (only two or three decades old in some cases), investigate these three possibilities: 1. use old materials from architectural salvage yards; 2. pay a premium for custom thicknesses and grades at specialty lumberyards; 3. make your own custom lumber with a machine called a thickness planer.

⇒ *Cosmetic alterations may impinge on mechanical systems.* The plumbing, heating and cooling, and electrical systems in a building are, for the most part, buried in the structure—out of sight, out of mind. But the mechanical guts of a building will quickly get your attention if you move a wall or widen a doorway, and encounter plumbing pipes and electrical lines.

And unless you or your contractor are very familiar with the structure, literally inside and out, locating these hidden obstacles before the walls are opened is just guesswork. But an experienced contractor should be able to make an informed guess, and make some allowance for the extra work or suggest a less cumbersome alternative.

In city and town settings, work on old buildings may have to conform to building or zoning regulations that control appearance, and preserve the character of the street and neighborhood. Also, countless details from wiring to plumbing may have to be upgraded, or replaced entirely, to meet modern building codes.

U.S. Forest Service

Here is a common problem for renovators and remodelers: termite and water damage above a window. Small, cosmetic jobs, such as plastering and repainting, can turn into major structural projects when you scratch the surface, and discover wet, rotted wood, and holes and tunnels made by termites in what used to be a solid wood header carrying roof loads.

It can also be a mistake to assume that existing mechanical systems can be tapped into or extended to feed a renovated attic or cellar, for instance. Electrical and heating systems have limited capacities that may already be stretched close to their limits. Certainly the demand for power by the panoply of modern appliances was not anticipated by electricians even 30 or 40 years ago. And covering an inadequate power supply with new paint and paper can be a fire hazard, necessitate tangles of extension cords, and damage appliances hooked into underpowered sockets.

Some do-it-yourselfers assume that tapping into an existing line, and adding outlets and switches in the renovated space will do the trick. But this only redistributes the power already in the house. You may have to bring in additional power, a job called *upgrading the service*, which is a more fundamental decision best made early on in the job.

▶ *Solving energy-wasting problems creates other problems.* It's easy to get information about saving energy by adding insulation, caulking, storm windows, and more. In the same breath you should consider, but don't often hear about, two potential byproducts of buttoning up a building: indoor air pollution and increased condensation. Older homes can develop severe cases of wet rot from trapped condensation, peeling paint inside and out, bad odors and damage from mildew growth in closets, bathrooms and laundry areas—all resulting from an incomplete energy retrofit. Promises of energy cost reductions based on further isolating the inside from the outside must be accompanied by a clear-headed plan to manage indoor air quality.

Computerized Kitchens
Future Appliances Will
Take Food from Shelf to Plate

Television viewers who grew up watching "The Jetsons" (or who see the reruns now), may recall how the space-age cartoon family prepared and served meals by simply pushing a few buttons. In a matter of seconds, piping hot dinners popped out of the wall and onto the table.

Such space-aged kitchen appliances that manage food from storage shelf to serving plate may be on the market by the year 2000. *Electronic House*, a magazine covering automation in the home, reports that several firms are developing these multi-task machines, called storage-delivery appliances.

In the last 50 years most advances in kitchen automation have been refinements of existing technology. For instance, adding "smart" computer chips to appliances allowed convenient timing and monitoring operations. Only one improvement has been fundamental, however. And it was invented by accident. In 1946, Dr. Percy Spencer, while experimenting with high-frequency radar waves, discovered a chocolate bar in his pocket had melted. That was the inauspicious birth of the microwave oven.

A few years ago, almost 11 million microwaves were sold, more than any type of appliance has ever sold in one year, according to the Association of Home Appliance Manufacturers. The microwave's super-fast cooking time has radically changed eating and cooking schedules, diet, cookware, kitchen layouts, and more.

The most advanced microwaves foreshadow the coming revolution in kitchen automation. Some are equipped with elaborate timers and remote sensors that feed temperature information to decision-making controls. Some can even be activated over the phone.

Appliance designers are now exploring two possible approaches to the next fundamental advance in kitchen design: robotics and storage-delivery appliances.

Robots are currently used in several industries. They have proven useful substituting for workers on heavy-duty, dangerous, or repetitive jobs. Bomb disposal units send robot crawlers with television cameras and mechanical arms to investigate suspicious packages. Automakers use robots to spot weld sections of car frames—the same spots, the same welds, again and again, which is perfect work for a robot.

Transposing this idea to the kitchen, however, could mean a very limited, robot-prepared menu. Robots might be good at dropping a "Lean Cuisine" through a slot in the microwave as you pulled in the driveway every night. But what about that sardine-onion-potato chip-mustard-ketchup sandwich you like to build on occasion? Robots may not be up to the nuances of creative cooking.

And there is the dark vision of a preprogrammed robot just slightly out of calibration. Picture a toaster-headed, spatula-handed contraption running amok in your kitchen, smothering scrambled eggs and bacon with peanut butter and jelly.

Although General Electric's Monogram series of appliances and cabinets presents a sleek, modernistic facade in the kitchen, the company has not yet produced consumer models of its multi-task, "storage-delivery" appliances. One such experimental machine is designed to pluck frozen foods from slots in a freezer, and shuttle them into an attached, preprogrammed microwave oven.

Storage-delivery appliances appear to be a more promising alternative. Jack Francis, an advanced design engineer at General Electric, says, "We've experimented with many systems to handle everything from food ordering and preparation to serving and cleaning up."

One machine was designed to pluck frozen foods from slots in a freezer, and shuttle them into an attached microwave oven. Another included a dishwasher built into a dining table.

But the designs most likely to reach the market will call for some human involvement. Francis says, "During the week, many two-career households require a minimum amount of time on food preparation and cleanup. But the same people often want to take over on weekends, preparing meals from scratch."

No single system seems to satisfy both needs. Also, an all-in-one appliance including refrigerator-freezer, microwave, and dishwasher, would tie consumers to the machine. In order to take advantage of all the conveniences, the family would always have to eat in the same place. GE's Francis says that's not what consumers want.

The heart of GE's current prototype is a computer. Consumers communicate with the computer using menus—the computer screen version, not the restaurant variety—on a pressure-sensitive television screen, and a light pen, capable of reading bar codes on food packages.

The experimental prototype's computer can manage a variety of tasks. It can subtract items from an inventory list as they are used, store recipes, time cooking, even print shopping lists with items organized by aisle in the supermarket. An infrared light pen picks up information about ingredients and preparation directions from package bar codes. (Current codes do not contain this information.) Draw the pen over the bar code on a package of frozen veal parmesan, and the computer automatically programs the microwave for proper cooking. The computer can even handle a complex cycle of defrosting time, cooking, and final browning operations.

Used with a very sensitive scale built into a countertop unit, the storage-delivery appliance will also turn exotic preparations with many ingredients into what GE's Francis calls "one-bowl recipes." Here's how.

As ingredients are added and checked off the computer menu screen, their weight is registered and displayed on the monitor. This means that flour, salt, seasonings, and other ingredients can be poured into the bowl directly from their bulk dispensers. Measuring cups and spoons aren't needed.

If a recipe calls for three eggs, for example, the scales can even detect if the eggs are slightly undersized. The computer responds by adjusting the liquid ingredient on the recipe screen and scale sensor to exactly balance overall moisture content. Yes, it's that slick.

And it all happens with astounding accuracy. Francis reports that with current technology the computer can detect an improper measurement of ¼ teaspoon in a mixing bowl already containing 6 cups of flour.

The system may sport other technological goodies, too. For instance, inventory software programs may "learn" the replacement frequency of common foodstuffs—how often you run out of milk, for instance—and automatically add them to the shopping list. The computer will also handle odd jobs such as monitoring the operation of all kitchen appliances and running self-diagnostic repair programs.

Current thinking at GE is that storage-delivery appliances will not offer much help with cleanup. But Francis anticipates that future food packaging will eliminate most of that after-dinner drudgery. The idea is to package frozen foods in attractive, "microwaveable," disposable containers.

The weakest link in the next generation of kitchen appliances may be their name. The revolutionary systems have yet to be dubbed with a suitably revolutionary title somewhat more memorable than "storage-delivery appliance." Maybe they could be called "Jetsons."

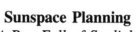

Sunspace Planning
A Box Full of Sunlight

Almost all households have a tendency to grow—either by adding members or possessions. To create more space, many homeowners have turned to open, energy-efficient rooms, or additions to existing rooms, called sunspaces. There are many possible approaches, ranging from adding windows and skylights to rooms without breaking down walls and pouring new foundations, to attaching a full-fledged greenhouse to the side of the house.

Several consumer surveys show that almost one in three houses now has some form of sunspace, tracing the popularity of these areas to energy-efficiency and exceptionally high resale value. A study conducted by *Remodeling Magazine*, an industry trade publication, that compared estimated costs of many home improvement projects to their short-term resale value, found that a typical sunspace addition netted 92 percent of construction costs. Several popular home improvements had a lower rate of return, for instance, remodeling a kitchen, which returned 80 percent of costs, and remodeling a bath, which returned 50 percent of costs.

A kitchen can be flooded with natural light, and expanded by sacrificing some wall and cabinet space to make an opening into a sunspace. Three-sided custom or prefabricated sunspace kits can be assembled on a concrete slab, and attached to the house wall. In this project, glazing was extended over the kitchen area as well.

Because there are so many options, planning a sunspace addition can be confusing. Basically, however, there are two ways to create the space: add windows and skylights in an existing room, or to a new addition built with conventional, solid walls and roof, or add a prefabricated glazed room, typically a three-sided unit, to the house. Here are some of the pros and cons of both approaches.

Converting an existing room to a sunspace has one obvious disadvantage: You don't get any more space. This is probably the least cost-effective way to make a sunspace.

You will experience all the disruption of a major remodeling project, and, typically, discover some unexpected problems—wires or pipes that must be moved, for instance.

Between this approach and building an entirely new room, however, is the possibility of converting a porch, deck, breezeway or patio. This type of project is very cost-effective if some or all of the major structural work (poured concrete foundations and slab floors, for instance) is already in place. However, bear in mind that most building departments require a building permit when the primary use of a space is changed, not only when building size is increased.

With this approach, you might be able to close in a porch by adding a *knee wall* (a short wall up to window sill height), and then a continuous row of windows. Combined with a series of skylights cut into the porch roof, solid structural components of the room become almost as unobtrusive as thin frames used between glazing panels in a greenhouse.

But leaks can be a problem. Every skylight and window makes a hole in the house. And although each unit has flashing and weatherstripping to seal out the weather, a row of skylights in particular is not unlikely to spring a leak. It might be wise to undertake such a project along with a new roof installation so that crucial skylight seams can be interwoven with new, watertight flashing and shingles.

The other, very popular approach, adding a prefabricated greenhouse, generally costs more, since, in order to use the enclosed space as comfortable, conditioned living space, you must go through most of the steps required to build a house in most cases: pour foundations and a slab, provide heating, possibly cooling, and wiring.

The big advantage is that the frame and the glazing components are made for each other. In many designs, extruded aluminum frames used to support glazing panels have built-in channels to carry off condensation, and to allow for movement as the glazing expands and contracts as it heats and cools.

There are many types of prefabricated sunspaces. Aside from aesthetic considerations, one basic difference is the type of glazing used. Glass is the traditional choice. It is clear, resists scratching and damage from ultraviolet rays, easy to clean, and available in many shapes and sizes. However, it is definitely breakable.

Alternatives to glass, including plastic, acrylics, fiberglass-reinforced polyesters, and other materials, are more flexible than glass but more easily scratched. Also, plastic glazing expands and contracts to a greater degree than glass when exposed to wide swings in temperature.

The clarity and strength of glass are important advantages, tempered (sorry) by another important consideration—how the glass breaks. Typical window glazing, called annealed glass, and ¼-inch plate glass in some larger windows, breaks into shards—jagged, pointed, razor-edged pieces. While some commercial greenhouses may use annealed glass, tempered glass is a must in residential sunspaces. This type of glass pebbles when it breaks, which greatly reduces the risk of serious injury. Some firms also offer more expensive laminated glass, which may eventually become the industry-wide standard. It consists of two pieces of glass sandwiching a resilient layer of polyvinyl butyral—a design used on automobile windshields that holds pieces of broken glass together in the sheet.

Whatever design you settle on, make sure to add it onto the house in a way that will allow you to use some of the heat collected in the sunspace. In winter, this can reduce fuel bills dramatically. Sunspaces open to living spaces will automatically heat up the house—so much so that elaborate summer shading could be required.

If the sunspace will be separated from the house by a wall, however, it makes sense to replace most or all of the partition with double-glazed sliding glass doors. You can see through them, so the space feels like part of the house even with the doors closed. And you can close the doors to keep out cool air at night, and open them during cold but sunny winter days when temperatures inside a sunspace can reach 90 degrees Fahrenheit or more.

In this adobe home (caught while still under construction by Adobe News, Inc.), full-height glazing on the first floor traps heat, which soaks into the masonry floors and walls. At night, as the temperature drops, the masonry gives off the heat. Even on small-scale projects, buying "operator" skylights that open, can help regulate temperature and ventilation.

Adding Space Up or Out

Q. We need to add on to our small, saltbox-style house, and have received conflicting advice about building up versus building out. We have space for either option: a roomy back yard, and a full, unused attic. Does one make more sense than the other?

A. There are so many variables. But each direction has some significant characteristics. Building out will probably be easier, even though your addition will require excavation, a foundation—every phase of new construction—since it will be a mini-house that just happens to be attached to your existing structure. The biggest bonus is that you will be able to continue living with only a normal amount of construction insanity and debris as the new rooms take shape in the back yard.

The main advantage of building up is that you do not have to start from scratch— usually. If you watch Public Television's "This Old House," you may have seen the expensive surprise encountered at the California house covered in a late 1988 episode of the series. Before building up, the entire house had to be raised so new foundations could be laid to support additional loads. A little miscalculation like that can add a nifty 30 or 40 percent to construction costs, crack interior walls, and open up woodwork trim. It can get ugly.

This unpleasant eventuality is usually covered by two words on the architect's plans: "Verify footings." That means you dig a few test trenches around the building to see exactly what's holding everything up. No small task. Hopefully, you find 10 inches of poured concrete, leading to a concrete footing well below the frost line.

In such cases, building up is almost always considerably less expensive than building out. But there are two drawbacks: you will live through every phase of the job, literally; and you will have to lose a bit of first-floor space to make a stairwell.

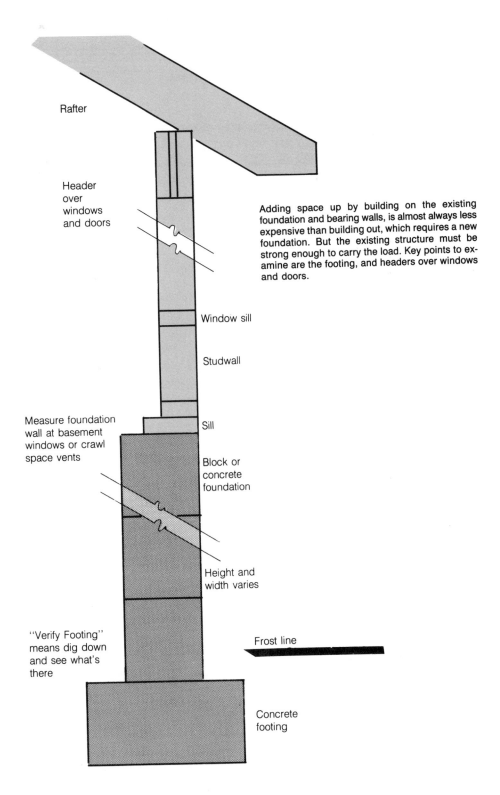

Rafter

Header over windows and doors

Window sill

Studwall

Measure foundation wall at basement windows or crawl space vents

Sill

Block or concrete foundation

Height and width varies

"Verify Footing" means dig down and see what's there

Frost line

Concrete footing

Adding space up by building on the existing foundation and bearing walls, is almost always less expensive than building out, which requires a new foundation. But the existing structure must be strong enough to carry the load. Key points to examine are the footing, and headers over windows and doors.

Three

PLANNING AIDS AND REFERENCE

Project Planners
Home Design and Planning Aids

Computers aren't really smart at all. They're quick. They can crunch numbers faster than a think tank full of geniuses. Some people even believe they can be programmed to find and destroy thousands of missiles whizzing through space. But computers are not very good at deciding something a lot more basic, say, whether your room addition should be 12 or 14 feet wide.

But there are several computer programs and other planning aids, such as scale-model furniture kits, that can help you explore building and remodeling design options before plans are drawn and decisions are set in cement. The planners may be well worth the price (from about $15 to $75), if you are patient enough to learn how to use them.

If you have not yet become user-friendly with a computer, you may not be aware that there is a flip side to all the quickness and precision. It is an inhuman absoluteness that few of us can relate to—at least when we first sit down at the keyboard.

Here is a typical example. If there is a program on your computer that keeps track of your family's birthdays called AGE, and, to activate it, you type in APE or ACE or ALE by mistake, or BIRTHDAY, or even HOW DO I ACTIVATE THE PROGRAM ABOUT AGES AND BIRTHDAYS, the machine just sits there.

If you sent these messages to a human, even a real dope, he would eventually get the idea that you wanted the AGE program about birthdays. But not a computer. Its response to your lack of precision would be a not very user-friendly message, such as BAD COMMAND OR FILE NAME, which, after you've been at it long enough to become thoroughly frustrated, reads like TRY AGAIN, DUMBBELL.

This is the paradox of even the friendliest computer programs: They do exactly what they are supposed to (most of the time), but only if you ask them in exactly the right way. With that in mind, you still might want to invest in a computer-design program, although you could stick with a more conventional scale-modeling kit. Here are a few of both types currently on the market.

❖ **Autosketch.** This software (for IBM-compatible machines) is a poor man's version of a computer-assisted design (CAD) system—poor in the financial sense since CAD systems used by architecture and engineering firms to produce complex blueprints can cost $5,000 or more. The basic version of Autosketch costs $79.95.

This drafting program is menu-driven, which means logical options are displayed so you can select the one you want. You don't have to memorize a lot of commands. Autosketch can be used from the keyboard or with a mouse (a device that runs a pointer around the screen in relation to how you move the mouse device across your desk). The program can produce straight lines, circles, arcs, boxes, even custom curves. It can zoom in on a small area so you can add more detail, rotate an object, and more.

In short, it does on a computer screen all the things you would be likely to do with a pencil on a piece of graph paper. Since I have been using the program for only a few days, I still do not have it communicating with my printer. I'm not sure whose fault this is. But the few questions I did have were answered clearly over the firm's tech support phone line (computer talk for a customer service department). This is a big plus. No matter how good the instructions are, and there are a few dabs of gobbledygook in Autosketch's documentation, almost everyone can use some help at first.

Well-known drawing programs for Apple or IBM (and compatible) computers, such as PC-Draw, can do about what Autosketch can do—generally for a few hundred dollars more. And the modest Autosketch program has some nifty twists. It transfers parts of one drawing onto another, copies repetitive parts of a drawing, for instance, stock-size doors and windows that appear throughout the plan, automatically draws dimension lines, figures area-square footage, and adds lettering.

The main bug I've encountered is a lack of precision in selecting lines and parts of lines to erase. Yes, even though the work is on a computer screen, you can still make mistakes. Also, custom curves and special lines made of dashes or dots slow down the program considerably. This drawback is solved by spending an extra $20 for a speed-enhanced version that uses a *math coprocessor*, if your computer has one, a board of computer chips that processes the drafting information about nine times faster than the standard version. The program is made by Autodesk, Inc.[1]

❖ **Plywood Planner.** This very specific program is typical of helpful software you can find by poring through computer magazines and electronic bulletin boards, which are like electronic libraries of computer information. You can tap into them with telecommunicating computers that can receive data over phone lines with a device called a *modem*. For instance, I used this method, called *downloading*, to get a file called CHEAPCAD—not that bad a drawing program, particularly considering it was free— from a bulletin board for IBM computer users on one of the more elaborate information networks called "THE SOURCE."

Plywood Planner costs only $19.95. It keeps track of pieces cut from sheets of plywood, which may seem like something only a lumberyard would want to do. But this program would enable you to type in all the parts on a plan for a piece of kit furniture, for instance, then see the most efficient layout on a sheet of 4-by-8-foot plywood. You would know how much wood to buy and where to make the cuts. The program even allows for saw thickness. Theoretically, this software could be applied to other projects, such as pattern- and dressmaking. It is also menu-driven, very straightforward, and very easy to use. Plywood Planner is made by Coiner Computer Systems.[2]

❖ **Project Planners.** Stanley Tools is now producing a line of planning kits covering different parts of the house, and a landscape design kit. Prices range from $14.95 to

---

[1]Autodesk, Inc., 2320 Marinship Way, Sausalito, CA 94965
[2]Coiner Computer Systems, 150 Robbins Station Rd., Suite 7, North Huntington, PA 15642

$29.95. The kits include a bluish-plastic base sheet with a layout grid onto which you can stick, move and restick a variety of graphic symbols to create colorful, readable, floor plan layouts. For instance, the Home Designer kit includes everything from house plants to a grand piano.

These kits are great if you are not comfortable with either pencil and paper or a computer, and if you like to change your mind a lot. They are incredibly easy to use and reuse. And the ¼-inch-scale furnishings, walls, windows, and other symbols can be photocopied. Such plans could make excellent preliminary or even finished plans to pore over with your contractor. Project Planners are made by Stanley Tools.[3]

❖ **Plan-It Kit.** This planning aid consists of miniature, three-dimensional styrene chairs, tables, couches, a piano, and other items—57 furniture pieces in all—scaled at one-half inch per foot. The kit, which costs $15.98 plus $2.50 postage, includes a floor grid, stick-on graphics of windows, doors, bookcases, and such, and cardboard wall panels. The idea is to create a three-dimensional model (an open-topped box) that

Stanley Tools Project Planners make designing your home improvement plans easy by providing a layout grid and dozens of precut, self-sticking graphic symbols. You can move them around, then photocopy the final version for discussions with contractors.

---

[3]Stanley Tools, 600 Myrtle St., New Britain, CT 06050

may provide a more realistic picture than a two-dimensional floor plan. Plan-It Kit is made by Plan-It-Kit Inc.[4]

Building by the Book
Reviews of Special Interest How-To Books

Learning about Japanese woodworking could get expensive if you had to start by buying a round-trip ticket to Japan. Figuring out how log cabins are built in Alaska wouldn't be much of a picnic either in the winter time if you had to be there in the flesh. But there is a less expensive alternative—reading a how-to book on the subject.

Sitting home in your socks, you may not hear the avalanches roar or the wolves howl as you turn the pages. But spending $10 or $20 for a how-to book, or getting your library to buy it and borrowing it from them, is a good way to test or develop your interest in a subject.

Here is a list of several specialty how-to books, some new, some older classics, and some perennial favorites that just have to make the list. The publication date is listed with older books to help you find them, since they may not be in book stores.

☐ *Japanese Woodworking*, by Hideo Sato (Cloudburst Press). Traditional American timber framing with complex mortise-and-tenon joints is practically child's play compared to the Japanese version. This book, which is heavily illustrated with line drawings, introduces and explains the use of Japanese woodworking tools (the saws and planes cut toward you), and the three-dimensional jigsaw puzzle of Japanese joinery. The drawback; no photos or color of the sculpture-like carpentry.

☐ *Audel Complete Siding Handbook*, by James E. Brumbaugh (MacMillan). Yes, the small but packed (this one has 434 pages) Audel guides are still going strong. The current versions are laid out cleanly with good line drawings. In this volume, each type of siding gets the full treatment: tools you'll need, different ways of handling corners and trim, and some features too many how-to books leave out—a list of trade associations and manufacturers, and a decent index.

☐ *Chip Carving and Relief Carving*, by Josef Mader (MacMillan). Step one: buy a good set of carving chisels. Step two: build up your hand and forearm muscles. Step three: start carving Acanthus leaves on chest drawers, rosettes on chair arms, flowers, stars, fish bladders, running dogs, cables, and other traditional patterns. The text is extremely modest. Just grab onto your chisels and go, with the drawings and sharp, working-stage photos as your guides. And in case someone asks you, fish bladders are generally circular arrangements of tadpole or teardrop shapes. Running dogs are generally linear patterns of interlaced S's or wave shapes.

☐ *Build-It-Better-Yourself Country Furniture*, by the editors of *Family Handyman Magazine* (Rodale Press). This is a book of old magazine stories. Most of the over 100 furniture projects are Colonial-style. Several are, by now, a little kitschy unless you're just gaga for knotty pine. But the treatment is traditional magazine how-to: di-

[4]Plan-It-Kit Inc., P.O. Box 664, Fairfield, CT 06430

rect, step-by-step text, exploded-view drawings and parts list—all very no nonsense. Some of the more complex projects, a full-height corner cupboard for instance, are helped along with working-stage photos, several of which reveal the figure of Rosario Capotosto, who wrote another book on this list, *Woodworking Wisdom*.

☐ *Country Living,* by Lewis and Nancy Hill (Rodale Press). This friendly book is filled with advice on country living—country as in raising your own fish and finding a suitable place to store manure. But what's particularly neat about this book is that the straightforward information about shade trees, growing your own Filberts (nuts) and a proper diet for pigs is geared to city folk who are thinking about moving and to newcomers—people who just may expect the livestock to find their own darn place to store the manure.

☐ *Wrought Ironwork,* by Cosira (MacMillan). Cosira is not a one-name author like Capucine, the one-name actress. The word stands for Council for Small Industries in Rural Areas, a group that provides craft training in Britain. The pages and pages of step-by-step how-to photos look fairly antique. But this is one subject where you don't have to worry that the original copyright is 1953. Iron hinges and scrolls and fishtails still heat up and bend the same way now as they did then.

☐ *I'll Buy That,* by the editors of *Consumer Reports* (Consumer Report Books). This is an informative, entertaining, offbeat home-consumer history book subtitled, "50 Small Wonders and Big Deals that Revolutionized the Lives of Consumers." The intensely illustrated, large-format book has most of the oldies but goodies—everything from

Subtitled, "50 Small Wonders and Big Deals that Revolutionized the Lives of Consumers," a *Consumer Reports* book called, *I'll Buy That* presents a photo history of some housing milestones, for example, the precut components of the first postwar prefab houses at Levittown in Long Island, New York.

Clarence Birdseye's first frozen foods that quickly doubled the average per capita consumption of vegetables, to Dow Chemical's first latex paint, sold in 1948 by the Glidden Company as Spred Satin.

☐ *Woodworking Wisdom,* by Rosario Capotosto (Van Nostrand Reinhold). Capotosto, who built a stainless steel pipe-trimmed platform bed I designed for a *Popular Mechanics* magazine story about 12 years ago, is a really good woodworker. He has participated in hundreds of how-to magazine articles and produced one of the most comprehensive, best-illustrated, shop woodworking books with fabulous how-to photos. It covers serious but doable, power-tool cabinetwork.

☐ *In Harmony With Nature,* by Christian Bruyere and Robert Inwood (Sterling). This unusual book of 12 country homestead case histories avoids preaching alternative-lifestyle dogma and offers practical guidance on country shelter instead. The energetic, realistic, annotated, almost comic book-style drawings make the book even more unique. One of the best "alternate lifestyle" practical books.

☐ *Country Woodcraft,* by Drew Langsner (Rodale Press). Use this straightforward, inviting book as a guide to handcraft hay rakes, brooms, baskets, and other tools and furnishings. No electricity is needed here where traditional hand tools and hand skills replace radial-arm saws and routers.

☐ *Building the Alaska Log Home,* by Tom Walker (Alaska Northwest). This thorough book on traditional, hand-hewn log construction has a warm, friendly text, and 175 pages of full-color photos of work at some amazing home sites. If you ever pictured your cabin by the lake and the mountains—ice-clear lakes and huge, pristine mountains— you will eat up the pictures.

☐ *One Man's Wilderness,* by Sam Keith (Alaska Northwest). This is a dream book. The inspiring story is based on the journals of Richard Proenneke, who moved to Alaska in 1950 and built a cabin in the wild. A revealing tale of the struggles and rewards— what might happen if you tried it, not how to lay up the logs. Fascinating.

☐ *Why Buildings Stand Up,* by Mario Salvadori (McGraw-Hill). If you are an amateur structural engineer, pounce. The challenging text at times just barely translates into layman's language. But, with some work, this book will give you a real understanding of building structure and its historical evolution.

☐ *Mr. Blandings Builds His Dream House,* by Eric Hodgins (Simon & Schuster, published in 1946!). This very entertaining book has some solid messages slipped in between the slapstick and sophistication. But it may be hard to find since it was published over 40 years ago. But on occasion the very faithful movie adaptation is shown on television. In short, Cary Grant and Myrna Loy move out of the city and, with the help (sort of) of Melvin Douglas, inspect, buy, tear down, redesign, build anew and move into a house in the country. What great fun.

Basic Building References
Review of Construction and Project Books

A good how-to book with a practical, understandable text and a lot of illustrations is still one of the best ways to learn about home building, restoration, woodworking, energy saving and the growing list of subjects consumers no longer leave solely in the hands of professionals.

If you have a special interest, in a particular style of construction for example, hands-on courses provide field experience no book can match. But a thorough how-to book can provide experience by osmosis, an informed overview, and confidence.

What follows is one slightly eclectic bookshelf selected from the hundreds of how-to books published every year. It includes some classic building references that may be hard to buy, and easier to locate in your library. I've found them practical, not full of textbook theory that looks good in print, but doesn't translate to field situations, and even readable—a characteristic that kept many how-to books off this shelf even though they are instructive.

☐ *Finding and Buying Your Place in the Country,* by Les Scher (Collier). A comprehensive, savvy guide to dealing with developers, real estate agents, attorneys, and the intricacies of deeds, land records, surveys, zoning and more. Written by an attorney in plain English, Les Scher explains every step from first searches to final closing. Even today, it will keep you out of countless country real estate potholes.

☐ *The New York Times Guide to Buying or Building a Home,* by William G. Connolly (Times Books). A decision-making book with chapters posed as questions on financing alternatives, new or old homes, neighborhood choices, self-contracting or hiring professionals, and more. Pros and cons of every option offer a well-rounded look at buying shelter.

☐ *The Complete Book of Home Inspection,* by Norman Becker (McGraw-Hill). Over 150 photos and drawings and a thorough text cover older homes and their problems. The author, an engineer and professional inspector, shows and tells what he looks for, and what he knows about the implications of rot, rust, and ragged edges.

☐ *Architectural Graphic Standards,* by Charles G. Ramsey and Harold R. Sleeper (Wiley). The classic architectural reference book is updated in a new edition every few years, adding to the 800 pages of measured drawings, tables, and extensive specifications of housing components, building systems, and construction material. It's very expensive; try the library.

☐ *Homeowner's Encyclopedia of House Construction,* by Morris Krieger (McGraw-Hill). A truly encyclopedic approach to tools, materials, and building systems, from acoustics to wood-frame construction. Many illustrations and an extensive text make this book a solid background reference, although you may well hunt for help on a particular topic that just isn't listed.

☐ *Housebuilding Illustrated,* by R.J. DeCristoforo (Harper & Row). Over 600 pages and 1,000 drawings and photos cover everything from building layout to interior trim,

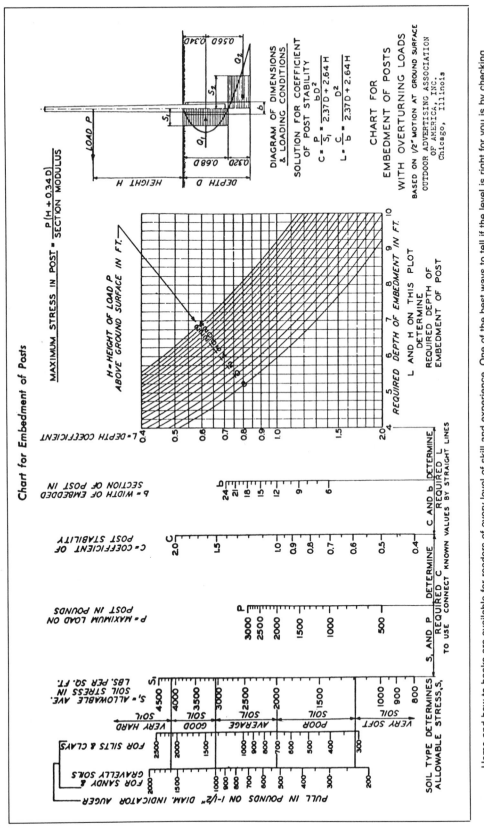

Chart for Embedment of Posts

CHART FOR
EMBEDMENT OF POSTS
WITH OVERTURNING LOADS
BASED ON 1/2" MOTION AT GROUND SURFACE
OUTDOOR ADVERTISING ASSOCIATION
OF AMERICA, INC.
Chicago, Illinois

DIAGRAM OF DIMENSIONS
& LOADING CONDITIONS

SOLUTION FOR COEFFICIENT
OF POST STABILITY

$$C = \frac{P}{S_1} = \frac{bD^2}{2.37D + 2.64H}$$

$$L = \frac{C}{b} = \frac{D^2}{2.37D + 2.64H}$$

$$MAXIMUM\ STRESS\ IN\ POST = \frac{P(H + 0.34D)}{SECTION\ MODULUS}$$

L AND H ON THIS PLOT
DETERMINE
REQUIRED DEPTH OF
EMBEDMENT OF POST

C AND b DETERMINE
REQUIRED L

S, AND P DETERMINE
REQUIRED C
TO USE CONNECT KNOWN VALUES BY STRAIGHT LINES

SOIL TYPE DETERMINES
ALLOWABLE STRESS, S,

Home and how-to books are available for readers of every level of skill and experience. One of the best ways to tell if the level is right for you is by checking some of the pictures and captions. In purely technical books, you might find complex pages—a detailed table that helps designers and builders determine how deep building poles must be embedded in the ground.

although practical tips of the trade are left to the reader. Voluminous coverage of all types of conventional construction.

☐ *Superhouse,* by Don Metz (Garden Way). The design and construction of earth-sheltered, double-envelope, and superinsulated houses; high-tech design is presented and evaluated by an experienced, innovative architect-builder.

☐ *Time-Life Home Repair and Improvement Series,* by the editors of Time-Life Books (Time-Life Books). A widely available series of books sold initially by subscription; accurate and basic, with clear drawings, although in several cases the artwork is unnecessarily large, as if it were meant to flesh out the text to book length.

☐ *Reader's Digest Complete Do-It-Yourself Manual,* Fix-It-Yourself Manual and Home Improvements Manual (Reader's Digest). The information-packed pages of these three books cover so much that the crisp drawings and practical advice tends to be generic—that is, your oil burner may not look like the one in the picture. When the Complete D.I.Y. Manual was published in 1973, I thought it was too generic to be really useful. But the newer manuals split up the broad coverage, which helps, and now I think they are quite good—maybe the best you can do without buying additional books on specific subjects.

☐ *Renovation,* by Michael W. Litchfield (Wiley). A comprehensive text by the founding editor of *Fine Homebuilding* magazine with 600 pages and 1,000 illustrations; content stresses thorough, quality work and covers planning, tools, materials, and structural and finishing jobs on every part of the house.

☐ *The Old-House Journal Compendium,* by Patricia Poore and Clem Labine (Dolphin). A 400-plus page presentation of the Journal's in-depth, monthly newsletters, covering restoration, maintenance and the full range of problems and questions associated with houses built before 1939. This is particularly helpful on city brownstones and row houses.

☐ *Home Energy How-To,* by A.J. Hand (Harper & Row). Missing a few of the latest advances, this book still offers a straightforward and balanced presentation of whole-house energy efficiency with step-by-step projects and practical evaluations of alternative energy sources.

☐ *The Home Cabinetmaker,* by Monte Burch (Harper & Row). Comprehensive coverage with over 500 pages and 1,000 illustrations on tools, materials, detailed step-by-step sequences and projects, plus a solid section on home workshops.

☐ *Woodworking Techniques and Projects,* by Rosario Capotosto (Van Nostrand Reinhold). Over 40 specific projects and 800 illustrations, including detailed sequences on tool use and procedures, plus an invaluable 40-page section on Capotosto's special-ty: all kinds of jigs, special setups and techniques that help a good woodworker with good tools produce professional results.

☐ *How to Build a Low-Cost House of Stone,* by Sharon and Lewis Watson (Stonehouse Publications). Another eye-opening case history, this one of a family who built a three-bedroom stone house in one summer for $2,000; worth reading even if you have no intention of building a stone house. This book offers a personal account of taking direct action to turn a dream into reality. (The book is self-published, complete with slightly scratchy drawings, and may still be available by writing Stonehouse Publications, Sweet, ID 83670.)

Home and Construction Books
Practical and Impractical Building Books

Books are not necessarily the best teachers. Among yet another crop of home how-to books there is one real winner (enjoyable even if you are not that interested in the subject), several thorough, workmanlike books on carpentry, woodworking, maintenance, and such, and an unusual clunker. Good news first.

☐ *The Timber-Frame Home,* by Tedd Benson (Taunton Press). When you are familiar with the top-notch design and construction work of the author, it is natural to expect a good book. It is rewarding to discover a terrific book, produced by Taunton Press, the company that also publishes *Fine Homebuilding* magazine, with the care of one of Benson's elegant timber-frame homes.

In the Taunton Press book, *The Timber-Frame Home*, by Tedd Benson, step-by-step assembly of framing "bents," and their details, are well covered.

Not surprisingly, the book is very much like the magazine—printed on glossy paper with clear line drawings, sharp black and white photos, and some of the richest color shots you'll find in a book. It's a visual treat.

While Benson's first book (*Building the Timber-Frame House,* Scribner's, 1980) was a nitty-gritty piece of work smothered in scratchy drawings and complicated construction formulas (a book for builders), this book is more for owners who will be working with a contractor, and timber-frame home buyers. It is filled with construction details, but presents them more as design options. Chapters cover all aspects of frame and home design, and the other not so minor details such as foundation work, wiring, and plumbing you need to know about before a large-scale timber frame becomes a house.

The book is the product of a matured designer-builder with 14 years of timber-frame construction experience—well past the point of alternative lifestyle carpentry.

It offers a thoughtful balance between modern, high-tech, energy-efficient building skins, insulation, and mechanical systems, and the classic simplicity of traditional timber-frame construction.

☐ *House Carpentry Simplified,* by Nelson L. Burbank (McGraw-Hill). This oversize paperback is filled with illustrations showing all types of wood framing, their construction details, and information on all other types of house carpentry such as installing windows, stairs, and molding.

The author is a former vocational school teacher, which shows in the methodical, step-by-step approach. The book is all about building and not at all about design. Many of the pictures are dated but the information isn't. (I haven't seen so many guys with crew cuts in a long time.)

☐ *The Woodturner's Art,* by Ron Roszkiewicz and Phyllis Straw (MacMillan). This oversize, thoroughly illustrated book seems best suited for amateur woodworkers who already have mastered the basics of operating a wood lathe and cutting tools. It concentrates on projects: making spindles, Shaker pegs, wooden bowls and goblets, molding, and many others. It is very thorough, covering every small nuance of cutting, shaping, and trimming in the text, and all key steps in either drawings or photos.

☐ *Radon,* by Bernard L. Cohen (Consumers Union). This book is still the best bet to help you understand a difficult subject. It offers basic, understandable explanations of complex scientific information about radon, a naturally occurring radioactive gas that can cause lung cancer. It is a serious and widespread problem. The book also provides practical information about testing devices and remedial action.

☐ *The Low-Maintenance House,* by Gene Logsdon (Rodale Press). This book is designed to minimize maintenance time and expense once you move into your home or start using your addition, by including low-maintenance features in the design. The lengthy text covers all types of structural and finishing materials, and features practical, easy-to-read charts comparing costs, expected lifespans, and other characteristics of material and design options. It attacks one specific aspect of home design, covering many possibilities, quite successfully.

☐ *Shortcuts,* by Cheryl Winters Tetreau and Carol Hupping (Rodale Press). This book is like a four-hour television mini series made up of 30 second sketches. The idea of the book seems to be to supply quick, short answers and advice on all sorts of home and other topics because we are all too busy for more thorough and detailed answers. "It's a wonder we manage to get through the day!" it says in the introduction.

The premise seems very contemporary, very hip. And the book covers a lot of ground, offering shortcuts on home maintenance, home repair, landscaping, gardening, and even hotter topics such as "A Fitter You," and a sort of catchall chapter, "A Better You," that includes shortcuts to "learning to beat the blues" such as the subsection "Do something cultural." Really.

Although Rodale is noted for books on home, garden, and health subjects loaded with practical information, many of the chapters here are fleshed out with bite-sized hints that are not exactly startling or useful—a shortcut in the marriage and family life section titled "Talk to each other." In the home improvement section there are tips on making a small room seem larger, but also several suggestions for making a large room seem smaller—not exactly a widespread problem in most apartments or houses.

When the text takes as much as half a page to shortcut you through "fine-tuning a radiator" more useful information is provided. But in the shortcut section on replacing a light switch, wire nuts, which come in many sizes and must be screwed over wires spliced in a specific way to be safe, are defined as "Used for wiring splices," which is not a whole lot of help.

A shortcut to scrubbing shower walls in the section on home management (a new phrase for cleaning) suggests that you can "eliminate virtually all weekly scrubbing by drying the shower walls after each shower." First problem: "virtually all" puts a tad too positive a spin on "some." It's advertising copy. Second problem: If you take a shower every day, using a sponge or squeegee and "wiping away all the moisture" has got to take at least as much time as washing the shower walls once a week. And if there are three of four people in the household, a few minutes spent washing the walls once a week will pale next to their collective man hours spent wiping the walls dry every time one of them takes a shower. It's just a dumb idea.

How-to books become valuable because they provide detail, explain options, offer pros and cons, and the measured judgment of the author's experience in the field. Quick fixes and easy answers may work on Wall Street or on pop psychology talk shows. But thorough information, practice, patience, trial and error and hard work—although they don't seem very contemporary or hip—sure get results.

Appropriate Technology Books

Q. I have a country cabin that serves as a proving ground for all sorts of improvement projects. Since I do, or at least attempt, all of them myself, I am interested in books that explain old-fashioned building and homestead skills. What is a good source for this kind of information, particularly geared for hand-powered tools and skills?

A. Your approach to homestead care and repair sounds like appropriate technology—a term that grew up to describe a commonsense approach to solving problems, for instance, providing an African villager with seeds and a hoe instead of irrigation software and a computer. The Intermediate Technology Development Group of North America[5] is one group trying to infuse low-tech, commonsense technology into the mainstream of American life.

Their new publications list for 1988 includes books that follow this approach in many different fields, including building, energy use, water supply, gardening, and sanitation—even some rarefied specialties such as thatching and rammed-earth construction. You can request the book list by writing ITDG/NA.

---

[5]ITDG/NA, P.O. Box 337, Croton-on-Hudson, NY 10520

Sometimes "appropriate technology" skills are practical despite improvements in building technology. Sometimes, it is just interesting to find out about them—for instance, how thatched straw roofs go together without leaking.

Estimating Building Costs

Q. Is there any way, other than getting several bids, to gauge whether or not building cost estimates are in the ballpark? For instance, how would you know if two estimates are both too high?

A. It would be difficult to know that unless you knew the ins and outs of construction costs, which underscores the sensible idea of getting several estimates (generally three or more) on jobs other than small, inexpensive repairs and improvements. An expensive bid will not stand out in a crowd unless it can be compared to two or three more reasonable bids.

But there are many factors influencing contractor bids, including time of year, interest rates, and general health of the economy. For example, builders who might have been ready to devote time and effort to an estimate in January when they were working inside and trying to line up projects for spring and summer, are less likely to be interested now. And interest rates are moderate, which means more people can afford to make improvements and build new homes. That means more consumers are trying to hire the same number of contractors.

When the law of supply and demand swings to the contractor's favor, and it certainly is swinging that way this spring, expect most bids to be increased somewhat. Consumers usually pay less buying out of season, whether it's Christmas tree lights in January or a bed and bath addition planned and estimated during the winter.

The *Means Home Improvement Cost Guide*, a large-format, 248-page book published by the R.S. Means Co. includes labor and materials for 74 different projects, covering variations with different materials and sizes.

While comparison shopping is still about the best way to uncover a particularly high or low estimate, there are several ways to cross-check costs. One is to convert the bid to a cost-per-square-foot and check that very approximate figure with local mortgage bankers, real estate agents, and other housing professionals. Bear in mind that jobs such as a new kitchen requiring a lot of mechanical work (plumbing, heating, cooling, and electrical) will cost much more per square foot than less-complex projects such as a new garage.

Tools
and
Materials

Four

LUMBER

Lumberyard Language
How to Ask for the Wood You Want

If there were only one kind of tree in the world, and all the lumber companies cut them up into one size, ordering a stick of wood would be as easy as ordering a glass of water. But forests are more diverse and complicated than that. Unfortunately, so is the language of lumber.

First of all, there are hundreds of wood species, from *Abura* (an acid-resistant wood used to make battery boxes and oil vats) to *Zebrano* (a West African wood with a striped, zebra-like pattern). But it's more likely that you'll need a less exotic variety such as fir, pine, redwood, spruce, or hemlock—an ironic choice (even though you can't drink it) for projects that prove to be particularly troublesome.

Different species of wood not only look different, they have different strengths and weaknesses. In fact, two pieces of the same type of wood can behave so differently that they are well suited for vastly different purposes. Their characteristics depend on what section of the tree they are cut from, how many knots they contain, and other factors.

For instance, a piece of Merchantable-Grade redwood contains large knots and softer, light-colored sapwood from the outer edges of the tree. This grade is recommended for fencing, trellises, and similar, rough, outdoor applications. But a beam of Clear All Heart redwood, an extremely dense, knot-free grade, is often specified for critical roof beams in homes situated in high-risk fire areas. The dense beams char slowly in a fire, sometimes retaining enough strength to keep a burning roof from collapsing.

Architects and engineers quantify the differences among wood species, and different cuts of the same species, in mathematical tables that must be consulted to find out if a certain size beam of a certain type of wood can adequately carry its load. At this level of detail, calculations might show, for example, that changing from one wood species to another or paying more for a better, stronger grade of the same species could allow an increased floor joist span and eliminate the need for a central support girder.

But in most cases you don't have to get this technical. For instance, if you want to replace a rotted, 2-by-4 wall stud you can simply ask for a 2 by 4 and expect to get a strong type of wood such as fir, commonly used for structural timbers. Lumber

Opposite: This particular type of circular saw is called a "worm-drive" saw. The position of the motor housing and handle behind and at the level of the blade makes it easier to guide the cut. Most circular saws have a top-mounted handle, which can leave you dragging the saw through the cut. The drawback to worm-drives is their weight.

companies wouldn't manufacture 2 by 4s out of a softwood such as balsa, which is great for model carving but lousy for holding up houses.

However, if a standard 2 by 4 rotted the first time, you might replace it with redwood or cedar that is more resistant to rot, or a pressure-treated 2 by 4 infused with rot-resistant chemicals. So instead of simply asking for a 2 by 4, ask the lumber dealer what type and grade of 2 by 4 would be best suited for your project.

Whatever wood you need is probably available in several grades and many sizes. Finish lumber, such as pine boards used for shelving, is graded by letter, from A (the best) to E (the worst, which many lumberyards don't stock).

As a rule, Grade A denotes completely clear, knot-free wood. Such pristine lumber is extremely costly and may be available only on special order. Grade B, often called ''clear'' although it has a few, small imperfections, should be more than equal to any piece of fine woodworking you have in mind. In fact, the two top grades are often combined into a category called Grade B & Better, meaning you get mostly Grade B with a few Grade A pieces included, maybe.

Grade C finish lumber has more visible blemishes but is still suitable for exposed moldings and woodwork. Grade D has visible knots and imperfections that cannot be completely hidden under a coat of paint. Of course, this grading system assumes that

---

TYPICAL LUMBER GRADE STAMPS

Treated Lumber

Construction Lumber

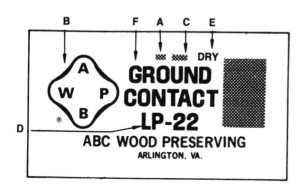

A–Year of treatment

B–American Wood Preservers Bureau trademark

C–AWPB quality standard

D–Preservative used in wood treatment

E–Condition of seasoning

a–Western Wood Products Assn. trademark

b–Mill number

c–Official grade name

d–Wood specie

e–Moisture content

Two pieces of the same type of wood, pine for instance, can behave so differently that they are well suited for vastly different purposes. These distinctions are stamped on lumber in the form of grade stamps made up by trade associations that represent groups of lumber producers, such as the Western Wood Products Association.

clearer, which is rarer and more expensive, is better. So if you like the look of knotty pine paneling, which is less clear and less expensive, you're in luck.

If in doubt, ask to see a sample. If the pine is for bookshelves, for instance, you might buy two, nearly clear boards for the exposed end panels and save money by using a knotty grade for the shelves. If your wood will have a clear finish such as polyurethane that enhances natural variations in the grain, clearer grades may look more subdued, uniform, and elegant. But if you plan to stain the boards, the appearance of knots and blemishes will be reduced instead of highlighted.

Common lumber such as 2 by 4s that, generally, are covered by other materials, are graded by number, from 1 (the best) to 5 (the worst, which is rarely used). Even Grade Number 1 has blemishes and knots, but they are sound and watertight. Number 2, and sometimes Number 3 are commonly specified for wood-framed buildings, while Number 4, suitable for temporary bracing and blocking, and Number 5 may not be stocked.

Now comes the fun part: specifying the size. Construction timbers such as 2 by 4s and 2 by 6s are sold by length, generally in 2-foot multiples from 8-foot lengths up to about 20 footers. Long lengths are more likely to be available at large lumberyards, while smaller, inner city yards catering more to homeowners and apartment dwellers than to builders may not stock timbers over 16 feet.

Heavier timbers, and boards such as 1-by-6-inch pine shelving may be specified by length, or by a confusing measurement system—the one used for pricing of finish and common lumber in most yards—based on board feet. Unlike measurement by length or square footage, "board feet" takes thickness into account. This makes the overall measurement of 1-inch thick wood completely different from the measurement of lumber which is the same length and width with a different thickness.

Technically, 1 board-foot is a 12-inch length of 12-inch wide, 1-inch thick material. A 1-foot length of 1-by-12 pine shelving would be one board foot, for example. But a 12-inch length of 2-by-6 timber would also measure 1 board foot. It's only half as wide, but twice as thick. In neat multiples this system is not too difficult to keep track of. Once you get into 2 by 10s, and mixed orders of 1-inch- and 2-inch-thick materials, hold onto your hat.

You can use this formula to sort out the different sizes:

width (inches) × thickness (inches) × length (feet) ÷ 12 = board feet

For example, if you were buying a 24-inch length of 1-by-12 shelving the formula would apply this way:

width (12) × thickness (1) × length (2)

Remember, length is listed in feet, not inches—divided by 12, which works out to 2 board feet.

The kicker to all this number crunching is that a 2 by 4 isn't really a 2 by 4; it's a 1½ by 3½. This difference between what the forest industry calls the "nominal" and "actual" dimensions is due to a lumber trimming and finishing process called "dressing," although "undressing" would be a more accurate description.

High-Tech Lumber
Improving On Mother Nature's Beams and Girders

All the king's horses and all the king's men may have been the first to try gluing an egg back together again. But no one is absolutely sure who first looked at a pile of sawdust and wood chips on a lumber mill floor and said, "Hey, I bet I could glue all that into a 2 by 12."

Most consumers have seen various types of 4-by-8-foot panels—generally known as particleboard—made of wood chips and glue. They are used for house sheathing, subflooring and furniture, when covered with a veneer of more attractive wood or plastic laminate. But few consumers have seen the newest advance in building technology, known as composite lumber—2-by-4 studs, 2-by-8 rafters, 2-by-12 joists, and larger structural boards made from different sizes and shapes of wood chips.

Prototypes for the increasing number of new, code-approved, composite lumber products were developed over the last decade. Much of the work was done at taxpayer expense at the USDA Forest Products Laboratory in Madison, Wisconsin, and resulted in a commercial product called "ComPly." Now, some of the people who were in on the development are out in the marketplace.

The new, composite form of a very old building material has several advantages over conventional wood timbers, and, when purchased in large quantities, is generally competitive in price. Engineers have discovered that they can reassemble a 2 by 6 to be stronger than the original, natural version. That means less wood can be used in a house, for example, where a 2-by-10 conventional floor joist can be replaced with a 2-by-8 composite timber that is just as strong. In some designs natural joists placed 16 inches on center can be replaced by the same-size composites at 24-inch centers. Since these engineered, glued-together timbers have no grain, they do not have the tendency to warp or twist that is built into many natural timbers. And since they have no knots, or cracks, or splits, there are no weak links. Composites also are available in very long lengths that can reduce labor and material costs required to splice shorter timbers or support them at mid-span.

One type of composite, called oriented strand board (OSB) is now being assembled and stamped out in huge, 1½-inch-thick, 8½-foot-wide, 36-foot-long sheets by Arrowood Technologies Inc.,[1] then cut into sizes equivalent to conventional framing materials. A typical Arrowood beam cut out and edged top and bottom with a narrow layer of laminated hardwood, is slightly heavier than normal timbers of the same size. Despite its somewhat strange and obviously manufactured appearance, however, you can still drive nails into it.

Another type of composite is called parallel strand lumber (PSL), and christened Parallam by the manufacturer, MacMillan Bloedel Ltd.,[2] one of the largest lumber companies in Canada. This surprisingly attractive composite has no capping or edging.

---

[1] Arrowood Technologies, 1000 Arrowood Drive, Roxboro, NC 27573
[2] MacMillan Bloedel Ltd., 1272 Derwent Way, Annacis Island, BC V3M5R1

ABOVE: Shouldering a 33-foot 2-by-10 beam would put a dent in almost anyone's shoulder—if anyone could get it off the ground. But manufactured, "engineered" timbers are much lighter while providing the same strength. BELOW: This Truss Joist floor beam has a laminated plywood top and bottom, and a long strip of plywood between.

It's all wood chips and glue, assembled from a random weave of 8-foot-long, ½-inch-wide, and ⅛-inch-thick wood strips, secured with glue and quick-cured by microwave.

Parallam is manufactured in a continuous process so that, theoretically, timbers can be as long as the building they are made in. Also, the thickness can be adjusted so that single composite timbers can be manufactured in, for example, 4½-inch-thick slices—the equivalent of three conventional timbers laboriously spiked together into a main girder. The manufacturer reports that Parallam timbers are 2½ to 3 times stronger than No. 2 Douglas Fir, a conventional framing material.

Some so-called advances in building technology, such as reducing the true size of a 2 by 4 to 1½ by 3½ inches, may have seemed a little one-sided to consumers. The changes may have saved time and money for builders but did little to improve the solidity and durability of a house. However, this is not likely to be the case with composite timbers. For one thing, they typically provide more strength and create fewer problems than the timbers they replace for roughly the same price. Even more importantly, composite timbers save wood. For one thing, you don't need to cut down big trees to make big beams. You can use small trees and scrap lumber that can't be used for anything else.

Bob McAlister, a Forest Products Technologist at the USDA Forest Products Lab, says that to conserve and preserve our forests, something had to change or we would have been in for "a really bad shock in the next 10 years as forest resources become more depleted." He adds, "People will never really know how close we came to a disaster."

Varieties of Pine

Q. How can I determine the variety of pine I am getting at the lumberyard: whether it is suitable for decking and other structural uses, or only for shelving and paneling?

A. Since there are many types of pine you'll have to ask which one you're looking at. Or, you could look through a book that shows pictures of many varieties. (One new book that shows most of the choices with color pictures of each wood species is *World Woods in Color*, William A. Lincoln (MacMillan, 1986).

Sometimes, a representative picture of, say, yellow pine, really looks like the piece at the lumberyard. Sometimes a few knots or fading can throw you off. It's confusing.

The subject is further complicated by the use of commercial and slang names for woods. For instance, American pitch pine, a structural quality wood approximately equal to Douglas fir, is also known by the commercial names of Florida longleaf or yellow pine, Georgia yellow pine, and slash pine. Other labels are pitch pine, longleaf pine, southern yellow pine, and southern pine.

LEFT: You might find pine boards this size in an old New England barn, but not at a lumberyard. However, there are some special-ty suppliers worth seeking out—particularly on restoration projects. BELOW: Nearly clear pine in 16-inch widths is available from some small mills such as Carlisle Restoration Lumber in Stoddard, New Hampshire. They can provide straight flooring and paneling with a variety of milled edges.

Morton, Cole & Weber

There are several commonly available varieties of pine to choose from. American pitch pine, which has alternating leaf-shaped patterns of light and dark yellow in its surface, is often used for heavy construction and in shipbuilding. Ponderosa pine, which is generally knottier with a redder, wavier grain than pitch pine, is used for interior paneling as a "knotty" pine, in window frames, trim, and other uses.

The "shelving" varieties you mention are likely to be one of two closely related and often confused species: Western white pine or yellow pine. Both have a pale, dried-out hue with fine brown resin lines along the boards. Both are uniform and straight-grained, which makes them easy to cut and work with in general. Western white pine is a little stronger.

Formaldehyde Glue in Wood

Q. Is there any product that does not contain formaldehyde that can be used in place of plywood for rough flooring over beams. A carpet and pad will be installed on top.

A. One alternative is a paper-based board made by Homasote, called the 4-Way Floor Decking System. It contains no formaldehyde. For 16-inch center framing 2-by-8-foot panels are $1^{11}/_{32}$ inches thick. ($1\frac{3}{4}$-inch thick panels are available for use over 24-inch center framing.)

The tongue and groove panels, which weigh 3 pounds each, are installed over floor joists with construction adhesive and nails. The company says they add up to an R-4.5 to floor insulation, six times the thermal value of $\frac{5}{8}$-inch plywood subflooring. (*R-value* is a measurement of insulation effectiveness, the higher the better.)

The company also manufactures a thinner board for use as an underlayment—a resilient layer between carpet and plywood subflooring.

Building Board Confusion

Q. What are the differences between Wonder-Board and Ultra-Board? We've had recommendations for both as the material to use behind ceramic wall tile surrounding a wood stove?

A. Wonder-Board, a trade name of the manufacturer, Modulars, Inc.,[3] is a concrete and fiberglass mesh building board that is often used as a base for tile. But it's main characteristic is resistance to moisture deterioration, for example, under tile on kitchen counters, behind back splashes, and other areas that get wet. It is used by many professionals as a replacement for traditional "mud set" installations in which tiles are embedded in mortar.

Ultra-Board, a British import distributed by Weyerhauser (available through a wide network of local dealers), is like fire-resistant asbestos board without the asbestos. It also is much less brittle than asbestos board, and, therefore, much easier to work with. Ultra-Board can be drilled, sawed, even planed and sanded. The material can be used inside or outside, and offers resistance to rot, insects, and moisture, as well as fire.

---

[3]Modulars, Inc., P.O. Box 216, Hamilton, OH 45012

There are several grades of Ultra-Boards. Chances are that either the standard board or the "FS" (for fire shield) grade would satisfy local fire codes. But it pays to check with your local building department. Do-it-yourselfers who make improvements without a building permit and an approved set of plans, may jeopardize their fire insurance coverage by inadvertently using a material or construction method that does not meet fire codes.

Rating Plywood Grades

Q. What are the specific differences between plywood panels rated from A to D? Picking through panels at the lumberyard, it seems that several grades are similar.

A. The A-to-D letters refer to the panel surface veneer, one letter per side, from best to worst alphabetically. The best possible grade would be A-A (also known in the trade as "good two sides"). Grades can also be mixed, for example, in an A-D panel (known as "good one side"). The minimum grade for use outside the building frame is C-D.

A is reserved for smooth-surfaced, paintable, and general furniture-quality panels. Some small repairs may have been made in the wood veneer by the manufacturer, but should be parallel to the grain and not glaring. A-grade sides should be presentable enough for cabinet doors and similar applications, even under a clear finish.

B denotes a solid veneer surface that has structural plugs inserted in place of natural defects. These football-shaped plugs (two to three inches long and half as wide), are set by machine at the factory. The panels also may have some minor surface splits and tight knots up to an inch across the grain of the panel. You could also make built-ins from these panels, but only if the surface was primed and painted to hide the plugs.

C is for panels with larger knots (up to 1½ inches across the grain), some knotholes (limited to the surface veneer, not completely through the panel), and evidence of several types of minor repair work by the manufacturer.

Finally, **D** is reserved for panels with large knots and knotholes. These panels are limited to use inside—over floor joists, for instance—and are commonly covered by another material such as finished hardwood flooring.

Treated Deck Joists

Q. I am having a porch built on piers that will have salt-treated girders and floor joists, pine floorboards, and a ⅜-inch plywood ceiling covered with lattice strips. I would like the wood painted, but a friend suggested applying some form of termite treatment and then stain. What process should I use?

A. The best way to "treat" termites is to keep them away from their food source, which is the untreated wood in your porch. The idea is to block off their routes to the food instead of making all the food inedible. This is done most efficiently with termite shields, typically sheets of aluminum set in tar that project an inch or so away and down from the tops of the piers, just below the main girders. Theoretically, termites can't crawl around these obstructions without falling off.

PRESSURE-TREATED GIRDER

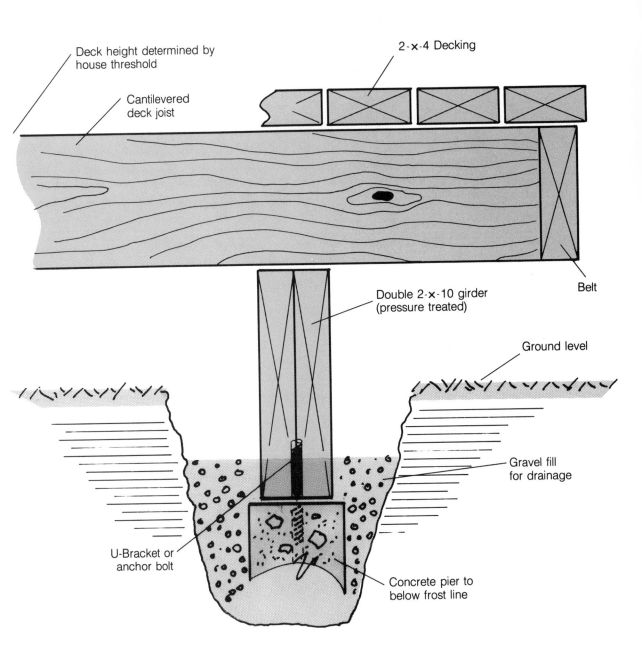

Deck height determined by house threshold

Cantilevered deck joist

2-x-4 Decking

Double 2-x-10 girder (pressure treated)

Belt

Ground level

Gravel fill for drainage

U-Bracket or anchor bolt

Concrete pier to below frost line

To keep a deck surface near ground level, a supporting girder must be buried. Even allowing for ventilation and drainage, such a beam should be chemically pressure-treated to last.

What you call "salt-treated" wood—a generic term for wood pressure-treated with copper chromium arsenate (CCA), which generally leaves a green tinge—is also a strong termite deterrent. Adding CCA floorboards would probably complete a very effective termite barrier. But if you use untreated pine, termites may tunnel over the treated wood to reach the pine, but they won't eat your treated girders or joists.

You can reduce the problem further by carting away any construction debris. Too often odd blocks of wood, plywood scraps and such are buried in the excavations created for foundations or piers. This may save carting time and expense short-term, but amounts to scattering food scraps for termites, which can lead to long-term infestation.

One part of your friend's suggestion does seem sensible, however. Generally, stain on wood exposed to the weather (even indirectly under a porch roof), requires less maintenance than paint. Stain soaks into wood; paint lies on the surface. Penetrating wood stains are available in all but the brightest and boldest paint colors, which you probably would not want on the porch anyway.

You might consider staining the plywood ceiling panels a dark brown or sky blue, and, prior to tacking the strips in place, staining the lattice a light gray or white or preserving the natural light wood tone under a clear sealer. (Lattice is also available in panels, by the way, which saves a lot of labor during installation.) Such two-tone effects can make the porch ceiling seem higher and make the space more detailed and generally more interesting.

BUILDING MATERIALS

New Product Development
Products That Succeed by Saving Time and Money

A recent article in *Builder*, a magazine for professional contractors, covered 12 new construction products and systems that save time and money, for builders. But saving time and money has also spawned such questionable innovations as aluminum wiring (to replace costly copper) and pumped-in foam insulation (to insulate without tearing open existing walls). Sometimes, saving time and money is not the best incentive for real progress.

Ideas for new building materials and methods of construction often germinate at government and industry research groups and at manufacturers. After limited testing they must start paying their way in the market place, and gain favor with professionals who monitor costs closely in order to survive much less succeed in a competitive and seasonal business so sensitive to economic trends.

It's difficult to launch a fundamentally new product or system in the building industry because, as *Builder* points out, "Few would accuse the home building industry of being overly innovative. After all, many of the last major breakthroughs—asphalt shingles and drywall, for example—occurred decades ago."

Following the basic market principle, "if it's not broken, don't fix it," most builders are reluctant to change a system that works, to adopt a new product unless it offers dramatic advantages over the one already in use. And since home buyers are generally more attuned to visible features than to methods of construction that could make the structure more durable and maintenance-free, there is little incentive for a builder to buy new tools and train new workers to install, say, a new corner framing system that could reduce the cracking seams and popping nails in wallboard joints. Other concerns, like an in-the-door ice maker, come first.

A builder has no incentive to change to an alternative system that is, so far as anyone can tell at this stage without long-term field tests, about as sturdy as the present system, but not obviously superior to it. But if such a system saves one stud on every outside corner and two studs on every partition wall corner (time and money) it suddenly becomes more attractive. And the more time and money a new system saves, the greater the temptation to overlook drawbacks such as a minor decrease in strength or longevity.

Here is a look at some recent innovations.

Flexible plastic pipes. Many builders and do-it-yourself owners became familiar with plastic pipe decades ago. The pipe could be cut with a hacksaw and easily cemented together. The newest version is polybutylene, which is just beginning to win acceptance

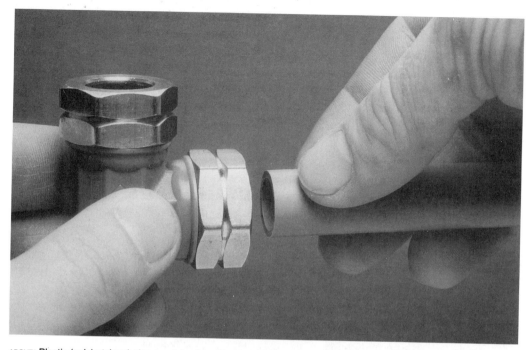

ABOVE: Plastic (polybutylene) pipe was introduced in 1979. The flexible piping can make gentle bends without the need for fittings. BELOW: To install elbows and tees simply insert the pipe into the fitting, then tighten down the locking nut with a wrench.

although it was introduced in 1979. It is flexible enough to bend around corners, which eliminates many elbow and tee fittings, and a lot of labor.

The National Association of Home Builders Research Foundation compared two houses: one plumbed with conventionally soldered copper, the other with code-approved polybutylene. The copper house took 1½ hours longer and cost $140 more than the plastic. Aside from time and money benefits, polybutylene is flexible enough not to crack if it freezes, and is inert, which means it won't react with the water flowing through it to create scaling and mineral deposits that can retard water flow.

Where fittings must be added to straight lengths of pipe, the method used in 90 percent of residential installations is crimping metal bands around the joints. But fittings differ slightly from one manufacturer to another.

Drywall clips. In the corners of every room two pieces of wallboard meet at right angles. The edge of each piece is typically backed up with a 2-by-4 wall stud. Without it, the edge of the drywall could not be nailed, and the corner joint could not be secured and covered over with joint compound. Similarly, 2 by 4s or other "nailers" may be added around the edges of ceilings for the same reason—to make a surface to nail against.

Instead of using timbers for nailers some builders are nailing only one piece of wallboard to the frame, and connecting the other with a U-shaped clip. This saves one stud on every outside corner, and two at inside corners, as much as 10 percent of the framing lumber on a 1,200-square-foot house.

This system relies heavily on two, and sometimes, only one piece of 2 by 4 to be straight and strong enough (and free of twisting or warping action common in moisture-laden studs as they dry out) to keep the corner joint together.

But this innovation has encountered a problem brought on by the degree of specialization in construction trades. Framers have to learn where to leave out a stud, while the drywallers have to nail on the clips that replace the missing stud and keep one edge of one of the panels from flopping around in mid air.

Short floor joists. Picture a side view of the floor framing in a house: 2-by-10-inch timbers span from the foundation wall on one side of the building to the other. On large houses, a girder, usually placed at mid-span, may be needed to prevent sagging. The floor joists are set in rows, 16 inches from center to center, strengthened with pieces of wood or metal banding called *bridging*, and by plywood subflooring, both of which tie the joists together.

A new lumber-saving system designed by a Washington state builder looks quite different. Smaller, 2-by-8-inch joists are spaced farther apart, 24 inches on center instead of 16 inches. Four feet in from the foundation walls, 4-by-8-inch support girders are set perpendicular to the joists on posts and concrete piers. The joists rest on the girders, and extend 2 feet beyond, halfway (yes, that's halfway) across the 4-foot space between the girder and foundation wall. Thick, ¾-inch flakeboard subflooring spans the unsupported gap between the ends of the joists and the foundation wall.

The system offers several cost-cutting advantages: the gap around the foundation wall makes a preformed nest for pipes and heat ducts; since the joists don't sit on the sill the house sits lower on the foundation, which saves siding costs; the amount of wood used for floor joists is cut in half.

Heavy-duty, ¾-inch-thick plywood sheets certainly make up for the increase in space between joists (from 16 to 24 inches), particularly when they are glued and nailed to the joists. Such a floor feels at least as strong and solid as a conventional floor built with ½-inch plywood over joists 16 inches on center.

But cantilevered joists (beams that project past their supports) have a certain liveliness and flexibility, and create unfamiliar uplift stresses away from the cantilevered section—a seesaw effect. Bookcases, couches, and other heavy furniture commonly placed near walls would load up plywood unsupported by floor joists, flexing cantilevered beams that could transfer the loads into an uplift force in the middle of the room.

Siding Systems
New Skins for Old Homes

Here's the situation—a real dilemma. The outside of your house definitely needs a face lift. But you are sick and tired of repainting every ＿＿ years (fill in your own number), particularly the darn double-hung windows, and even more particularly the overhangs where, no matter what you do, paint drips down your arm and into your eyes, and your back aches like crazy by the time you finally finish.

On the other hand, like many homeowners you may not want your home to be covered in pot and pan material, to radiate a metallic glint in the sunset like a car roof, or to dent when hit by a snowball. Houses should not dent. Of course, like other homeowners you may think that the problem with another alternative, vinyl siding, is that it looks like vinyl siding.

Now, before any angry letters are written extolling the virtues of synthetics and criticizing me for being prejudiced against them and in favor of wood, let me beat those letters to the punch and say that I am prejudiced against them and favor wood. My only excuse is that I used to be a carpenter, which, to me, always meant working with wood.

In addition to these limitations, the two most popular "maintenance-free" siding materials have been up on enough homes for enough years for many owners to discover a few flaws in those two magic words. Some owners even have to wash their aluminum homes with soap and water. And some, after 20 years or more in most cases, even do the unthinkable. They repaint.

What to do?

There are many possibilities: simple cleaning, performing a sort of face tuck instead of a full lift by covering only trim, overhangs, soffits, and other maintenance headaches, and complete re-siding in a variety of materials—even wood.

Cleaning a painted exterior with warm water, nonabrasive household detergent, and a soft brush (about ⅓ cup liquid detergent to a gallon of water) sometimes can be almost as effective as repainting. As dirt accumulates on siding over several years, you may not notice the gradual increase in dinginess—until you wash one of the dull spots and find surprisingly bright paint underneath.

If part of the building is not exposed to much sunshine and natural ventilation, you may need to add bleach (up to 1 quart bleach to 3 quarts water) to disinfect mold and mildew formations. (Do not combine bleach and ammonia, which produces dangerous fumes.)

Another appealing alternative is to recover a wood house with fresh wood. For instance, several lumber companies manufacture relatively thin hardboard panels configured like individual clapboards in a variety of patterns. Or, you could re-side with a ½-inch-thick plywood panel such as Texture 1-11, which comes in 4-by-8-foot and larger sheets with vertical grooves (simulating shiplap siding), every 4 or 6 inches. If you have done enough exterior painting for one lifetime, consider staining the new wood siding with a penetrating oil-base stain. It may fade slightly over the years. But it won't chip, peel, crack, and require regular stripping and repainting—a chronic problem on older homes.

No matter what material you choose, avoid the most common re-siding mistake of wrapping the house in foil before applying new clapboards or vinyl, or anything else.

Foil is an impervious vapor barrier. It is valuable on the inside of the house frame, just below the interior drywall, where it keeps moisture produced inside from seeping into the walls. Once any moisture gets into the walls, however, it should not be stopped by another barrier. This can create maintenance problems with paint and wallpaper on interior walls, cause bad odors, mold and mildew formations, soak insulation batts in wall cavities, and foster wood rot. It's a genuinely bad idea. (For more on re-siding, see Chapter 20.)

One common rap against vinyl siding is its appearance. But this solid vinyl re-siding job using Bird & Son, 4-inch clapboard panels maintains the building's classic colonial look.

All varieties of re-siding are a staple of shelter magazines and home improvement books. In addition, many companies and associations produce helpful literature. Here are just a few sources:

ALCOA BUILDING PRODUCTS
P.O. Box 716
Sidney, OH 45365

This company, a major manufacturer of aluminum and vinyl siding, estimates that only 3 percent of wood-sided homes are re-sided with wood.

THE VINYL SIDING INSTITUTE
355 Lexington Avenue
New York, NY 10017

This association produces many booklets for consumers on the installation process, including help with tools, trim, and fasteners.

THE RED CEDAR SHINGLE & HANDSPLIT SHAKE BUREAU
515 116th Avenue, NE, Suite 275
Bellevue, WA 98004

This organization can provide information on how to cover over old wood clapboards, wood shingles, stucco, and brick with new wood shingles.

Nail Sizes

Q. Why are nails ordered by "penny" instead of by length, and how do you compute "pennies" into inches?

A. Ordering nails by pennyweight instead of length, is a holdover from days when nails were priced in pennies per hundred. Longer, heavier nails cost more pennies per hundred than shorter, lighter nails. Now, "penny" refers only to length. Here are the equivalents between length and the commonly used pennyweight sizes. (Incidentally, the convention is to notate "pennyweight" with a "d," for example, 10d common nails.)

Large, 16d nails for nailing beams and girders on framing are 3½ inches long. 10d and 8d common nails used for most framing work, deck building, and such, are 3 inches and 2½ inches long respectively. Starting with a 4d, 1½-inch nail, each "penny" added increases the length by ¼ inch. A 6d nail, for example, is 2 inches long, 2 "pennies" more than the 4d nail, and 2 "pennies" less than the 2½-inch, 8d nail.

You didn't mention the other confusing issue: How many nails, whether ordered by pennyweight or length, do you get per pound? Unfortunately, each type of nail produces a different answer. You get about 11, 6-inch-long nails per pound, but about

850 1-inch common nails. Your best bet is to check one of the general how-to books—the *Reader's Digest Complete Do-it-Yourself Manual* has a chart of number of nails per pound—or just ask at your local lumberyard or hardware store.

NAIL SIZES
Pennyweight Size

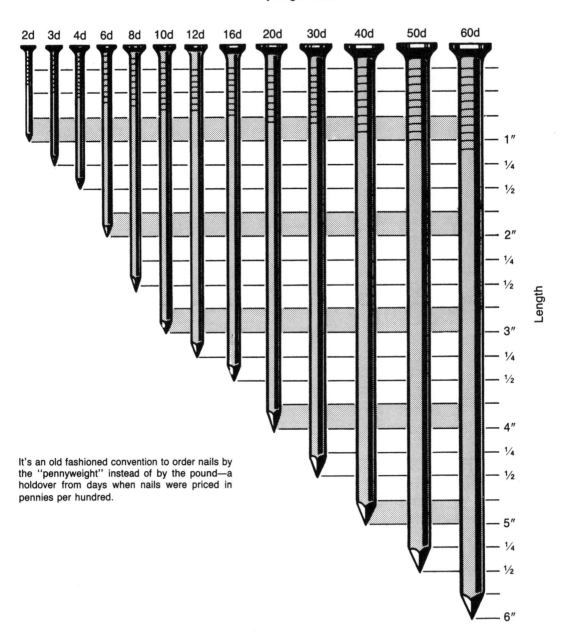

It's an old fashioned convention to order nails by the "pennyweight" instead of by the pound—a holdover from days when nails were priced in pennies per hundred.

Nailing Drywall

Q. How many nails must be used on a standard panel of drywall? It seems that more nails provide more holding power, but also more holes to spackle. And that leads to more maintenance later on as nail heads pop through the spackle and paint.

A. For ½-inch-thick, 4-by-8-foot sheets of gypsum drywall (the most common size used in residences), use 1¼-inch, diamond-point nails. Start nailing from the center of the panel, pressing it flat against the framing as you work your way toward the edges. This avoids building in stress that can later force nails to pop. Space nails 7 inches apart on ceiling panels, 8 inches apart on walls. And keep them at least ⅜ inch from the edges of panels.

You can minimize taping, and maintenance later on, by driving the nails perpendicular to the board, not at an angle. Finish each one off with a hammer blow that seats the head just below the board surface, but not deeply enough to puncture the surface paper.

Spacing can increase to about 14 inches on ceilings and 16 inches on walls if a continuous bead of construction adhesive is applied over framing members. Check label directions on the adhesive tube before using, as several products require use in well ventilated areas within a limited temperature range.

With more professional equipment you can use drive screws instead of nails. These pointed, threaded fasteners have more holding power. Also, they are much faster to use than nails if you have a power screwdriver—basically a ¼-inch electric drill with a special head that turns the screws in place, then releases at a preset torque level. This method is also much neater than nailing, and produces very small, uniform dimples in the drywall surface.

If you have a fair amount of drywall to place, try to rent a power, drywall screwdriver. You'll get used to it quickly. From then on, you'll save a lot of time, and get better results—not a bad combination.

Beam-Hanging Hardware

Q. I'm building a deck using 2-by-8 floor framing. Many of the right-angle connections can be nailed securely through one board into the other, but this won't be possible on the joints up against the house. Isn't there a piece of hardware that will do the job?

A. Yes, there is. In fact, the general term is beam hardware, in this case, a deep U-shaped bracket with a surrounding flange. For your application you would ask for a joist hanger or a stirrup (more of an old-time phrase). There are configurations made to strengthen almost any framing joint, between 2-inch, and even 4-inch-thick timbers.

In some areas building codes require beam hardware in addition to face nailing. But if the floor beams of the deck are perpendicular to the house you must use hardware on joints against the house because there is no room for nailing face nailing—not unless you assemble the frame, and then push it against the house, which is another option.

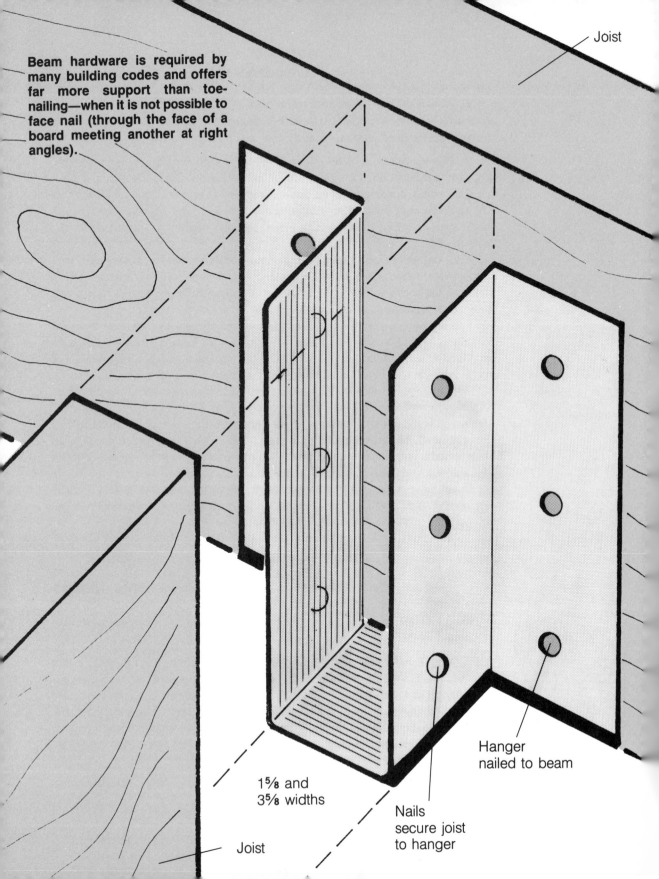

Joist

Beam hardware is required by many building codes and offers far more support than toe-nailing—when it is not possible to face nail (through the face of a board meeting another at right angles).

Hanger nailed to beam

Nails secure joist to hanger

1⅝ and 3⅝ widths

Joist

Joist

Toenailing, or angling a nail through the edge of one piece into another, is, by itself, not acceptable for this kind of frame connection. But on the end of the joists away from the house you can easily drive three, ten-penny nails through the face of a 2-by-8 belt piece and into the joists butting against it.

Although the joists would hang on the nails alone, for extra strength and durability, if not to satisfy building codes, drive two face nails to secure the connection, and continue to set all the joists. Then check for levelness, and make any small adjustments required to produce a level frame. After that, nail a beam hanger into place, reinforcing each connection.

Small holes (for box nails, which are thinner than common nails used on framing) are prepunched in the metal flange and serve as nailing guides. Several nails connect the hanger to the beam and the hanger to the 2-by-8 belt running at right angles to the floor joists. You should be able to find this hardware at any lumberyard or home center.

PVC Lattice

Q. Between the floor of our wraparound porch and the ground we have latticework to close off the irregular space. Although it looks very good when repaired and freshly painted it is a constant maintenance problem. Is there some coating or lattice-size wood that will last longer?

A. The best plan, at least from the point of view of reducing maintenance and repair time, may be to replace the wood with PVC lattice. Several sizes and colors are available from Cross Industries, Inc.[1] The panels are made with polyvinyl-chloride strips that do not need paint or sealer. Dirt splattered from rain or dripping gutters for instance, can be washed off with a hose.

Granted, the material is plastic, not wood. But the lattice grid is likely to be a more prominent characteristic than the uniform texture and finish of the individual strips. The plastic can be cut with hand or power saws (a fine-toothed plywood blade will produce the neatest cuts) and nailed without predrilling.

Vinyl Siding System

Q. What is a good way to cover a chronically damp, rough, and unattractive basement cinder block wall? The area is so damp, I'm worried that even a new wall will soon show mold and mildew deposits.

A. Increasing ventilation, or running a dehumidifier, will decrease moisture and help preserve whatever wall you build. Adding vent fans in basement laundry rooms, lavatories, and other moisture sources will also help.

But when a wall seems beyond cosmetic repair, though still structurally sound, it is reasonable to bury it. For instance, you could build a wood-frame wall of 2-by-2

---

[1]Cross Industries, Inc., 5262 Peachtree Rd., Atlanta, GA 30341

ABOVE: Most vinyl siding can be applied directly over existing walls, to recover a garage, for instance—without burying existing window and door trim. BELOW: Specialized vinyl siding systems include board-and batten configurations, and clapboard styles. Most systems, such as this one made by Vinyline, a Marion, Ohio firm, use preformed moldings, trim pieces, and end caps to enclose vertical or horizontal vinyl sheets.

studs, insert rigid foam insulation between the studs or under the entire frame, cover with a plastic vapor barrier, then add a finish surface of wallboard or paneling. This avoids nailing into the wall, which sometimes leads to leaks and other problems.

Since the basement climate is a chronic problem, though, you might be interested in a new type of vinyl siding, suitable indoors and out. The Vinyline system uses trim pieces top and bottom, and narrow vertical cover strips every 16 inches. These strips must be secured to the wall or to furring strips. Flat vinyl panels fit within this framework.

The board and batten design, applied over a layer of rigid insulation, should provide a dry, room temperature, easy-to-clean surface. But the manufacturer (General Plastics Corporation, contacted toll-free at 1-800-833-6000), has altered the design somewhat, and now offers a clapboard-style (horizontal) configuration, although you may be able to track down some board-and-batten stock.

Fancy Cut Shakes

Q. I need to replace some irregular wood shingles on my bungalow, but can't find a supplier. (The exposed ends are tapered like bird feathers.) How difficult is it to cut your own, or is there a supplier I haven't found?

A. Cutting more than a few shakes would be tedious. And the bird feather shakes you describe sound like octagonal cuts, included with several other stock "fancy cuts" made by Shakertown Corporation.[2] They offer a variety of special shapes, including an arrow, fish scale, diamond, and others.

Information on shakes is also available from the Red Cedar Shingle & Handsplit Shake Bureau.[3]

Many unique patterns can be made by alternating styles in different courses. For instance laying a course of pointed, diamond shakes over a course of round-ends makes a teardrop pattern. This is the kind of architectural detail difficult to recreate when residing with low-maintenance materials such as aluminum or vinyl.

Wood Heat Registers

Q. What is the best way to hide, or at least disguise, the series of dark-colored, metal, hot-air registers around the perimeter of a living room floor? The furniture is grouped away from the walls in the large room, which makes the registers stick out like sore thumbs against a light-toned oak floor.

A. The easiest way to make the registers less obtrusive is to repaint them in a lighter color—maybe a shade of one of the darker pieces of oak in your floor so that they do not stick out like sore thumbs by being too light. Lift the registers out of their pockets (some types are secured with screws), scratch up the visible surfaces with steel wool

---

[2]Shakertown Corp., Box 400, Winlock, WA 98596
[3]The Red Cedar Shingle & Handsplit Shake Bureau, 515 116th Ave., NE, Suite 275, Bellevue, WA 98004

to improve paint adhesion, and then spray paint. You could use a brush, but spraying in two coats produces a more uniform finish, and makes it easier to cover the grill slats.

Another option is to install wood registers. One company, Grill Works[4] makes 2¼-by-12-inch and 4-by-12-inch wood registers in red oak, white oak, and maple. The small size retails for $32; the larger size for $36. Price includes the hardwood register and frame.

The very attractive units sit in wood frames flush with the floor. It is a pretty slick detail. And the bottom of the wood grills are recessed so you can reset the original metal vent onto the plywood subfloor just beneath the wood register. This feature is handy if you have metal registers with an adjustment to control air flow, although most homeowners don't adjust the registers very often, if ever.

Instead of installing modern, slatted floor registers in an old house, you might prefer more decorative versions, such as this brass model made by Reggio Register of Ayer, Massachusetts.

---

[4]Grill Works, 22060 Stratford Place, Shorewood, MN 55331

Six

TOOLS

Tool-Buying Guidelines
Selecting the Right Tools for the Job

Selecting a practical, reliable, and efficient set of hand and power tools can be as complicated as ordering dinner for eight from a large-scale, four-page, fine-print menu. There are so many possibilities to choose from: hundreds of different hammers—with different-shaped heads, in different weights, made with wood or fiberglass or rubber handles. And that's child's play compared to the complexities of saws.

Some tools are made to last a lifetime, or longer, while others are called "throwaways"—even by their manufacturers. There is no single type, or degree of quality, or combination of tools that is correct for everyone. The selection depends on the work you want to do with the tools, how often you'll use them, to some extent how good you are at using them, and, of course, how much you can afford to spend. Many good tools are expensive.

While a heavy-duty collection like the one above might be right for a log builder (the huge circular saw will slice through a 4-inch-thick log in one pass), most do-it-yourselfers are more comfortable using more manageable sizes.

But one common piece of bad advice about tools is that all good ones are expensive. Not true. One of the most accurate, durable, and useful construction tools is an extremely inexpensive water level, used for jobs such as making sure that one end of the foundation is level with the other. This unfailingly accurate tool consists of some clear tubing, which may cost a few cents per foot. You supply the water that fills the tubing and levels itself.

The other common but no more helpful piece of advice is that you should always buy the best. Baloney. Sometimes a cheap and inexpensive throwaway tool is a good choice. For example, an expensive bristle brush is unnecessary when adding a touch-up coat of wood stain to a few old railroad ties beside the driveway.

Even though it might be nice to buy the best—accepting for a moment the misguided premise that money is no object—buying top-of-the-line tools is often an unrealistic and unnecessary investment. They may be attractive, intricate, imported, and even useful. But while buying chisels with good Rockwell hardness numbers may have some impact on the work of an experienced cabinetmaker, having the ultimate cutting edge is not a prerequisite for typical do-it-yourself repair and improvement projects.

The truth is that a novice do-it-yourselfer or an inexperienced carpenter will get mediocre results despite using the best tools. But a good carpenter will somehow get reasonably clean cuts with even the crummiest handsaw. A higher quality saw would keep a keen edge longer, work more efficiently, and make the carpenter's job easier. It would not make the carpenter more skilled. Like most tools, a saw simply goes where you push it. So don't be coaxed into a high price range by a salesperson who suggests that the tool, and not the person using it, makes the difference.

Here are a few guidelines that may help you accumulate a practical collection of tools:

• Generally, avoid the most and least expensive models. The most expensive tools often include "gee-whiz" features that do not enhance performance or durability. The least expensive models often have fundamental, built-in problems, or are too flimsy to withstand even normal use.

• Avoid tools with painted metal surfaces. This is a common method of disguising inferior manufacturing. When the body of a plane, for example, is manufactured by casting, molten steel is poured into a mold of the tool's shape and allowed to cool. This allows bubbles to form in the steel, which weakens it. When a metal tool fractures when dropped, particularly in cold weather, or a wrench handle simply snaps under pressure, the fault was probably built into the casting. This manufacturing process can often be recognized by rough edges of steel that looks unfinished—unless it is disguised by a coat of paint.

• Where accuracy is important, on cutting tools such as planes, for instance, look for symmetrical grain lines in the metal surface which indicate a manufacturing process called *machining*. In this case steel is heated, then squeezed between heavy rollers to remove most of the weakening bubbles trapped as the original ingot was formed. The tools are then machined, or ground out of the rolled steel like a sculpture chiseled from a block of stone.

• Where strength is important, on tools that must deliver and withstand impact forces such as hammers, the best method of manufacture is called *drop-forging*. In this process the tool is stamped out of the rolled ingot with a huge, heavy, molded hammer. This process exerts even more pressure on the steel than rolling, further reducing the presence of bubbles. It produces tools that can withstand great concentrations of stress.

- Generally, avoid multi-purpose tools, except for situations where having the right device is crucial, and the fact that it may be mediocre quality, or built into a clumsy handle along with 8 other devices isn't important. For example, a combination screwdriver-pliers-socket wrench covered with reflective tape to serve as safety markers may be a reasonable, space-saving choice for your car. But most tools do one job well, two jobs not quite as well, and so on.

- Include mail-order catalogs in your comparison shopping for tools. Several mail-order firms (some also maintain retail outlets) carry interesting collections, and may offer a greater variety than small stores and even some large home centers. But mail-order tools are not necessarily less expensive than their store bought counterparts. Some firms are considerably more expensive than others.

Here are just a few of the well-established and reliable sources for general purpose and specialized mail-order tools.

BROOKSTONE HARD-TO-FIND TOOLS
127 Vose Farm Road
Peterborough, NH 03458
(Now with many retail outlets as well.)

FINE TOOL SHOPS INC.
20 Backus Avenue
Danbury, CT 06810

FRANK MITTERMEIR INC.
3577 E. Tremont Avenue
Bronx, NY 10465

U.S. GENERAL SUPPLY CORPORATION
100 Commercial Street
Plainview, NY 11803 (800-645-7077)

WOODCRAFT SUPPLY CORPORATION
41 Atlantic Avenue
Woburn, MA 01888

Circular Saws
Power Saws for Production Cutting

A circular saw is the most basic power tool, used by do-it-yourselfers and professionals on everything from bridges to bookshelves. With a small, fine-toothed blade it can cut hardwood floor trim. With a huge, carbide-abrasive blade it can cut through reinforced concrete.

Until 1810, sawing was strictly a back and forth operation. Every timber, every clapboard, every piece of trim was sawn to its shape by hand. And about half of all that motion was wasted. Saw teeth are sloped forward slightly, and shaped and sharpened in a way that makes them cut into wood on the forward, pushing stroke. The return stroke just repositions the saw for the next cutting stroke. (Incidentally, on Eastern saws, even modern Japanese handsaws, saw teeth slope back toward the handle, the pull stroke does the cutting, and the push stroke is the return.)

In 1810, in a Shaker settlement at Harvard, Massachusetts, that wasted effort prompted Sister Tabitha Babbitt to invent the circular saw. After watching Shaker brothers sawing boards, Sister Tabitha rigged up a prototype circular saw by fitting a toothed circular blade cut from a tin sheet to her spinning wheel.

Modern circular saws are more accurate and much faster than handsaws. And instead of buying several handsaws with cutting teeth matched to different tasks, one circular saw can be used with any number of specialized and interchangeable blades. The round blades with fewer teeth than handsaws are much easier to sharpen. In fact, if a blade begins to dull from repetitive cutting through plywood, for instance, the teeth can be touched up with a file on the spot. It is much more difficult to touch up a handsaw, which generally requires professional attention. And if you happen to destroy the cutting edge, it's less expensive to replace a circular blade than an entire handsaw.

Despite all the advantages you may not really need one. If you rarely do home repairs or improvements, much less woodworking projects, you probably don't. But because a circular saw can be adjusted to cut through wood at different angles, and through different thicknesses of wood without splintering the edges, it is a very versatile tool and valuable on all sorts of jobs. On a renovation project such as paneling a room or building a deck, it's a necessity. It is ideal for production-type projects requiring many cuts, for cutting long straight lines—trimming the edges of a new deck, for instance—and preferable to a handsaw for cutting plywood.

Plywood is particularly hard on handsaw blades because it is tougher than a normal piece of wood. Different layers of wood are laid with grain at right angles, and joined with glue that hardens. While a large-toothed saw would be a good choice to minimize cutting time through plywood, a fine-toothed saw is needed to avoid splintering the outermost layer of wood, particularly on veneered plywood used for shelving and furniture. A portable, electric-powered circular saw with a fine-toothed ''plywood'' blade combines speed and a neat cut.

Deciding which saw to buy is a simple matter for the most gung-ho do-it-yourselfers. Generally, they want the best, even if they don't really need top-of-the-line quality. But buying even a basic power tool such as a circular saw can be confusing to less-crazed home repairers and improvers. When prices range from several hundred dollars for a large, heavy-duty model to only thirty or forty dollars for a small, almost toy-like version, it's difficult to select a saw with features you really need and an appropriate level of quality. This guide should help.

Size. For all-around work use a 7½-inch model (saw size is given in the diameter of the blade). Smaller saws don't have the depth of cut needed for standard timbers such as 2-by-4-inch wall studs. Larger saws are best suited to production cutting, and are too heavy and unwieldy for most people. Motors rated less than 2 horsepower are sufficient for odd repair and improvement jobs, but not powerful enough for heavy-duty production cutting.

Second Handle. This nice but unessential extra commonly takes the form of a knob mounted toward the front of the saw. Most will be quite awkward for lefties who may have to reach across the blade path for the second hand hold. But in many cases two hands are better than one, when working at shoulder height or above, for instance. And it's far safer than holding the motor housing, which gets hot, or any part of the saw near the blade.

Balance. Few stores allow a powered test with blade. But you should at least simulate cutting motions to get a feel for the saw. The handgrip and trigger must be comfortable and provide efficient leverage as you direct the saw. A handle position directly above or slightly forward of the motor can cause fatigue and inaccurate cutting by forcing you to drag the saw through the cut.

Adjustments. To hold different settings of blade depth and angle of cut, a saw requires easily tightened, positive-locking controls. Large levers or knobs work best. Avoid small wing-nut locks, which are tough on the fingers.

Blade Guard. You can't buy a circular saw without a retractable guard. It covers the blade teeth, telescoping into the saw housing during a cut. But to make plunge cuts, starting in the middle as opposed to the end of a board, the guard must have a small handle so it can be retracted safely before the blade digs in.

Automatic Brake. This extra, generally reserved for higher-priced saws, stops the spinning blade as soon as the trigger is released. The useful safety feature can prevent accidents resulting from careless handling, but, on some models, makes a startling screech when it engages. If you use the tool the way you're supposed to, you don't need it.

Arbor Lock. This feature enables you to change blades safely. It prevents blade rotation while the nut holding the blade on the saw is loosened. Without it, the blade turns as pressure is applied to the nut. Home-made "stops" such as little blocks of wood, or a stick, are generally unsafe substitutes.

Blades. Many saws are sold with a 24-tooth combination blade, good for overall cutting. Fewer teeth produce a rougher but quicker cut. More teeth produce slower but cleaner cuts. Look for taper-ground blades, which offer smooth operation because the circumference where the cutting teeth are is slightly thicker than the rest of the blade. This reduces friction and drag as the blade travels through the wood. Top-of-the-line carbide-tipped blades hold their sharpness much longer than standard blades, but are more expensive. Also, they cannot be touched up by hand and require professional sharpening.

Carbide Blades

Q. Are carbide-tipped saw blades much better than regular blades and worth the extra money they cost; and how do you sharpen them?

A. They are more durable, which is better if you are a carpenter or use a circular saw on a regular basis. For example, Black & Decker claims a lifespan up to 50 times longer for its Piranha carbide blades than for standard steel blades.

Normal blades can be sharpened to as fine an edge, but won't keep the edge as long. Since they are less expensive than carbide-tipped blades, they are a reasonable choice for do-it-yourselfers. Also, standard blades can be touched up easily if you mistakenly cut through a nail, for instance. Carbide-tipped blades must be resharpened by a professional with special equipment.

One application where the extra expense for carbide can pay off is on a table saw. For example, if you are building cabinets or furniture using plywood or particleboard (the glue in these materials is particularly tough on blades), a 36- or 40-tooth carbide-tipped blade can consistently produce very clean cuts without ragged edges that need a lot of sanding. But for run of the mill circular saw jobs, a standard blade is fine.

Japanese Saws

Q. I have been tempted by a set of unusual-looking Japanese saws that I have seen in several mail-order tool catalogs. The ads say they are very sharp, very durable, and easy to use. But the saws have long straight handles unlike any I've ever used. Do they really work well, or are they just conversation pieces?

A. They work very well if you are Japanese and grew up using them. Of course, Western saws are probably just as unfamiliar to Japanese due to several differences in design. For instance, the Japanese saws, which range from knife-like keyhole models to large, rectangular-bladed crosscut saws, have small diameter, straight, bamboo-wrapped handles.

Although the saws have a beautiful simplicity characteristic of Japanese design in general, handling them is an adventure. Even after a few go rounds you half expect to find a frying pan at the end of the handle instead of a saw blade. Western-style, open-handle-grip designs seem to offer more control by making the saw more of a direct extension of your hand. But then I've built houses using ''our'' saws, and only dabbled in using ''theirs.''

Another fundamental difference is the saw tooth direction. Japanese saws are made to cut on the pull stroke (our rest or retrieval stroke), and to rest on the push stroke (our cutting stroke). Even trying to discount experience and habit, it seems a lot more logical to put your body weight behind the more forceful cutting stroke, allowing your hand to provide more guidance than power. Pulling back through the cut just seems wrong; it takes you away from the action instead of toward it.

However, I have kept the Japanese keyhole saw in the tool box. It has a smaller, slightly bent and "user-friendly" handle, and a very thin, very sharp, pointed blade. Truth be told (and probably to the horror of woodworking purists), I'm afraid I have found this tool perfect for plunge-cutting through gypsum drywall, and making neat, quick, and accurate cutouts for switch boxes, and other obstructions. It is much faster and safer than a drywall knife, for instance.

I think you might find the keyhole saw (called a *Hikimawashi*), and the dovetail saw (a fine-toothed, thinner, more rectangular version of Western dovetail saws called a *Dozuki*), enjoyable and serviceable on small-scale hobby and shop projects. The larger, construction-scale Japanese saws are just too bizarre, and take too much getting used to.

Laying Out Saw Cuts

Q. I want to cut an octagon coffee table top out of a sheet of plywood. How do you mark the sheet so the sides will be equal?

A. The first job is to draw the octagon on the plywood. Second, is marking and cutting the lines consistently so that the width of saw cuts (each may be less than ⅛-inch thick), does not distort the layout.

Here's how to mark up the square. Lightly sketch two diagonals connecting the corners. Adjust a length of string attached to a pencil (like a giant compass), so the fixed end of the string is at any outside corner, and the pencil point rests on the center of the board where the diagonals cross.

Swing arcs across the board holding the string at each corner. Connecting the points where the arcs cross the outside edges of the square will produce an octagon.

Once these points are located, trace the octagon perimeter with a sharp pencil. If the point fattens out as drawn, producing a thick line, sharpen it. Then, decide on a margin for cutting. For instance, some carpenters cut the line off, meaning the inside of the saw blade just barely erases the pencil line. Others prefer cutting up to the line. Whichever method you choose, try to keep the same relationship between pencil line and saw blade.

Wallboard Saw

Q. What's the easiest way to make a small cutout in a piece of wallboard? I need to install several light switches and am having a tough time using a drywall knife.

A. Even a sharp drywall knife will have to be drawn along the cut lines repeatedly before slicing through ½-inch-thick gypsum panels. And the blade is likely to bind before cutting through. The job is easier if you cut a narrow V-shaped trench through the panel—the same idea as notching a tree instead of sawing straight through.

But since the V-cut is wide—it must extend into the piece of wall you intend to remove—this system can easily lead to mistakes in dimensions.

Many contractors use a keyhole saw instead, although sawing through gypsum will dull the blade and make it unusable on wood. It is a narrow, tapered, toothed blade that makes a lot of dust, and leaves a slightly ragged edge. But it is fast, accurate, and less dangerous than using a drywall razor knife.

Chainsaws

Q. I am going to buy a chain saw and would like to know the pros and cons of a gasoline model versus an electric. Which one makes more sense for a person cutting up about a cord of wood into small, stove-length logs?

A. I would stay away from an electric model for anything but occasional, light-duty cutting. Even though you wouldn't have to deal with gas and oil mixtures and dirty carburetors—there is no combustion with an electric model—you would have to deal with the cord. It follows you everywhere, providing one more item to trip over or cut through accidentally. Running a chain saw is tricky enough without another potential obstacle, no matter how convenient it may be.

Cutting Laminates

Q. I have been trying to apply a new layer of laminate over our old kitchen cabinets. But there is a problem along the edge of the cabinet doors. When I run a router along the edge to trim the laminate corners between the side panel and the face, the side panel becomes darkened—almost scorched. What's wrong: me, the router, or the laminate?

A. The scorching comes from excessive friction as the guide pin protruding below the router blade spins against the laminate. It is possible that you are being too careful, and pulling the router along the seam too slowly. But if speeding up starts to chip the laminate, or overloads the router (the pitch of the motor will deepen noticeably), your blade may be dull.

Since plastic laminate is hard and brittle, a sharp, fine-toothed blade is required to avoid chipping. This Skil saw offers another advantage on tight corners—a rotating blade head.

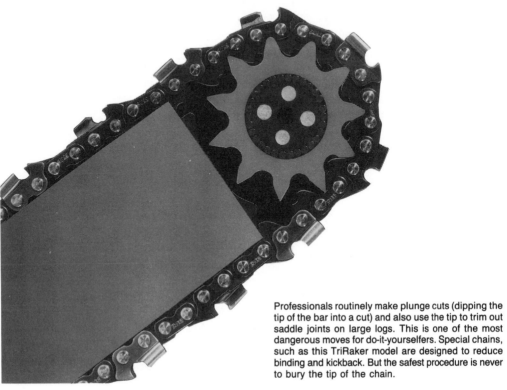

Professionals routinely make plunge cuts (dipping the tip of the bar into a cut) and also use the tip to trim out saddle joints on large logs. This is one of the most dangerous moves for do-it-yourselfers. Special chains, such as this TriRaker model are designed to reduce binding and kickback. But the safest procedure is never to bury the tip of the chain.

There is a special type of router blade made for this job which should eliminate the problem. The guide pin portion of the blade—the part that travels along the edge of the cabinet door and is scorching the laminate now—is surrounded by a ball bearing guide. The ball bearing rolls slowly along the edge while the guide portion of the blade spins inside, eliminating the high-speed friction.

Paint Brushes

Q. I'm not in the habit of throwing out an electric drill or a hammer after I use them, and don't see why I should use a cheap paint brush that sheds bristles just so I can throw it away when I'm done. Since I plan to take reasonable care of the tool, I'd like to buy a really good bristle brush. What should I look for?

A. While a nylon brush is the best choice for latex paints, a natural bristle brush seems to provide the best results for oil-base and alkyd paints, stains, varnish, shellac, and similar finishes. Other more subtle characteristics, such as the amount of paint the brush can pick up and hold, then spread evenly, and how comfortable the brush feels, may depend more on who uses the brush and what type of surface they paint.

There are three primary qualities, though, that do separate a really good brush from the rest of the pack. First, is a configuration called *tipping*. "Tipped" means the ends of the bristles are pointed like a needle. This encourages an even release of paint. Second, is a second treatment at the end of the brush called *flagging*. "Flagged" means the ends of the bristles are split, which helps the brush hold more paint and spread it more evenly. High-quality synthetic brushes can be specially treated to simulate a flagged and tipped bristle brush.

Although no brush can compete with a roller on large flat surfaces, brushes are used almost always on trim. To "cut in" around windows and doors a 3-inch wide, long-handled trim brush works well. Its long, flexible bristles can be articulated with great accuracy, allowing even a do-it-yourselfer with limited experience to draw a straight line of evenly applied paint along the edge of a piece of molding. Expect to pay top dollar for a long bristle, long handle, 3-inch, flagged and tipped brush, known in the trade as a "sash tool."

Paint Rollers

Q. I'm using what the paint dealer calls a "masonry surfacer" over the concrete block walls of the cellar, and a flat latex paint on the wallboard ceilings. Can I use the same roller for both jobs, or do I need a brush for the masonry?

A. Look closely at the rollers in the paint store and you'll see that they are sold in different lengths and nap textures. "Nap" refers to the thickness of the roller mat—the surface that holds the paint. Fine-nap, mohair rollers create a smooth surface. They would be a good selection for applying high-gloss oil paint to kitchen cabinets, for example.

For the rough-surfaced concrete block you should use a similarly rough-surfaced roller. In the trade these wooly rollers are called "bulldozers" because they hold so much paint, and even thick material like a masonry surfacer, and push it ahead of the roller like a bulldozer. The thick nap is needed to thoroughly coat all the little crevices in the block surface. On smooth walls fine-nap rollers leave a flat finish, and heavy-nap rollers leave a textured finish.

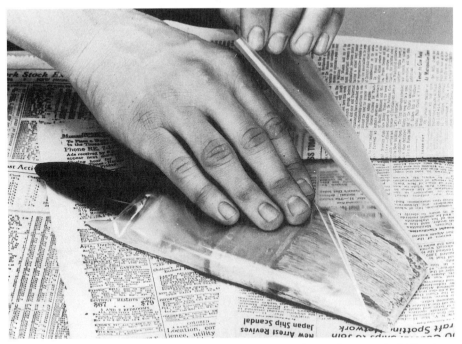

Buy good brushes but take the time to clean them thoroughly at day's end. Store them by folding them neatly into a plastic bag, turning over the excess plastic, and closing the opening with tape or rubber bands.

Portable Electrical Screwdrivers

Q. Are battery-powered screwdrivers really useful or just another case of adding a gimmick to a simple tool that increases the price?

A. This new twist on an old design can be very useful in some situations. The models I've tried all work well on driving modest-sized screws in predrilled holes or in soft wood like pine. When there isn't much resistance, and you have a lot of screws to turn (when assembling predrilled, knock-down furniture kits, for instance), using a power screwdriver can make the job easier and much faster.

The main limitations are bulkiness and lack of power to turn big screws through thick or dense woods. The bulkiness cuts down on the feedback and sense of touch through the tool. It's more difficult to keep the screwdriver bit in the screw slot and "feel" when it's running off center or otherwise out of kilter.

However, since the tools are handy for some jobs and cost only about $20 you might consider buying one, but using another form of power screwdriver to handle heavier-duty projects. For instance, you can simulate most of the capabilities of a professional-quality electric screwdriver by locking a screwdriver bit into a standard ¼- or ⅜-inch drill chuck.

This works pretty well on a drill with variable speed control so that you can control the turning and slow down to apply more push on the drill as the screw seats. And then there is the old standard—a semiautomatic, nonelectric yankee screwdriver, which turns screws quickly as you compress the long barrel of the tool, then finishes them slowly as you lock the barrel down for the final few turns.

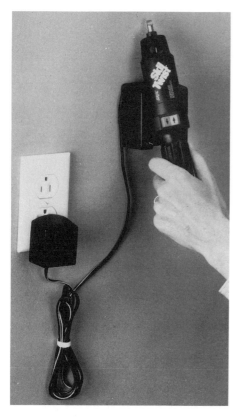

The "Twist," made by Skil, comes with a plug-in recharging holder and provides enough power to turn at a relatively slow and controllable 130 RPM. The handy tool is rated to drive up to No. 10 wood screws.

In any case, the battery-powered units are selling like hotcakes. Skil, which makes a model called Twist, says its cordless, battery-powered, 1 pound, reversing screwdriver, sold with a plug-in recharging holder, is the most successful new power tool ever introduced by the company.

Hammer Handles

Q. Which works better, a hammer with a wooden handle, a fiberglass handle, or a rubber handle?

A. There's no way to answer without offending several manufacturers of hammers, even though the answer is only my choice, and not based on anything like scientific stress tests on hammer handles. I like wood best because it combines the best qualities of fiberglass and wood. That's reasonably tactful, right?

Fiberglass handles are supposed to be stronger than wood, which doesn't matter too much unless you hit the nail with the handle—a bad move. And in any case, I have seen fiberglass handles break at the hammerhead, which only shows that no material can withstand misuse. Rubber handles—usually a rubber sleeve around a steel shank connected to the hammerhead—are more resilient than fiberglass, not as strong, and more prone to scarring. Also, when sweat from your hand gets onto the rubber sleeve it becomes very slippery.

Wood is naturally resilient, but not as bouncy as rubber, and durable, but not as rigid as fiberglass. If you use a hammer often enough it begins to fit your hand in a way a molded rubber handle never will. The only drawback with wood is that the grain soaks up sweat and dirt, which can make the handle difficult to grasp. This problem can be solved by scuffing up the sides of the handle with rough sandpaper or even with a finishing saw, then sanding off any potential splinters with fine paper. With this process you can customize the grip, and make the wood handle easier to hold under all conditions.

Drill Bits

Q. When I drill or saw through a piece of wood the edges on the top side of the cut or hole are smooth, but the edges on the bottom are ragged. How can this be prevented? I am building a room divider bookcase where both sides of the boards will show.

A. Wood grain on top of a board does not splinter under the pressure of sawing or drilling because it is supported and stabilized by more wood grain beneath the surface. But this support is missing at the bottom layer of wood where even a sharp saw or drill bit is likely to bust through, instead of cut through, the wood.

There are several ways to minimize this common problem. First, is to provide support to the bottom layer by tightly clamping a second board beneath the first. For example, if you are sawing through a piece of ¾-inch-thick pine shelving, clamp on a scrap piece of same material and cut through both boards at once. Holding a board against a workbench cannot substitute for the uniform, stable support of a clamped board.

Using sharp tools also helps. Dull tools apply more pushing force against the grain, the force that causes splintering. Sharp tools transfer more energy to cutting through the grain.

Special bits can also greatly reduce splintering on the bottom edges around holes in wood. Forstner bits have a circular cutting wheel with a single raised tooth around a central sharp point. As the point penetrates the grain, the circular cutter slices through the grain around the perimeter of the hole. When the bottom of the board is reached, this circular wheel tooth slices through the last layer of wood just before the center of the drill pushes through.

Although these bits are more expensive than conventional twist drill or wood-boring bits, they are standard tools of the trade for carpenters working on jobs such as installing oak stair treads, and for furniture makers who routinely use fine hardwoods on which holes that accept spindles and other connecting pieces are visible.

Contracts
and
Contractors

Seven

ESTIMATES AND CONTRACTS

Contract Benefits
Protection for Home Remodelers

It is reasonable to think of a contract as a binding agreement—reasonable, but often misguided. For example, there are contracts with defense contractors to build ships and planes for specific, agreed-on prices, and cost overruns. There are contracts for new model cars, and surprise changes due to last minute price increases on the new model.

In fact, so many contracts are broken so often, that you may well wonder if there is much point to drawing up one with a home improvement contractor. Consider this worst case, but not altogether unheard of, scenario.

Your $20,000 remodeling project is nearly complete. You have reserved a final payment of 10 percent—a combination carrot and stick—to induce the contractor to complete a lengthy checklist of unfinished items. To get your money's worth, you intend to stay home the final week of the job and make sure that every item is attended to properly.

But your contractor is ready to start his next job. And he has already taken a fair amount of profit out of your project. Sure, he would like the $2,000. But, looking over the checklist, he can see many expenses, mainly labor costs, that will shrink the profit in your final payment. He decides that it's not worth leaving the crew at your home for a week to make everything perfect. So he leaves.

Aha! You have a contract, you say. He leaves anyway. You won't pay him the $2,000. He knows that already. You won't recommend him to other consumers. There's so much work now that he doesn't need your recommendation. So you will activate the contract provision about arbitration. He doesn't need to arbitrate anything. He's gone. Okay, you'll haul out the big gun. You'll take him to court.

So this great binding agreement has left you with a house full of unhinged doors and unpainted trim. After many months, if not years, of legal delays, chances are that if the fellow is still in business and still in the area, you might come face-to-face with him in court. At that point, your recollection of events may be pitted against what seems like a practically hallucinogenic version from the contractor. And the issue will be decided by someone who doesn't know you, or your house, or the number of mosquito bites you got and the hours of sleep you lost because you never got the screens you

---

Opposite: On this project, the foundation is waterproofed, insulated, and backfilled. The finished roof should come next—to protect the frame and floor, then walls, windows, and doors.

were supposed to get with the new windows. Spectators in court may wonder why you look so ready to kill.

Aren't contracts terrific?

Despite their lack of airtightness, home improvement contracts are essential. Conventional wisdom says they will provide legal safeguards against consumer catastrophes such as the vanishing contractor. Sometimes they can. But a good contract probably cannot improve the character of a dishonest contractor. He may vanish no matter how many times the contract says he is not allowed to vanish.

But if consumer and contractor can make a reasonable contract before the job begins, they are unlikely to need the contract as the job progresses. That truism—that reasonable contracts are made by reasonable people—is one of the best reasons for translating the details of your project into contract form.

In a very real sense, home improvement contracts are tests of honesty, reliability, and professionalism. Chances of making a complete, airtight, fair and honest contract are greatest with a fair and honest contractor who is least likely to violate the provisions. You are most likely to need a solid contract, and least likely to get one, with an unprofessional contractor who will use every available loophole. If you can't draw up a fair agreement with the contractor, you're probably dealing with the wrong contractor.

Despite all the concrete, framing and wallboard, a few finishing touches left undone often can undo an otherwise successful project. Watch out for lingering special orders—a wood-grained finish panel for the dishwasher, for instance, that will match surrounding cabinets.

Also, writing a detailed contract is a good way to plan the job and to discover trouble spots on paper, ahead of time. Considering the complexity of construction and remodeling work, it is natural that you and the contractor would have slightly different ideas about details of the project.

For instance, he might assume that a few pieces of pine painted to match surrounding siding will do nicely around your new windows. But you may be thinking that he will carefully remove all the old window trim, scrape off all the paint, then reattach it around the new windows—a considerably more time-consuming task.

In the process of reducing your ideas to writing, misunderstandings—even understandable, honest misunderstandings that can create ill will and delay the project—can be avoided.

There are three basic contract options: Write your own; use preprinted forms; or hire an attorney to write one.

The desirability of each option depends on job complexity and cost, and on your penchant for consulting lawyers. In general, large projects that cost a lot of money—whatever "a lot" is to you—should be covered by a professionally prepared contract, one drawn up by an attorney, or one modified from preprinted home improvement contract forms. On smaller, straightforward jobs you can write your own contract in the form of a letter of agreement.

<hr/>

Budget and Schedule Control
Keeping Track of Home Improvement Projects

Few home consumers still cling to the hope that their carefully planned improvements or remodeling projects will be completed on schedule and on budget. Realists know that home improvements almost always take longer and cost more than expected.

Some surprises may be inevitable. But there are several ways to minimize cost overruns and delays—two of the most common complaints from consumers who tackle a nearly impossible mission: transforming the place where they live, and continuing to live there at the same time.

Obviously, a key component of any home improvement contract is the price. Theoretically, if you budget enough to cover that bottom line there shouldn't be any financial surprises. But there usually are, mainly from two sources: changes in plans or materials that cost more than the originals, and "extras" that you expected to be included in the overall contract price.

To protect against costly changes, specify in the contract that any change can be made only after your written approval. Suppose, for instance, that instead of enclosing the space beneath a deck with 2 by 4s and solid wood siding, the contractor uses widely-spaced lattice strips.

They might be easier to install, and cost less. That could be good news if the contractor passes along the savings, but bad news if you planned to use the under-deck space near the pool as a changing room and didn't want see-through walls. Even well-intentioned alterations should be agreed to in writing, in order to avoid situations where the contractor makes a change thinking, mistakenly, that it's to your advantage.

Making changes in writing is a relatively standard provision of home improvement contracts. So is another phrase that governs material substitutions: "or equal." For example, the contract may specify a certain brand and model number of window. But in case the window is out of stock, or a better price is available on a comparable unit, the contract makes provision for switching to a unit of equal quality.

Since quality is a subjective judgment, all supposedly equal material substitutions also should be approved in writing. Every once in a while, a contractor will substitute a less expensive, inferior product, and pocket the savings. You should have the opportunity to compare construction features and warranties as well as prices.

Even more protection may be offered by amplifying the "or equal" phrase with language saying that written agreements about substitutions must specify charges for labor and materials. With this language, even if you did not mind the loss of privacy in your changing room, you would see from the estimate for the substitute lattices, that the change would save time and money, entitling you to a reduction of the overall contract price.

Unexpected extras are the other main source of cost overruns. These may include all kinds of items: steps to a deck that you thought were part of the deck, storms on the windows that you thought came with storms, a stone hearth for the wood stove. Everyone knows you can't just sit the wood stove on the wood floor, you reason, as the contractor points to the contract specification about a wood stove, and you search in vain for the part about the hearth.

One component that is useless without another may, even in arbitration or a court case, be assumed to be included in the contract, for instance, an electric line to power an exterior floodlight. But in a good contract, even the most obvious component is covered. It may be covered specifically—a list of materials and dimensions for the deck steps. It may be covered in brief, referring to a certain type of window including storms. Or it may be covered by a catchall, performance specification, for instance, that the wood stove shall be installed in accordance with national and local fire codes. These include elaborate controls on the use of potentially combustible building materials near the stove, including hearths.

The point is, everything, but everything should be covered. If you read the contract and can't find anything about that birch countertop you talked about with the contractor, don't be too surprised if you don't get one, or that if you do get one, it's listed on the "extras" bill as N.I.C. (Not In Contract).

Another common complaint of home consumers is that the improvement project never seems to end. Some extensions are inevitable. But there are steps you can take to minimize delays. For instance, order materials ahead of time, particularly appliances, and any custom material such as special-pattern tile.

The most important safeguard is to establish regular communication with the contractor. Of course, you probably will talk every day. Certainly you will talk when problems erupt. But with good communication you can calmly discuss potential problems before they erupt.

On lengthy projects such as room additions, try to schedule at least one meeting a week, allowing a good hour to cover current job status, finances, materials on order, any changes, and a tentative schedule for the upcoming week.

Instead of shooting for one completion date far off in the future, and possibly missing it by a wide margin, striving for several intermediate dates offers many opportunities to recognize and recover from minor delays.

Letters of Agreement
Home Improvement Contracts: Is What They Say, What You Get?

Every spring the backlog of home improvement projects simmering on drawing boards during cold weather finally coalesces. That increases the number of jobs, making more work for about the same number of contractors. And that creates a seller's market in which it can be more difficult for consumers to make a reasonable agreement with the right contractor at the right price.

For many consumers it's a catch-22, in fact, almost a conspiracy. Now that the economy is healthy, inflation and interest rates holding, and they can finally afford to build the deck or remodel the basement, they can't find anyone to do the work.

Conditions that have spurred new and existing home sales as well as renovation and remodeling work, favor contractors in their dealing with consumers. The law of supply and demand dictates that many contractors will now be able to pick and choose their projects. Estimates that might have been trimmed to the bone last year, may not be so free of fat now. And consumers, happy to find any contractor, may not look as hard at the contractors they hire.

The greatest risk is overlooking the basic protection offered by a fair job contract. In a seller's market it is even more important to reproduce in writing every verbal promise about job price, starting time, materials, and job quality. This protects your interests and reduces the number of honest misunderstandings between contractor and client.

Reducing a series of general conversations about a project to several cogent paragraphs does not necessarily require the services of an attorney. However, it is self-evident that an attorney is better equipped than most consumers to write a contract. Not all contracts require an attorney's expertise. But every job requires a contract, whether a preprinted form or a document you write yourself, called a letter of agreement.

The raw ingredients of this letter are facts and figures from the contractor's estimate, and common sense. Both parties should have ample time to consider the provisions before signing. And neither party should take offense at provisions included to cover situations that almost certainly will not arise—a complete work stoppage, for instance. That word "almost" is why you need provisions for extreme cases.

Remember during this process that you are the one with the money. That gives you the right to ask questions and get reasonable answers before signing. An established contractor should be able and willing to document work experience with blueprints, photographs, and names of satisfied customers. You should verify this documentation, and make the obligatory checks for complaints at the local Better Business Bureau and Consumer Protection Agency before proceeding.

Preprinted contract forms are available from the American Institute of Architects.[1] Their "Abbreviated Form of Agreement Between Owner and Contractor" contains language that is standard in the trade, based on years of research and experience. It is used for projects up to and including major additions. A more complete form is used for new home construction.

Obviously, such forms must include some generic language; they cannot anticipate the specifics of your project. You and your contractor must fill in the blanks. And you may have to strike some provisions that do not apply, such as a clause defining the role of the architect if one is not involved.

Supplanting a material and labor estimate with a more detailed, official-looking document may alienate some contractors no matter how large and complex the project. On small-scale projects completely reputable contractors may balk at all the fine print, which is understandable if contract negotiations and signing ceremonies loom larger than the job itself. In such cases a letter of agreement is a reasonable alternative.

The idea is to write the specifics of your own project in your own words, following this 7-item format.

1 Record names, dates, and identify the purpose of the document, stating, for example, that the letter is an agreement regarding the work of reroofing a garage. Include the contractor's license number, if required, and starting and completion dates for the job.

2 Describe the work area and its limits, for example, that the garage roof includes the breezeway, and that shrubbery by the garage must be protected against damage during construction.

3 Describe the work itself, listing, for example, that the existing shingles will be removed and new felt paper laid. If this information isn't on the contractor's estimate, and the contractor feels compelled to keep the process a secret, talk to another contractor.

4 Describe the materials, including trade names, model numbers, dimensions, or other characteristics. This prevents the substitution of inferior materials later on. Record any product warranties, for instance, that manufacturer's shingle guarantee.

5 Include the contractor's guarantee of both personal liability and property damage insurance. "I'm covered," or "I'd never sue," or any other verbal promise is worthless.

6 List everything the contractor provides including, for example, all materials, equipment, and labor required to complete the reroofing job in a timely and professional manner. On larger projects involving subcontractors (for example, a painter and a roofer who work for your contractor), specify that each contractor turn in a form called a waiver of mechanic's lien rights. This prevents subcontractors from suing you for money you paid to the contractor that he did not pass on to them.

7 List total cost and method of payment. Reduce the first payment to no more than 15 or 20 percent, and increase the final payment to at least 15 to 20 percent. On time-consuming projects such as a room addition, divide payments to coincide with the completion of major portions of the work. For example: 20 percent up front, 20 percent when the masonry and rough carpentry is done, 20 percent when siding, roofing, windows, and doors are in, 20 percent when the plumbing, heating, and electrical work

---

[1]The American Institute of Architects, 1735 New York Ave., NW, Washington, DC 20006

On highly designed projects such as this bath redo, only experienced builders will have the connections to locate special lamps, tile, mirrors, countertops, not to mention a partition made of glass block. Contracts for such jobs should nail down materials by name, size, and model so that no substitutions are made.

is done, and 20 percent after all work is completed, including the cleanup. At any rate, if you finance the job your bank will probably insist on a similar system of staged payments. Never pay a large percentage initially. Never make final payment prematurely. (For more on contractual agreements and contractor-consumer relationships, see Chapters 8 and 13.)

Comparing Estimates

Q. Is it considered unethical or bad consumer strategy to show one contractor estimates from another? It seems that showing the expensive contractor a bid from the inexpensive contractor on the same job might result in a price reduction.

A. Asking one professional to comment on the proposal of another is an interesting tactic. It may ruffle some feathers, but could provide useful information, and, maybe, even a modest reduction of a high bid—but only if the proposals are very similar in all respects except price. If not, you will be comparing apples and oranges, and the high-end contractor will be able to justify his price by pointing to materials and plans in his estimate not even mentioned in other proposals.

There is nothing unethical about it. What you suggest is, after all, simply an extension of what the contractors are doing anyway: competing with each other. If you question a contractor on his selection of a particular type of window, he may say no more than they are good, and he always uses them. But these pat answers will not work if you ask why he uses them instead of another, less-expensive type suggested in a competing estimate.

The high-end contractor's more detailed justification of the more expensive windows may make a lot of sense; maybe the extra money buys extra features well worth paying for. But if the high-end contractor provides no more than pat answers to a series of challenges over lower labor costs, an earlier completion date, better lumber grades, a longer warranty period, and other job issues presented in competing proposals, it would probably be wise to discard his bid.

The drawback to this competitive tactic is that one contractor may dismiss any recommendation other than his own as unprofessional. There may even be some name-calling ("Everyone knows that so-and-so contractor is no good"), which is why it is prudent to photocopy the competitive estimates with names and addresses deleted. But even this type of blustering response can be educational.

You might be better off with a contractor who presents a good plan, and, instead of trashing the competition, clearly explains the differences between one bid and another, and shows you why his plan is the best one.

Eight

WORKING WITH CONTRACTORS

Self-Contracting
Managing a Home Improvement Project

Buying direct and eliminating middle men is a sure way to save money. It seems like a very good idea. If you know what you want and where to get it, you can often bypass services and profits at the retail level and order direct from a manufacturer, major distribution, or factory outlet.

Many consumers take the same approach to major home improvement projects. Instead of hiring an architect to design an addition, they draw their own plans. Instead of hiring a general contractor who orders materials, hires subcontractors, and supervises the work, they take charge of the project themselves.

Being your own architect and general contractor certainly saves money, maybe as much as 30 or 40 percent of the cost of a room addition. But you may have trouble filling in for these construction middlemen. Even if you have a clear picture of your project, and even if you know where to buy the materials and where to find the subcontractors, bypassing the professionals can be a risky business.

You may be able to sketch out a picture of the deck or dormer. But to get a permit for the job, your building department will want to see some very specialized pictures called *working plans*. Typically, these include a plot plan showing your existing home and proposed alterations in relation to the property lines, framing plans with details, and cross sections of critical areas and connections, and elevations (side views).

On small jobs, some building inspectors may grant you a lot of leeway and approve a nonprofessional set of drawings. But whatever you scribble on the back of an envelope must still show how the structure will be put together, the depth of the concrete footing, the size of the floor girder, the location of all major timbers, and other details.

Of course, architects are trained to do more than draw. Even if you have a clear idea of how the improvement should look, an architect should be able to execute your idea efficiently, if not improve on the concept. It's no surprise that someone who designs homes for a living would see a few pitfalls you don't, and build in a few money- or maintenance-saving features you would overlook.

Another option is to order stock designs from one of the many firms that sell working plans for full houses. (Several advertise regularly in home how-to magazines.) Fewer offer plans for room additions or specialized alterations. But if you are adding a known quantity such as a prefabricated sunspace, the manufacturer should be able to provide working drawings that will satisfy a building inspector and a contractor you hire to attach the structure to your building.

Marley Continental Homes

ABOVE: Instead of trying to do everything yourself (particularly if you have never built a house before), a sensible alternative is to buy a kit or prefab home. Experienced crews put the structure together, including, in most cases, insulation, plumbing, and wiring, all assembled under controlled conditions at the factory. BELOW: Working inside a closed-in home, new owners can tend to decorating and finishing work.

Marley Continental Homes

With permit and plans in hand the next job is to hire subcontractors to execute the design. This requires an exhaustive process of interviewing masons, framers, plumbers, electricians, and others, receiving and evaluating competitive estimates, then drawing up contracts with each one. If you hire a general contractor (G.C.) you have to go through this process with only one person. The G.C. is responsible for assembling the materials and many specialists who will complete the project.

This raises the issue of overall job responsibility. When you work with a G.C. or an architect who is also providing supervisory services (as opposed to a set of drawings only), you effectively make one person responsible for the finished product. Without one of these supervisors on the job, you are in charge. And even though each subcontractor you hire (electricians, plumbers, framers, roofers, and others) is responsible for a particular piece of the job it's up to the general contractor (you) to make sure all the pieces fit together.

For instance, you have to make sure the mason allows for the soil pipe opening in the foundation. Otherwise, the plumber putting in the pipe will have to take the time to knock a hole in the block. You have to make sure the subcontractors show up in order, for instance, that rough, in-wall piping and wiring is completed before drywallers arrive. You have to make sure that the subcontractors accommodate each other—that the framer leaves out a few floor timbers so the furnace and oil tank can be moved into the cellar.

Construction is a cooperative effort. But not all subcontractors are cooperative. And on a one-time job working for you they are missing the powerful incentive of satisfying the general contractor who hires them for many jobs during the year.

In short, when you pay a general building contractor to run the job, infighting, scheduling, and other job details are handled by the G.C. If you're in charge and the drywaller blames cracking wallboard seams on the wet wood used by the framer, you get caught in the middle of the argument—maybe without the expertise to understand their explanations and excuses, and without the authority or clout to settle the dispute.

If you have been through several home improvement projects and feel familiar enough to cope with the managerial and technical aspects of your current project, there is still another hurdle: time. As a rule, running a construction or home improvement job takes more time than most people have, particularly if they work full-time.

It's true that experienced architects and general contractors may have several jobs running simultaneously. That doesn't mean that managing your project yourself is a part-time affair. The professionals can tend to many projects because they know what to expect, and have already seen and solved most of the problems that will crop up—problems that may be unexpected and unfamiliar to you. Also, the professionals are probably dealing with familiar subcontractors who know what the architect or G.C. wants.

Maintaining any semblance of normal day-to-day living can be difficult enough even when an architect or general contractor is in charge. Tending to household responsibilities, a job, and supervising a construction project is taxing on a very practical level.

For instance, many subcontractors start work early—at 7:00 or 7:30 in the morning. That's the time when they may need to talk about materials, job progress, and other matters—just as you're getting ready to leave for work or getting kids ready for school. And by the time you get home after work the subs are long gone. If you can't be on-site all day you still must be accessible over the phone to consult on unexpected matters such as a delivery of screen doors that were supposed to be glass doors. It can be difficult to manage the job from a distance, over the phone, and under the gaze of your employer.

If you haven't yet tried managing a home improvement project, it is wise to gain experience on one or more relatively small projects before tackling a room addition or similar major alteration.

Home Builder Profile
Who's Building All the Houses

Don't expect home building contractors you interview to show up in overalls with pencils tucked behind their ears and crumpled pads where they jot down a few notes and dimensions. If this picture ever were true it certainly isn't any more. It's more likely now that the builder will be in a suit and tie (97 percent are male) and feed data about your job into a computer that will spew out estimates, blueprints, job progress plans and payment schedules.

It's likely that the builders you talk to about your new home or room addition have switched their collars and their majors: from blue collar carpentry to white collar business administration. They have had to in order to survive in an increasingly competitive market in which there are fewer builders and increasingly expensive homes. (The average nationwide price of new and existing houses in 32 major cities surveyed by the Federal Home Loan Bank Board was about $125,000 in 1988.)

That's part of the picture of modern home builders that emerges from a recent survey of over 17,000 builders conducted by *Builder* magazine and the National Association of Home Builders, a major trade association.

It is clear from the survey that the chances of finding what many consumers still think of as a typical home builder—an independent carpenter who employs a small crew and puts up one house at a time—is decreasing. In 1969, there were about 129,000 home builders and about 100,000 today. And two-thirds of the homes built in this country are constructed by large firms that put up 100 or more houses a year.

Although there are fewer builders they have more experience. Their median age is only 42. But most have been in business 14 years or more (a decade ago the median of experience was only 8 years), according to the survey. Almost 30 percent have been in business 20 years or more. But even 14 years on the job should provide perspective since it covers periods of building booms and busts. A few bouts with hard times certainly thinned the ranks of many laid-back carpenters who got the idea in the 60s that it would be nice to work with their hands, man.

One of the most significant trends in the home-building business is an increase in more sophisticated business practices to improve efficiency and cut costs, and an increase in computerization, particularly for planning and estimating, although larger firms also use costly computer programs for design and drafting.

These changes are reflected in the educational background of home builders today. While 18 percent are high school graduates (3 percent are not), 25 percent have completed some college, 34 percent are college graduates, and 20 percent either have completed some graduate work or hold graduate degrees.

As management becomes more important, more builders are doing less of the actual building work themselves. According to NAHB statistics, 40 percent of builders subcontracted more than 75 percent of all construction work in 1969, compared to 61 percent now who use specialized subcontractors to handle jobs such as building foundations, installing plumbing, electrical, and heating and cooling systems, applying roofing and installing drywall.

Although the builder is responsible for the work of his subcontractors, it is typical now for three-fourths of the work done on your home to be done by people you don't know, who do not compete directly with other roofers or drywallers you interview, who do not submit to you bids that can be compared with their competitors' estimates.

The increasing distance between the businessman builder and the fieldwork only emphasizes the importance of selecting a builder carefully and choosing someone whom you trust to make the right decisions about people as well as job quality and cost. Some building contracts include provisions that give the owner the right of refusal over the selection of subcontractors. But few owners are in a position to exercise it knowledgeably.

Another important provision, called a *Waiver of Mechanics' Lien Rights*, prevents the builder's subcontractors from dumping their financial problems with the builder on your doorstep. Specifically, it prevents them from suing you for money owed them by the builder.

How much are builders making for their efforts? *Builder* magazine reports that almost 75 percent of the heads of small companies (with annual construction valued at less than $1 million make less than $50,000 a year, while their construction supervisors (the people you're more likely to see on a regular basis) make between $25,000 and $30,000. In big firms with construction totaling over $100 million annually the company presidents make over $350,000 with bonuses and the construction supervisors makes about $50,000.

Home Improvement Contractors
Finding Out about Home Improvement Contractors

When it comes time to find a contractor, you are likely to encounter a classic home improvement truism: Jobs always take longer and are more complicated than you thought they would be. This holds true from the very beginning, when you are trying to get out of the planning stage and find someone to make the plan a reality.

Locating and hiring a reliable contractor is often a time-consuming and difficult process. But it is a crucial part of any project. An inexperienced, flaky, untalented contractor can foul up the most foolproof set of blueprints, while a good contractor can get surprisingly good results with only mediocre plans and materials. That should be no surprise.

But you may not expect to spend so much time locating one of the good guys. It's likely to take some detective work—developing leads, tracking down referrals, verifying recommendations, conducting face-to-face interviews, putting all the pieces together, and drawing conclusions.

Ideally, someone else would do it all for you. Occasionally, that is a realistic option, for instance, if a contractor is highly recommended by a trusted friend or neighbor who has just had work done that is very similar to the job you're planning. Your friend can tell you about costs, schedules—even the contractor's attitude. And you can see the results for yourself. How handy.

But in most cases you must conduct the search. Here are some guidelines that should help.

• Develop a list of candidates using referrals and recommendations. Referrals are simply names you get from ads and professional societies such as state or local home builder or remodeler associations. Recommendations are names that include an evaluation, for instance, a contractor who gets rave reviews from your neighbor. If you have trouble collecting names, ask people in housing-related fields such as your home insurance agent, real estate agent and mortgage banker.

• Put all the names on your list through the most basic checks with local consumer protection agencies and the Better Business Bureau. Although these agencies don't recommend contractors, they can tell you if a contractor is licensed, where required, to do business, and report on the record of consumer complaints against your candidate.

• Check for the contractor's affiliations with professional groups. Of course, a National Association of Homebuilders home builder is not necessarily more talented than a nonaffiliated builder. But such affiliations are usually a plus. It's safe to assume that fly-by-nighters are not likely to spend the time or money to join, even if the professional group could be fooled into accepting them.

• Ask each contractor for both consumer and professional testimonials. An established roofer, for example, should have no problem providing the names of several satisfied customers, and the name of a lumberyard or supply house where he buys materials. Making a few telephone calls can help to round out your picture of the contractor as you discover that he is highly regarded, or barely known.

• Find out how long the contractor has been in business. Experience does count. It means the contractor has had more practice, seen more one-of-a-kind construction details, and solved more problems. In general, firms in business a decade or more must be doing something right.

• Find out what type of contract each contractor normally provides. You may find surprising variations, from the briefest, most general estimate that is essentially worthless, to a comprehensive contract that lists materials, dates, payment schedules— everything about the job.

A professional contractor will not balk at translating into writing what he is promising about the job, for his own protection as well as yours. For instance, stay away from someone who does no more than specify a "high-quality" window. A reputable contractor will list the window manufacturer, model number, size, and if screens and storms are included or extra.

• If you are hiring a general contractor who will use specialized subcontractors on parts of your project, find out if your general contractor has a long-term business relationship with the subs, which is normally the case with established and successful general contractors.

Even so, you may want to make a few brief checks on the electrical or plumbing subcontractor, for instance—just as a way of double checking the general contractor's judgment and veracity. You should avoid a general contractor who can't provide names of subs, or expects you to find and hire them.

• Avoid contractors who engage in any of these very questionable practices: Someone who applies pressure or offers special inducements to sign a home improvement contract; someone who is reluctant to produce a license where required; someone who demands a large up-front payment to buy materials—more than 15 or 20 percent (10 percent is standard); someone who says that you don't need any kind of building permit on projects where foundation and structural alterations or additions are planned; someone who demands payments in cash.

Bunco Home Scams
Debunking "Bunco" Consumer Scams

"Bunco" sounds like something Sgt. Joe Friday would have talked about on "Dragnet." Although it may sound dated, police still use the term to describe a variety of theft-by-trick crimes, including all sorts of phony sales, fake charity solicitations, confidence swindles, and other con games. But many of the most successful bunco crimes are directed at homeowners, including a host of home repair and improvement rackets.

Although everyone is a potential victim of a bunco con artist, the principal victims are often elderly and alone. But any uninformed consumer may fold under the slick, high-pressure techniques of a bunco artist when they are caught off guard, one-on-one, for instance, at home after everyone else in the house has left for work or school.

And in some cases, consumers whose judgment is clouded by greed, are not exactly innocent victims. Some forget about asking basic questions, or getting a written contract, and participate willingly in scams designed to take advantage of someone who is looking for a deal that is, in fact, too good to be true.

The "pigeon drop" is a classic example. In this scam, bunco artists may plant a wallet with money in it, and arrange to "discover" the wallet in your presence. The con man (or woman, young or old, neat or scruffy) may offer to cut you in on their find, but only if you put up an equal share of money as a sign of good faith, or if you supply cash for travelers checks or another valuable item in the wallet. Whatever the excuse, you are supposed to bring money into the deal in hope of getting even more money in return. Such deals turn sour when the bunco artists disappear with your cash, and the money from the wallet that was counted out and placed in an envelope turns out to be Monopoly money, or the travelers checks turn out to be phony photocopies.

Such schemes take advantage of the victim's desire to make money or save money because of some special deal—a unique set of circumstances that will finally enable them to get even for all the change lost in pay telephones and soda machines. That is often the approach used with two of the most common home repair scams: resurfacing roofs and driveways. Here's a typical scenario.

The nice-looking fellow at the front door says he is contacting several of your neighbors. He's noticed that their shingles, like yours, are a little worn out and probably about to start leaking, if they haven't already. But this is your lucky day. His crew just finished laying a fantastic new roof coating at a house nearby and they have material left over. Since the crew is here and the material is ready, they can give you the deal of deals. And one last thing: Since they are practically taking a loss on your job, maybe you could pay them in cash. *Dum da dum dum.*

If you haven't checked out your shingles lately and don't know much about roofing, a friendly ''expert's'' offer to solve potential problems for a bargain price might seem

Magical roof coatings that can transform a leaking roof or skylight into a waterproof shield are favorite scams of home improvement con artists—in part because it is difficult for owners to climb up on the roof to check the work. But slapping some tar around a leaking skylight will only fix the problem temporarily.

attractive. But the life-extending shingle coatings, which may be slopped onto the roof in a matter of minutes, normally turn out to be some thinned down mix of old engine oil that looks good over slightly worn shingles or a blacktop driveway for a very short time. Such mixes will wash away in the rain, stain siding, kill nearby grass and generally produce a mess that costs much more to fix than the "bargain" installation price.

One of the crudest bunco home schemes is to cajole a homeowner into providing a cash advance against materials for a job that is never done. The "salesman" simply pockets your deposit on materials and leaves. Another common scam is to gain entry by offering some sort of free prize or inspection service—the proverbial "something for nothing."

For example, bunco artists may arrive at the door saying they are conducting free safety inspections of home furnaces. Some may flash a phony badge and purport to be from a local government agency. Others may say the free service is simply a goodwill gesture to make friends for their new company.

Once inside, the phony inspector may bang on pipes, disconnect oil supply lines, drop a marble into the furnace fan, which makes quite a racket, or create some other problem. Then they offer to fix the problem for a price—maybe only $25 or $50 for removing a marble from a fan. Someone alone at home can feel so threatened by the bunco artists, who are now becoming very argumentative and talking about explosions and fires, that just getting them out of the house seems worth almost any price.

These final warning signs and your common sense should prevent bunco artists from running one of their scams. Beware of:

- Unsolicited orders
- Deals that coincidentally seem to offer services or products at incredibly low prices
- A demand for cash instead of a check
- Pressure to conclude the deal quickly; No written estimate or contract
- No business card, no main office or business phone number, and no references

Presented with those circumstances, your response should be simple: "No deal"

Mediating Consumer Disputes
Mediating Disputes: What to Do When Things Go Wrong

After the new roof sprung a leak the homeowner contacted the roofer who came back to install several new shingles. The leaking stopped. But the light-pink shingles the roofer used for repair tended to stand out against the dark-brown shingles he had used on the rest of the roof. When the contractor refused to make another change, this case became one of the 35,000 or so complaints reported to Better Business Bureaus every year.

Few were as frivolous. Over 60 percent were settled in a mediation process, and, unlike this case, in which the roofing company argued that the contract said the roof shouldn't leak but nothing about color, did not go to court.

To get good results with all sorts of home repair and improvement projects, and to avoid litigation, consumers receive a lot of advice and instruction about how to deal with roofers and mortgage bankers and other home professionals. The premise is that if they follow the guidelines everything will work out satisfactorily. Sometimes everything does. Because the advice is supposed to work, however, little effort is spent on what to do if it doesn't.

The following advice assumes the worst. It is based exclusively on the premise that everything will not work out—that plans for new additions, a new bay window, and many other efforts will go awry.

In the worst case, against the most intransigent contractor, you can, in the end, always take them to court. This is the easiest advice to give a consumer, and often the most misleading.

Taking a contractor to court should be the last resort. It is time-consuming and expensive. Depending on the jurisdiction, a suit over $5,000 worth of work on a $25,000 job could linger in litigation for 3 or 4 years. Few people can stay angry enough about warped doors or flooded basements to propel such a case through the legal system. The appearances and postponements can become more harassing than problems on the original job.

Even if you stick with it you may not win—even if you're right. But many consumer advisers don't mention that. Details that seemed so clear and important at the time, are often supplanted by a colorless paper record of the job. And a company that told you to take a hike at the time, may now say they tried to help but you were never home. In almost all cases it is more reasonable and practical to negotiate some kind of settlement without going to court.

Most of the home repair and improvement complaints received by the Council of Better Business Bureaus are triggered by consumer dissatisfaction with quality (of labor or materials or both), and timing—typically a job that drags on and on.

When the end of a job is in sight it becomes clear to the contractor how much or how little he will really make. At the same time, the consumer starts to see the kinds of details that will be left undone, and may be surprised when finishing touches turn out to be extras.

At this point cold cash can be more potent than reason. As a practical matter, often regardless of what the contract or contractor promises, a final payment turns out to offer the best hope of settlement: You want the last $2,500? Let's sit down and draw up a written list of jobs that we agree will be done before you get it. Obviously, if only a token amount is left for the final payment, reason may have to prevail on its own. Generally, final payment should be at least as large as the downpayment, or 10 to 15 percent of total job cost, whichever is higher. It must be enough money to maintain the contractor's interest in the job.

Communication, with or without a financial carrot backing it up, is the best defense against problems over time or money. As the job draws to a close, schedule regular meetings if you have not already done so. The idea is to parcel out the remaining work in manageable bundles that can be adjusted, priced, even traded.

Use regular progress reports to uncover trouble spots while they are molehills instead of mountains. Informal, ongoing conversations are no substitute for an official sit-down meeting (once a week on large projects, more often on smaller ones), where owner and contractor (and architect or other involved professional) review the job.

On large projects, a contract provision called a *work stoppage clause* can help. The clause defines when a delay becomes a stoppage, permitting you to use construction funds to hire a second contractor (after legal notification) without financial liability to the first.

But more often a contractor or supply firm is willing to talk. Generally they too would rather close the books on the project, even if they have to give up a bit of labor and material to do it. This may be possible in face-to-face discussions. But Diane Skeltis of the Council of Better Business Bureaus says, "The issues are often clouded with emotions. The problem is in someone's home; they're faced with it all the time. Our complaint reports show they can get pretty riled up about it."

In such cases a third party can be helpful. The Better Business Bureau (BBB), for example, offers a mediation service. As third party to the dispute a BBB representative can edit out some of your heavy-duty adjectives when they talk to the other party, make suggestions, help both sides to zero in on what appears to be common ground.

While mediation is voluntary, there is another step, called *binding arbitration* that has the force of law without taking the parties into court. The Better Business Bureau, the American Arbitration Association and other groups offer these services. Typically, both parties agree to present their case to an arbiter, and to abide by his decision—just the way professional baseball players and club owners do it. Although not always successful, the BBB program, for instance, has a 60 percent settlement rate in the home improvement and repair field.

More information on arbitration services is available from the Council of Better Business Bureaus.[1]

The Grievance Process
How to Complain Effectively

Page one of the *Consumer's Resource Handbook*, published by the U.S. Office of Consumer Affairs (OCA), is titled "How To Be A Smart Consumer." That's a tough assignment given the number of competing brands, clever sales pitches, extravagant advertising claims, extended warranties, service contracts, and other complexities that accompany many consumer purchases. So it's only fitting that page two is titled, "How To Handle Your Own Complaint."

Complaining is something just about everybody does at one time or another. It's natural. But few people can channel their anger or disappointment about a new wood stove that smokes or an air conditioner that clunks into a level-headed complaint letter in a way that gets action and solves a problem.

To this end the OCA book makes a positive start by avoiding the easy answer given too often by too many advisors to too many consumers when something goes wrong: take them to court. Instead, the Office of Consumer Affairs proposes a 5-point plan you can undertake without legal help (or expense), culminating in an effective letter

[1]Council of Better Business Bureaus, 1515 Wilson Blvd., Arlington, VA 22209

of complaint sent to someone in a position to help.

In addition, the 90-page book provides a lengthy index of federal, state, and local consumer agencies and services, industry trade associations, Better Business Bureaus, third-party dispute-settling programs, and a directory of corporate consumer contacts at hundreds of companies ranging from AAMCO Transmissions, Inc. to Zenith Radio Corp. Here's the 5-step plan:

• *Identify the problem.* Zero in as much as possible on what's wrong, while avoiding editorial comments about an installers unfriendly attitude and other subsidiary complaints that will only cloud the issue. Decide what you believe would be a fair settlement, if you want your money back, a repair, or an exchange.

The first step in effective complaining is to identify the problem clearly. In this case poor drainage, a downspout releasing water in the wrong direction, and an inadequate footing cause the dirt beneath a concrete slab to wash away very quickly. Undermining is also a problem when contractors fail to compact excavated soil before pouring. Without support, cracks will appear in the surface, then even a reinforced slab will crack open as one edge of the slab sinks.

• *Gather documentation.* Gather originals (and make copies) of sales receipts, repair orders, warranties, canceled checks, contracts, and other pertinent paperwork. A written reference to the problem, or an acknowledgment of the problem by a repairman, for instance, is particularly valuable.

• *Start at the point of purchase.* As the OCA booklet puts it "Calmly and accurately explain the problem" to the person who sold you the item or performed the service. If you don't get help at this level, ask for the manager or supervisor and try again, calmly. The Office of Consumer Affairs reports that a large percentage of consumer problems are solved at the supervisory level, by someone—maybe the only one—with the authority to make changes and adjustments.

- *Don't give up.* Many companies have several levels of management above a local supervisor. Follow the chain of command through regional and national headquarters (the type of contacts in the OCA index).
- *Write an effective letter of complaint.* Include your name, address, and home and work phone numbers. Type the letter, if possible, and keep it brief and to the point, including product serial numbers, and where and when you bought the item. State what you want done and set a reasonable time limit for a resolution. Include copies, not originals, of the paper documentation.

Remember that the person reading your letter is not the one who left a hose clamp off your washing machine or packed your new microwave oven without a door handle. Don't "yell" at them. Be reasonable and persuasive.

The Office of Consumer Affairs suggests the following form for a complaint letter. For clarity, remarks about the letter's suggested text are set off in capital letters inside brackets.

YOUR ADDRESS
YOUR CITY, STATE, ZIP CODE
DATE

APPROPRIATE PERSON
COMPANY NAME
STREET ADDRESS
CITY, STATE, ZIP CODE

Dear Appropriate Name:
[DESCRIBE YOUR PURCHASE] Last week I purchased (or had repaired) a [PRODUCT NAME WITH SERIAL OR MODEL NUMBER OR SERVICE PERFORMED]. I made this purchase at [LOCATION, DATE, DETAILS OF THE TRANSACTION].

Unfortunately, your product (or service) has not performed satisfactorily (or the service was inadequate) because [GIVE HISTORY OF PROBLEM]. Therefore, to solve the problem, I would appreciate your [ASK FOR SPECIFIC ACTION]. Enclosed are copies of my records.

I am looking forward to your reply and resolution of my problem, and will wait 3 weeks before seeking third-party assistance. Contact me at the above address or by phone at [HOME AND OFFICE NUMBERS]

Sincerely, [EVEN IF YOU DON'T MEAN IT]

Although it is reasonable to offer a waiting period before seeking third-party assistance (an intentionally vague reference to a dispute-settling program, or possibly legal action), be prepared to seek help at as many agencies as you can find. For instance, if you do not receive help at a local level, you can duplicate your complaint, with a copy of your letter, to the Better Business Bureau, local consumer agencies, trade associations, and other groups.

Credit Schemes

Q. Once a credit rating has deteriorated can the record really be cleaned up by firms advertising this service? The cost, which includes a promise to arrange for charge cards, is about $150.

A. Although the Fair Credit Reporting Act does offer consumers a way to obtain copies of their credit record, and a way to challenge inaccuracies, it also allows private credit reporting agencies to list most negative information, such as late payments and loan defaults, for 7 years. Bankruptcy can stay on the record for 10 years.

Generally, "credit repair" firms can do no more than an individual consumer to improve his own record. For instance, working with a local bank, it may be possible to establish an account with a mandatory balance against which limited credit is extended—like securing your own loan with your own cash. Plans like this cannot wipe the slate clean, but can build a positive record that may eventually counterbalance the negative aspects of a report.

The Federal Trade Commission (FTC) has charged several firms in the credit cleanup field with misleading and deceptive practices. In one recent case the Credit Establishing Bureau, which charged $95 to improve a credit rating, and another $75 to help consumers get credit cards, was charged with "misleading consumers by falsely and deceptively claiming the company could improve their credit records and arrange for them to receive major credit cards." The FTC also charged that the firm often did not even attempt to deliver the promised credit services, had no way to obtain credit cards for $75, and rarely provided guaranteed refunds.

Anne Price Fortney, associate director for credit practices at the FTC, notes that this type of firm advertises locally and nationally. She says, "These businesses can relocate with little effort or expense, making law enforcement difficult."

New Construction

Nine

FOUNDATIONS AND MASONRY

Concrete Work
Pouring Concrete That Lasts and Lasts

Mortarless masonry was the only way to build structures as durable as the pyramids and the Parthenon until 200 B.C. when the Romans invented a long-lived mortar that would help hold individual blocks of masonry in place. That mortar evolved into early forms of concrete—the preeminent twentieth-century building material used for roads, bridges, dams, airports, houses, skyscrapers, and more. (During World War II there were even experimental, concrete-hulled boats.)

In a way, improved mortar and concrete were responsible for the decline of fine stone work in which edges were precisely chiseled for strength and to keep out water. The improved mortar, a mixture called *pozzolana* made largely of prehistoric volcanic ash, made it possible to use small, irregularly shaped stones without sacrificing the strength of large, uniform blocks.

Roman engineers developed concrete to add strength by adding mortar to the rubble core of stone-face walls. The widespread construction system called for a 1- to 2-foot layer of small stones to be covered with mortar that was rammed into the pebbles, then another layer of stone, and mortar, and so on—a process that amounted to mixing and pouring the concrete in one step. During construction, the core was held in shape by rough boards pinned to vertical stakes—the equivalent of our forms commonly made of plywood backed by 2 by 4s.

Roman techniques such as building up concrete walls in two foot high layers, called *lifts* today, are still good concrete practice. It pays to have faith in builders who poured massive concrete arches at the amphitheater in Pozzuoli 2,000 years ago, because even after their protective layer of facing brick has eroded and fallen away, the arches remain intact. That kind of longevity is one heck of a recommendation.

Today, concrete technology has made it possible to adjust mix ratios to suit different engineering requirements—to build large, relatively thin slabs and massive walls to hold back earth and water. Special ingredients, called *admixtures*, make it possible, though not very comfortable, to pour a house foundation in below-freezing winter weather.

Opposite: Rob Roy, a builder specializing in earth sheltered homes, uses chains and the bucket arm of a backhoe to set large rocks that will provide a natural retaining wall. If boulders this size are firmly seated, no amount of groundwater should dislodge them.

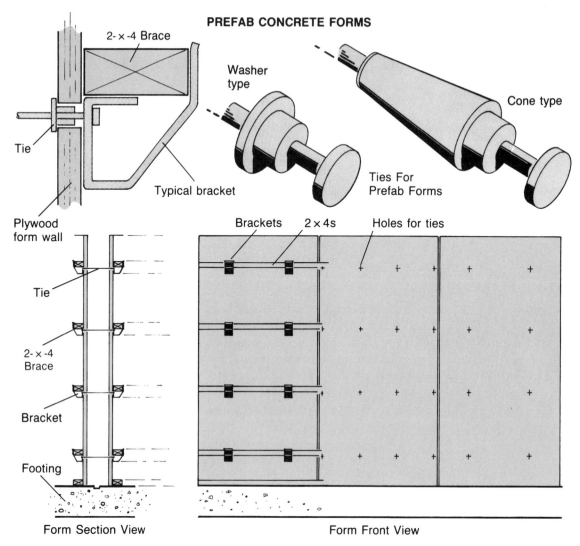

PREFAB CONCRETE FORMS

2- x -4 Brace

Washer type

Cone type

Tie

Typical bracket

Ties For Prefab Forms

Plywood form wall

Brackets   2 x 4s   Holes for ties

Tie

2- x -4 Brace

Bracket

Footing

Form Section View

Form Front View

On large projects general building contractors normally subcontract the foundation to specialists who use prefabricated forms. Some advanced do-it-yourselfers rent their own, erecting reusable, fiberglass-faced plywood sheets, and compression ties to hold the walls in place—usually 6 or 8 inches apart. Brackets hold horizontal 2-by-4 braces called whales. They stiffen the plywood sheets.

Whether you or your contractor use concrete for a wall, a slab, or a small set of steps, some practices will make any job stronger and longer-lasting. Of course, special sites and designs may require complex engineering solutions.

Preparing the Site. To minimize compression the foundation must be supported by compacted earth. The process is called *soil consolidation*, and like concrete, it is an ancient practice that grew out of the need to locate strategic structures on strategic sites, even if they did not have stable soil.

Soil consolidation was first accomplished by driving 6- to 10-foot wooden pilings by hand into soft ground. Any soil under concrete should be tamped or rolled, packed

Some contractors make their own forms. This pier under construction by Rammed Earth Works, a California-based firm that builds homes of a compacted mix of sifted earth and cement, is held by plywood sheets backed with wooden braces and secured with pipe clamps.

down as firmly as possible. Digging deeper, past layers of loose topsoil, doesn't help much unless a different, more stable soil is uncovered. On a house footing, for example, approximately 80 percent of settlement that can cause structural faults results from soil compression within a depth of only 1½ times the footing width.

Planning footing depth. Where concrete is used to support a structure, whether a whole house or a small patio, it must reach below the frost line—the level at which ground water freezes in winter. This depth is quite different depending on regional and local climate and on site conditions. The local building department is the best source of information on the subject. You should ask them, and your contractor, for the average depth of frost penetration, and start building at or a bit below this level.

Proportioning cut and fill. The proportion between the amount of earth excavated and the amount filled in is crucial to highway engineers. Ideally, the dirt from the hill fills in the next valley creating a level road. In residential construction, however, the problem often becomes where to put all the dirt. Excavating a full cellar measuring 60 by 40 feet with 8-foot walls protruding 1 foot above grade, means removing 16,800 cubic feet of earth, enough to spread 4 inches of fill over a football field.

Figuring the volume. Concrete is measured and sold by the cubic yard—enough concrete to fill a 3-by-3-by-3-foot cube. If you mix ingredients by hand, figuring that the small set of steps won't require trucked-in concrete, remember that one wheelbarrow-sized load will be less than 3 cubic feet. Renting a portable power mixer for small projects is often a more reasonable alternative than hand mixing.

The trick is to measure the area of the form carefully—at least twice, or until the totals agree. For example, if a deck plan calls for 10 concrete piers, each 1 by 1 by 4 feet, convert the formed space to cubic volume (4 cubic feet per pier, 40 cubic feet total), then divide by 27 (the number of cubic feet in 1 cubic yard) to find the number of cubic yards to order—in this case, 1.48, or 1½ cubic yards. To simplify calculations and build in a reasonable excess factor of about 8 percent, change the conversion factor from 27 to 25.

Mix ratios. In most situations the best policy is to order concrete from a ready-mix company. On your own, concrete for typical structural use, such as footings, follows this recipe: 1 part Portland cement, 2½ parts sand, 4 parts gravel, and 5½ gallons of water per bag of cement. But no mix ratio can be followed without considering environmental conditions. For example, on a very hot day, more water will be needed.

The key proportion is water-to-cement. The more water you add, the easier it is to mix the ingredients, but the weaker the results. In standard-mix concrete adding 7.3 gallons of water per bag of mix produces concrete with a compressive strength of 2,500 pounds per square inch (psi). Adding only 4.3 gallons produces 4,500 psi concrete.

Curing. Concrete becomes solid, then gets stronger and stronger as a chemical reaction of the water and cement occurs, a process called *hydration*. If the concrete dries too quickly, when left exposed to the sun and wind, for example, hydration slows or stops. The first 3 days are most crucial.

During that time a concrete patio, for example, should be covered with plastic sheeting, or one of the proprietary curing compounds that are rolled or sprayed on like paint. Coverage standards are 150 square feet per gallon for wax-base compounds, and 200 square feet per gallon for resin-base compounds. With proper curing, here's what happens to general-purpose concrete. At 3 days the concrete reaches 2,100 psi; at 7 days, 3,200 psi; at 28 days, 4,500 psi; at 90 days, 5,000 psi; and at 365 days, 5,600 psi. Without proper curing 28-day strength can be reduced 50 percent.

A few final tips. Make way for the ready-mix truck. They are large and heavy. You might have to tie back tree branches, for instance. And don't expect the driver to get 10 yards of concrete from the end of the driveway to the new addition at the back of the house. That's your responsibility. If you are hand-mixing, invest in rubber gloves. Concrete is very rough on hands. Also, ease into the project if you are not used to heavy construction. Mixing and placing concrete is heavy-duty work. It's also a great way to get in shape and build your patio at the same time.

Foundation Drainage
Keeping Water Out of the Basement

Spring thaws and April showers should pose no problems if your home is built on an elevated, naturally draining building site. Unfortunately, almost all such natural sites within commuting distance of metropolitan areas were used up decades ago. And despite storm drains and other large-scale plumbing systems, completely dry man-made sites are difficult to construct. Groundwater often goes its own way, even straight through your basement, despite the best laid plans of housing developers and builders.

The worst cases can cost thousands of dollars to correct. But most basements leak only after heavy rains, or after the ground is saturated from the final thaw of a mammoth snowfall. This kind of occasional leaking often can be stopped by one or more modest home improvements that decrease the water load against the foundation. The best bet is to start with easy and inexpensive solutions. If the problem persists, you can opt for a more expensive fix such as new foundation waterproofing or an interior drainage system.

Water diverters. Before calling in professionals to fix a wet basement try something so simple many homeowners overlook it. Extend the downspouts to deposit rain water from the roof well away from the building. Attach an elbow fitting to the downspout, then add a short length of drain pipe leading away from the house. The water can be deposited on a masonry splash block that spreads the flow onto the ground, or into a diffuser—a perforated hose that dribbles water onto the ground to reduce erosion.

For houses built on a slope, where water from downspouts on the high side of the house runs back to the foundation, high-side downspouts are normally fitted into underground drains. But if you don't have these buried drain lines, or if they are broken, downspout pipe can be laid on the ground next to the foundation to reach the low side of the house.

Surface regrading. The foundation water load can also be decreased by filling in gullies around the house with compacted soil, and creating a slight slope away from the foundation.

You may not hear about such simple solutions from waterproofing firms that sell complex and costly pipe and pump systems. In fact, several years ago a Washington consumer group, Washington Consumer's Checkbook, set up a controlled experiment in a test house with a wet basement. An independent group of experts purposely created wet conditions that could be solved by regrading and extending downspouts—work estimated to cost $300. When dozens of unsuspecting basement waterproofing contractors were called in to bid on the job of solving the problem, the majority of estimates ranged from $1,200 to $2,000.

Dry wells. You can build more water-holding capacity into your yard by routing downspouts and other drains to a dry well, typically a large hole in the ground, say 5 or 6 feet deep and 3 or 4 feet round, filled with rocks. A layer of burlap or other ground filter fabric can be laid over the rocks and covered with sod to hide the well completely.

Water that would have overflowed against the foundation now drops into the extremely porous well and filters back into the surrounding soil gradually. Obviously, the bigger the well, the greater the capacity. But given the variety of soil types, water tables, and other factors, there is no rule of thumb about exactly what size a dry well should be.

Area drains. Area drains intercept the flow of groundwater before it gets near the house, for instance, at the edge of the yard. A typical drain includes a shallow trench, maybe three feet deep and a foot or two across, lined with black plastic, several inches of gravel, perforated drain pipe to collect the water and channel it away, and finally, more gravel up to ground level. Area drains may be covered with a dirt filter fabric, and then surface sod to blend in with the lawn.

The trench should be placed as a shield between the normal direction of water flow and the house. A gradual slope must be built in so that water collected in the trench pipes will flow to release points where it cannot double back against the foundation.

Foundation cracks. Some water will still reach the foundation and may work through the weakest links in deteriorated foundation waterproofing. Major cracks from which water pours during heavy rains can be closed with hydraulic cement, a dense masonry mix that swells slightly as it hardens to make a tight seal. Before using such mixes cracks should be scraped out vigorously and cleaned.

Foundation coatings. Obviously, any new, full-surface asphalt foundation coating can be applied only after the house foundation is reexcavated—a costly and messy job that usually destroys most landscaping near the house. Systems that avoid excavation by pumping a clay-type mixture into the soil have been judged by many experts and an in-depth study in *Consumer Reports*, to be of little or no value.

If you must reexcavate consider adding a hydrostatic barrier (one trade name is Enkadrain) over the asphalt coating. The material is made of a resilient, open mesh about an inch thick—like a loose tangle of springs covered with a filter fabric that keeps out dirt but lets in water. The idea is to relieve hydrostatic pressure against the layer of waterproofing by providing an exceptionally porous channel of mesh straight down to the foundation drains.

FOUNDATION DRAIN MAT

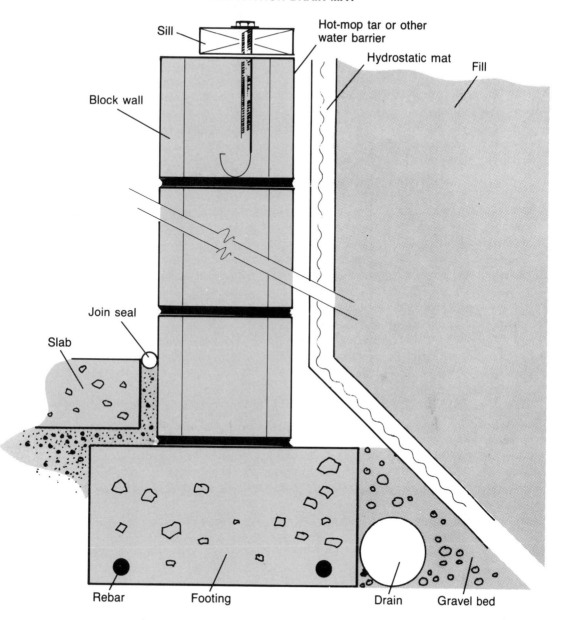

The chronic problem of wet basements can be avoided by interrupting the flow of water against the foundation with a hydrostatic barrier. These sheets have a filter fabric on the outside to let in water but keep out dirt.

CreteCore Foundation System
A New Package for Good Old Concrete Foundations

Concrete makes strong, long-lasting foundations. It can be ordered over the phone and arrives in a truck ready to pour. That's the easy part. What's time-consuming is building the forms that hold the soupy mix in place as it hardens.

On most jobs, plywood panels that are held in place by timbers form the wall. Basic carpentry skill will suffice on straightforward jobs. But the work is much more complex when walls turn in and out, rise up and down to create different floor levels, and contain many openings for windows and doors. And after the concrete hardens all the carpentry work is stripped away. Professionals have heavy-duty wood or metal systems that can be used again and again. But for do-it-yourselfers and small-project contractors, all the wood used in forming is generally of no further use. Often it becomes a liability—unwieldy trash that's hard to dispose of.

A forming system called CreteCore [1] can make this process a lot easier. The lightweight, modular forming system, which is used by professionals, also makes concrete forming a much more realistic job for do-it-yourselfers.

The system is about 20 years old, although it was lost in a corporate shuffle until recently. The system was originally called Foam-Form of Canada. According to Diane Meyer, the owner of CreteCore, the original firm was bought more than a decade ago by a large Canadian conglomerate that went out of business shortly thereafter, taking the small firm down with it.

Now, there are two CreteCore firms, one in Rochester, NY, and one in Albuquerque, NM. Both were franchised plants of the original firm, brought back into operation by new owners.

The CreteCore system has a lot of commonsense characteristics. Here's how it works. Large plywood sheets are replaced by stackable, two-sided, molded polystyrene blocks. The blocks are 48 inches long, 16 inches high, and either 9 or 11 inches wide. The side panels are spaced apart and held together with reinforcing wire. This leaves a hollow core where the concrete is poured.

The inside surfaces of the foam blocks are shaped to produce a solid concrete wall that has a waffle pattern on both surfaces. (You never see this because the polystyrene, which has a high insulating value, is left in place.) The indented waffle pattern is as strong as a uniformly thick wall, but uses 30 percent less concrete.

On a typical job the interlocking blocks are stacked over a footing (a layer of concrete wider than the foundation that rests directly on the ground). The polystyrene blocks are easy to handle. Depending on size, they weigh between 4 and 5 pounds each.

The interlocking blocks are self-supporting, but some bracing is required to withstand the force of concrete as it is poured. Typically, a vertical 2 by 4 tied to 2-by-4 braces that slant down to the ground every 4 feet will do the job.

---

[1]CreteCore Corp., 17 Tree Brook Drive, Rochester, NY 14625

ABOVE: Builders, and their suppliers, are endlessly fascinated with systems and materials that do two jobs at the same time. One example is CreteCore, a foundation forming system that uses rigid foam insulating materials as the forms. BELOW: Large blocks are interlocked row to row to create a continuous channel for concrete and rebar reinforcement.

But even with conventional forms care must be taken with concrete as it comes out of the concrete truck chute. Released from an elevation well above unbraced forms, concrete can pack enough of a punch by the time it reaches the forms to knock them over.

After the foam blocks are stacked, reinforcing bars are set vertically to tie the wall together. Then concrete is poured in layers, called *lifts*, of up to 4 feet. Since the foam material is easily cut, even with a handsaw, corners can be mitered at neat, 45-degree angles, and tied together with reinforcing wire.

At this stage of a typical job, the advantages of CreteCore really begin to show. For one thing, there are no plywood forms to strip and cart away. For another, the concrete wall is already insulated inside and out. And both surfaces are ready for finishing. Drywall can be applied to the inside, and a stucco finish can be troweled on the outside.

To make finishing with wood siding easy, the manufacturer offers blocks with 2-by-4 nailing strips already embedded in the foam 24 inches on center. Plywood or clapboard-style siding can be nailed in place just as it would be on a wood-framed wall.

A typical finished wall, with ½-inch drywall inside and ⅝-inch plywood siding outside has an R-value of approximately 25. (*R-value* is a conventional measure of insulating value; the higher the better.) Typical 3½-inch insulation in a wood-framed wall is rated at approximately R-13.

The foam blocks costs from $9 to $10.50 each, depending on size and whether nailing strips are included. It is difficult to compare costs with other systems because there is no waste (plywood forms that are discarded) and no additional labor or material costs for insulation. However, several contractors using the system report that it compares favorably with the costs of building a foundation out of concrete blocks, a labor intensive process.

This system also makes it easy to estimate the amount of concrete needed for a job. As mentioned earlier, concrete is sold by the "yard"—actually a cubic yard, or 27 cubic feet. Figuring width times depth times length of your foundation, minus openings for windows and doors, plus an allowance for waste, can be tricky. With CreteCore, estimating is simple: 1 yard of concrete fills 10 large blocks (11 inches wide), or 14 small blocks (9 inches wide).

Masonry Mixes
Tips on Using Mortar and Concrete

Stone, in all shapes and sizes, has been used in construction throughout history. Whether cut from a quarry to make a pyramid, or simply picked up off the ground to make a primitive hut, masonry was the traditional choice for strength, safety, and durability. It still is.

But today, massive cut stones have been replaced by a variety of mixes using aggregates such as sand and gravel. Some aggregates are used for fill, others to cover driveways and walks. In a variety of combinations aggregates are most widely used to make many types of mortar and concrete. By altering the ingredients and proportions, these masonry mixes can be tailored to the job at hand. And they are less expensive, more accessible, and a lot easier to handle than large cut stones.

Smaller aggregates, used as fill and in mortar and concrete mixes, are divided into coarse and fine categories. Coarse aggregates include gravel and crushed stone ranging in size from approximately 2 to $\frac{3}{16}$ inches. Fine aggregates include small-sized stone and different types of sand, from washed and sanitized white sand suitable for a child's sandbox to coarse sand used in concrete.

Almost all aggregates are sold in both very small and very large quantities. Small loads are likely to be priced by weight or by the bag. Even gravel normally delivered by the truckload may be available in 40-pound bags, an expensive, but convenient, way to buy just enough stone to fill some muddy depressions in a driveway, for instance. Sand, mortar for blocks and bricks, and concrete mix also can be purchased by the bag.

For many do-it-yourselfers the convenience of using premixed bags containing all dry ingredients is worth the cost, especially after considering the alternative: feeding a rented power mixer with bags of cement and shovels of sand and stone from piles dumped in the driveway.

Like concrete, larger quantities of ready-mixed aggregate are sold by volume: by the cubic yard, or 27 cubic feet. Ready-mixed concrete delivered by truck ready to pour can be ordered for projects such as a concrete patio or foundation for an addition.

Orders are normally accepted in full, and sometimes in half yards. So if the width times depth times length of your foundation calls for a bit more than 3 yards, you may have to order $3\frac{1}{2}$ or possibly 4 yards from the ready-mix company. Concrete sold by the bag can be more convenient for smaller jobs—building piers for a deck, for example. Although there is no rule of thumb about when to mix your own concrete and when to order ready-mix, bear in mind that one contractor's-size wheelbarrow of concrete is less than 3 cubic feet. You'll need approximately nine such loads to make only 1 yard of concrete.

Mortar used for projects with concrete block and brick is also available in premixed bags. The ingredients include a binder, such as cement or lime, sand, and water. For most construction work with brick or concrete block a proportion of 1 part binder to 3 parts sand will suffice. But there are many variations. Proportions range from an all-cement mix, which is very water-resistant and very strong, to a lower-strength mortar for nonloadbearing interior walls, called "Type D," consisting of one part cement, 2 parts hydrated lime, and up to 9 parts sand.

The most common type of sand, the type we like to stretch out on by the ocean, happens to be the worst kind to use in masonry mixes. Its salt content is corrosive to metal reinforcement, weakens the mix, and retards drying. Sand for masonry mixes should be clean, dry, and free of dirt and other foreign matter. To make an on-the-spot test, squeeze a handful of the sand. Damp, workable sand for concrete should form a ball without leaving excess moisture or stains from silt or other matter on your hand.

Working with raw ingredients, combine the cement and clean sand, then gradually work in water. Too much water makes a soupy mix that will be forced out of mortar joints under the weight of bricks and concrete blocks. If the sand is very wet, less water is needed; if it's very dry you'll have to add more. Even the weather can have an effect. On a hot, breezy day more water will be needed to compensate for evaporation.

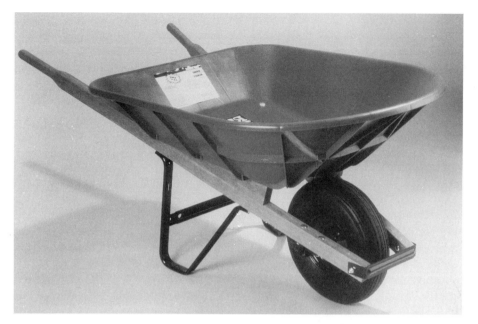

The all-purpose mixing bin for small-scale concrete projects—pouring one or two concrete piers for a deck, for example, is a contractor's wheelbarrow. A hard plastic container section makes cleanup easy. One tip is to thoroughly mix dry ingredients—even out of a premixed bag—before adding water.

So rather than follow a strict formula, add water gradually, even though stirring a thick mix is more difficult than stirring a watery mix.

As stated earlier in the chapter, the most crucial proportion with concrete is often the water-to-cement ratio. As with mortar, the more water you add, the easier it is to mix the ingredients, but the weaker the results.

Even when using preproportioned mortar mix in bags, it pays to observe the time-honored rule of thoroughly mixing dry ingredients before adding water. This ensures that clumps of sand or cement that could weaken the mortar are broken up and spread evenly.

Q & A

Estimating Block

Q. How can I estimate the number of concrete blocks and mortar mix needed to build a storage shed? The building will be 16-by-12 feet with 4-foot-high masonry walls and a wood frame with siding above.

A. If you are using conventional 8-by-8-by-16-inch block, figure 113 blocks per 100 square feet of wall area. Your building has 56 linear feet of block 4 feet high, or 224 square feet of wall, and would need about 260 blocks. Figure 8.5 cubic feet of mortar per 100 square feet of wall area.

Since that is a lot of block, and you plan to build a short wood-frame wall above it, consider the possibility of building the entire wall of wood. Even if a portion will be below ground you can use exterior grade or treated plywood sheathing covered with plastic waterproofing.

To finish a concrete block wall, a special grouting tool is raked along the mortar joints. Several patterns are available, which leave various patterns of mortar in the joint. But do-it-yourselfers could simply use a piece of pipe (for a round, concave joint), or the square edge of a piece of angle iron, for instance, to make a V-joint.

New Foundation for Addition

Q. Recently, I watched an episode of "This Old House" in which a house in California the crew was remodeling needed a new foundation. We are facing the same problem adding a second story to our 1900 house that is supported by brick pillars in a partially dug cellar. The question seems to be if we should pour a new perimeter foundation, or use a new post and beam framework under the house?

A. I think your local building department, which authorizes construction permits, will solve this dilemma for you and insist on a new perimeter foundation capable of supporting the existing house and new second floor. Enclosing the cellar crawl space also will provide an opportunity to control ground-floor temperature and moisture.

Theoretically, you could support both stories with a framework of posts and beams in the basement. Another option would be using a pole structure, in which posts with the girth of telephone poles are sunk into the ground, and a network of beams to support the house is bolted to them. The problem is, the darn house is in the way. You can't set poles in the ground, or reasonably build many piers to hold posts that would hold new beams to carry the new loads.

And even with a new perimeter foundation, the building inspector may point out that at least some of the second-story loads will be transferred down through bearing walls inside the house. This is most likely where full-length, second-story floor beams are truncated at the stairwell.

So, at best, and in addition to the perimeter work, you may have to convince a contractor to wriggle into your partially dug cellar and build a pier or two to support some new, intermediate beams that will carry additional internal loads.

The potential problems in adding a second story over an older home are so severe and costly that such jobs should be thoroughly analyzed by an architect or structural engineer before plowing ahead. Generally, homes with beefy footing and foundations—8- to 10-inch-wide concrete walls sitting on a concrete footing below the frost line—can support a lot more than one story. In such cases building up can be very economical.

However, since the original builder probably did not anticipate a second story, someone has got to excavate portions of the masonry support system. Once you know for sure exactly what's there, an architect, engineer, experienced building contractor, or building inspector ought to be able to tell you very quickly if adding a second story is economically, if not physically, feasible.

Ten

BUILDING FRAMES

Strengthening Building Frames
Framing Extras That Tie a Building Together

When a car door closes against the chassis with a solid, rattle-free thud, buyers take it as a sign of overall quality. This not very scientific test actually provides some practical, sensory feedback about the car's frame strength, and maybe even its durability. In the same way, door slams can tell you a lot about the frame, and maybe even the durability, of a house.

Many homes wouldn't pass a door-slam test. But they might with the addition of some key braces that make almost any frame stronger and more durable.

To build a true building frame, one cardinal rule is to brace every major timber and wall during construction. Braces on this gable-end wall extend out and down to the ground, and back into the building. Also, the bottom section of the gable-end truss is tied to the next truss with more braces.

Extra door bracing. Exterior walls in a wood-frame house are normally built with 2 by 4s spaced 16 inches center-to-center. This structural system is interrupted by windows, and, even more so, by doors. Since exterior doors are often 3 feet wide, two wall studs (spanning 32 inches), may have to be removed to make way for the larger opening.

Common sense suggests that if the framing system calls for a wall stud every 16 inches, a 36-inch door opening without wall studs could be a weak link in the frame. In fact, it is. To prove the point, just slam a solid wood, 36-inch-wide exterior door. In many houses, nearby windows will rattle and picture frames will jump off the wall. If the house were a car, you might describe it as a rattle trap—missing that solid thud of strength and durability.

To strengthen the opening and support the door, typical door openings are surrounded by four, 2-by-4 studs, two on each side of the frame. But you can do better by backing up these studs with two, 2-by-4 braces.

The braces are set about halfway up the wall, wide side parallel to the floor, and toenailed (when nails are driven through one board into another at an angle) between the 2 by 4s surrounding the door frame and the nearest wall stud. This ties the double 2 by 4s surrounding the door to the framing system.

Such braces are even more important at very wide openings for sliding glass doors. Many "sliders" create 6-foot openings in the framing system; some have two, four-foot-wide glass doors, making an 8-foot opening. Since the panels are normally made of insulated glass (two panes sandwiching an airspace), they are heavy. Also, many people tend to close these doors by simply giving them a shove in the right direction— sort of a controlled slam.

But a vigorous push can turn a glass slider into a runaway freight train heading for the bumper at the end of the track. As these minor collisions are repeated day after day, the seal between glass panes may be broken. Also, the frame in which the doors slide can shift out of alignment. Surrounding wallboard can crack. The door frame may even come apart at the corners. Bracing, say two 2 by 4s spaced about 2 feet off the floor and ceiling, helps to absorb the shock, spreading it into adjacent 2 by 4s in the framing system.

Corner bracing. Anyone who has assembled a set of economy steel storage shelves will remember how rickety the structure is until diagonal braces are bolted across the back. Triangulating the rectangular structure makes it much more stable. That's what let-in diagonal corner bracing does for a building frame. It used to be standard practice. But on many new houses plywood sheets nailed over the studs are considered sufficient.

And they are. But shouldn't the structure of your average, $100,000-plus house be more than just "sufficient"? Corner bracing is installed after corners are carefully plumbed and aligned by tacking a 1 by 4 to the outside surface of wall studs. The board runs from the top of the corner down, at approximately a 45-degree angle, to the bottom of the wall frame. After the position is marked, a series of pockets are cut in the 2 by 4s so the brace lies flush with the outside of the wall. Run down the lines with a circular saw set to the depth of the brace board, and knock out the pocket material with a chisel. Then, when the brace is nailed on, crucial corner posts where opposing stresses meet are joined to several adjacent studs.

On large timbers and critical joints between smaller beams, connecting hardware usually can provide far more support than nails. There is stock hardware available for almost every conceivable type of timber connection. Some connectors are even left exposed on open roof beams.

A similar system can be used to strengthen the outermost rafters in a roof—the only rafters not tied into at least two other rafters in the roof frame. Diagonal bracing, or 2-by-4 blocking (wide side down), can be set an approximately 45 degrees between the outside rafter and the roof ridge board (where the rafters meet at the roof peak). A second brace known as a strut when used this way in the roof frame, can be set toward the low end of the roof, between the rafter and the outside wall.

Minimizing loss of structural strength. The structural value of any timber can be undermined by mechanical installations on-site. (''Mechanical'' is the overall trade term for plumbing, heating, cooling, and electrical work.) Since ducts, pipes, and wires are unsightly, it is common practice to run them between framing members.

This works well when a 4-inch-diameter drain line, for instance, runs parallel to floor joists. But pipes, wires, and ducts also must cross framing members. In houses with full basements, mechanical lines are sometimes installed just below the floor joists. This leaves the floor structure untouched, but cuts down on basement headroom.

Too often, one mechanical installer after another punches holes in framing timbers to hide pipes, wires and ducts. Careful professionals will not sap the strength of a timber by cutting oversize holes, or bunching them together. But some professionals aren't too careful. And, frankly, not many plumbers, electricians and heating contractors are known for their careful carpentry.

Overbuilding. The trend in modern construction is to minimize the structural margin of error—to use a timber just strong enough for the job. But since timber is, at least for now, a good buy, slight overbuilding throughout the house frame is a reasonable step.

Area Screening Walls
Building Yourself Some
Inexpensive and Unobtrusive Privacy

Forty years ago a compact, 2-bedroom house in Levittown, Long Island, one of the first postwar subdivisions, sold for $6,990, with no money down and monthly installments of $65 a month. Postwar real estate was such a good deal that it was not uncommon, even over the next 2 decades, to buy ''protection'' when you bought a house. The protection was an adjacent building lot, kept empty to preserve a view or a secluded back yard, to protect the sense of privacy.

Such protection is prohibitively priced in today's real estate market. But with screen walls you can secure some privacy inexpensively and unobtrusively. Screen walls are an intentional architectural compromise. They are not solid; some light and air can get through. But a plain view is obstructed, or screened.

The walls can be built in all shapes and sizes, made of wood, masonry, or synthetics. Screen walls can be made of vertical slats, like a picket fence, horizontal slats like a shutter, normally solid materials such as masonry blocks cast with perforations, even with plastic strips woven through security chain link fences.

Unfortunately, screen walls cannot be adjusted like Venetian blinds. Ideally, slats could be closed down for a private summer dinner on the patio, then opened up during the day to flood the area with sunlight. But the degree of privacy, light transmission, and air circulation is fixed by the degree of openness in the design. There are many options.

Vertical slats can be nailed top and bottom to horizontal rails, such as 2 by 4s. The rails are then nailed to posts, such as 4 by 4s that are set into the ground every 6 or 8 feet. Vertical or horizontal screens can have narrow slats, such as lattice strips or 1 by 2s, or wide slats, such as 1-by-4 or 1-by-6 boards.

A structural framework can also be filled in with a variety of prefabricated lattice patterns available at most lumberyards. Up-and-down and diagonal lattice weaves are sold in inexpensive woods such as fir, in pressure-treated strips, and even in polyvinyl chloride (PVC) plastic. Pressure-treated and PVC materials are the most durable. Mud that splatters on ground level, prefinished PVC screen walls can simply be hosed off.

Although some sites may require special planning, in most cases gaps between screening material should be no larger than the material itself. For example, if you decide on a horizontal screen using 1-by-4 rough-sawn redwood, the maximum gap between boards should be about 3½ inches, the actual width of a 1 by 4.

This deck behind a row house uses two types of screen walls. To the left, vertical boards are angled to block a view from the side, while allowing a screened view into the yard—like a Venetian blind turned sideways. Fencing provides privacy at chair level, and keeps people from falling off—even though they might land in the pool below.

Logic suggests that this 50-50 proportion of material to empty space will provide about 50 percent more privacy. It's not that a passerby will see only every other person on your patio, or precisely half of each person. But it may be about twice as hard to see what's going on—to put together all the pieces fragmented by the screening boards. Small gaps—closing the gaps between 1-by-4 boards to 2 inches, for instance—make more of a barrier and provide more privacy.

Another crucial factor is the distance of the screen wall to the most likely location of passing traffic. The closer you are to the screen, the easier it is to make sense of the images well beyond the screen. You can focus on bigger, more coherent chunks of the vista through each gap, which makes it easier to visualize a complete scene. The further you are from the screen the harder it is to see what's happening just behind it.

Photo by Balthazar Korab; Courtesy of the California Redwood Assoc.

This suburban back yard deck built of long-lasting heart redwood uses solid screening walls to provide complete privacy to the sides. Shoulder-height walls (about 5 feet) usually offer more than enough protection, and still let in sunlight and summer breezes.

So if you have a view worth preserving, but still want to increase privacy, the ideal configuration would be an open screen design, say, 50-50 proportion, on a wall built close to the private area, and far from the nearest vantage point.

Although screen walls are not adjustable, you can make them directional by using vertical slats set at an angle. With such designs the screen wall almost disappears when you see only the edges of the boards from one side of the yard. But from a position at the other side of the yard the slats appear full-face and form an almost solid screen.

Screen Porches
A Room with a View—and a Breeze

Whether you are moving summer meals out of a stuffy kitchen onto the porch, or just rocking away a lazy afternoon and watching the world go by, almost any porch activity is more pleasant without the most annoying type of uninvited guests: bugs. Floor-to-ceiling screens will keep them out and go a long way toward making the porch a comfortable, usable living space 24 hours a day.

One of the most economical ways to screen in a porch is to use the existing framework of corner posts, beams, and balustrades to support custom-made, removable, wood-framed, or in some cases, aluminum-framed screens. This design approach has a minimal impact on the structure and appearance of the house, since the frames can be removed and stored after the bugs leave.

There are several ways to design and build removable frames. In most cases, large, flat, floor-to-ceiling frames (divided in half horizontally for extra stiffness), can be made of ⁵⁄₄-by-3- or ⁵⁄₄-by-4-inch lumber. (Ask for "five quarter" at the lumberyard.) Obviously, very large openings and other unusual designs may require heavier, stronger frames. But as a rule, floor-to-ceiling frames can be made from good grades of lumber smaller than clunky looking 2 by 4s. Such structural timbers are not required since the screen frames do not support the porch roof or siding or glass. They simply provide a surface against which screening can be attached.

Aluminum frames are commonly used on openings the size of conventional house windows. While the strength of most aluminum frames is not sufficient for floor-to-ceiling installations, they could serve on porches where open spaces are subdivided by a network of posts. Many hardware stores and home centers sell aluminum screen components. Lengths can be mitered (cut at 45-degree angles) and fitted together with corner locks that slide into channels in the opposing mitered frame pieces. The frames have a narrow channel along the inside edges into which screening can be forced with a putty knife or similar tool. It is held fast with a plastic or rubber spline forced into the channel on top of the screen.

Wood frames can be assembled with a variety of complex carpentry joints. But novices may prefer to simply abut the top and side sections at a right angle, and then to screw down a right angle mending plate or corner iron (flat, strong pieces of metal with predrilled screw holes). This fastening system isn't very elegant—it should face in instead of out—but it can be thinly disguised under a coat of paint. Frames can also

Sunspaces, which collect heat and reduce the furnace load during the winter, can become too hot, and burden the air conditioner in summer. Aside from shading, one solution is to install removable glazing frames that can be replaced with screens set into channels in the main support timbers.

be joined with long wood screws, corrugated miter joint fasteners, wooden dowels, or a combination of these and other systems.

Additional woodwork can be avoided by simply stapling the screening to the frames and covering the screen edge and staples with a strip of molding. For a neater but more difficult version of the same basic application, a channel can be cut along the inside edges of the frame. Screening is stapled into the channel and covered with molding that sits flush with the frame.

If frames are built to fit snugly between floor and ceiling, they can be held in place by only four wood screws turned into a strip of molding along the porch ceiling or floor, or into existing parts of the porch structure. To unmount the screens in the fall, simply remove the screws.

There is one weak link in this simple installation—the floor-to-ceiling joints between frames. You can keep the frames aligned by installing butterfly latches (like a wing nut that turns around a central screw), or even a short stub of wood screw mounted on the frame. The latch or piece of wood is pivoted from its mount on one frame across the joint and over the adjoining frame, maintaining alignment between the two boards and keeping out the bugs.

Screen installation tips. To avoid wrinkling and a loose fit, staple the sides first, working from the center toward the top and bottom. Staple across the center divider last. To get a tight fit bow the screen slightly while stapling. You can create this slight, temporary curve in the frame by inserting blocks of wood under the top and bottom sections and weighting or clamping down the center divider. When the bow is released, energy stored in the slightly bent frame works to tighten the screen for a neat fit.

Tips on patching screens. Tiny punctures can be sealed with clear waterproof glue on metal screens, or an acetone-type glue on plastic screens. Larger holes on metal screens can be sealed with sections of screen. Bend the end wires of the patch down so they go through the screening surrounding the hole, then rebend the end wires flat to hold the patch in place. Plastic patches can be sewn or glued in place.

Leveling Techniques

Level-Headed Solutions for Flat Floors and Decks

Carnival fun houses are built with curved walls, crooked corners, and cockeyed floors. They're supposed to be out of kilter. But if your house were lopsided instead of level, it wouldn't be entertaining for long. Even slightly sloping floors and decks can upset your equilibrium, make you feel unsure of your footing and uncomfortable. Subtle slopes also can be annoying, make a coffee table wobble, or have you chasing peas to the ''downhill'' side of the dinner plate.

There are several tools and procedures that can help change lopsided to level— whether you're building a 30-foot deck or a 3-foot bookshelf.

The most common leveling device is a *bubble level*—a bubble of air suspended in liquid inside a glass tube. When such an assembly is carefully mounted in a 2- or 4-foot-long carpenter's level, or an 8-foot-long mason's level, it provides very accurate readings. Even slight adjustments, as little as $\frac{1}{4}$ inch up or down over a 4-foot length, can move the bubble past its centering lines on a good level.

As a rule, in tools of equal quality, measuring accuracy decreases with the length of the level. Ideally, you would use a 10-foot level on a 10-foot shelf; a 2-foot level on a 2-foot shelf. That would provide the best reading, measuring level from one end to the other. But if you level a 10-foot shelf with a 1-foot level, a marginal error over 1 foot could be multiplied by 10 into a noticeable error over the full shelf.

For this reason, extremely short, multipurpose gadgets like a roll up ruler with built-in midget level, are almost worthless, even when leveling a short bookshelf. Sometimes, you are better off leveling by eye, in context of the surroundings.

Suppose you use a level to install a shelf about halfway up the wall between two windows. No matter how level the bubble is, the shelf won't look level unless it relates symmetrically to the window sills and casings, which may not be level or plumb. Situations like this illustrate that carpentry is not a precise process, but one of intelligent, commonsense accommodation.

Don't follow the bubble blindly. It might be better to position the shelf by measuring up equal distances from the baseboard, or from the sill of each window. If the shelf will be high on the wall, you might measure down from the ceiling, or from the top window casings, in each case, relating the shelf to the context in which it will be seen.

Then, double-check with a level to make sure the goldfish bowl won't slide off onto the couch.

Larger-scale construction projects, a deck, for example, demand more accuracy than your eye can provide. The most accurate tool is a piece of sophisticated optical equipment, generally known as a *transit*. It is used by many professional contractors—a reassuring sign of professionalism on big jobs such as an addition or house. Once the instrument is planted firmly in a level position on the ground, it can establish perfect levels anywhere on the job within view of its magnifying eyepiece. Unfortunately, its cost is prohibitive for do-it-yourselfers—$250, $350, and considerably higher for top-notch optics.

A 4-foot carpenter's level, starting at about one-tenth the cost of a transit, could be a good investment on a substantial project, and handy on future jobs. It can reliably level beams three and four times its length. But what about leveling widely spaced objects such as piers for a deck, or the ends of a long retaining wall?

Aside from a transit, you could try an inexpensive line level—a small bubble vial that can be suspended on a string stretched tightly between stakes. But its accuracy depends on whether the string actually is a straight line between two points. Slight sagging, even a little wobbling in the wind, can alter level readings.

More impressive for its accuracy and simplicity is the water level, which works on a most basic principle of physics: Water always seeks its own level.

Instead of leveling each joist on this deck, which could create a wavy outer edge and railing, it makes more sense to level the main support girder, and a corresponding beam against the house, called a ledger. Once the two main carriers are level, joists of the same size will automatically provide a true floor.

This tool consists of a length of thin, clear plastic tubing, and some water, period. Fill the tube with water, hold each end upright—10 feet or 100 feet apart—and the water level at one end of the tube will settle to be exactly even with the level at the other end. Nifty.

Some water level kits include a container of red dye, which makes it easier to read the water level, and to spot bubbles that could distort the reading, plus a few clips to attach the tubing to wooden pier forms, beams, and such. It is a very simple tool.

Another advantage is that the tubing can snake around obstructions, over girders, down into holes and back up again, and still produce perfectly accurate readings.

Floor Framing
Strengthening the Subfloor

Ceramic tiles make durable floors particularly well suited to high-traffic, rough-use, and potentially wet areas such as entry halls, baths, and kitchens. Quarry tile, for example, is routinely specified in hospitals and commercial kitchens because it is difficult to damage and easy to keep clean. But tile floors are only as good as the subfloor they rest on.

In wood-frame buildings subflooring is commonly ½-inch-thick plywood nailed to wooden floor joists, usually 2 by 8s or 2 by 10s, set 16 inches apart. Depending on the joist size—the deeper the beam and the shorter the span, the stronger the floor—a typical assembly is strong enough to be left as is and covered with wall-to-wall carpeting. Such a floor may flex a bit when a large person strides across the room. But this movement doesn't hurt the floor or the carpet.

Vinyl sheet flooring may also be resilient enough to withstand slight flexing without tearing. But ceramic tiles, vinyl tiles, and even some hardwood flooring, are not flexible enough to move with the floor. Movement in the frame disrupts grouted seams between tiles—a disaster in kitchens and baths where water seeping through the crack delaminates and rots plywood subfloors. To build a long-lasting tile floor the frame and subflooring must be brought up to the high-strength level of the ceramic tile covering.

When there is access to floor beams from a crawl space or basement, the frame can be strengthened. Before work begins on the floor surface, double up floor joists by applying another 2 by 8, for example, against the existing joist. Cut the new beam to length, apply a liberal bead of construction adhesive (sold in cartridge tubes and applied with a caulking gun) in a snaking pattern, clamp the new beam onto the old, then nail with 8d common nails, called eight-penny nails, actually 2½ inches long.

In cases where plumbing pipes, or electrical lines block access for a full-size beam, notch the new beam to accommodate the obstruction. If the existing joist is joined to adjacent joists with bridging—either X-pattern braces or short lengths of timber the same depth as the floor joists, called *solid bridging*—remove the bridging, then double up the joists.

It is not necessary, or required by model building codes, to reinstall bridging, according to the Technical Services Division of the National Association of Homebuilders

(NAHB) and the Department of Housing and Urban Development (HUD). Even though bridging seems to strengthen a series of joists by tying them together, NAHB field tests show it has no structural value, with two exceptions. First, when floor joists are more than 12 inches deep, bridging is required to prevent the joists from twisting. Second, when the bottom edges of joists are uncovered—outside under a deck as opposed to inside on the second floor where the bottom edges would be covered with gypsum panels—some form of stiffener, even a surface nailed 1-by-2 strip run perpendicular to the joists, is needed to minimize twisting.

This may be news to many do-it-yourselfers, and to some carpenters, too. Individual members in an unfinished floor frame wobble noticeably until bridging is added. Bridging seems to knit the house frame together. But applying subflooring, either plywood inside or 2 by 4s or other decking outside, more than compensates for the lack of bridging. While the effect of adding bridging to uncovered joists is obvious, it is difficult to make a practical comparison between the two approaches, adding or not adding bridging, since it makes no sense to remove bridging after surface flooring has been laid.

Despite the convincing evidence, I have always solid-bridged outside decks, even when relatively small timbers such as 2 by 6s, unlikely to twist, were used. Also, given the propensity to twisting in many moisture-laden timbers, delivered along with acceptably dry beams from most lumberyards, bridging should help to prevent disruption of seams in flooring, tile, baseboard molding, and other materials, as wet lumber dries out inside the house.

In some cases, doubling the width of existing floor joists will not add the strength needed to support tile. If the existing floor is underbuilt, for example, 2 by 6s were

Instead of butting two girders together over a support post, an interlocking connection, called a scarf joint, is used. Such joints distribute construction loads more evenly. Notice that above this heavy-duty girder, beams join at the center of the joint, spreading the load between the two girders below.

BLOCKING HARDWARE

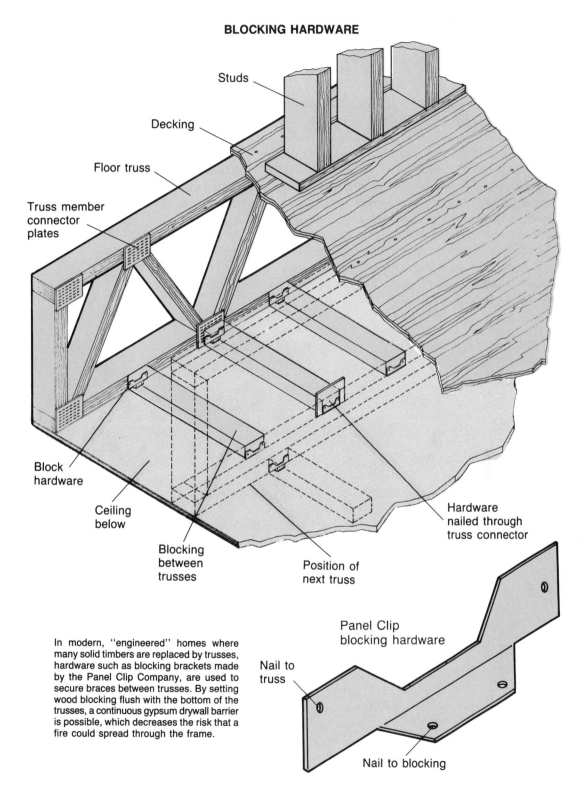

Studs

Decking

Floor truss

Truss member connector plates

Block hardware

Ceiling below

Blocking between trusses

Position of next truss

Hardware nailed through truss connector

In modern, "engineered" homes where many solid timbers are replaced by trusses, hardware such as blocking brackets made by the Panel Clip Company, are used to secure braces between trusses. By setting wood blocking flush with the bottom of the trusses, a continuous gypsum drywall barrier is possible, which decreases the risk that a fire could spread through the frame.

Panel Clip blocking hardware

Nail to truss

Nail to blocking

used instead of the 2 by 8s required by codes, the correct timber should be added to the existing joists, even though its greater depth protrudes below the existing beams.

The most economical way to increase beam strength is to make a beam deeper. For example, making a 2 by 8 into a 2 by 12 is much better than making a 2 by 8 into a 4 by 8 (actually 3 by 7½ inches) by doubling up the beam. However, since replacing smaller beams with larger beams is impractical, and almost impossible without tearing apart the house, doubling up, even with a deeper timber, is the more reasonable alternative.

Floors also can be strengthened by doubling up the plywood surface. A good choice for the second layer of plywood (called an *underlayment*) in areas exposed to water and moisture is ½-inch-thick, exterior-grade plywood. It's layers are joined with glue designed to resist delamination when used on exterior sheathing.

These panels should be laid with the grain of facing layers perpendicular to the floor beams. Architectural nailing specs (recommended nailing guidelines as opposed to what seems to be about enough nails) call for 6d common nails (called six-penny nails, actually 2 inches long), set every 10 inches over intermediate joists and every 6 inches along panel edges.

Eleven

ROOFING, WINDOWS AND DOORS

Roofing Details For Durability
Building in Roofing "Extras"

Attention to detail is a sign of quality and durability in house construction, often devoted to trim, tile, and other highly visible finishing touches. Focusing some extra attention on crucial components like the roof, which preserves everything below by keeping it dry, is a sign of common sense.

Four out of five houses are covered with asphalt shingles—a straightforward system of interwoven, overlapping, water-shedding layers. Nailed down over asphalt roofing paper without any special attention, the shingles should keep your house dry. But there are many details, too often treated as "extras," that can make a roof more watertight and more durable.

Heavyweight shingles carry the longest warranties. They are thick enough to show the shadow lines normally thrown by wood shakes. This Bird & Son shingle is rated at 345 pounds per square—roofing parlance for enough shingles to cover 100 square feet of roof.

Backup protection. Normally, asphalt roofing paper is laid beneath the shingles. It smooths out irregularities in the roof deck and could prevent damage from a protruding nail head or splinter. But its main purpose is to catch and shed any water that seeps through the shingles.

Tar paper is inexpensive and easy to install. Maybe that's why it's sometimes laid down a little haphazardly. Ripped sheets may be left in place. Horizontal edges may have the most minimal overlap of only an inch. A small overlap (3 or 4 inches) would be sufficient on perfectly even runs of tar paper without rips. But 5 or 6 inches provides more room for error, and more protection.

Ideally, each horizontal strip would be a single sheet. If water did get through, it would run from one layer to the next until it reached the gutter. But for the sake of economy, it is accepted practice to make at least 4-inch vertical overlaps where partial sheets join. If this eliminates a trip into town to buy one last roll of paper, I suppose one or two vertical seams won't hurt. But don't overlap 3- and 4-foot scrap sections, creating a patchwork of seams, just to save a few dollars worth of tar paper.

Another good tip is to install tar paper with roofing nails or staples driven through "buttons," the nickname for half-dollar-sized slivers of aluminum that greatly increase the holding power of each nail or staple. This "extra" can be crucial on windy days, when a gust can lift and rip the paper.

Protecting exposed roof edges. The gable ends of the roof, the sloped edges between peak and gutter, are vulnerable since the edges of the shingles are exposed.

There are three ways to protect against roof edge leaks. First, add a full-width, vertical strip of tar paper along the roof edges—a backup to the backup layer. Second, cover the edges of horizontal layers of tar paper with strips of flashing. These long, L-shaped aluminum strips, called *drip edge*, cover the exposed edges of plywood roof deck and wooden fascia boards used to trim the gable ends. Also, they keep water from flowing around the edges and back under the shingles. Third, overlap shingles beyond the drip edge by ¼ to ⅜ inch to discourage back flow.

Protecting freeze-prone eaves. Ice dams that can raise shingles and cause severe leaks in winter, occur when heat rising through the attic warms the roof deck just enough to melt snow. The dams develop along the eaves (the unheated, gutter end of the roof that overhangs the house walls) when the water flows onto the cold roof surface.

Although dams may be prevented by adjusting insulation and ventilation, or installing heat cables along the eaves, it is wise to build in extra protection. One tip is to fit lengths of aluminum J-channel around the raw, exposed edge of plywood roof deck adjacent to the gutter. This protects the porous end grain from soaking up water, warping, or rotting.

Also, you can install double layers of tar paper over the eaves, or one of the new, rubberized asphalt and polyethylene membranes. One such membrane is called Ice & Water Shield, made by W.R. Grace & Company.[1] This self-adhering material bonds directly to the roof deck and seals itself around punctures from nails protruding through shingles. (For more on roofing, see Chapter 19.)

---

[1] W.R. Grace & Co., Construction Products Division, 62 Whittemore Ave., Cambridge, MA 02140

Framed Wall Openings
Solid Framing for the Holes in Your House

Most homes are not designed by the people who live in them. Except for those fortunate enough to work with an architect who translates their thoughts into blueprints, owners and renters must adjust to someone else's idea of adequate closet space and room size and everything else.

In the planning stage, walls can be moved with an eraser. After construction these drastic alterations are impractical at best and, sometimes, nearly impossible. But dramatic changes are possible by adding openings in existing walls, either interior passages or exterior doors and windows.

Granted, removing entire walls is not a job for novice do-it-yourselfers. The same is true of making openings in solid brick or masonry exterior walls. But for wood-framed walls, on the building perimeter or interior partitions, making a structurally sound framed opening is a reasonable weekend project.

Before cutting through the wallboard or plaster though, remember that individual 2 by 4s, 2 by 10s, and such are part of a framing system. Some pieces carry more of the overall structural load than others. So haphazardly pulling out several 2-by-4 wall studs can be a bit like pulling one can from the bottom of a pyramid display in the supermarket.

One way to understand how a framing system works is to think of it as a network of rivers and streams along which structural loads flow from the roof, through the building and foundation, and into the ground. The network gathers loads the way a stream gathers water drained from surrounding terrain. Like water, loads tend to take the path of least resistance in accordance with the law of gravity; they go where you'd expect them to go. In the same way that water won't run uphill overflowing some upland creek, structural loads from a rafter, say, don't jump out into midair to appear magically on the opposite corner of the building. They flow down the rafter to the stud directly beneath the rafter.

Structural loads collected and transmitted through the frame include the weight of building materials, called a *dead load*, the weight and stresses added by the building's inhabitants and their furnishings, called a *live load*, and other types of environmental loads, for example, a snow load, which accounts for extra weight on the roof. The architect's or engineer's job is to anticipate correctly all conditions that could reasonably be expected at the site.

In different situations, ''reasonable'' can mean very different things. In a project to determine the possible design of a breakwater surrounding a nuclear power plant off the coast of New Jersey, the U.S. Army Corps of Engineers had to anticipate potential storm damage. While the Corps routinely uses 50- to 100-year time spans for these estimates, a 1,000-year period was used for the nuclear project. (Incidentally, the worst possible weather in 1,000 years was characterized as a double hurricane—when a passing hurricane doubles back to join a second, approaching storm raising the most extreme wave height from 31 to 48 feet.)

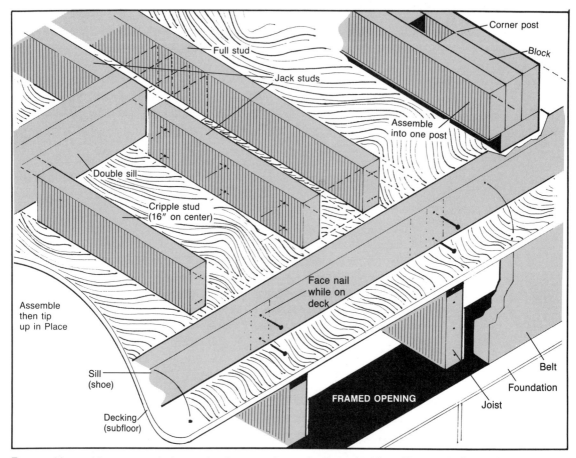

To assemble wood frames securely, lay out the pieces on edge on the plywood subfloor. That permits face nailing through the bottom of the sill into the ends of the studs. The jack studs support the ends of window sills and headers over openings.

In houses, potential loads and stresses are more standardized. In special risk areas, a fire or earthquake zone for instance, special engineering is required. For example, floor systems are generally designed to support 40 pounds per square inch. That includes you and the chair you're sitting in. The system won't break under 41 pounds. But the beams will start to bend. Since wood is resilient, the frame can absorb extra strain as you get out of the chair and do calisthenics. The standard limit of bending, called *deflection* in a building beam, is $\frac{1}{360}$ of the span. Statistically, that means if the floor joists were 360 feet long, they would have to be strong enough to bend no more than 1 foot when loaded with people and furniture.

Holding the idea of active loads and stresses flowing through the frame may make it easier to understand the fundamental part of any frame opening, the header. This is the horizontal beam, often made of two pieces of wood nailed together, that collects loads formerly channeled through ceiling to floor studs that are now truncated where the window or door or passageway is cut into the frame system.

While local building codes always supersede general rules, the following guidelines can be used to produce safe and strong headers. Note that where 2-inch-wide timbers are used, which actually measure 1½ inches, it is necessary to sandwich a piece of ½-inch-thick plywood between the timbers so that the header equals wall frame thickness. For horizontal openings up to 3½ feet the header should be two, 2 by 6s; for 5-foot openings two, 2 by 8s; for 6½-foot openings two, 2 by 10s; and for 8-foot openings—as wide as the largest standard-sized sliding glass or patio doors—two, 2 by 12s.

Here is the basic sequence for building an opening for a window, which is a bit more complicated then building a simple passageway, since it must accommodate the specific dimensions of the window unit.

Step 1. Determine the rough opening (supplied by the window manufacturer), generally the complete frame unit plus ½-inch space for adjustment within the opening.

Step 2. Nail a full-height, floor-to-ceiling stud 1½ inches outside the limits of the rough opening. It may be possible to leave a full-height, existing stud in place, while relocating one of the removed studs to form the other side of the opening.

Step 3. Nail together two, 2 by 4s to form the frame sill—the horizontal member supporting the window—and nail it between the full-height studs.

Step 4. Follow the same process with 2 by 6s or larger timbers as required, to assemble the header—the horizontal member across the top of the windows—and nail it between the full-height studs.

Step 5. Use the removed studs (to save material) to cut short sections of 2-by-4 wall studs and nail them between the ceiling and the new header, and also between the floor and the new sill. These short timbers, called *cripple studs*, help to stiffen the horizontal timbers, and support siding and wallboard nailed back in place around the opening.

Step 6. Short sections of 2 by 4 should also be nailed against the full-height studs. These timbers fill up the 1½-inch space per side allowed on the original layout, and help the nails to support the new horizontal timbers framing the opening.

Don't be surprised (particularly if you uncover the frame in a relatively new house) to discover openings built with considerably less material than described above. Single piece, 2-by-4 sills and double 2-by-4 headers, even on openings wider than 3 or 4 feet, are often used to save wood and labor.

But it is also not surprising when openings framed this way produce cracks in wallboard and plaster, often in the telltale form of jagged breaks running at an angle away from the upper corners of windows and doors. Using more material, particularly the 2-by-4 sections, called *jack studs*, nailed against the full-height studs, may even be considered wasteful by some builders. But adding them is a cost-effective preventive measure that can eliminate scraping, spackling, sanding and repainting later on.

Roof Valley Protection

Q. Which is preferable when using standard asphalt shingles, a closed or open valley?

A. One is not better than the other, although closed-valley construction, in which shingles meeting at right angles where two sloping roofs intersect are interlaced, is faster. In open-valley construction extra felt paper and metal flashing that can withstand direct exposure to the elements must be installed, while shingles running up to the flashing must be cut back at an angle.

As to appearance, some like closed valleys because it knits the different roof sections together, while others like the architectural definition exposed valley flashing gives to the roof lines.

Wood Shake Roof

Q. When installing wood roof shingles, should tar paper be laid over the entire roof, or should a roll be laid over each course of shingles as they are nailed down?

A. The second method is the correct one. As a rule, a full, 36-inch-wide sheet of at least 15-pound roofing felt paper (what most people call tar paper) should be laid along the eaves. It is covered with a double layer of shakes consisting of a short, 15- to 18-inch starter course, and a course of standard 18- or 24-inch shakes.

After this double layer is applied an 18-inch-wide roll of felt paper should be laid over the top of the shakes, extending over about a third of the shingle, and onto the roof sheathing. This process is repeated on each course, which weaves multiple layers of felt paper into multiple layers of wood shakes.

Roof Cap Shingles

Q. What is the best way to match and replace several of the small shingles that cover the joint between both sides of a roof along the ridge? The sides of shingles near one end of the roof have broken away.

A. You make these cap pieces by cutting them from full-sized shingles. If you don't have leftovers for an exact match, you may have to buy a bundle in a similar color. Although these new cap pieces will be a bit brighter than surrounding shingles that have aged, the difference should not be noticeable--at least not from the ground.

Each small cap shingle is actually one tab section of a full-size, three-tab shingle. To cut the cap sections, cut from the top of the space separating the tabs, called the

Priced competitively with natural cedar shakes, Masonite "Woodruf" shakes are made of compressed wood fibers. The cap shakes are overlapped enough to cover the nails used to secure each one. Water should step down from one to another without ever encountering a nail head.

key, to the top of the shingle at a slight inward angle. This makes the hidden portion (the part without granules) narrower than the visible section, and makes a neat line along the ridge.

Unlike full shingles placed flat on the roof, the tabs must bend over the ridge. Bending should not be a problem in warm weather. Still, work them in place gradually. Two nails secure the cap pieces, one toward each edge, just above the visible, granular section. As each cap piece is nailed in place, it covers the nail heads of the preceding piece. However, since the nails will be exposed on the final piece, you should cover those last nail heads with roof tar, or set the last cap piece in a full bed of roof tar without nails.

Installing Skylights

Q. We are planning to have a skylight installed in our kitchen. Which type of skylight would be better and easier to install: a fixed unit, or one that opens to let out trapped heat?

A. As long as you are going to cut a hole in the roof, you might as well pay the extra money for what's called an *operator skylight* (the industry's way of saying it opens). Added fresh-air ventilation and light is welcome in most kitchens.

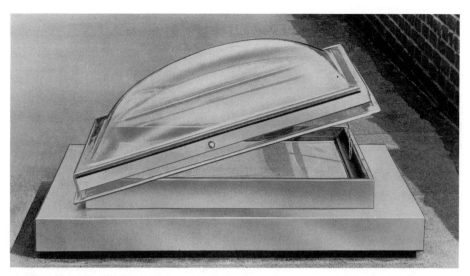

Installers must control potential leaking between the skylight and the roof. But it is up to the manufacturer to make skylights such as this Ventarama unit watertight. Some of the best units have one-piece copper flashing extending from the lip of the opening (under the opening dome), and completely over the frame.

Aside from inexpensive all-plastic bubbles, which can be difficult to keep in place since they expand and contract so much, most quality skylights have a glazed section attached by the manufacturer to a frame that raises the glazed section several inches above the roof. There are two basic types of operator skylights: bubbles, which are hinged on the high side and open a few inches at the bottom, and "windows," which are flat frames that pivot about halfway up the frame. In both cases the entire assembly, frame included, is installed in the roof.

So no matter which type you use, the installation consists of attaching the frame of the skylight on the roof. Both fixed and operator, frame-mounted skylights should install in approximately the same amount of time and require the same amount of maintenance.

I am not a fan of all-plastic units that are molded with some type of flange along the sides instead of a frame. They are inexpensive. However, expansion and contraction with changes in temperature stresses the site-built seam between the roof and the bubble, even if the installer sets the bubble on some type of frame added to the roof. Movement at the critical seam between glazing and frame is accounted for by the manufacturer in skylights with an integral frame.

As long as I am spending your money so freely, you might also consider two other options: some type of shade or blind built into the unit to block out direct sunlight on hot summer days, and a removable screen to keep out bugs when you open the skylight to increase ventilation.

Door Fitting

Q. What is the best way to make wooden doors, which swell up in the summer and don't fit or close easily, work without sticking?

A. It is easy enough to sand or plane the rough edges a bit, or even lop off ¼ inch or so with a saw. That will make the door work easily now, and leak like a sieve next winter. As Shakespeare's Hamlet would say facing the same problem on his house, "Aye, there's the rub."

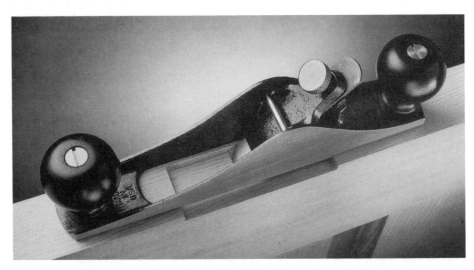

To mortise hinges and lock hardware, most manufacturers provide paper templates to use as cutting guides. But woodworkers who appreciate fine shop tools might like this butt mortise plane, which can cut a perfectly flat mortise with square corners. The tool is available from T.S. Wheeler (Box 52, Wilmette, IL 60091), for about $40.

Bad puns aside, the trick now, once the door has swollen, is to take just enough off the offending edges of the door to get a tight fit. The best way to find the right compromise between summer tightness and winter looseness is to pare down the door gradually.

Some doors have adjustable flashing that covers seams between the door and jamb; some have interlocking flashing with enough give to withstand some swelling and shrinking without either sticking or separating. Cutting back your existing door and adding such flashing systems is one drastic but effective solution to seasonal swelling.

A simpler solution is to reduce the door until it works properly (waiting for a few days of low humidity will reduce it some without any sanding or planing), then protect the wood from absorbing moisture that causes the swelling by sealing it with paint or a clear sealer such as polyurethane or varnish. Two coats of marine-grade spar varnish, which is good enough for exposed woodwork on boats, will help to keep the door one size year-round.

Hanging Doors

Q. Does it make sense to save money and buy a door, frame, lock, and hinges separately and install them myself, or pay more for what the lumberyard calls a "prehung" door?

A. Unless you have done this job before a few times, spend the extra money. It's not that any one particular skill required to hang a door is all that difficult. But handling all of them well enough so that the door actually opens and closes, locks, and keeps out the weather is another matter. It's much easier to pop the preassembled door and frame of a prehung unit into an opening in the wall.

Happily, major door, sidelight, and fanlight assemblies such as this elegant unit made by Marvin Windows, can be ordered preassembled. In general, do-it-yourselfers will find that ordering prehung doors (already in jambs with hinges mounted) is well worth the extra cost.

Twelve

OUTDOOR STRUCTURES

Porch and Deck Piers
Pier Pressure from Porches and Decks

Piers that hold up porches, decks, stoops, and stairs are like masonry tree trunks supporting a network of timbers above. If the piers are strong, solid, and well rooted in the ground, then the joists, decking, rafters, and roofing they support are likely to stay where you put them. But if the piers crack, crumble, tip, or sink, even the strongest framing that rests on them can be torn apart.

Piers provide the primary working platform. They establish levels and boundaries for the entire structure, and bridge the gap between empty space and construction space. Their design can vary greatly, ranging from a simple concrete pad supporting a treated construction pole to a monolithic block reaching 5 or 6 feet below grade. But several basic building principles apply to almost every type of masonry pier.

Establishing a level. The final elevation of a deck or porch surface is usually the controlling design feature. Normally this level is within 6 or 7 inches (a single step) of the inside floor level. The joist and girder dimensions beneath the porch or deck floor are controlled by the size and design of the structure as specified by an architect or contractor and verified by a building inspector.

On elevated structures such as second-story decks and balconies, it would be unreasonable to pour a full-height concrete support pier. Instead, a wood post is used to transfer girder loads down to standard concrete piers at, or a few inches above, ground level. In such cases the surface levels of a series of piers do not have to be the same. Discrepancies of even a few inches can be compensated for by cutting the wood posts a bit longer or shorter.

Excavation. Telephone companies dig holes for their poles with a powered auger mounted on the back of a truck. Chances are you don't have such a handy machine and will have to use some other exotic tool—like a shovel. Digging a deep but small-diameter hole is surprisingly difficult. The job is much easier with a hand-held posthole digger, basically two opposingly hinged minishovels. To minimize settling of the pier, soil at the bottom of the hole must be compacted, a process called soil consolidation. Pound the dirt down with a heavy metal tamper or even the end of a 2 by 4.

Pier depth. As mentioned in Chapter 9, if concrete is used to support a structure it must reach below the frost line—the level at which ground water usually freezes in winter. This depth varies depending on regional, local, and even on-site conditions. In the process of obtaining a building permit for the project, an inspector can tell you exactly how deep the pier must be.

Photo by Karl Riek; Courtesy of the California Redwood Assoc.

Three, 6-by-6 wood posts carry almost all the weight on this cantilevered, redwood lattice "porch-deck" in Berkeley, California. To prevent twisting, and distribute the load more evenly, angle braces are added between the girder and each side of the posts.

Concrete volume. Concrete is measured and sold by the cubic yard—enough concrete to fill a 3-by-3-by-3-foot cube. Figure the volume of concrete needed by totaling the volume of each pier. For instance, on a large deck requiring ten, 1-by-1-by-4-foot piers, multiply 4 cubic feet per pier times 10 piers, which equals 40 cubic feet, then divide by 27 (the number of cubic feet in one cubic yard), to find the number of cubic yards to order—in this case, 1.48, or 1½ cubic yards. To simplify calculations and

PIER FORM ON GRADE

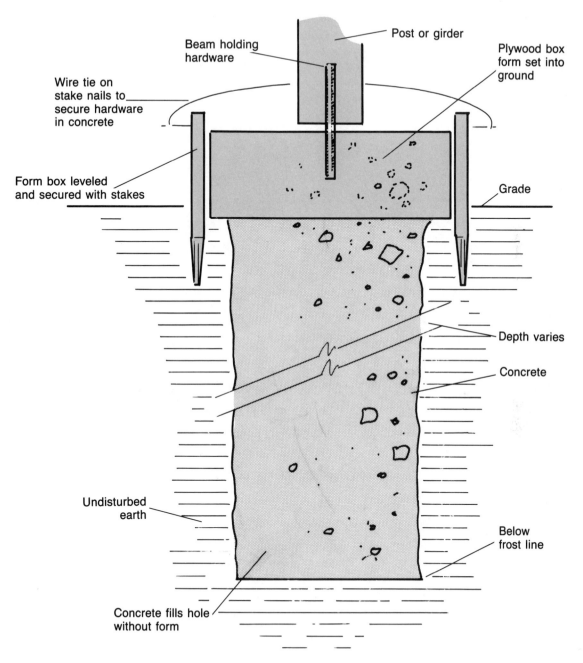

Beam holding hardware

Post or girder

Plywood box form set into ground

Wire tie on stake nails to secure hardware in concrete

Form box leveled and secured with stakes

Grade

Depth varies

Concrete

Undisturbed earth

Below frost line

Concrete fills hole without form

On modest-sized piers common in deck construction, you can save time by digging a neat hole, and building only a small form that sits on the ground. Undisturbed earth holds the concrete, while the box, staked in place, forms a neat projection to keep girders out of the mud.

Photo by Karl Riek; Courtesy of the California Redwood Assoc.

From the deck you can see the ingenious system of traveling lattice screens—seen at floor height from the street, then raised to eye level against the late afternoon sun. Rafters sandwiching support posts are bolted in place, a system that works well for floor joists, too.

build in a reasonable excess factor of about 8 percent, change the conversion factor from 27 to 25. (See Chapter 9, p. 126 for directions on proper concrete mixing.)

For many do-it-yourselfers the convenience of using premixed bags that contain all dry ingredients is the best alternative. Always mix the dry ingredients before adding water. This ensures that clumps of sand or cement that could weaken the mortar are broken up and spread evenly. On larger projects it is possible to use a rented power mixer with bags of cement and shovels of sand and stone from piles dumped in the driveway. On much larger jobs concrete can be ordered ready-to-pour from "ready-mix" firms.

Forms. Normally, ½-inch plywood boxes are built to hold concrete. But you can save on materials by digging neat holes, which can contain the concrete below-ground. In such cases, a small plywood box securely braced and staked into the ground around the hole, can contain the portion of concrete above-ground. Extending the piers at least a few inches above the ground keeps the girder out of direct constant contact with mud and snow.

Tying piers to girders. The transition from masonry to wood is a crucial structural connection. In many designs it is a point where all the structural loads are channeled into one, large wood girder that rests on the piers. To solidify this connection some type of steel tie is normally embedded vertically several inches in the concrete, with several inches protruding. The girder is nailed or lag-bolted to the protruding section.

Even short lengths of reinforcing bars will do. The idea is to bore holes in the bottom of the girder (and flood them with wood preservative), then set the girder onto the steel rods. It is easier to work with steel straps, which allow for repositioning the girder somewhat. It can be difficult to place a large beam if a series of holes must be perfectly aligned with a corresponding series of steel rods.

Deck Design and Planning
Popular and Cost-Effective Deck Additions

Building a deck is one of the most satisfying and hassle-free home improvement projects for owners and do-it-yourselfers. A wide variety of designs are possible using several different materials and only basic carpentry tools and techniques. Somehow, rough edges that are mistakes on wood inside the house become inconsequential on larger scale deck timbers used outside.

Different types of wood, timber sizes, application techniques, changes in level, and overall shape and dimension can be combined to make a practically infinite variety of final designs. This variation is only one reason decks are one of the most popular spring projects.

Many of the difficulties associated with projects inside the house, notably the complexities and costs of wiring, plumbing, and cabinetry common to bath and kitchen renovations, are eliminated outside. Unlike interior alterations that are constrained by the shape of existing rooms and complicated by floors that are out of level and walls

This back yard redwood garden shed combines storage closets, a potting workbench, and built-in seats—all shaded under a lattice roof. The deck extensions in the foreground are built in modular sections, and can be moved to make new configurations.

Outdoor living on a multi-level deck is also possible in the heart of Brooklyn, New York, where architect David Hirsch built this compact deck with two landings and stairs into the back garden. Double redwood horizontal beams tie the network of support posts together.

that are out of plumb, decks are built in unencumbered free space. Normally, decks attach to a building near a door and near the floor level. But aside from these minor limitations there are no restrictions.

Also, deck building is less time-consuming than most other major home improvements. A typical kitchen remodeling job, for example, has many phases, including carpentry work, wiring, plumbing, cabinetmaking, and many surface finishing operations. But with decks the structure itself is the finished product.

Building a deck is also a popular choice for the majority of homeowners who may not have the time or skill or inclination to build it themselves. Decks are highly rated features in surveys of home buyers. They are a good investment. A new survey of remodeling projects by *New Shelter Magazine* (now *Practical Homeowner*) shows that decks contribute to resale value more than many other major home improvements, returning 82 percent of labor and materials costs. (For a rundown on the most cost-effective home improvements, refer to Chapter 13, p. 185.)

Cost data supplied by the R.S. Means Company, a publisher of construction cost and estimating books, indicates that the average national cost for decks is $3,320, or about $15 per square foot. Costs include an average of $1,003 for materials, a labor-to-material ratio of about 3 to 1.

While materials, shapes, sizes, and costs can vary widely, there are several design decisions common to almost every deck project.

Although most decks are simply wood platforms raised above the yard they are an extension of the house—more like living space than yard space—even though they are outside. Replacing a solid wall with sliding glass doors leading to an expansive deck is a quick and relatively inexpensive way to make any inside room seem a lot larger. Considering connected inside and outside space as one unit, deck additions are likely to be most appropriate and useful added onto living-family areas and kitchen-dining areas.

Since wood decks are exposed to the elements year-round, the wood must have weather-resisting characteristics built in or brushed on. Common framing material such as construction-grade fir, is more than strong enough and can be treated with penetrating wood stain, clear wood preservative, or both to resist deterioration. In most regions, particularly the Northeast, this protective coating should be reapplied every 2 or 3 years. I built a fir deck in New Hampshire almost 20 years ago that has been drenched in clear preservative every few years and shows no signs of rot.

Another option, pressure-treated timbers, have chemical preservatives injected throughout. Although it may take several seasons for the greenish tint to weather into a more mellow and natural tone, this type of decking has a long life and requires little maintenance.

For more money—sometimes a third or even half again the cost of fir—more exotic species such as redwood or cedar can be used. They are more naturally resistant to the elements. But although these woods have an extraordinary appearance when first installed (some select redwood has a unique pink-orange hue), they will weather. Most woods used for decking eventually turn a driftwood gray color. Redwood may turn much darker unless protected with a clear sealer. Even then it gradually changes to an elegant silvery tan.

Most decks have four structural levels. From the top down they are: the surface, usually 2 by 4s, and sometimes 2 by 6s on large decks; the joists, at least 2 by 6s and as large as 2 by 12s, usually set 16 inches on center at right angles to the surface boards; one or more girders such as a 4 by 10 at right angles to and supporting the joists; and posts or piers that support the girders and transfer loads to the ground.

The final level of the deck surface is usually the controlling feature. Since it ties into the house the surface level is often most convenient at or only a few inches below the house floor level. The joist and girder dimensions are controlled by structural requirements specified by an architect or contractor and verified by a building inspector. The posts are the only easily adjustable element, taking up as much or as little space as required between the girder and the ground.

Decks are also among the easiest home improvements to commit to paper, even if you do not have drafting experience. A preliminary and basic measured drawing on graph paper will help to define what deck design will be most attractive and most useful, and help to clarify communication with contractors estimating the job.

However, areas defined on clean, uncluttered scale drawings tend to look larger than they actually are in real life. To avoid disappointment transfer the scale drawings to the actual building site using stakes driven into the ground connected with string to outline the deck. Because deck labor is two to three times as costly as materials, extending the deck using 12-foot instead of 10-foot joists, for example, has little effect on labor costs, increases material costs only marginally, but may increase the usefulness and sense of space dramatically.

Sand-Set Patios
Masonry-Surfaced Patios on a Bed of Sand

Watching a sandcastle melt back into the beach as waves lap gently at its foundations, you might not think that sand would make much of a patio or walkway. And, by itself, it doesn't. But it makes an excellent base on which you can lay bricks, flagstones, pavers, or other materials hard enough to withstand foot traffic.

The sand system makes sense for many amateur carpenters and masons. That's a tactful way of saying that building a wood deck with piers, girders, and joists, or pouring a concrete slab with reinforcing mesh and control joints, might be a little out of reach for some people.

Sand, on the other hand, is manageable and forgiving. If you put a little too much over here, or not quite enough over there, you simply keep raking and leveling. No 60-dollar 4 by 12 ever gets cut 2 inches too short. No load of concrete ever hardens where the drain was supposed to be.

To start with, no special tools or building experience is required. Also, if sand, bricks for the surface, and pressure-treated 2 by 6s for borders are delivered, you can move them into place in pieces that won't slip your disc.

First, estimate the amount of materials you'll need, including coarse building sand for a 1-inch-deep patio base, black plastic, or asphalt paper to keep down undergrowth and prevent erosion of the sand base, and border material.

Sand under this herringbone-pattern floor has been carefully leveled and smoothed. To secure the bricks, fine sand is spread over the surface, then swept back and forth until it sifts into the irregular spaces between pavers.

Estimate the sand using the ratio of 9 pounds per square foot of patio surface area. The amount of surface stone or brick you'll need will vary according to the material and the pattern. If you plan to use a material not of uniform size, such as slate or flagstone, ask the masonry supply yard for help with your estimate. If you plan to use a standardized material—brick is the most popular choice—use this ratio: 4½, 4-by-8-inch brick pavers per square foot of patio surface.

Excavation is the next step. Strip off the surface layer of sod, which may come in handy elsewhere if you remove thick chunks that include grass roots. The plan is to wind up with a relatively flat, compacted surface. Since dirt compacts itself very nicely over the years, you can save yourself a lot of compacting work by digging down to, but not past, a layer of undisturbed soil.

If removing a few rocks creates pockets, fill them in with dirt, and pound down each shovelful with a metal tramper or the end of a 2 by 4. The final, compacted soil base should be free of stones and other debris. Remember that loose, aerated soil, which may be good in the garden, is rotten under a patio. It will sink irregularly, taking your level surface of stones or brick down with it just as irregularly.

The next step is to smooth out and grade the 1-inch or slightly thicker sand base (thickness is not crucial). To aid in drainage, try to create a slight slope of ¼ inch per linear foot. This is important if the patio is set in a normally damp area, which is not the best location, although sometimes your choices are limited. If the site is normally dry and does not puddle, don't worry a whole lot about the slope. Just try to make the darn thing level, and you'll probably get a little slope anyway. That's fine.

To keep the sand and bricks in place, and for a neat appearance, pressure-treated wood borders can be set into the ground. If you set the borders first, leveling them carefully, they can serve as guides, called *screeds* in the business, for the sand and surface brick.

Whatever edging you choose, brick standing on end, for instance, should be deep enough to contain both the surface material and the sand base. Otherwise, sand can wash under the edging, undermining the surface.

To border the patio with treated wood, you are likely to need 2-by-6-inch timbers. Secure the edging with treated wood stakes, such as 1 by 3s, every 3 or 4 feet. Once the layout line has been established, drive the stakes slightly below the grade level on the outside of the patio, which will keep them hidden once you pack in sod or flowers around the patio. Secure the borders by driving galvanized nails from the outside of the stakes into the 2 by 6s.

Next, spread a layer of black plastic or asphalt paper over the sand base. This prevents vegetation from disrupting the patio, and prevents sand erosion as rain water washes between the surface stones. The surface stone or brick is laid over the plastic. You could pack together bricks or flat stones, and leave them as is. But some are likely to be a little wobbly. For a more stable surface, sweep sand onto the surface and into the joints.

Since not all types of brick are rated for exterior use, ask for an exterior-grade brick with resistance to freeze-thaw cycles. Supply yards should be familiar with several types, such as C902-SX and C216-SW—the type commonly used in exterior walls.

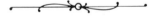

Deck Specialties
Small Points That Make an Average Deck Special

Using elegant, high-quality decking materials such as cedar and redwood is one sure way to make a deck look good. It also is an easy way to empty your checking account. But even plain, construction-grade fir 2 by 4s, complete with knots and rough edges, can be joined with some high class carpentry and design detailing to make an elegant structure.

In carpenter's language "elegant" refers to a good-looking synthesis of form and function—the innate beauty of mechanically efficient structural systems and techniques. Some of these fine points are easy to incorporate into any deck project.

Without careful attention to the spacing and nailing of 2 by 4s on a deck surface, even a simple and symmetrical design can present a haphazard appearance. Typically, 2 by 4s are attached to larger supporting joists with two, 10-penny (3-inch-long) galvanized common nails driven through each 2 by 4 at every point where it crosses a joist. It is a time-consuming job. Although one nail at each crossing point would hold the board in place, it would allow the board to cup, or turn up at the edges. Two nails, placed about ¾ of an inch in from each edge, are used to keep each board flat.

There are many such crossing points, even on a small deck. Without a system for this kind of repetitive work both do-it-yourselfers and professionals have a tendency to lose concentration after a while. It may seem like splitting hairs, but such lapses can create irregular gaps between boards, and erratic nailing patterns.

Experienced carpenters can repeatedly and accurately gauge such distances by eye. But many use a low-tech, distance-estimating system anyway. For example, to create an even gap between boards, drop a nail into the space between 2 by 4s, or tack a nail onto the joist. Since the nail shanks are the same size. They create a uniform spacing between boards—about ⅛ inch for good drainage.

To nail at the same margin from the edge of the 2 by 4s it is convenient to use some form of human measuring template. For instance, you might grip the nail between thumb and forefinger just below the head, rest your thumb at the edge of the 2 by 4, then press down on the head to leave a slight depression where the nail should be driven. Using this type of human engineering can be surprisingly accurate. Mechanical aids such as rulers or premarked nailing templates are too cumbersome in this type of operation.

A more time-consuming but totally concealed nailing system called Dec-Klip, uses T-shaped clips nailed onto the joists. One flange of the clip is toenailed (nailed at an angle) through the 2 by 4, while a spur on another flange secures the adjoining board.

California Redwood Assoc.

Using structural-grade timbers such as 2-by-6s to make benches, allows an elegant, free-floating design. Ample seating is built in without overshadowing the ground-hugging effect, since the timbers are pinned to the deck floor frame and float at the corners without the help of posts.

The system is made by G.L. Field Manufacturing, Incorporated.[1]

When viewed from a location perpendicular to the run or direction of the surface 2 by 4s, decking generally appears to be neat and clean. Parallel to the run, however, rough cut, end-grain sections of each 2 by 4 can present a ragged appearance. There are two basic ways to tidy up this loose end.

Most decks are face-nailed, which hurts when you buy cedar or clear redwood. One answer is to use concealed nailing hardware such as Dec-Klips (made by G.L. Field Manufacturing, Inc., P.O. Box 51188, Wedgewood Station, Seattle, WA 98115).

The easiest finishing touch also saves time during the job. Instead of precutting each board to length (you'll never get them all the same, anyway), simply leave the outside ends of the boards uncut. On many deck designs the uncut outside edge will be irregular. For example, different stock lengths may be needed to accommodate changes in the perimeter of the house where it joins the deck.

To create a neat edge, wait until all 2 by 4s are in place. Then, allowing for a small overhang of an inch or so beyond the outermost joist, make identical measurements out from the joist at each end of the deck. Snap a light chalk line (a standard, inexpensive carpentry tool consisting of a line doused in powdered marking chalk) held at these marks. This leaves a precisely straight cutting guide so that every 2 by 4 will overhang the joist by the same amount.

---

[1]G.L. Field Mfg., Inc., P.O. Box 51188, Wedgewood Station, Seattle, WA 98115

Set a circular saw so the blade depth is just slightly greater than 1½ inches (the actual thickness of a 2 by 4). After trimming the deck edge (the sharper the blade, the neater the cuts), clean the board ends if necessary with sandpaper or a sharp block plane. A beveled top edge (angled instead of sharp and 90 degrees square) is another nice finishing touch. The bevel can be added easily with a plane or a belt sander.

After trimming the 2 by 4s at the chalk line, rough end-grain sections can be completely concealed behind a piece of trim made out of the same decking material. In this case you might use a 2 by 2 (actually 1½ by 1½, the same thickness as the 2 by 4 decking) nailed perpendicularly to the deck boards. To present a thicker, more substantial edge, you could use a full 2 by 4 turned on edge. There are many possible "boxed in" designs.

Despite these and other nice pieces of carpentry (such as laying 2 by 4s across joists on a diagonal), green-tinted, pressure-treated timbers, selected for their resistance to deterioration, often leave a very inelegant appearance. Although such boards do not require a surface sealer, the glaring green can be softened by an application of light gray, semitransparent stain. Eventually, the green tint will be softened by the weather. This application simulates this visual softening immediately.

Decks rarely ever look as good as they do just after the last nail is set. There is a natural desire to preserve this snapshot indefinitely. Unfortunately, it isn't possible. No exterior clear sealer will preserve forever the hue of clean, freshly sanded wood. At best, repeated applications only retard the inevitable weathering process.

At some point in the future, however, you could resand the deck with a floor sander (after checking that no nail heads protrude enough to tear the sandpaper belts), and restart the weathering process from a second fresh surface.

Below-Grade Girders

Q. What material should I use for a girder that will support deck beams? The girder will be partially underground at one end. Also, how should it be attached to the concrete piers it sits on?

A. Even pressure-treated wood (lumber injected with wood preserving chemicals) should not be buried unless absolutely necessary. Since you will have to dig holes for the concrete piers, extend the excavation far enough and deep enough to keep soil away from the wood. The mini trench can be filled with gravel so that surface water flows quickly to the bottom, and does not sit against the girder.

There are many ways to attach the timber to concrete piers. Proprietary hardware is available that has a metal rod at one end (embed it in the wet concrete), and a U-shaped pocket at the other (to surround the girder).

Also, you can simply set a piece of common threaded rod into the concrete, and support it as the concrete sets, then drill a hole into the bottom of the girder to accommodate the rod. Flood the hole with wood preservative for good measure. Generally, the considerable weight of joists and decking above, will keep the girder from traveling.

Retaining Walls

Q. A retaining wall between the lawn and driveway has started to tilt out at the top, making small cracks in the concrete block. How can I prevent more tipping and damage?

A. It is sometimes possible to force a wood frame back into place, but difficult to nudge masonry even an inch without breaking it. Usually the only realistic goal is to prevent more tipping. The most likely cause is hydrostatic pressure—dirt and ground water behind the wall pushing against it. To relieve the pressure, retaining walls need weep holes, small drainage channels made, for example, by building in pieces of galvanized pipe every few feet along the bottom of the wall.

If your wall has weep holes they may have clogged. Use a plumber's snake or similar tool with a jet of water from a garden hose to clear out fine silt and dirt. Sometimes screens covering the pipe inlet to prevent clogging, clog themselves. If all else fails it may be necessary to excavate a trench along the wall and install a larger-capacity drainage system to relieve the pressure, for example, a 6-inch-wide, full-height bed of gravel with drain tile or perforated pipe to carry off the water.

Home Improvement Primer

Thirteen

REMODELING BASICS

Remodeling Possibilities
Discovering Room for Improvement

Most people would like to have a brand new house, including many owners of older homes. Imagine, no more cracked plaster. No more cold, leaky windows. There would even be an energy-efficient heating system and real water pressure. Wow, running the dishwasher and taking a shower at the same time!

The efficiency and convenience built into a new house are strong arguments for buying a new house. But remodeling an older home can be a less expensive, and sometimes more rewarding, alternative. You may be able to wind up with more space for less money, and dramatically increase home value by remodeling.

Who should remodel? If you already have a house it's a difficult decision: Should you exchange a low mortgage rate, a familiar neighborhood, a comfortable, lived-in home—even with all its little quirks—for a new house? It's called "trading up," or using the equity built up in an existing home to buy a newer, bigger, and supposedly better model.

For first-time buyers, the question is easier. Older houses that need remodeling work are less expensive than new homes. The average price of a new, single-family house, within commuting distance of most cities, is over $100,000. But diligent buyers who take the trouble to search neighborhoods a bit off the beaten track can do better. The best buys are often priced well below neighborhood averages. They may have fewer rooms and amenities than most other houses in the area. Because there is room for improvement, they are the most affordable, and the best candidates for cost-effective remodeling.

Remodel the old or build the new? Builders will undoubtedly mention all the advantages of owning a new house. But unless your older house is architecturally noteworthy, or so old it is a candidate for historic preservation, no one may speak up for the alternative of improving what you've got instead of moving.

Financially, remodeling is almost always a better bet than buying another house, new or old. You save the considerable hassle and expense of moving, for one thing. And you save closing costs, which, not counting any real estate broker fees, average about 4 percent of the house price. On a $100,000 new house, that's $4,000 worth

---

Opposite: Short of converting an entire extra bedroom or den, specialized furniture can provide a mini-office almost anywhere. This oak piece (also available in kit form from Craftsman's Corner, P.O. Box AP, Des Moines, IA 50302), holds computer equipment with a printer and paper unit mounted on full-extension slides.

Nearly 80 percent of the 61 million single-family homes in America are over 18 years old, and prime candidates for some form of remodeling work. Replacing rotted deck boards, and adding a new railing are typical upgrades. In 1989, remodeling expenditures should total $89 billion in this growing field.

of quarry tile, new windows, or bath fixtures for remodeling projects that vanishes instead on various one-time real estate, banking, and legal fees. Unlike tile, windows, and bath tubs, have no tangible value once you move in.

With many house designs, even major ''whole-house'' remodeling projects take place within the existing building shell, for example, turning an attic into two beds and a bath, or a garage into an office or den. Building the same spaces from scratch in a new house would be much more costly, requiring masonry foundations, framing, roofing, and other components already in place on an existing house.

Many existing houses built 20 or more years ago may also be fundamentally more sound than a new house. Maybe that shouldn't be true. But new is not necessarily better. Rising construction costs (including labor, materials, builder financing, insurance, and more), have forced builders to keep a very tight rein on labor and materials. Otherwise, their houses might be priced out of reach of most buyers.

Many new houses are built with the minimum amount of materials. For instance, wall studs in a new house measure 1½ by 3½ inches, shaved down from the true, 2 by 4s in older homes. There is some truth to the various homilies about ''the good old days when there was time to do the job right.'' And unless the new house is unusual, its architecture style may be rather bland. Rich details such as cornice moldings and real mullions subdividing double-hung window panes (instead of clip-on plastic grills) may be missing.

The remodeling industry. Remodeling is now a huge business, ranging from small, cosmetic home improvements to major, whole-house overhauls. And as the nation's housing stock ages—60 percent of the country's residential and commercial buildings are over 22 years old—the business continues to grow. Many homes considerably older than 22 years have structural components and other characteristics worth preserving as part of a remodeled house that is more energy-efficient, and easier to maintain.

According to a recent report prepared by the Sweet's Division of McGraw-Hill Information Systems Company, more money is now spent on remodeling work than on new construction. Remodeling expenditures were only 20 percent of total construction costs in 1960, but up to 42 percent by 1980. Some remodeling groups estimate that expenditures are now close to 80 billion dollars a year.

Remodeling motivations. There has been a gradual change away from the traditional American dream of owning your own new home, to a more realistic process of buying, remodeling, and maintaining an older existing building. This alternative is not only a practical reaction to rising costs, but also a response to changing lifestyles. There are three key reasons for the shift away from new construction to renovation.

First, homeowners who traditionally cashed in their appreciated value in home equity to buy a newer, bigger house, are not willing to trade 7 or 8 percent conventional mortgages for new loans at higher rates. Instead, they add rooms and upgrade the existing, low-rate house with home equity loans.

Second, homeowners are often reluctant to change school districts, leave familiar, established, and stable neighborhoods, and extend commuting time by moving.

Third, as rising costs of new construction have been countered with smaller room sizes and other cut backs, many older homes with pantries, deep closets, and other such features have become more appealing. For instance, few new homes have 9-foot-high ceilings that add an immeasurable feeling of spaciousness to a house. This appeal is coupled with home buyer's increasing appreciation of handcrafted construction details, soundproof plaster walls, high-quality hardwood floors, and other details that are generally too expensive to duplicate in new homes.

There is also an increasing awareness of construction quality on the part of remodeling homeowners. Contrary to the routine, hold-the-line repair and maintenance work normally associated with home ownership, there is more emphasis on ''doing it right,'' using first quality, energy-efficient, durable methods and materials.

But before you spend your share of the remodeling billions, there are several decisions to make. You have to select the right professionals to help you, or figure out how to do the job yourself, and choose a plan that makes the changes you want in a cost effective way.

The key to running a successful remodeling project is thorough planning and preparation before the job begins. Even so, some part of the project will probably go awry. Expect it, along with a general upheaval as new lumber, pipes, paint, and paper are put into place.

In the end, putting a new face on the old building is likely to be a smart move that pays for itself many times over. You start to enjoy the changes and the immediate jump in home equity as soon as the paint dries.

———◆———

Project Planning
Changing Your Mind is Okay, on Paper

If you have never lived through a major remodeling project, the disruption it causes may come as a shock. Even resurfacing projects—refinishing floors and repainting walls, for instance—produces enough of a mess to unhinge normal routines. Major remodeling will produce changes in your schedule and in the contractor's schedule.

Southern Forest Products Assoc.

The Southern Forest Products Association built this scale model to show consumers how its underfloor air circulation systems works. Less elaborate models can help visualize living space that doesn't quite ring true when you look at faded blue lines of construction drawings.

Good planning can't eliminate the hectic by-products of remodeling. They're normal. Good planning can ensure that the finished job will closely resemble what you had in mind before the work started. Changing your mind after materials are locked in place is inconvenient and costly. Better to experiment with various designs and alternative materials in the planning stage, when windows and doors can be moved by pencil point and eraser.

Planning on paper. Beneath layers of paint and wallpaper, all sorts of surprises may await. But dealing with unexpected pipes and wires is a job for your contractors. You pay them to carry out the remodeling plan. Your responsibility is to transmit an accurate version of the plan to the people doing the work. But you have to know what you want before you can tell someone else to build it.

On large, complex house overhauls you can get professional help from an architect or designer. Some large stores also provide design and decorating services, although it shouldn't surprise you if the firm's wares are a prominent part of the plan.

But on most remodeling projects alternatives can be worked through at home, on graph paper, allowing one square on the paper per foot of floor space. Paper plans, cardboard models, and any other facsimiles, complete with fabric swatches and paint chip samples, will help. But paper plans can also be deceptive.

It is common when building new houses to frame outside walls first, then close in the house against the weather before splitting up the space with interior partition walls. Until the floor space is subdivided most houses look quite roomy. Then, as the builder or designer, you start to resent the intrusion of hallways and closets on the sweeping space. By the time partition framing is covered with wallboard, a house that seemed spacious can appear hopelessly chopped up into minuscule apartments. And that's before any furniture is moved in. Architectural space seems bigger on paper than it does in reality.

Scale-model planning tools. Professional blueprints drawn up for the office space of commercial clients include furniture layouts. But blueprints for residences commonly do not. That can leave you guessing if your expanded and remodeled space will accommodate new furnishings and new traffic patterns.

For a modest investment, scale-model planning kits can help you get a more realistic picture. "Plan-A-Flex Home Designer" is a kit of 500 reusable furniture shapes at ¼-inch scale. Stylized symbols for windows, doors, appliances, electrical outlets and other furnishings can be positioned, and easily relocated, on an accompanying layout board. The kit is made by Procreations Publishing Company.[1]

Pitfalls good planning can avoid. Timing is a crucial part of any remodeling plan, determining, among other things, when the job starts and ends. On a typical project the activities of many people must be coordinated. You have to make way for the invasion of workers. General contractors have to estimate the duration of the job and schedule a sequence of appearances by various subcontractors (plumbers, electricians, and others). Making periodic payments is likely to require cooperation from a banker.

As more and more people become involved in the project, the risk of delays and other problems may increase. Any one cog in the remodeling wheel that runs amok, for instance, a material supplier who can't locate those special windows he promised, can bring the wheel to a halt. (For the windows, which keep out the rain, the floor can't be laid. For the floors the molding can't be applied, and so on.)

---

[1]Procreations Pub. Co., 8129 Earhart Blvd.,, New Orleans, LA 70118

In the planning stage, rooms may seem large enough. And as you tour the construction site, floor-through spaces may seem more than adequate. Then partition walls go up, carving the space into little boxes. Making scale models, even laying out the space in the yard, can help provide a more realistic picture.

Also, most jobs take longer and cost more than planned. But laying out a detailed job schedule with your contractor can save many delays. The idea is to divide the project into phases, each with its own time frame. This compartmentalized approach can help identify molehill problems before they become mountains.

Like a ship's captain you should also make a plan for damage control. Sawdust, paint splatters, general construction debris, not to mention noise, have a way of escaping the immediate work space. If a particular area must continue to function normally, a home office for example, make a point of this restriction and spell out work area limits and any special protection required in the job contract.

Even when remodeling projects are limited to seemingly minor alterations, other work on the building structure beneath the skin may be necessary. Thorough planning must include this possibility. For instance, moving a wall or widening a doorway can be costly and complicated when the wall contains plumbing pipes and electrical lines. But an experienced contractor should be able to make a reasonable allowance for the extra work, or suggest a less troublesome alternative.

Balancing what you want and what sells. You may never move to another house. But most people do make a change, on average, every 7 years. Naturally, your remodeling project should serve your needs and look the way you want it to look. But it is wise to balance what you want with what will make your house sell if you do move.

Generally, any remodeling project that brings your house in line with area norms will be very cost-effective. For example, if your home is one bath and one bedroom shy of most houses in the neighborhood, a bed-bath addition will pay off handsomely. Adding two bedrooms above area norms is likely to limit the number of potential buyers.

A recent survey of remodeling projects by *Practical Homeowner Magazine* found that, among the 20 most popular home improvements, a general interior face-lift had the highest rate of return on investment, returning 107 percent of labor and material costs immediately after completion. (Obviously, such improvements are likely to add considerably more value to the home long-term, and may appreciate in value to many times the initial cost before the property is resold.)

The next best jobs were general attic and basement conversions, both inexpensive methods of increasing the usefulness and value of a home by converting dead space or storage space that already exists to living space. Number four on the top 20 list was a new fireplace, the only specific improvement, returning 85 percent of costs, rated ahead of a new deck, which returns 82 percent.

In comparison, much publicized window replacement projects were found to recoup only 43 percent of costs short-term, while one of the most expensive projects on the list, a new swimming pool, returned only 46 percent. (Additional statistics on the cost-effectiveness of various remodeling projects can be found in Chapter 32, pp. 439–444.)

By allowing adequate time to plan the job, options and alternatives can be explored. Ideas can be raised and revised. You can uncover a shortage of closets or counter space on paper. Of course, all remodeling jobs run into a few problems. But good planning can keep them to a minimum.

Financing Options
Four Basic Ways to Pay for Your Project

You may have thought the hard part of a remodeling project would be selecting from an endless number of possible designs and materials, or finding the right remodeling contractor. But financing is likely to involve even more confusing possibilities.

At first blush, financing may seem straightforward. There are only four basic options. But each one has many permutations. The advisability of following any one option may depend in part on your income, the project cost, and other variables such as prevailing interest rates.

Now add another ingredient to this confusing brew: tax laws that change on a regular basis. Changes in the tax code have created uncertainties about deductions for different types of loans. Worst of all, Congress (of any political makeup) shows no signs of sticking to any one policy about real estate investment, improvement, and resulting deductions. But it is doubtful that they would ever try to do away with one of the cornerstones of home ownership—the mortgage interest deduction.

Cash on the barrelhead. Amid the financial confusion one alternative is clear. You could always pay cash. That would eliminate all decisions about financing (well, almost all). In a nation accustomed to personal and federal debt, it is refreshing to hear at least one consumer group make just that suggestion. The Consumer Federation of America (CFA) advises against financing where possible because of the extremely high ratio of consumer debt to personal income. The CFA sees many consumers as already financially overextended. (And you can't order up new debt limits and new taxes the way the government can to "manage" its debt.)

Obviously, this recommendation depends on personal income, savings, and job cost. No group suggests that you should liquidate important financial assets such as a fund for college education, or that you should incur penalties by cashing in securities prematurely.

The most important consideration may be where the remodeling cash comes from. For example, paying cash with money from a low-interest account may make more sense than borrowing money at a much higher interest rate. Withdrawing a few thousand dollars from, say, a money market fund paying 5 or 6 percent, could make more sense than borrowing the money with a consumer loan at, say, 10 or 12 percent.

But what seems like the best idea to one financial expert can seem like the worst idea to another. As an example, here's the other side of the same proposition. Leaving the money market funds in place might net 6 percent interest, which effectively makes the 12-percent consumer loan a 6-percent loan.

Depending on your resources, paying cash may be most cost-effective for projects costing less than $5,000. Above that very approximate guideline, some form of financing is generally more appropriate, if not essential. There are three basic possibilities: a home improvement loan, a home equity loan, and mortgage refinancing.

Consumer loans for home improvements. Home improvement loans are likely to carry the highest interest rate. One explanation is that the bank making the loan is likely to be second in line in case you have financial problems. If the loan is collateralized by your home, the lender holding the first mortgage is repaid first from a foreclosure sale. The home improvement lender must wait in line, and hope there is enough value left over to repay the loan.

However, home improvement loans have a distinct advantage over home equity and refinancing plans. There is no flat fee, known as "points" (one point is 1 percent of the loan amount), charged to make the loan, and no settlement costs normally charged when mortgages are refinanced.

When comparing options, remember that when these one-time charges are added to the cost of a low-rate, home equity loan, they may drive up total loan costs to an overall rate roughly equal to a home improvement loan with a higher interest rate but without the one-time fees.

For this reason, home improvement loans are considered most appropriate on remodeling projects in the $5,000 to $10,000 range. Many lenders will not make these loans for larger amounts in any case.

Cashing in home equity. About $220 billion in home equity loans was owed by the end of 1988—about $90 billion in "line of credit loans," in which consumers dip into funds as needed, and about $130 billion in lump sum loans. Home equity loans are appropriate for the next level of financing above-installment home improvement loans—past the approximate guideline of $10,000. In this range, one-time settlement costs, which are relatively constant regardless of the loan amount, represent a smaller percentage of the total loan. This can make them a bit easier to swallow.

A home equity loan is a form of second mortgage. But "points" (one point equals one percent of the loan amount) and settlement costs are commonly charged for making the loan. It irks many homeowners that some of these costs, for example, for a title search, are charged even though ownership has not changed hands since your last title search. You may have to comparison shop among many lenders before finding one that will forego such excessive fees.

For many consumers, home equity is the most readily available source of financing. It often represents an owner's largest financial asset—money accrued by appreciation of property that probably would not have been salted away out of a paycheck week by week.

The Mortgage Bankers Association estimates that there is currently about two trillion dollars in unencumbered equity in this country—pure home value that could collateralize a loan. Most lenders will grant up to 80 percent of a home's value once the amount of any unpaid mortgage is subtracted.

Some versions of home equity loans offer a credit line based on equity. Although terms may vary widely from one lender to another, the general idea is to apply for a loan, which is granted in the form of credit. You don't pay interest on the loan until you dip into the funds. It's a bit like a giant credit card. But there may be a hidden twist.

You may pay points or settlement costs as you would on a more conventional home equity loan. But if the loan money sits unused as a credit line, or if you wind up using only a small portion of the amount, settlement costs may loom large. Once the loan charges are paid, the loan money should sit in your account, drawing interest, until you need it, not in the bank's account.

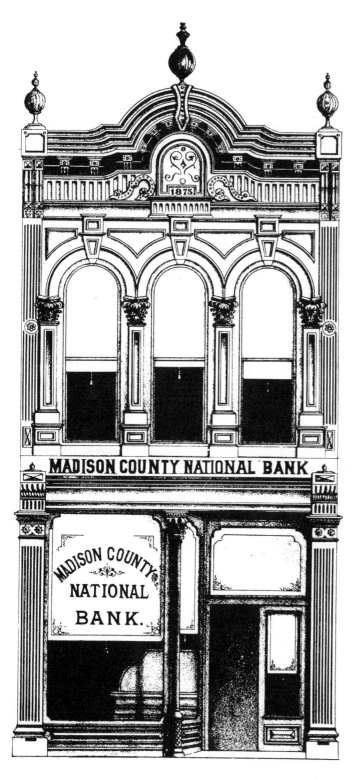

When banks looked like this, homeowners and loan officers may have been neighbors—on a first name basis. Lending, and lenders, have become more sophisticated since 1875 and offer all sorts of financing. Currently, owners have borrowed over $200 billion in line-of-credit, and lump-sum home equity loans—all collateralized by their homes.

"Take-out" money from refinancing. Refinancing (making a new mortgage), is another option. When mortgage interest rates decline, lenders are sometimes flooded with refinancing applications from homeowners anxious to trade in high-rate loans, or adjustable-rate loans, for the old fashioned security of a long-term, fixed-rate mortgage.

Several years ago, when record-high interest rates finally retreated from close to 20 percent, homeowners with high-rate loans, say, 15 percent and above, were more than willing to incur closing costs—even for a redundant title search—to take advantage of much lower, long-term lending rates. They paid a premium to refinance. But the long-range savings were well worth the price.

While the majority of refinancing applications are made solely to take advantage of lower rates, some are for what bankers call "take out" loans. For instance, instead of exchanging a high-rate $50,000 mortgage for a low-rate $50,000 mortgage, a new mortgage is made for $75,000, taking out an additional amount that can be used to pay remodeling costs.

But no matter what option you choose, always comparison shop for financing. Lenders in the same area may have a surprising range of terms and rates. Also, do not limit yourself to financing offered by a remodeling contractor. Although there are exceptions, it generally makes sense to talk to a contractor about remodeling issues, but a banker about financial issues. Several groups, including the Consumer Federation of America, advise consumers against shopping for remodeling and financing services at the same source.

Job Progress
Greasing the Wheels of Your Remodeling Job

If you have not yet been through a major remodeling job, you can gain valuable insights into the process by thinking about an airplane flight or getting a haircut. They have a lot in common with remodeling—really.

The most action and excitement on a flight is in the beginning and at the end. It's the same with remodeling jobs.

What about the time in between? That's where the haircut comes in. You give the barber a set of general directions, then tend to nod off in the chair as the clipping proceeds. But if you leave all the details up to the barber—a new barber as unfamiliar with your hair as a remodeler is with your house—and there may be a few surprises when you look in the mirror.

After the flurry of activity in the beginning of a project, it is natural to relax a bit once the work is underway. But relax too much and the work may take unexpected turns.

Most jobs start with great expectations, some apprehension, and a fair amount of confusion. There are a lot of strangers traipsing through the house. You're meeting with architects, contractors, subcontractors, and bankers. Your well-organized daily routine is a shambles. It's all a common by-product of remodeling.

As the job ends, details that may have been glossed over in a contract and estimate come into focus. It can be a tense time. But there is a lot you can do to make the job run smoothly, and get the results you're paying for, even if you have no experience with the nuts and bolts of construction.

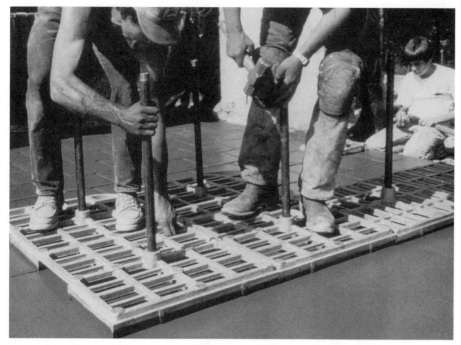

Many jobs seem to progress in fits and starts—even though the crew shows up for 8 hours every day. Masonry work is usually slow going, while framing is faster. But on this Rammed Earth Works job in California, masons use steel forms to quickly turn a concrete slab into a "tiled" floor.

Helping versus butting in. There is one area where a hands-off policy is the best policy: helping the contractors do their jobs. Unless you have made a gigantic mistake and hired rank amateurs, it's safe to assume they do their jobs better than you can, hopefully much better. Trying your hand at a few shingles Saturday morning may be kind of a kick for you. But it puts your contractor in a bad position.

I've had a difficult time saying, "No. Thanks anyway." After all, how can you refuse the person who is paying all the bills? And, no matter how you phrase it, the owner-assistant carpenter takes offense. Too many owners don't seem to see the parallel—how they would feel if the remodeler showed up to "help out" in their office.

Instead of trying out the hammer and saw, spend your time on really helpful, if menial, jobs. For instance, sweeping up a work area, gathering up construction refuse, supplying coffee and soda, and other such contributions make the remodeler's work go more smoothly. That helps get the job done.

Also, most remodeling crews have established routines and work habits. The crew may take a coffee break or run power equipment at times that are inconvenient for you. They may play the one radio station you hate all day. It's reasonable to ask for an occasional accommodation, but try not to interfere on a regular basis. Often, this framework of activity is a firmly established and essential part of getting the work done, and done right.

Dealing with changes and surprises. Remodeling work has a mysterious side not found with new construction. Who knows for sure what lurks beneath those walls: unexpected pipes and wires, wet rot, termites? On projects that require more than a cosmetic face-lift, it is routine to uncover unexpected problems.

In some old houses, opening up the walls is like opening up a Pandora's Box of home repair problems. You may discover that the linoleum covered cracked vinyl tiles, which covered plywood, which, in turn, covered a stained and scarred hardwood floor. Surprise, surprise. All that excavation work for nothing.

Most of the work can be covered by explicit blueprints and detailed specifications listing every type of window and paint in unmistakable detail. Still, you may have to make some changes or additions to the contract.

Make all changes in writing, complete with a mini estimate including material and labor costs for the change. If you are working with an architect, interior designer, or other design professional, involve them in the decision.

Constant communication. On substantial jobs lasting more than a week or so, arrange to have regular meetings with the remodeler. Daily chitchat is no substitute for a sit-down meeting once a week. During these progress reports owner and contractor (and architect or other professional) should review the job. A typical agenda might include payments due, materials on order, problems uncovered, and other items that affect the work.

Progress reports can provide an early diagnosis of trouble. There will inevitably be some unexpected twists and turns. Most start as remodeling molehills. Regular progress reports can prevent them from growing into mountains before the job is completed.

Parceling out payments. Profit is the remodeler's primary incentive and reward. A periodic reward is invigorating, and only fair. But some incentive should remain until the job is completed. For this reason money due for most types of construction work is divided into partial payments. The payments coincide with completion of major stages of the job.

Here's how total payments might be dispensed during the job: 10 percent up front; 25 percent when new structural work is completed; 25 percent when mechanical work (plumbing, heating and electrical) is done; 25 percent when all finishing work (painting, papering, floor sealing) is completed; 15 percent after the final checklist of items and cleanup is attended to. (See also "Letters of Agreement" in Chapter 7.)

If you finance the job your lender is likely to make similar arrangements. No matter how you parcel out interim payments, follow these guidelines. *Never* pay a large percentage initially. *Never* make final payment prematurely.

End-weighted payments are a good idea, if you can get them. Instead of making equal payments, say 15 percent of the total, to start and finish the job, end-weighting alters the proportions: 10 percent to start, 20 percent to finish. This saves more incentive for the end of the job, the time when irreconcilable differences are most likely to arise.

Concluding the Job
Loose Ends Could Unravel the Entire Package

Strange things can happen as remodeling jobs draw to a close. Clients and contractors who have been concerned about the same issues suddenly part company.

Too often, here's what happens. Clients are used to seeing major changes in the way their home looks. There are obvious signs of progress. New windows, new colors and other dramatic changes overshadow surrounding details, for instance, the trim around the windows.

As the job winds down, however, there are no more transformations between the time you leave for work and the time you get home. Sometimes, it's hard to find any changes. That's because the remodelers are tying up loose ends. Naturally, your focus changes from the big picture to the small details within the picture. You may start to find defects, like gaps in the window trim, you never noticed before.

Your apprehension about the remodeler and the quality of work grows. Instead of seeing all the work that's been done, your eye zeros in on missing light fixtures and closet shelves and a seemingly endless number of small puzzle pieces not yet fitted into place.

While your vision is refocusing from the large to the small, the remodeler's vision is going in the opposite direction. Finally, after endless hours concentrating on detail after detail, the job is coming together. A few details still need attention, sure. But they pale next to the transformed overall picture.

An impartial outsider, hearing the concerns of both parties, might see a few problems ahead. Somehow, the people involved rarely see the other person's point of view. That can really cause trouble.

Loose-end checklists. A checklist, sometimes called a punch list, is simply a list of jobs still to be done. The twist is, both parties have to agree to the items on the list. Typically, it includes items such as adding a piece of trim, touching up paint, refinishing stair treads damaged during construction, and such. Checklists are not intended to describe substantial parts of the project.

Chances are your list will be a lot longer than the remodeler's. The job architect can mediate differences. Without a third party you'll have to thrash out the details. Start by including everything. But be prepared to forego some touch-ups in order to get other, more important jobs done. The goal is to come up with a mutually agreed upon list—jobs the remodeler is agreeing to do, in writing.

Three deadly words. The contractor may grumble a bit about adding special hardware in the kitchen cabinets, getting screens for the windows, and taking care of other details. You may do more than grumble when you get the bill.

The bill? What happened to the contract? How can this work be extra?

The explanation is probably right on the bill, in the form of three letters: N.I.C. They stand for "Not In Contract." They denote extras, not figured in the original estimate, not listed in the specifications, not drawn on the plans.

Details that make the project for you are likely to be the items that make a checklist at the end of the job. Typical loose ends are one-of-a-kind built-ins such as a cabinet with wine rack, lazy susan storage bins for corner cabinets, and any special order materials such as tile and cabinet hardware.

Sometimes these initials are used to gouge consumers. For instance, it is reasonable to expect that drawers will have drawer pulls, that linen closets will have shelves. Yet, technically, if these details are not spelled out in the contract, they are extras. But in most cases, N.I.C. charges represent a change of some sort—upgrading materials, for instance.

Before making a change, or requesting an addition to a piece of work already in place, check first to be sure it's covered in the contract. If not, get a written estimate for the alteration, broken down into labor and material costs, before proceeding.

Protective contract clauses. There are some steps you can take in the initial contract stage that can help at the end of the job, too. There are several contract clauses worth considering. Problems may be avoided without invoking these punitive clauses, but the fact that they could be invoked may be enough to get everyone past some particularly rough points.

Penalty-bonus clauses are one option. They seem to offer a financial carrot (bonus money you pay to the contractor) for finishing on time or ahead of time, and a financial stick (deductions from the job price) if the contractor finishes late. But these provisions may be fatally flawed.

Quality work takes time. Rewarding speed encourages slapdash contracting. On the other hand, penalties for delays may turn problems into disasters. If the contractor is late, his only remaining incentive is the final payment. Start chipping away at that payment, and the incentive (along with the contractor) may evaporate. (For more on contracts, see "Mediating Consumer Disputes" in Chapter 8.)

Although legal protection is important, it is an option you should try not to use. It's difficult to browbeat someone into turning out really fine carpentry. Negotiation is almost always a better option. It may be difficult to restrain your anger or resentment in the heat of the moment. But rarely is the client completely right and the professional completely wrong. Give a little, and you may get most of what you want.

Regular communication, and, if need be, patient negotiation, can keep the job out of the hands of lawyers. It pays to remember that lawyers work with words, and probably will not come to your house to complete the unfinished wiring. Better to keep the job in the hands of people who will get the job done so you can enjoy the changes, and get on with your life, finally free of paint chips and sawdust.

Fourteen

MAKING SPACE

Using Dead Space
Finishing Unfinished Living Space

Living space is costly, about $50 per square foot nationally, and much more in many bedroom communities serving major cities. But if you are fortunate enough to own a building, there may be another way to gain living space aside from buying it at new construction prices. For many owners it is less expensive and more convenient to improve and finish unfinished living space they already own.

Here are the most basic pros and cons. Buying new space entails a detailed real estate search, a full dose of paperwork and legal fees for financing (maybe at a higher rate than your present mortgage), and the expensive ritual of closing a real estate purchase.

When all that is done you still have to move, usually a time-consuming and expensive operation. Of course, you get to walk into a larger, maybe newer living space for all the effort.

One alternative—finishing unfinished space in your existing home—does entail some disruption. Depending on the scope of your renovation, the house could be crawling with contractors for weeks, maybe months. But you don't have to spend time searching out new homes in unfamiliar neighborhoods, and you won't have to move. If you're a bit of a pack rat, this issue alone can tip the balance in favor of staying where you are.

Also, using home improvement or home equity funds based on your existing mortgage is often easier and less expensive than putting together a new financing package. Staying put also postpones paying capital gains almost all homeowners are subject to when they sell.

The largest unclaimed parcels of dead space can be found in attics and basements. But there are odd lots, too. For instance, oversize entry ways or halls could hold floor-to-ceiling storage closets, freeing floor space eaten up by bureaus and cupboards. (Remember how rooms that looked spacious when you viewed the house without furniture seemed to shrink after you moved in?) Unused areas under cathedral ceilings could hold a partial second story of loft space for a home office or guest room.

Substantial savings may not be possible if unfinished space is converted to kitchens or baths. Such rooms require concentrations of costly electrical and plumbing work, and even in new houses, cost much more per square foot than other living spaces.

Many homeowners don't think of using their dead space because there are roadblocks in the way. The potential living space may be inaccessible, uninsulated, and unpresentable. On the other hand, since the space is already enclosed, work can start any time of year and progress uninterrupted by bad weather.

Accessibility is most troublesome in attics reached by a trapdoor or pull-down stairs. There may not be enough room in narrow, second-story halls to install a conventional permanent stairway. But space for stairs (even a 2-foot width will do in a pinch), may be stolen from an adjacent bedroom, or a built-in closet. Another option is to gain access with a circular stair. Many firms make "library" stairs in diameters as small as 4 feet that can fit into an alcove or at the dead end of a hall.

With this kind of extra space, who needs more closets? On the other hand, this attic has enough headroom along the wide center aisle to provide a few bedrooms. Lighting could come from dormers or skylights. Storage would be relegated to the low, nonwalkable space under the eaves.

Insulating attics and cellars calls for the most careful planning. Normally, insulation and a vapor barrier are installed in the attic floor. But when the space is finished the insulation envelope must extend to the roof. Blankets of thermal insulation called *batts* can be stapled between rafters with the foil side (the vapor barrier), facing in. If paper-backed insulation is used, plastic sheeting should cover the batts on the inside.

But some ventilation space, at least an inch, should be left between the top of the insulation and the roof. This space should be vented to the outside through vents in eaves overhanging the house side walls. This keeps moisture from forming in the roof structure. For more protection, ¾-inch-thick rigid foam insulating panels can be applied over the insulated rafters, directly under a finished surface such as drywall or paneling.

Most attics are shaped like triangles. The lower corners, where rafters slope toward the outside wall, do not make good living space—not for grown ups, anyway. This limitation can be overcome by building dormers, which also let light into the attic space. Another solution is to make the attic living space narrower than the attic floor. Although the ceiling will be sloped, it will not meet the floor. Dead space behind inset attic walls can be used to house built-in bureaus, storage drawers, and closets.

In many ways basements are easier to finish than attics. Even rough, irregular masonry walls can be covered with a grid of 1-by-2-inch furring strips, and covered with foam board insulation, a plastic vapor barrier, and either drywall or paneling to finish.

However, masonry nails used to hold the strips to the wall can create a fault line that attracts structural stress. This may be the first step in turning a dry cellar into a wet one. But the problem can be eliminated by replacing the furring strips with a stud wall built with 2 by 2s. It stands on its own next to the masonry, and also provides a bit more room for insulation.

While drywall or paneling provides a workable finish surface for walls and ceilings, wall-to-wall carpeting over a pad is an excellent choice for floors in attics and basements. Like insulation over the masonry walls, a carpet pad insulates the cool masonry floor from warm interior air that might otherwise cause condensation to form. Also, a carpet and pad combination makes a hard masonry floor much more comfortable.

In the planning stage there are many options to consider. Before forging ahead, however, consult your local building department. Even though you are not building a new structure, such as a room addition, local codes may require a building permit, a set of building plans, and periodic inspections.

In part, this is necessary because attic floor joists, for instance, may not have been designed to carry people. It's not that you'll fall through the floor. But 2 by 6s, for instance, that may have been more than adequate to hold up the second floor ceiling, could bend excessively under the weight of furniture and foot traffic.

An Office at Home
Creating a Working Environment

Ideally, you shouldn't have to spend all that time on a bus, or a subway, or eating the exhaust of an untuned diesel that came to a halt just in front of your car in the morning or evening rush hour. Theoretically, you should be able to tie into your workplace with a computer terminal, and commute every morning from the kitchen table, all the way down the hall—in your socks, with a cup of coffee that won't spill into the tape player—to your home office. Wouldn't it be loverly?

Exchanging commuting time for work time, or just sleeping later, is the most obvious advantage of setting up a home office. If you travel about 45 minutes each way for work, a home office can save you almost eight hours of travel time, or 1 work day, every week. That's a lot of time—about 4 work days a month, 48 per year, which is about 2½ months, based on a 5-day work week. There are other, less staggering advantages, but also a few drawbacks you should consider.

There are pros and cons about the two most basic concerns: the physical plant, a spare bedroom, section of the cellar, or corner of the kitchen that must be set up and maintained; and the home employee. That's you.

Since there are a large number of different businesses that can be operated out of a home office, and no two homes or occupants exactly alike, there are no pat answers and standard, detailed home office designs. But here are some of the many considerations.

Climate control. Most modern office buildings have windows that cannot be opened. This design makes it easier to control the interior climate efficiently. Your home may be comfortable enough for you already. But is it "comfortable" enough for papers and computers and other equipment that, in most offices, is kept at a stable relative humidity and temperature 24 hours a day?

In many cases, particularly if you intend to set up in a basement, humidity is a devilish problem. You may find it too dry with static electrical buildups in winter, and too wet with condensation that can corrode computer circuit boards in summer. If you are allergic to mold and mildew, as many people are, the problem may be insurmountable without a dehumidifier, an air conditioner, and an air filter—all running almost all the time. And it can be difficult to install a through-the-wall air conditioner in a masonry basement with walls that are mostly below ground level.

To start with, scrub masonry walls with a proprietary mold and mildew cleaner, or a mix of warm water and approximately 25 percent household bleach (1 part bleach to 3 parts water). Don't combine bleach and ammonia, which produces irritating and potentially dangerous fumes. A thick carpet and pad can help prevent even marginally warm, moist air from condensing on masonry floors, while making basement work space more attractive, more comfortable, and a lot more quiet.

Before repainting walls and ceilings coat any greenish dots where mold and mildew formed with pigmented white shellac. In potentially damp areas, it makes sense to use a glossy paint premixed with a mildewcide agent.

If the office area has windows you can reduce climate control costs by installing shades, drapes, or blinds to keep out sunlight and heat in summer, and either storm windows or more temporary, heat-shrink plastic, to reduce heat loss and drafts in winter. Adding storm windows also reduces noise transmission by about 50 percent, which may be important if the windows face a busy road.

Electricity. To run climate control appliances, and other office machinery, it is likely that you will have to modify household wiring. You can add up the power requirements of all the lights and machinery to determine if a nearby 15- or 20-amp branch circuit can handle the load. But if you will be bringing in new machinery, it is sensible to make a simple list of the equipment, and solicit estimates from electricians for running a separate circuit to the office that can handle the load. Computers can be particularly sensitive to peaks and valleys in a power supply. But if the only additional load is an electric typewriter and a desk lamp, you might not have to make any alterations to the circuitry.

Telephone. If you have children who know how to talk and know how to dial there is no question about it; your home office will need a separate phone line with its own number. If you will use phone lines on a regular basis to send or receive information with a computer, it may be necessary to install yet another line with its own unlisted number, since incoming calls can disrupt the transmission of data.

Insurance. It is essential that you contact your home insurance agent before opening a home office. Almost certainly you will need changes in your existing policy or a separate policy to include equipment and furnishings used professionally at home.

Although there are other questions of design, construction, and maintenance, perhaps the most important question is not about the physical plant at all, but about you— whether or not you are suited to work at home.

In many households, home office employees are subject to many more interruptions than they experienced at work. Instead of a fellow employee breaking in to check some fact or figure, the break at home may take the form of a Little Leaguer who needs a ride to practice. It is difficult for family members to realize that Mom or Dad is really at work when they are just down the hall, just one ''Hey Mom, have you seen my sneakers'' away.

Some of these issues are discussed in an interesting, 48-page booklet produced by the U.S. Small Business Administration (SBA) called ''Starting and Managing a Business from Your Home.''

It includes a series of questions that can help you make up your mind, for instance, ''Do you get up early and find yourself at work while others are still getting up? As a kid, did you have a paper route or sell lemonade? Do you trust your hunches and find it easy to make decisions? Do you keep new ideas in your head and do you remember people's names and faces?''

A number of affirmative answers may, according to the SBA, indicate that you could become a successful ''at home'' employee who commutes to work by walking down the hall.

More Closet Space

Q. Even though I rotate summer and winter clothes from a small but deep bedroom closet to a storage closet downstairs, it seems that there is never enough room. Aside from the wire rack and basket systems, which may provide more organization but not more usable space, what is the best way to make awkward closet space more accessible?

A. Although different types of construction and floor plans can dictate different solutions, here are a few ideas. One is to make the entire front of the closet into doors. In a typical closet, deep or not, space to each side of a central door can be hard to get at. Widening the opening and installing either one large door or a pair of doors that meet in the middle of the opening makes the out-of-the-way spaces more accessible.

Another approach is to mount existing doors on heavy-duty hinges (three instead of the standard pair), and attach storage shelves to the backs of the doors. With this plan you can reduce the depth of closet shelves by 6 or 8 inches (even by 10 or 12 inches with heavy-duty shelf hardware), while transferring the same amount of space to a much more accessible location on the door.

The ultimate solution could be provided by White Home Products, the company that developed those amazing rotating clothing racks that snake across the walls and ceilings of dry cleaning stores. The firm now makes several residential versions— motorized oval tracks around which hanging hardware circulates.

The smallest unit fits in a 4-foot-by-6-inch-by-7-foot space. For information on this model (it retails for a whopping $2,150 without accessories such as wire storage baskets that revolve along with the hanging sections), and residential models up to twice the size contact White Home Products, Inc.[1]

Built-In Murphy Beds

Q. In order to gain more full-time usable floor space in my apartment I want to turn a postage-stamp-size bedroom into a study. That means finding a substitute for the double bed. Is there something other than a convertible couch, like a Murphy bed, that can be built in?

A. There is even an actual Murphy bed, made by The Murphy Door Bed Company,[2] a company started in 1900 and still under Murphy family management. In this case, necessity was definitely the mother of invention. William Murphy, the company's founder, lived in a one-room apartment in San Francisco, and experimented with a folding mechanism to gain room for entertaining. He also invented a pivot bed, pulled out of a storage space like a door and then lowered, and also a compact kitchen unit called the Murphy Cabrinette.

The heart of the current bed design is a built-in counterbalance mechanism that allows a conventional innerspring mattress to be tipped up on its head against a wall, covers and all. Approximately 70 percent of all Murphy beds (sold through a network of dealers) are built into a prefabricated cabinet. Many dealers can install the bed mechanism in custom cabinets—as part of a storage wall for example. The beds are available in all conventional sizes.

[1]White Home Products, 2401 Lake Park Drive, Atlanta, GA 30080
[2]The Murphy Door Bed Co., 5300 New Horizons Blvd., Amityville, NY 11701

Improvements and Repairs Inside

Fifteen

WALLS

Installing Drywall
Tips on Carrying, Cutting, Installing, and Finishing

Drywall, also called wallboard and Sheetrock (the U.S. Gypsum Company trade name), is made from a liquid slurry of gypsum poured between two sheets of paper and baked in an oven until dry and hard. The finished panels, available in many sizes with a variety of special features, cover the walls and ceilings in over 30 percent of all new houses and apartment buildings.

Some architectural purists argue that drywall can't match the durability, sound-deadening quality, and beauty of plaster. They may be right. But it is a lot easier to find a drywall installer than a plasterer—and less expensive to hire one, too. And while plastering is a difficult and time-consuming hand craft, installing drywall is, for many, a reasonable do-it-yourself job.

A successful drywall installation depends on many factors, including the alignment and stability of wall studs and ceiling joists the panels are fastened to. To build a strong, durable frame, and avoid all-too-common drywall maintenance problems such as cracking seams and popping nails, follow these three basic guidelines.

First, the supporting frame must be straight; its surface must provide a uniformly flat plane. Even small, ¼-inch misalignments between framing timbers can create ridges and depressions in the drywall surface, or build in stresses that cause maintenance problems later on.

Second, the frame should be reasonably dry. Wet wood can shrink dramatically while losing excess moisture during the first few heating seasons. This shrinkage twists and turns framing timbers, disrupting the surface drywall. Technically, ''dry'' means timbers should have no more than a 19-percent moisture content. As a practical matter, ''dry'' includes all but excessively waterlogged boards, for instance, 2 by 4s that are obviously much heavier than others.

Third, drywall panels must have structural support behind all edges. On walls, one panel reaches to the center of a 2-by-4 wall stud, while the adjoining panel rests on the other half of the same stud. Along the joints between walls and ceilings, however, blocking must be added between joists so that the edges of drywall panels do not ''float'' from one timber to the next.

Opposite: Texturing walls does not require any high-tech equipment. A variety of patterns can be created by dragging a brush, a comb, or even a wet sponge through sand-textured surfacer, Free-form, natural hand motions are imperfect, but uniform enough to create an overall pattern.

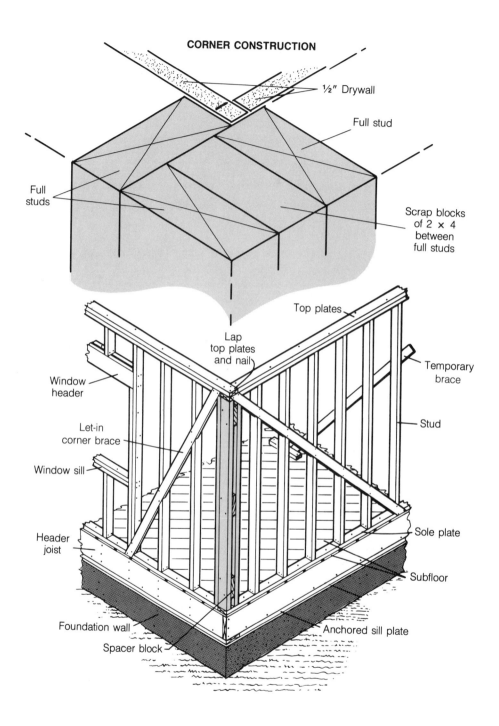

CORNER CONSTRUCTION

½" Drywall

Full stud

Full studs

Scrap blocks of 2 x 4 between full studs

Top plates

Lap top plates and nail

Temporary brace

Window header

Let-in corner brace

Window sill

Stud

Header joist

Sole plate

Subfloor

Foundation wall

Spacer block

Anchored sill plate

Many framing tricks avoid using three full studs plus blocking at corners. But the old-fashioned method provides great strength and durability, keeping taped drywall corners where you put them. Also, old-fashioned let-in diagonal bracing ties the corner across the frame.

Standard wallboard panels are 4 feet wide, ½ inch thick and 8 feet long. Longer lengths can be ordered that reduce the number of seams in the wall. But larger panels are difficult to handle. Whenever possible, arrange for the supplier to deliver panels inside, where they will be installed. Some dealers even have fork-lift cranes that can deliver stacks of panels to the sill of second or third story windows. That sure beats carrying them up the stairs.

If possible, avoid carrying panels by yourself. (They're too heavy for most people.) Also, watch out for wind that can sweep you and a panel off your feet, and beware of cramped halls or stairwells. Maneuvering through them is difficult without damaging panel edges. And that makes it more difficult to make concealed seams later on.

Standard panels can be ordered with two special features that are useful in special circumstances. Water-resistant panels, often notated on blueprints as W/R panels, and easily recognized by a green surface tint, including an asphalt mix in the gypsum core and a chemical additive in the surface paper. They are ideal in kitchens, baths, and laundry rooms where moisture is produced.

Fire-retardant panels also have a specially formulated core that increases the amount of time wallboard stays intact when exposed to fire. These panels are a worthwhile and only marginally more expensive alternative in furnace rooms and in kitchens, two likely spawning grounds of a house fire.

After careful measuring, drywall can be cut with a drywall knife—a stubby-handled tool with a triangular, razor-sharp blade. Cuts are made most easily by scoring the panel once or twice through the surface paper, folding the back of the panel toward itself so it snaps along the cut line, then completing the cut from the rear of the panel, slicing through the paper backing.

Professionals use a special drill to drive sharply pointed, Phillips-head fasteners called drive screws to hang drywall. These produce a neat dimple in the wallboard surface that is easily filled with joint compound. Most do-it-yourselfers use trusty, old-fashioned hammer and nails.

Testing by gypsum manufacturers shows that long nails driven deeply into the wood frame will protrude more than shorter nails as the wood dries. Since shorter nails have less holding power, resin-coated nails with wide heads and a series of rings on the shank were developed. A 1¼-inch, ringed drywall nail is recommended for ½-inch panels.

Drive nails at least ⅜ of an inch from the ends of panels. Work from the center out, pressing boards against the framing when nailing. Keep the nail shank perpendicular to the drywall, seating the nail with a final hammer blow just below the board surface without breaking the paper. Space nails approximately 7 inches apart on ceilings, 8 inches on walls. If you use drive screws spacing can be increased to 12 inches on ceilings and 16 inches on walls.

Generally, using adhesive reduces the number of fasteners by 50 to 75 percent, although different manufacturers make different recommendations. Extra holding power is provided by a continuous bead of adhesive applied over the framing. Check label directions before using adhesive, as several products require use in well-ventilated areas within a temperature range of approximately 50 to 100 degrees Fahrenheit.

Drywall is finished with a three-coat taping job. First, a narrow base coat of joint compound is spread with a trowel over the seams between panels, and a layer of paper

DRYWALL SEAM

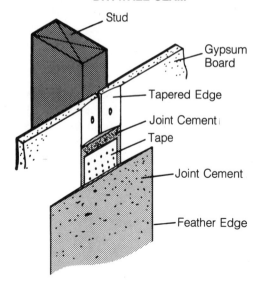

Stud

Gypsum Board

Tapered Edge

Joint Cement

Tape

Joint Cement

Feather Edge

Cracking and nail popping of taped wallboard can be traced to two causes: wet framing lumber that twists as it dries out, and a skimpy, two-coat taping job. Three coats are needed: one to embed the tape, one to widen and fill the seam, and a final, feathering coat.

tape and fill the depression at the seam built in to accommodate the tape and joint compound without creating a bulge in the wall. After sanding again, apply a thin, wider finishing coat of compound, sanding lightly again to finish.

With practice, compound can be applied smoothly, without most of the little cuts and ridges that require sanding. It helps to mix the compound to a soupy consistency and to keep trowel blades very clean.

Taping Gypsum Drywall
Turning Individual Panels Into a Smooth Wall

Paper-covered gypsum wallboard (drywall) is the material of choice on walls and ceilings. It is used by professionals almost exclusively in new houses and apartment buildings. Most do-it-yourselfers also find drywall a lot more forgiving than plaster.

But a wall of individual gypsum panels, complete with seams every 4 feet and rows of nail heads every 16 inches (sometimes every 24 inches), would not look very good without a three-coat taping job—the finishing process that covers seams and nail heads and, under two coats of paint, makes a wall of individual panels closely resemble plaster.

It helps to install the gypsum panels correctly. But a three-coat taping job can rescue uneven joints, excessively large dimples around nail heads, and punctures, tears, and crumpled wallboard corners that sneak into many do-it-yourself installations.

Before you take out the spackle knives, however, here are some tips on installing gypsum panels that can make the taping process much easier.

▮▮▶ Use resin-coated, ringed, 1¼-inch, drywall nails for standard, ½-inch-thick wallboard, working from the center out, pressing the panel against the wood framing as you nail.

➤ Avoid flexing the panels during installation. This can inadvertently build in stresses that disrupt taped seams later on. When working on ceilings where panels are most likely to flex due to gravity, call in a few helpers, or use a "deadman"—a bracket made of 2 by 4s that can be tipped up to support one end of a panel at ceiling height while you start to nail.

➤ Drive the nails straight into the sheet. Finish with a hammer blow that drives the wide-headed nail just below the panel surface without breaking the paper. The resulting "dimple" should look like a very shallow crater with the nail head at its center.

➤ For extra holding power you can use construction adhesive (applied with a caulking gun), in a continuous bead over the framing. Check label directions before using. Several products require use in well-ventilated areas and moderate temperatures.

➤ You can also increase holding power and prevent nail pops later on by attaching the panels with drive screws—pointed, Phillips-head fasteners set by electric screwdriver (or drill with a Phillips head bit). These wide-thread screws produce a neat, small dimple in the wallboard surface.

After the last nail is driven, check the wall for protruding nail or screw heads by drawing a spackling blade over every dimple and seam. If you detect even a slightly protruding piece of metal (you should feel and hear the contact when it hits the blade), take the time to drive it deeper so it will not hit the blade during taping and spackling.

At this point the drywall should be finished with a three-coat taping job to strengthen and conceal joints, fasteners, reinforced corners covered with metal corner guard, and to give the wall a smooth, flat, uninterrupted surface.

Although some professional-quality tools can make this job more efficient, do-it-yourselfers can do well with basic tools and materials: ready-mix joint compound; paper tape to cover and reinforce seams; at least one 4-inch spackling blade (preferably one 4-inch and one 6-inch blade); and a wider, 10-inch blade used to smooth wider beds of compound over taped seams.

Ready-mixed joint compound is a smooth mixture used over seams and nail heads. Using ready-mix eliminates debris and various other contaminates from impure water or dirty mixing containers that could foul the taping process if you mixed your own compound at home. The material has a creamy consistency and stays plastic as long as it has not been stored in an unheated space over the winter. (Repeated freeze-thaw cycles make the compound unusable.)

The taping job consists of three steps, in which tape is embedded in a bed of compound over seams between panels, the shallow depression built into the edges of each wallboard panel is filled with a second coat of compound, and a final coat smooths out and finishes the seam. The compound should be left to dry at each stage, after which a light sanding can reduce any unwanted ridges and bumps. Naturally, the better you are at handling spackling blades, and less sanding you will have to do to correct mistakes.

Here is how the process unfolds.

1 Fill the seam between panels, spreading compound to a width slightly wider than the paper tape. This is the first, embedding coat, which should be smoothed and level before tape is rolled over the seam.

2 While the compound is still wet, embed paper joint tape (sold in rolls) by drawing a spackling blade over the tape at a 45-degree angle with light pressure. Drag the blade along the edges if necessary to remove ridges of excessive compound. The paper tape must make constant contact with the compound. Tape that bridges small depressions in the compound will probably form a bubble in the final wall and have to be cut out and respackled.

3 The final step in this first course is to cover the tape with a skim coat of compound immediately after embedding. You will still see the tape. Then allow the seam to dry completely, for 24 hours under normal conditions. At the same time apply the first coat of compound to nail head dimples.

4 Before starting the second and third coats, make sure your spackling blades are clean. Otherwise, small, hardened bits of compound will foul the soft compound. Use one of the wider blades to feather the second layer of compound beyond the tape by about 2 inches. The tape should disappear under this coat.

5 Light sanding may be necessary to remove ridges before applying a thinner, still wider third coat, which extends approximately 2 inches beyond the width of the second coat, fully filling the depression built into the edges of wallboard panels to accommodate the tape and compound. A final, very light sanding may be necessary before paint is applied.

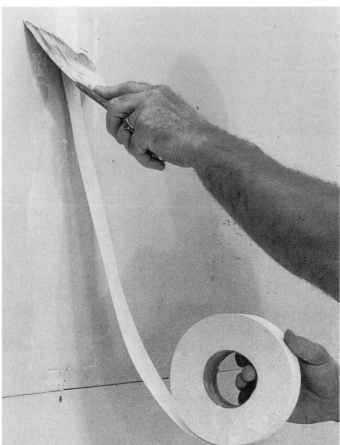

After checking for protruding nail heads by running the blade along the joint, spread compound evenly over the seam. Then roll out drywall tape and press it in place gently with a spackling knife. Areas of the tape not in contact with compound will bubble and crack.

Georgia Pacific

Efflorescence on Masonry
A Low-Salt Diet for Masonry Walls

''Efflorescence'' sounds like a costly housing option—something extra like flocked wallpaper or crystal chandeliers. But it's not. Efflorescence is the cause of countless problems on masonry surfaces. It contributes to the erosion of solid concrete foundations, masonry block walls, and mortar that bonds together courses of bricks. It is also the most common cause of peeling paint on brick, masonry block, and concrete.

Technically, efflorescence is a crystalline deposit of water-soluble salts. It usually takes the form of a scaly or sandy-whitish film on a masonry surface. Wash it off, brush it away, or paint over it, and only a few weeks later it may reappear.

The formation of efflorescence on masonry is analogous to the formation of ''salt rings'' you may notice on shoes after a walk on snowy streets that have been salted. The salt helps to melt ice and snow, and also dissolves in the slush that soaks into your shoes. As the water evaporates dissolved salt migrates to the edges of the wet area where it is deposited. The same kind of process occurs on masonry walls.

The two main ingredients of efflorescence are salt and water. The soluble salts are in or on the masonry, for instance, in the concrete or mortar mix of a foundation wall. The water may come from any number of sources, including rain, leaks from roof gutters or plumbing pipes, or condensation. Both ingredients are present in, and often difficult to eliminate from, conventional masonry construction.

Salts found in efflorescence may come from sodium and potassium in cement, and from chlorides sometimes used as special additives in concrete, called accelerators, used to quicken the hardening process. They may even come from such an unlikely source as sea water contaminating the sand used in a mortar mix.

Water propelling the soluble salts out of a masonry wall can often be traced to rain or snow that contacts exposed masonry outside the house. But even when a masonry foundation is thoroughly waterproofed from the outside before dirt is backfilled against the building, efflorescence may occur as condensation forms within the wall.

In this complex process moisture produced inside the house from such mundane activities as washing and cooking works its way through a masonry wall toward the cold, dry air outside. But as the warm, moist air encounters the cold wall, it may condense, bringing a fresh supply of soluble salts back to the interior masonry surface.

Efflorescence is not an unexpected problem on new masonry construction. In the trade this initial blush of surface salts on a new building is called a ''bloom.'' The condition is relatively common since it is difficult to protect a structure from the weather completely during construction. Rain that soaks into an exposed masonry block foundation wall, for instance, can later carry salts in the mortar to the surface.

Efflorescence is usually not damaging to the structure, although it is the cause of many nagging maintenance problems. Ongoing repairs stemming from efflorescence can be minimized two ways: limiting the soluble salt content of building materials (an option during construction only), and limiting contact between masonry and moisture.

During construction, samples of masonry can be tested for efflorescence by contractors with the idea of using materials such as low-alkali portland cement in mortar mixes, and avoiding the use of calcium chloride accelerators that also can corrode metal reinforcement. The Brick Institute of America notes, ''Admixtures for mortar are generally not recommended.''

Water contact can be minimized by applying waterproofing on outside surfaces, directing the flow from gutters and downspouts away from masonry foundations, and grading soil around the building on a slope to shed water away from the walls. Inside, condensation can be reduced by venting excess moisture with exhaust fans in baths, kitchens, and laundry areas, installing a dehumidifier, and insulating masonry walls.

Reducing the two main ingredients of efflorescence is an essential part of the solution; the other is to remove the deposits. New ''bloom'' deposits on exterior surfaces are likely to be washed away in the weather. It is not advisable to wash efflorescence from newly built surfaces because this just adds more moisture to the wall that may bring more salts to the surface.

In most situations it is better to remove the deposits with a dry brush, or for more severe cases, by wire brushing or light sandblasting. Particularly stubborn deposits may respond to a scrubbing with muriatic acid, used with caution in a proportion of 1 part acid to 12 parts water.

Applying a silicone or acrylic coating is often suggested as a remedy for recurring efflorescence. Such coatings can greatly reduce the amount of moisture that penetrates the masonry. But there is a catch. Sealing the wall without stopping the sources of deposits can lead to deterioration that is far more damaging than efflorescence.

For example, when water leaking through from the ground outside hits such a water-resistant barrier on the inside, salts can be deposited just below the wall surface. There, crystalline growth can exert enough pressure to break apart the masonry surface—a condition called *spalling*. Since it may be difficult to eliminate all leaks, industry groups such as the Brick Institute do not recommend coatings for treating efflorescence.

After efflorescence had been wirebrushed off the wall, a masonry water-resistant (not really ''waterproof'') compound can be applied. The material is like a very thick paint. However, if water continues to enter from the outside, scaly deposits are likely to return inside.

To help pinpoint the source of the problems, consider the age of the masonry. If the building is less than a year old efflorescence is probably of the new "bloom" variety, stemming from salts in cement combined with water that infiltrated the structure during construction. Surface scrubbing and time may solve the problem.

If the building is over a year old check for leaks that let water into the wall. When the deposits appear for the first time on older surfaces, a new source of water, from a broken downspout drain, for example, is often the source of trouble.

Quieting Common Walls
Building Partitions to Absorb Sound

If you live in a building built like a tin drum, it pays to have neighbors with similar tastes in music. You can all tune in the same radio station and create cavernous, wall-to-wall stereo. Realistically, you may know more about your neighbor's tastes than you care to, because many common walls between attached homes (or between rooms in the same house), do little more than muffle the sounds of everyday living. When your neighbor sneezes, you may be tempted to say "gesundheit."

Older buildings may offer more privacy. In many, interior walls were built with somewhat larger wall studs than those used today (2 by 4s that actually measured 2 by 4 inches), creating airspaces covered with sound-deadening lath and plaster on both sides. But there are several ways to make less substantial structures more soundproof.

Where existing walls cannot easily be opened up to add sound-deadening insulation, foam or fiber boards can be applied beneath new paneling, for instance. When walls are deteriorated, it sometimes is cost effective to bury the cracks and tears, instead of trying to repair them.

For one thing, you can redecorate to make a room acoustically "soft" by filling it with spongy, irregular surfaces that soak up sound. Minimalist modern rooms with glass-faced exterior walls and sparse furnishings are likely to be noisy echo chambers, bouncing sound from one hard surface to the next. Crowded, bookcase-lined, Victorian rooms with overstuffed chairs, rugs, drapes, shades and fabric wallpaper are much quieter since the whole room is like a huge acoustic sponge.

Since sound tolerance is a question of degree, one or more "soft" additions may suffice. For example, a sparse room can be dramatically quieted by covering the hardwood floor with a pad and wall-to-wall carpeting. But even an area rug is better than nothing at all.

Given a choice, it would be best to locate a large bookcase against the common wall. Bookshelves could be fastened in place with screws and angle brackets using rubber washers to minimize direct contact with the wall. From the sound-deadening point of view, a wall of books is an ideal, very thick layer of paper insulation.

There are many other decorating possibilities. But, as general guidelines, fabric hangings are better than glass-faced picture frames; padded chairs better than bare-boned Windsors. For peace and quiet the rule for furnishings is the softer the better.

But what about the noisy neighbor? The best bet is to isolate your room from the incoming sound waves. The most elaborate sound-reducing design is a double-stud wall with staggered 2-by-4 studs that eliminate all solid connections between drywall panels. This kind of structural disconnection makes attached homes audibly unattached as well.

But building an independent stud wall is an elaborate home improvement. Also, it uses up about a 4-inch-wide strip of valuable floor space. A furring strip system uses less space and is a more reasonable project. Nail 1-by-2 furring strips across the wall parallel to the floor about 16 inches apart. Fill the spaces between strips with insulation, such as ¾-inch-thick rigid styrene board, before covering with drywall or paneling.

To reduce the amount of direct contact between your new wall and the old one, furring strips can be mounted on strips of felt, large rubber washers, or another slightly Rube Goldberg method of dead-ending sound waves coming through the wall. The key is to disconnect the surface on your side of the partition that emits sound from the other side of the wall.

Similar furring systems can be used on ceilings. But if you can afford to lose more headroom, a suspended ceiling works even better, and provides more dead space that can be filled with puffy, sound-deadening insulation batts. Before recovering a ceiling with anything from new drywall to antique tin ceiling tile, you could nail up furring strips on felt strips of rubber washers, cover the furring strip grid with a ¾-inch layer of rigid insulating board, and then apply the finished ceiling material. This design would incorporate only minimal connection to the structural ceiling, a dead air space, and new insulating material.

On floors the most sensible sound-proofing is a pad and carpet. Although false raised floors offer even more isolation, they can create more problems than they solve, for instance, you can't open and close any doors unless they are cut down or rehung.

On new construction work adding insulation to interior partition walls is unnecessary for energy-saving but does reduce sound transmission. Adding storm windows on outside walls also reduces the effect of street noise by about 50 percent.

The same principles apply to specific sound sources, such as a noisy air conditioner in the bedroom. Although some people can happily nod off to the hum and thump of an air conditioner compressor, many find it annoying, particularly after a long day when the compressor seems to kick in every time your eyes close.

You can't dampen the sound by covering the air conditioner or packing it with insulation. That would block the flow of air. But you can reduce vibration, and reverberations into the house frame by mounting the unit on a wide strip of heavy felt or hard rubber placed over the 2-by-4 sill. Even a layer of styrene insulating board will help, although the weight of the machine will compress it somewhat.

Drywall Tape Shadows

Q. Why does drywall tape over wallboard seams show through after being painted with an enamel paint? Walls in my kitchen are showing shadows in stripes every four feet along the seams.

A. The shadow lines could be caused in several ways. Discoloration could result from differences in suction of paper on the gypsum panels and the joint compound used in the seams and both under and over the tape. The same effect occurs when you repaint a wall that has had cracks filled with spackle. If the spackle is not primed, it absorbs the paint more than the surrounding wall and creates a slightly dark blemish.

On drywall, this problem can also result from excessive sanding along the spackled joint. This can roughen the paper along the joint edges, which makes them soak up paint like a brush. The solution is to sand carefully and seal the wall joints before painting again. Joint darkening also can occur when color-tinted paints are used (as opposed to white), and is most severe when paint is applied in humid conditions or when the joint compound is not fully dried.

Tests by one drywall manufacturer, U.S. Gypsum, indicate that a joint taped at 70 degrees F. and 85 percent humidity won't be dry for 2 days. The solution is to allow adequate drying time and to use a good-quality alkyd flat wall paint and a latex- or solvent-base primer sealer, which also must be fully dry before repainting.

Drywall Repairs

Q. How can I repair several small dents and surface scrapes in gypsum drywall, including one large hole about 1 foot square? If there are dozens of damaged areas does it make more sense to recover the walls?

A. Although there is no hard rule about when to recover and when to repair a room that is in really bad shape, bear in mind that recovering an existing surface, even with ¼-inch or ⅜-inch panels, is almost as much work as installing the first layer of wallboard. It requires a lot of cutting and fitting, then a three-coat taping job plus paint to finish. One reason for the popularity of prefinished paneling is that the finishing steps involved with wallboard are eliminated.

Extensive repair work can be time consuming, but usually is preferable to resurfacing. Small depressions are easy to fix. Simply apply successive coats of a spackling compound, allowing each coat to dry before recoating. On deep holes, fill in stages to avoid cracking. Don't use one thick coat.

Scrapes can be more troublesome. It's ironic that this kind of surface tearing is often more difficult to fix than a hole. The edges around surface tears become frayed and often will not lie down under a coat or two of compound. Generally, you can get better results by neatly trimming torn surface paper to a straight edge with a razor knife, then filling in the shallow paperless section with compound.

Through-the-wall holes can be repaired three ways. On minor punctures, you may get away with stuffing chicken wire or screening into the wall cavity so that the mesh material provides a form against which you can apply layers of compound. This system is the least likely to last without cracking.

On larger holes, cut the damaged area into a rectangle, then make a patch piece of drywall bigger than the cut-out area that will just barely fit through the cutout when slipped into the wall cavity on the diagonal. The idea is to hook a string or a nail into the patch piece, "butter" the edges that will overlap the hole on the inside with construction adhesive (or even joint compound), then pull the patch against the back of the existing gypsum panel. This forms a support for a second patch piece that is set flush with the existing wall surface and taped.

For very large holes the best policy is to cut out a section of the drywall panel up to the center of wall studs on each side of the hole. In most homes these studs are set 16 inches on center. This way a new piece of drywall can be nailed securely in place, then taped and painted.

Basement Leaks

Q. Aside from one flood on a day when everybody on the street was flooded, our cellar has been dry until recently. The roof drains, which empty into underground pipes that go to a drywell are all intact, and the foundation has no visible cracks. How can I stop the intermittent flow from the seam between the floor and the foundation? Should I install a sump pump or an inside drain system?

A. All cellars can keep out at least some ground water. But even a small increase, for instance, from a change in area drainage caused by construction nearby, can supply enough extra water to push a dry cellar past its waterproofing limits.

The best approach to solving the problem is to remove, or at least decrease the water load against the foundation with small, relatively easy and inexpensive steps. Then, if the problem persists, you can opt for a more expensive solution like new foundation waterproofing or an interior drainage system.

If the leaks are near the corners of your house, it is reasonable to suspect the underground drain pipes. After years in the ground they can become separated or cracked. While the gutters and downspouts appear to carry the water away safely, some of the flow may be spilling from the underground drains that are close to the cellar wall.

After diverting roof downspouts and taking other measures to decrease the flow of ground water against the foundation, hydraulic cement is worth a try—even in wet cracks.

Also, drywells don't last forever. They become filled with silt, lose much of their capacity, and simply spill roof water into the soil, where it may be flowing back against the house. You could dig a new drywell, or simply connect the downspouts into an above-ground pipe that slopes away from the house. The trick is to release the water at a point where it will continue to flow away from the cellar.

Other simple steps include regrading around the house, filling gullies that often form from rain drips off the roof edge. This also encourages water to drain away from the building. Finally, try filling the leaking seam with hydraulic cement, a dense cement mixture that expands as it hardens.

Tub-Wall Seam Caulk

Q. How can I keep the seam closed between the tub and the surrounding tile? It seems to need recaulking on an all-too-regular basis.

A. It's not surprising that the tub-tile seam is so difficult to close permanently. The tile is attached to the wall, which is subject to one set of stresses, while the tub rests on the floor, which is subject to different forces. Also, the tub may actually move a bit when it is loaded down with water—and a person, too. That combined load is often enough to flex the joists and subfloor on which the tub rests.

This sinking problem can be minimized by beefing up floor joists and subflooring beneath the tub during construction or remodeling. Another good tip is to load the tub with water or cinder blocks resting on some towels before the water is hooked up. This trick stresses the connection between tub and tile the way it will be stressed later on and builds in resistance to sagging that can open the joint.

The best you can do working on an existing joint is to follow this sequence. First, vigorously scrape out layers of caulk, including old grout between the tiles. Second, let the area dry. (You can speed up this process with a hair dryer.) Third, fill the tub-tile seam liberally with a flexible silicon- or polyurethane-based caulk, colored to match surrounding grout.

Resilient caulks such as silicone are water-resistant like grout but far more flexible across a joint between different materials under different stresses.

Plaster Ornamentation

Q. What are the options for repairing or replacing plaster ornamentation such as cornice moldings and ceiling medallions? In some areas water damage has made large sections of the plasterwork so loose and crumbly that they seem beyond repair.

A. Washing crumbling plaster with a solution of 1 pint white household vinegar in 1 gallon of water may strengthen some surfaces. It's a simple enough job, and worth trying. Rebuilding plaster detailing is considerably more difficult. Aside from patching small cracks and chips, larger, complex shapes must be recreated with wooden molds.

In a typical repair sequence a plasterer might use a contour gage to duplicate a molding profile in wood. Then, after clearing away bad plaster and building up a base of fresh, wet plaster, the idea is to drag the wooden profile over the plaster, gradually scraping away excess, and leaving a molded shape. You can imagine that this operation requires some finesse. Some experience doesn't hurt either.

Another option is to replace richly detailed and nonlinear patterns such as ceiling medallions with synthetic recreations offered by several companies. They advertise regularly in restoration shelter magazines such as *Victorian Homes*.

Plaster Repairs

Q. Repairing a large section of plaster wall, I discovered that there is old-fashioned wood lath over the wall studs. I want to use wood lath to make the repair, but I'm not sure how much space there should be between them. The old ones are about ½ inch apart. Is this correct?

A. A ⅜-inch space between horizontal strips is customary. But as the old strips have dried out shrinkage may have increased the spacing a bit. Replace the damaged section with standard lath made of a soft, straight grained wood such as white pine, spruce, or fir, cut to ⁵⁄₁₆ by 1½ by 48 inches. To allow for movement in the wall frame and to prevent buckling, the joints between 4-foot strips in a single row should also have a small space between them—about ¼ inch.

If you run into trouble, a good alternative to old-fashioned wood lath is gypsum board lath (commonly available in ⅜-by-16-by-48-inch sheets). If you can't find new, clean wood lath, use the gypsum board instead of old, plastercaked lath, which does not provide a secure surface for bonding new plaster.

Sixteen

FLOORS

Finishing Wood Floors
Sanding and Sealing Worn Out Wood Floors

Hardwoods such as oak, one of the most common flooring materials, can last several hundred years, as long as the wood fibers have a protective coating. In a forest, bark separates the fibers from the elements, which could soak the wood, causing swelling and rotting, or dry the wood, causing shrinking and cracking.

In a house, a sealer separates the fibers from the elements. It has to be tough like bark to protect the fibers from foot traffic and ground-in dirt. And it has to be weathertight to prevent swelling from moisture in summer and to prevent shrinking from dry air during the winter heating season.

Three coats of polyurethane, a standard floor finish today, may accomplish all that and last 20 years or more in the corner of the room where nobody walks. But resanding and adding a new protective coating is often the only alternative out in the middle of the room—particularly along the pathways from room-to-room that people tend to follow again and again. Architects call them "traffic patterns." It's usually easy to spot them—the strips that are a little grayer and not as shiny as the surrounding wood.

Of course, there are other reasons to resurface a hardwood floor. You may have to repair a large area that is stained or cracked. Or you may discover that a previous occupant who preferred vinyl to real wood laid vinyl tile or linoleum over what turns out to be a beautiful hardwood floor.

Whatever the motivation, there are two ways to go about resurfacing a wood floor: pay a professional, or do it yourself with rented equipment. To find out how much money you can save working on your own, compare the cost of rental equipment plus about $50 for polyurethane, extra sanding belts, a roller and a brush, to the job costs estimated by several contractors.

It is more difficult to analyze whether or not you should try to tackle the project. But be prepared for some heavy-duty work moving furniture out of the room, which must be empty to do the refinishing job properly. Running a modern drum sander is not as much like controlling a bucking bronco as it used to be. But running these powerful machines does require finesse—skill that comes from experience.

Stopping and starting is the hard part for do-it-yourselfers. A stationary machine with a sanding belt spinning at high speed chews away wood at a surprising rate. So in order to remove only the thin, top layer, the sanding machine (not just the belt) must be in motion, tracking in line with the wood grain, as soon as the sanding drum begins to rotate.

Whole-house renovation and remodeling projects may include new built-in shelves, new windows and sliding glass doors, a new fireplace, and, of course, new furniture. But the existing strip oak floor can stay. It will respond to a light resanding, and two or three new coats of polyurethane.

That sounds simple: turn on the machine and start moving. But even a brief delay—a fraction of a second when you start the machine or stop at the other side of the room—can leave a depression as the rotating belt digs into the wood.

The depressions would not pose a hazard. You wouldn't ever trip over them. But you would see them—like gentle waves on the wood, or lap marks on a poorly painted wall. Eliminating these depressions and running the machine smoothly is what separates professional floor finishers from do-it-yourselfers.

If you rent tools, you'll need a large drum sander, a rotary edger (a small machine for corners, edges and stairs) and sanding belts. The best type of machine by far is a lever-action drum sander. While some sanders must be tipped on edge to break contact between the spinning belt and the floor, lever-action machines have a tip-up lever (sometimes called a clutch) that raises the drum only.

This feature makes the job much easier and reduces lap marks. You can raise the drum with two fingers, instead of wrestling the machine up on edge. But whatever type you rent, be sure it does not require a power supply (25 amps for some machines) that is beyond the capacity of circuits in your home.

Here's how a typical job would go, no matter who does the work. First, the room must be cleared, along with any obstructions on the floor, such as heating registers or nail heads that could tear the belts. Most sanders have a dust bag. But some very fine sawdust always escapes—enough so that you should block doorways into adjacent rooms, and consider wearing a respirator mask to keep the dust out of your lungs.

A two-step sanding will suffice on most floors. The procedure is to cover the floor with the drum sander and then the edger using medium and then fine sandpaper. A pass with coarse paper is normally needed only on badly worn floors with dirt ground deeply into the wood grain. Conversely, floors in relatively good shape may need only one pass with fine paper.

After vacuuming thoroughly, seal the wood with at least a two-coat surface finish. There are many possible finishes, although the traditional covering, wax, which requires regular maintenance, has been largely replaced by longer lasting polyurethanes. Such clear sealers can be applied over bare wood, or over a coat of stain. For instance, to warm up the tone of old floors, which tend to gray tones even after sanding, apply a light brown stain before sealing.

Polyurethane is the most popular sealer for several reasons. It can be rolled on, dries overnight, and is available in a variety of sheens from high gloss to a low-luster satin. The trick is to apply the viscous liquid without trapping air bubbles. Do this by applying the polyurethane slowly with a fine-napped mohair roller.

FLOOR PLUGS

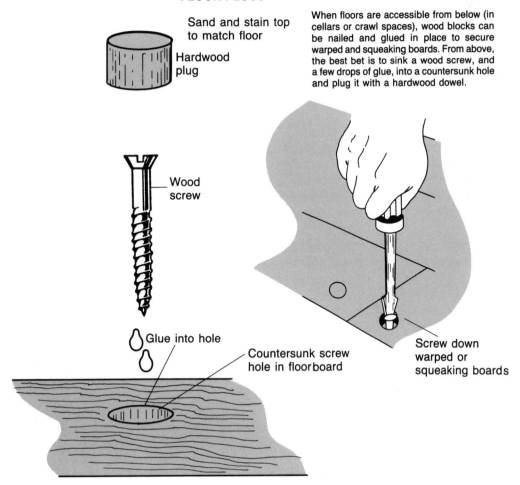

Sand and stain top to match floor

Hardwood plug

When floors are accessible from below (in cellars or crawl spaces), wood blocks can be nailed and glued in place to secure warped and squeaking boards. From above, the best bet is to sink a wood screw, and a few drops of glue, into a countersunk hole and plug it with a hardwood dowel.

Wood screw

Glue into hole

Countersunk screw hole in floorboard

Screw down warped or squeaking boards

With the new surface protection in place, vacuuming and an occasional buffing to remove scuff marks should suffice. You may want to rewax (or use a combination cleaning and buffing liquid) once or twice a year to maintain a shine, even though some polyurethane manufacturers say waxing is not required.

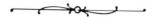

Caring For Quarry Tile
Maintenance Tips for a "Maintenance-Free" Floor

Quarry tile, one of the most popular varieties of ceramic tile, is commonly used on floors that take a beating—in entry halls where people track in mud and snow, in kitchens and baths, greenhouses, and other rooms where elements from outdoors are likely to get indoors.

The stock size, 6-by-6 or 6-by-8-inch, generally earth-tone tiles are extremely durable. Over a strong, nonflexing subfloor, such as a concrete slab, or an overbuilt, reinforced wood frame, quarry tile should last indefinitely—an unusual characteristic for finished floors.

Resilient sheet flooring can become brittle, punctured, torn, or so dull and dirty that cleaning and rewaxing can't rescue the material, and replacement finally becomes the only alternative. Vinyl tiles suffer many of the same problems, including a tendency to lose adhesion to the subfloor due to condensation problems in installations directly over uninsulated concrete slabs.

Wood floors are more forgiving. After years of wear have left graying traffic lanes throughout the house, even in oak, the most common wood flooring, you can make an almost new floor by sanding off the top layer of wood and refinishing.

Replacement and resurfacing are not reasonable options with quarry tile. But there are several procedures and products that can be used to keep a clean, durable surface finish on practically indestructible quarry tile. The following regimens are suggested by one of the largest tile manufacturers, American Olean Tile Company[1], including recommendations for widely used commercial-duty products made by other companies that have produced excellent results in tests by American Olean's technical services division.

For everyday cleaning, quarry tile can be swept, vacuumed, or dry-mopped like other floors. Foot marks and small spills can be removed with a damp mop or sponge. For periodic cleaning, American Olean recommends a product called Hillyard Super Shine-All, made by Hillyard Floor Care Company.[2] Mix one-third cup into a gallon of water and wash with a two-bucket cleaning system: one with clean solution, one with dirty solution removed from the floor. After damp mopping (or wet vacuuming), let the floor dry without further rinsing.

[1]American Olean Tile Co., Lansdale, PA 19446
[2]Hillyard Floor Care Co., P.O. Box 909, St. Joseph, MO 64502

After grout has been troweled into the seams, excess residue on the tile surface is wiped away with a wet towel. With cement grouts, which become harder with curing, the floor should be mopped with clean water twice a day. Building paper can be laid to retard evaporation.

For high-strength cleaning of extremely dirty quarry tile floors, American Olean suggests a product called Holcomb Creme-Scour, made by J. I. Holcomb Manufacturing Company.[3] This cleaner can be used most effectively (and with the least amount of elbow grease) with an electric floor-cleaning machine with nylon scrubbing pads. (Many hardware stores and home centers rent such machines.) After scrubbing in the cleaner, mop and rinse to remove the scouring residue, let the floor dry, then damp mop to remove final white traces.

Although this type of thorough surface cleaning usually suffices, sometimes the grouted seams between tiles, which are often more porous than the surrounding tile, need more attention, even regrouting.

During the original installation, or regrouting, most grout materials leave a residue that can be cleared off the wet floor surface with a rubber squeegee. Any thin film that remains can be wiped away with a damp rag. Another method of finishing grouted seams is to sprinkle some dry grout over the still-wet tile joints to make the grout surface more durable—a process called *densifying*. Then, slightly damp pine wood shavings are wiped over the area with a piece of burlap, followed by a final pass with dry shavings.

When standard white or gray grout traces remain on the floor, reapply a small amount of Holcomb Creme-Scour and scrub vigorously with a nylon pad to remove the film. Then, damp mop or sponge away the scouring residue, rinse and let dry.

Despite thorough cleaning, some stubborn stains and spills may remain. For instance, paint may spill or splatter on the quarry tile while you are renewing the other surfaces in the room. Try to scrape off hardened paint with a razor blade. If you wipe up a splatter while it is wet but a thin film of paint remains, you can use paint remover, following manufacturer's directions. After cleaning up the film, scrub the area with a detergent such as Spic-'N-Span or with Hillyard Super Shine-All mixed with hot water.

[3]J. I. Holcomb, Mfg. Co., 4415 Euclid Ave., Cleveland, OH 44103

Oil and grease stains, often the most persistent because they seep into the quarry tile, can be dealt with several ways. First, try scrubbing with a household detergent or Super Shine-All (1 part to 8 parts of hot water), then rinse. If the stain persists mix the detergent with hot water into a paste, and allow it to cover the stain overnight. Remove the paste, which may blot up the stain, by wetting, scrubbing, and rinsing.

If the oil or grease still won't budge, American Olean suggests a unique solution. Place several paper towels over the stain and heat them with an electric iron. (The iron should be set at a temperature that will not scorch the paper.) The idea is that heat from the iron will thin the oil or grease after about 5 minutes, which encourages the blotting action of the paper towels.

Cleaning Glazed Tile

Q. How can I clean glazed tile on bathroom floors without scratching the surface?

A. The tiles should need only a damp mopping to remove floor marks, spills, and such. However, for heavy-duty cleaning of built-up dirt, try this regimen:

First, mix a solution of 2 cups Hillyard Clean-O-Lite or Hillyard Re-Juv-Nal to 1 gallon of hot water (a 1 to 8 proportion). Second, use a soft scrub brush to loosen dirt, particularly in grouted joints. Third, remove the dirty solution with a wet vacuum or mop, working on one small area at a time before starting with more cleaning solution. Fourth, for the most stubborn buildup, try Holcomb Creme-Scour, testing in a small inconspicuous area to be sure the scouring will not scratch or dull a worn glaze. Then mop and rinse to remove the cleaning residue, let the floor dry, and damp mop to remove the last white traces of scouring.

These specific brand names are only some of the alternatives, but they continue to be strongly recommended in the comprehensive Maintenance Guide Manual prepared by the technical department of American Olean Tile Company.

Sealing Time for Wood Floors

Q. During a remodeling project when is the best time to lay and seal the oak flooring? Should we wait until the different subcontractors are finished, or seal the raw wood right away and protect the floor with paper or drop cloths until the job is done?

A. Generally, flooring, like all surface finishing work, should be started only after other jobs that could reasonably be expected to do some damage are completed. For example, new kitchen appliances or a new furnace should be moved through the room while plywood subflooring is in place. Scratches and dents won't ruin it. All prefinished flooring, such as parquet tile that comes stained and sealed, should be installed as late in the job as possible.

I've seen some jobs where unfinished flooring is laid but left unfinished as paint and trim and other finishing jobs are done. The idea is to wait for the dust to settle, then sand off any scuffs and scratches, and seal.

However, raw, kiln-dried hardwood can absorb enough moisture before it is sealed—even sitting in bundles before it is laid—to cause cracking, cupping (a U-shaped twisting across the grain), and crowning (an inverted U-shape) later on. Certainly it pays to wait until excess moisture produced from masonry or plaster work has evaporated.

When raw flooring absorbs excessive moisture through subflooring below, the resulting expansion pushes the floorboards together, raising the joints, which creates peaks at the seams and valleys in between, called ''cupping.''

In this condition a final sanding before the floor is sealed cuts off the peaks and everything looks fine. But as the floor dries out and the bottom sides of the oak strips flatten out, the joints (the former peaks) are pulled down below the floor surface, which produces crowning. This condition may require yet another sanding, which means re-refinishing. So the most reasonable course is to wait for heavy traffic from construction to end before laying the floor, but then to seal it right away.

Cleaning Wood Floors

Q. What's the best way to care for and clean oak hardwood floors that have accumulated a variety of stains and scuff marks, without resanding and refinishing the entire floor?

A. On a well-sealed floor routine vacuuming, and an occasional buffing to remove scuff marks, should suffice. Depending on the amount of wear, it may be necessary to rewax (or use a combination cleaning and buffing liquid) once or twice a year to maintain a high luster. Don't use water to wash or damp-mop hardwood floors. This can leave other stains and cause warping.

Although some manufacturers of polyurethane, a moisture-resistant surface sealer, say waxing is not required, the Oak Flooring Institute[4] recommends waxing over polyurethane for improved wear resistance and appearance.

To clean most scuff marks rub vigorously with a rag or fine steel wool and a floor cleaner; then wipe dry and polish. To remove darker stains and blemishes that penetrate more deeply (from ink stains or burns, for example), scrub the area with fine steel wool and either a floor cleaner or mineral spirits. Then wash the stain with household vinegar, allowing it to sit for three or four minutes. Deeper sanding or an application of oxalic acid may be required for penetrating stains. (Oxalic acid, a bleaching agent should be used with caution, with rubber gloves, according to label directions, typically in a proportion of 1 ounce to 1 quart of water.)

Finally, blend the bleached spot into the surrounding floor by rubbing with fine steel wool, applying a matching stain where required, then waxing and buffing.

---

[4]Oak Flooring Institute, 8 N. Third St., Suite 810, Sterick Bldg., Memphis, TN 38103

Raising a Sunken Floor Girder

Q. A girder that supports floor beams on the first floor has apparently sagged over the years. Short of rebuilding the first floor, is there some way to raise the beam about ¾ of an inch?

A. Girders can be raised small amounts with adjustable steel columns. These posts have a threaded end at the top that can be turned to make the column longer.

If you don't have such columns in place, a temporary support system would have to be built on each side of the existing girder so that old posts can be removed and new, adjustable posts inserted. The idea is to make very small adjustments (on the order of half a turn every few days), over a period of weeks. And you may hear some creaking and cracking as the house frame moves.

There are two potential problems to look for during this operation. First, the post may exert enough pressure to break a concrete floor unless it is supported by a footing. This means it is not wise to position a new post a foot or so away from an old one, which, most likely, has a footing beneath the concrete floor.

The second problem is compression at the wood beam (the technical term for squashing the wood). A pressure plate on top of the post may compress the beam or dig into it instead of raising the floor. Either symptom is a good indicator that you have moved beyond the province of doing it yourself, and should call in a carpenter.

Leveling Unlevel Floors

Q. The subfloor in my kitchen is very uneven with sometimes an inch difference between two places only a foot apart. How can this be corrected before a new floor is laid?

A. A subfloor out of level by that much cannot be buried successfully beneath new finished flooring, or even under a new layer of rough flooring laid over a carefully constructed series of wedge-shaped shims that fill up or bridge the low spots.

There are two possible causes for the unevenness. The plywood subfloor itself could be so warped (from water and dampness in the kitchen) that, although the floor frame below is level, the plywood sheets are buckling and delaminating. This means the plywood is not usable. It would have to be removed and replaced by new plywood.

The other, more serious cause could be in the floor framing beneath the plywood. The subfloor may be only reflecting discrepancies in supporting joists that are weak, undersized, rotted, sagging over a center girder or wobbling up and down for some other reason, all of which would require stripping away the existing subfloor, repairing or, more likely, rebuilding the frame, then adding a new subfloor.

As a general rule it never makes sense to add a new surface material (on floors, walls, roofs, or anywhere else) where the base is not sound. For a short time, maybe only a few days, the fresh material, say, a new quarry tile floor, may look okay. But then the problems buried underneath start to surface and the improvement project may be a total loss.

Seventeen

PAINTING, PAPERING & FINISHING

Painting a Room
Preparing One Room at a Time

Painting is one of the easiest do-it-yourself jobs and one of the least expensive ways to change a drab, dingy, messy-looking room into a bright, clean, neat-looking room. But the truth is that actually applying paint is the smallest part of the job.

The real work is preparing to paint—maneuvering the furniture away from the walls or out of the room entirely, spreading drop cloths so you won't have hours of cleanup, then spackling the cracks and sanding the blisters, all before you put a drop of paint on the walls.

The job would be easiest if the room were completely empty. Since this ideal is almost always impossible to achieve, try to limit obstructions to one pile in the middle of the room. For example, pull out the bed and use it as a storage platform, stacking drawers from bureaus and desks on top so you can move the lightened desk and bureau frames out of the room easily. Pile on drapes, window shades, coats from the closet, everything that would get in the way and have to be moved or covered once painting is underway.

Even though you will be careful climbing around the room and leaning off ladders once the job is underway, there is a temptation to use any surface for a foothold in a pinch, just to reach a little farther to cover that last bare spot on the ceiling without moving the ladder again. So it is a good idea to take fragile items such as glass picture frames out of the room. Also, since spackling and sanding create a lot of dust, it is wise to remove televisions, stereo equipment, and computers.

The next step in preparing to paint is to cover the surfaces that won't be painted. Again, although you will be careful not to splatter and drip and kick over buckets accidentally, somehow paint finds its way onto floors, chairs, and any other exposed surface. Professional painters use heavy cloths, real "drop cloths," to blanket the floor and furnishings completely. Do-it-yourselfers usually substitute plastic sheeting, which isn't as expensive but is not nearly as tough. You have to be careful not to puncture or tear the filmy sheets moving a ladder around, for instance.

It helps to use masking tape to fix the sheets in place. They are so light that even a breeze through the window can set them sailing. Cover the floor first, then drape another sheet over the mound in the middle of the room. Finally, put down a few thick sections of newspaper to make a substantial, cushioned, absorbent central paint platform where you can leave the cans, fill the roller pan and stir paint without worrying so much about tearing the plastic or spilling the paint.

When this part of the preparation is complete you may notice that it is closer to lunchtime (maybe even dinnertime) than you might have thought, and that the room seems a lot bigger than it did when the furniture was in place. The moral is it pays to start early in the day, even in a small room.

In some rooms, particularly kitchens, the fresh paint will almost certainly adhere better and last longer if you wash the walls with a household detergent, or a mix of about 1 quart of household bleach to 3 quarts of water, which is effective against mold and mildew.

To make a smooth surface, be vigorous scraping out cracks. Use a screwdriver or a can opener to dig away loose material. Fill in deep cracks in stages. Now is the time to be meticulous so you don't have to interrupt the painting process later on to scrape, spackle, and sand as you go. If you do that, too much debris will find its way into the paint and mar the surface.

Some blemishes, such as stains from a roof leak that contain traces of asphalt, will show through fresh paint, even after sanding. Such stains should be primed with a coat of pigmented white shellac, a dense white mixture with tremendous hiding power.

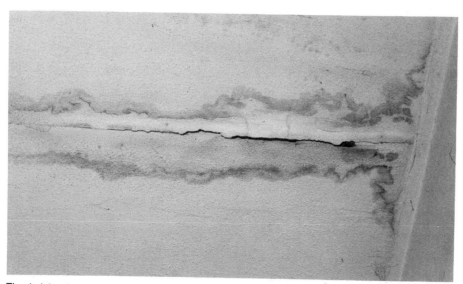

The dark border edging this ceiling stain indicates a roof leak. The stains result from traces of asphalt picked up by the water and must be "stain-killed" before painting.

Although several painting sequences are possible, one of the easiest for do-it-yourselfers is to cut in the edges of a section of wall or ceiling with a brush—a strip a few inches wide up to wall trim or a joint between the wall and ceiling. While a nylon brush is the best choice for latex paints, a natural bristle brush seems to provide the best results for oil-base and alkyd paints, stains, varnish, shellac, and similar finishes.

Then, before the cut-in edge has dried if possible, use a roller to apply paint, lapping over the cut-in edge. For a flat finish use a roller sleeve with a fine, flat nap. Furrier roller sleeves provide a more textured finish.

For best results, double-roll the paint, laying it on in bulk straight from the roller pan or a wide, 2-gallon bucket, with horizontal strokes several inches apart. Then, before the paint can set and begin to harden, finish the process with lighter vertical strokes, drawing the roller handle ahead of the sleeve if possible, instead of pushing the sleeve into the paint from behind. This helps to make a smooth layer of even thickness. And that can reduce wrinkling and other problems later on.

If complete preparation has taken most of the daylight hours and the sun sets before you have finished, bring several lamps into the room so that you can continue to paint under reasonably bright light. Surfaces that look satisfactory, without the small gaps professional painters call "holidays," under the glare of unshaded overhead and table lamps will generally look quite good under more natural, subdued lighting.

---

25 Quick-Paint Tips
Tips for a Successful, Last-Minute Face-Lift

Nothing can transform a room so quickly and inexpensively as a fresh coat of paint. Under ideal conditions, a thorough repainting job allowing enough time for spackling, sanding, and priming, can take several days, even for one room.

But in a pinch—during the holiday season, for instance—a faster face-lift may be in order. Some preparation is still necessary, of course. But the following tips are designed to get the best possible results in the briefest possible time.

Tools. For most jobs the most convenient tools are a 10-inch roller for large flat surfaces (particularly ceilings uninterrupted by the doors and windows on walls), a 6-inch roller for smaller areas, and a 2- or 3-inch brush for trim. Short-napped rollers produce the flattest finished surface. Long-napped rollers leave a more textured surface.

Materials. Although clean up is a lot easier with latex than with oil paint, the best policy for durability is to stick with the type of paint that's already on the wall. In general, paints with the same bases adhere best to each other.

Light colors. Ceilings painted lighter shades than walls seem higher; those painted darker seem lower.

Accent colors. Using starkly contrasting colors on moldings or "accent" walls, chops up a space, which should be avoided in small rooms. To achieve a subtle sense of contrast in small spaces, accent with complementary pastel colors, or switch from a flat finish on walls to semigloss on trim.

Making room to work. Use filmy, inexpensive plastic sheets over furnishings grouped together in the middle of the room, but invest in more substantial plastic drop cloths to cover the floor area where you'll be working.

Splatter protection. Either encapsulate electronic equipment in plastic (even to the point of taping the seams), or remove it. Otherwise fine dust from sanding may gum up the delicate works.

Visibility. Paint under a lot of light. A surface that looks only satisfactory under unshaded overhead and table lamps will generally look quite good under more natural, subdued lighting.

Wall washing. In many rooms, particularly kitchens, it pays to wash walls with soap and water before painting. Use about 1 quart of household bleach to 3 quarts of water and a nonabrasive household detergent to deal with mold and mildew.

Scraping. If patching is called for, clean excess patching material from the wall with scrapers before it dries to save a lot of time and mess with sanding later on.

Contractor credits. A qualified contractor should be ready to supply recommendations of satisfied customers, and to show how long the business has been around; the longer the better.

Estimators. It's best to talk with the person who will put the paint on the walls, not an estimator whom you'll never see again.

Contractor checks. Call your local consumer protection or consumer affairs department and local branch of the Better Business Bureau to inquire about the contractor's record and license, where required.

Agreements. Every contractor should be willing to provide a contract for work, listing names and addresses of all the parties, the amount and method of payment, a detailed job description, and the materials to be used.

Preparation. You can save time and money by preparing the space for the contractor. Remove everything that's portable and not too heavy.

Isolation areas. Use drop cloths or sheets to carefully screen off areas of the house or apartment that will not be painted.

Paint check. Make a last minute check to be sure the paint brought to the job is the paint specified in the contract.

Sequencing. Don't scrape, spackle, and sand as you go. Too much debris will find its way into the paint and mar the surface.

Wet edges. Keep a wet edge, which means you shouldn't pause long enough to let one section of the wall dry. If you do, a lap mark will be left where you continue.

"Stainkilling." Seal stains and blemishes that could bleed through fresh paint by spot coating them with pigmented white shellac.

Priming. Prime raw surfaces, such as newly spackled patches, with a thinned coat of paint, which soaks in quickly and prevents flat spots in the finished surface.

Plaster work. Try rescuing powdery plaster by washing with a solution of 1 pint white household vinegar in 1 gallon of water. Repeated washings may be needed to harden the plaster surface. If this rescue attempt works, sponge the surface with clean water, let dry, then prime and paint.

Drywall work. Prime joint compound used to seal seams on new panels of gypsum drywall before painting. First, clean off the fine dust produced by sanding.

Painting wallpaper. Before painting over wallpaper, wipe a small section of the paper with a damp rag to see if the color is set fast or if it will bleed into the paint. Beware of reds, pinks, and metallic silvers and golds.

Wallpaper tests. Prime and paint paper with the same base paint. Check closely for bubbling and a general loosening of the paper when testing a latex paint. Always test paint a small patch of paper.

Double rolling. For best results and a quick job, double-roll the paint by laying it on the wall in bulk with horizontal strokes, then spreading the film evenly with lighter vertical strokes.

Wallpaper Solutions
Solutions for Bubbles, Bumps, and Bulges

Careful planning and measuring is usually the key to a successful wallcovering job, whether you use wheat paste on large sheets or small prepasted squares. But, as it is with many how-to projects, small problems can detract from an otherwise successful venture. Here are some of the most common problems, and ways to avoid them, or fix them, so your papering job looks better and lasts longer.

The pattern doesn't match across seam. Distinct patterns can help to disguise imperfections in the wall. But mismatched panels can make the seams stand out, fragmenting the room into vertical stripes.

Assuming that the pattern matches from roll to roll, there are two likely sources of trouble. After pasting or soaking, wallcoverings are generally put aside for a short time as specified by the manufacturer. Depending on the material, a paper may expand or shrink a little as it absorbs the adhesive paste. If one strip is hung immediately without curing time next to a cured strip the discrepancy may show up in a pattern mismatch.

Stretching the paper can cause the same problem. If the panel isn't positioned properly, it's natural to move it by pulling on the edges. Depending on the type of material, this can stretch a sheet of wallpaper by ¼ to ½ inch. To minimize this stretching problem, shift the panel of paper by pushing on it with the palms of your hands.

Overlapped seams between sheets don't adhere. This is a common problem on vinyl wallcoverings, caused when regular vinyl adhesive is used to bond the panels to the wall and to each other where panels overlap. Special vinyl-to-vinyl adhesive is required on overlaps, or you can avoid this somewhat inferior method altogether. Inevitably, the double thickness overlaps will show up as slight ridges on the wall.

A neatly butted seam between two panels is made by a process called *double cutting*. With this system panels are overlapped by an inch or so, and the pattern is matched. Then, with a straightedge and a sharp trimming knife, a cut is made through both panels down the center of the overlap. When the excess strips are removed the resulting seam should be perfect since both panels were cut on the same line.

Air bubbles form under the paper. This common problem can result from the wallpaper drying too fast, usually because an area of the wall was not primed, for instance, where a damaged area was spackled. In these spots moisture from the wallpaper adhesive soaks into the wall. This dries out the paste and reduces its holding power.

Of course, any areas not covered by adhesive cannot be expected to stick to the wall. For example, rolling paste on quickly may leave small, uncoated spots. The same is true for prepasted panels that are not completely wet when applied. If the glue is not activated by water it simply won't stick to the wall.

If you notice bubbles before the paste dries, smooth out the paper to move glue into the raised area. Depending on the wallcovering surface you may do this with a brush, roller, or squeegee, follow the manufacturer's recommendation. As a last resort, burst the air bubble with a pin, then smooth-paste into the area gradually. If the paste has dried, cut an X across the bubble with a razor, peel back the corners, apply adhesive to the wall and paper, press down, and smooth.

Paste bumps won't smooth out. Bumps may form when too much paste is applied, or applied unevenly so that it bunches up in little ridges. Start from the finished side of the wall and smooth out the sheet until the excess reaches the uncovered edge and can be removed. Small bubbles that appear in prepasted wallcoverings should reduce themselves as the paper dries and soaks up the paste. But any lumps or stray objects in a batch of mixed paste will show up beneath the paper. Better to deal with them before they harden.

Wallpaper edges curl up. Often this is caused by excessive rolling that removes too much paste from the seam. The edges need just as much paste as the rest of the paper. But since it is easy to roll paste onto the middle of the paper, it's natural to apply a liberal amount, while in an effort to be neat applying paste to the edges, it's common to apply less.

To remedy this problem before the adhesive sets, roll back a curled corner, lay a scrap piece of paper between the underside and the finished section of the wall, and roll on an even amount of paste.

Mildew spots appear in the paper. Vinyls, foils, and other nonporous wallcoverings will trap moisture in the walls behind them. To prevent mildew spots from forming use a quick-drying adhesive. Once the spots appear (small, dark, gray-green dots) the best solution is to remove the paper, wash the wall with a fungicide that will kill mildew bacteria, then rinse and let the area dry completely before resealing the wall and applying new paper.

Short of this drastic step you might try another approach that, unfortunately, is almost as drastic. Drill a few ½-inch holes in the wall sill and plate—the top and bottom horizontal members of the wall frame that may be accessible only from a cellar or attic below or above the wall cavity. This can help excess moisture escape. Even a few holes drilled into the wall cavity through the wall surface—they could be concealed by a vanity or towel rack—may help.

Before hanging paper on a wall subject to condensation, several precautions will minimize the risk of mildew problems later on. First, keep the area well ventilated. Second, use wallboard panels designated WR (they have a greenish tinge) that are chemically treated to resist moisture. Third, wash existing walls prior to hanging paper with a fungicide (a brew of 3 parts water and 1 part household bleach will do).

Wood Finishing
Matching Materials and Methods to the Job at Hand

Before wood becomes lumber it is protected in the wild by bark. This tough skin keeps out the elements and seals in moisture so the wood stays supple and strong. But when a tree is cut into lumber, the wood loses this natural protection. Left uncovered and unsealed, it can crack, warp, buckle, swell, and shrink.

To prevent these forces from ruining trim and furniture, exposed wood needs a protective coating—a man-made substitute for bark. There are many possibilities.

The most basic finishes have only one ingredient. Linseed oil, for instance, adds tone and protects wood at the same time. Other finishes call for several ingredients, for example, stain to add color, a sealer to close the wood grain, and a protective top coating such as varnish.

Here are some of the qualities to consider when selecting a wood finish, and a rundown of the finishes themselves.

Fast-drying finishes. These are the most convenient. They combine a relatively small amount of solids (the actual coating), and a large amount of thinner (the liquid in which the solids are dissolved). When the thinner evaporates solids are left in place to protect the wood. But brush strokes may set in the surface as it dries, before the finish can flatten out.

Also, lap marks will show if the wet edge dries during application. This is most troublesome on a large surface such as a wood door. You have to move quickly to "pick up" the wet edge. Fast-drying films are also relatively thin, since they have a small proportion of solids.

Slow-drying finishes. These finishes, boiled linseed oil, for example, have more solids and less thinner, or none at all. They tend to dry to a tacky condition when the thinner evaporates. Then, the remaining protective film absorbs oxygen and hardens gradually—a process called *polymerization*. In general, 6 to 12 hours of drying and hardening are needed before the surface can withstand contact without marring. The hardening actually continues for a much longer period, from a day to a week, depending on the finish.

Finishes with a greater proportion of solids form thicker protective skins. But this does not necessarily mean they are better than fast-drying, thinner-skinned finishes— just different.

Special consideration must also be given to finishes on surfaces used for food preparation, and on infant's furniture. Babies seem to make contact with an object, even a chair or the edge of a table, by sucking and chewing on it. Finishes on such surfaces should be lead-free (most modern finishes are), and also free of other metals used as drying agents. If in doubt, read the label and contact the manufacturer.

Spar varnish. This very thick, very slow-drying varnish provides a dense surface coating that provides excellent protection against water and moisture—ideal for wood trim on a boat, for instance. Since spar varnish is likely to darken and yellow somewhat it is not suitable for furniture for cosmetic reasons. But it offers excellent protection on window sills that regularly become flooded with condensation from windows.

Latex varnish. This water-based version of varnish is fast drying, but produces a thinner protective film than conventional varnish with reduced moisture resistance acceptable for furniture and trim not exposed to water or excessive moisture.

Shellac. Shellac has a very fast drying time (within 30 or 40 minutes on thin coats) and good wear-resistance, but because it has little resistance to water, shellac is acceptable for use only on interior wood surfaces. Several layers (usually at least three), are needed to provide good protection. Single, heavy coats become brittle and crack.

Shellac is now used primarily as a sealer, to make wood grain accept stain more uniformly, protect porous end grain, and prepare wood for final, very fine sanding. White shellac is the most common. Orange shellac can be used to darken and seal wood.

Allow 24 hours drying time after the final coat, depending on weather conditions, of course, then rub with fine steel wool, apply paste wax, and buff.

Polyurethane varnish. Polyurethanes dry slowly compared to shellac but provide a very durable and moisture-resistant surface. They are the most popular all-around clear finishes, available in high and low gloss, and a good choice on floors and other surfaces subject to wear and tear and wetness. On floors and other large, flat surfaces, apply with a short-napped mohair roller to avoid trapping air bubbles. Overnight drying is normal.

ABOVE: Clear polyurethane is available in three finishes: high gloss, medium gloss, and a low luster (sometimes called satin finish), that simulates the sheen of wax. BELOW: Raw wood takes at least two thin coats. Three coats should be enough to bead water spilled on the surface.

French polish. This is a common finish on antique furniture. It produces a fine patina but water-spots easily and is time-consuming to apply. The process uses shellac cut with a touch of boiled linseed oil, applied parallel to the wood grain, with a balled-up rag dipped in the mixture. When dry, the surface is rubbed with fine steel wool. Then a second application, this time with a bit more oil in the shellac, is rubbed on. This process is repeated several times with increasing amounts of elbow grease to bring up the uniquely "deep" shine.

Lacquer. This evaporative finish is also fast-drying, and, like shellac, must be applied in multiple layers to provide adequate protection.

Prepare wood for a lacquer finish with successive sandings of increasingly fine paper, finishing with a cabinet-grade silicone carbide. After sealing with a mixture of lacquer diluted with an equal part of lacquer thinner (or a lacquer sanding-sealer), resand to "kill" raised grain. The resulting white surface clears under the next coat of lacquer. The resulting finish can be buffed and polished with paste wax to produce a high shine.

Boiled linseed oil. This thick but soft-skinned finish seeps into the wood grain to provide good moisture resistance but little protection against surface abrasion. The hand-rubbed finishing system has faded in popularity due to the amount of labor involved—generally 6 to 12 separate coats applied over a period of weeks.

If time is no object, apply the oil liberally with a brush or rag, wait about 15 minutes for the oil to soak in, wipe off the excess, then start rubbing. Work on a small section at a time, rubbing hard and fast enough to heat the oil by friction and raise a deep luster. Allow approximately 48 hours for drying time, then repeat the process.

Rescuing Wood Trim
Removing Layers of Paint from Wood Trim

Wood trim sets off and defines windows, doors, cabinets, and walls. It is the obvious target of decoration, which may include a conglomeration of coverings and colors, from flowery wallpaper border panels to high-gloss, primary-color paints. Once wood trim is covered up with paint, there is a tendency for each new occupant to add yet another layer, until the job of recovering the original finish seems impossible.

While accenting trim calls attention to an area, it also tends to fragment a room into individual spaces. This kind of decorating scheme can make a room seem smaller and visually busier than a room of the same size where the trim is close to the hue of larger surfaces. Removing bright colors and other eye-catching finishes is one low-cost way to increase the sense of space in a room.

Another good reason for removing layers of paint is to expose the fine wood below. Certainly, there is always some risk in stripping and refinishing, particularly on furniture where paint may be covering inferior wood grades with many knots and blemishes. The safest procedure is to uncover a small sample area before launching a major refinishing project.

But, as a rule, exposed wood trim such as window and door moldings, are made of select grades free of knots and discolorations. While light-toned woods such as pine are commonly used today, there may be oak or another elegant hardwood hidden beneath paint in older buildings.

Exposing rich mahogany doors, and other valuable woods used in cabinets and trim is not likely to cost much money, even though it will probably increase the value of the property. But it is likely to take longer than planned. The tedious job of clearing old paint from small grooves in molding can seem overwhelming compared to the simple job of washing the surface, then wiping with steel wool to renew an existing painted surface before repainting.

But the amount of elbow grease needed for refinishing can be minimized by using the right tools and materials. For example, in many older buildings woodwork was sealed with shellac, which can be removed with its solvent, alcohol. If the existing finish dissolves rapidly when wiped with a rag dipped in alcohol, the finish is shellac. In this case, spray or wipe on denatured alcohol and wipe with fine steel wool. (Work on small sections as alcohol evaporates quickly.)

On painted wood surfaces there is disagreement about the best removal method. There are five basic alternatives; draw-scraping with a sharp, curve-edged scraping blade; applying chemicals that cause paint to bubble and soften so most of the coating can be scraped off; or heating the surface to be scraped with a propane torch, a heat gun (like a high-powered hair dryer), or an electric paint remover, which is like a flat-iron. Each method has its pros and cons.

Draw-scraping may suffice on a thin coating of poorly adhering paint on a smooth surface—paint that is almost ready to separate from the wall on its own. A typical draw-scraper has a long handle with a sharp U-shaped blade set into the end. Working at a low angle to the surface, the idea is to push down on the handle while drawing the tool towards you. Ideally, this method will peel continuous strips of paint. The tool is less effective on multiple layers of paint. However, there are no chemical or fire hazards. Used with strength and control, this method can achieve very good results.

Chemical paint strippers also are most effective on thin coatings over smooth surfaces. Since they are caustic enough to bubble paint, they must be handled with caution, kept from contact with skin, and used only in well-ventilated areas. (As always, read label cautions before using.) On thick layers of paint, several chemical treatments may be necessary, each one removing some but not all of the paint. Aside from the time and trouble involved, this can use up a lot of costly chemicals.

Heat is often the best treatment for removing heavy coats of paint over wood. A propane torch provides more than enough heat for the job, but can be difficult to control. The flame must be played over a section of trim just long enough to soften and bubble the paint, but not long enough to cause scorching. Also, working with an open flame presents a fire hazard and risk of injury not associated with the other tools that do approximately the same job.

One is an electric heat stripper. Most are shaped like the bottom plate of an iron. They are drawn slowly over the paint with one hand while a flat scraper held in the other hand is used to peel away the sticky strips of paint. Since this tool is flat it works best on flat surfaces. A heat gun, which looks and works like a portable hair dryer, does not apply as much heat as directly to the painted surface as a flat heat iron, but it is superior on intricate moldings and in tight spaces.

Some consumers report success using chemical "mats"—plastic-like gauze that embeds itself in paint, and, theoretically, peels it all away when the gauze is removed. Unfortunately, failures seem to equal successes with this approach.

Whichever method you use, remember that the heating tools and the paint residue they produce become hot enough to burn whatever they touch. (Electric heat irons become red-hot.) That includes your hands, clothes, and the walls and floors.

So many stock molding shapes are available that by combining them you can create, if not duplicate, older moldings that have deteriorated. More architects and designers are using built-up moldings to give an old-fashioned sense of detail to custom-built homes.

BUILT-UP MOLDINGS

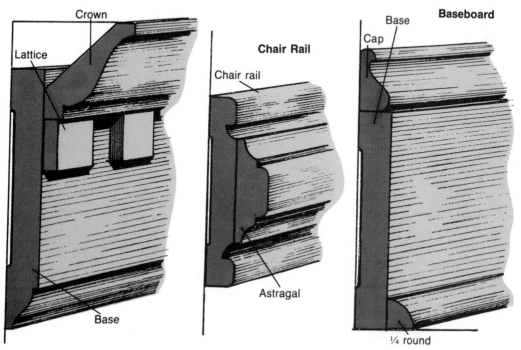

Bases

Rounds and Caps

Crowns and Astragals

Ceiling Cornice

Crown

Lattice

Base

Chair Rail

Chair rail

Astragal

Baseboard

Base

Cap

¼ round

Even when using the right tools and materials, it is unrealistic to expect every trace of paint to disappear. Inevitably, some paint will remain embedded in the wood grain just below the surface, and in crevices and corners. On flat surfaces final traces can be removed by sanding with fine paper, or by rubbing with steel wool, following the direction of the wood grain. Small scrapers, chisels, carving knives, or similar tools can be used to shave the last remnants of paint from joints and beads in molding.

Resurfacing Kitchen Cabinets
Skin-Deep Remodeling to Recover Old Cabinets

Maybe you can't judge a book by its cover. But sometimes an improvement that's only skin-deep can make a big difference—whether it's a face-lift over good cheek bones or a coat of paint over solid walls. This kind of resurfacing approach to home remodeling is being used increasingly on kitchen cabinets that are still solid and serviceable but out of style, or just plain ugly.

The idea is to apply a combination of solid wood cabinet doors, drawer fronts, and thin wood veneers over the visible parts of the old cabinets. Such a project should be tackled by at least moderately competent do-it-yourselfers, particularly if you buy stock sizes of solid woods and veneers, and custom cut and fit each piece in place. Assembling the raw materials, then cutting expensive hardwoods or veneer plywoods to make doors and drawer fronts generally requires good tools (including a table or radial arm saw for accuracy) and woodworking experience.

However you don't have to be a wood surgeon, even though this project amounts to a kitchen cabinet face-lift. One alternative is to hire one of the growing number of kitchen cabinet resurfacing firms. But the project can be handled as a considerably less-challenging do-it-yourself job if you use a kitchen cabinet resurfacing kit. A series of widely available kits in which several different door sizes and styles are offered are produced by The Masonite Corporation.

The step-by-step sequence using a kit may vary somewhat from a more unusual custom resurfacing job. But the basic approach and process is about the same whether or not you use a precut kit or assemble your own parts.

If your kitchen is similar to the typical American kitchen, which, according to Masonite, has 15 cabinet doors and 11 drawer fronts, resurfacing with a kit should take from 16 to 24 hours and save up to 70 percent of the cost of installing all new cabinets. The kits, which you assemble from parts in several cabinet door sizes and raised panel designs at the retailer, cost about $600 for an average kitchen. Masonite Solid Oak Cabinet Front Resurfacing System is made by Gamble Brothers Division of Masonite.[1]

The overall job can be divided into three basic parts: replacing cabinet doors, adding veneer, and replacing drawer fronts. In brief, here's the sequence: remove old cabinet doors and hardware; match new door fronts to the cabinet openings (or add framing strips to decrease the size of the openings); apply self-sticking wood veneer over the

---

[1]Gamble Bros. Div. of Masonite, P.O. Box 14504, Louisville, KY 40214

visible frame edges and exposed side panels; then stain, seal and finish the ¾-inch-thick, solid oak fronts and oak veneers to suit.

A similar sequence is used on the drawer fronts: first remove the drawers and hardware; cut the existing drawer fronts flush with the top, bottom, and sides of the drawers; glue and clamp the new, solid oak fronts over the cut-down drawers; then finish to suit and apply new hardware. Here is a closer look at the sequence.

A typical precut resurfacing kit includes peel-and-stick oak veneers, and ¾-inch-thick, solid oak drawer fronts and cabinet doors (available in several sizes) and either a square or rounded, raised panel pattern.

Start the resurfacing project by removing existing doors, hinges, and catches. Although a number of standard door sizes are normally available in kits, you may have to down-size your existing openings. Do this by nailing framing strips (made from ¾-inch pine, for example) around the door openings. Later, they will be covered by veneer. Another option is to screw a board to the back of one of two doors that meet at the center of one opening (instead of narrowing the overall opening). Or, you could add a vertical center stile in a wide opening to make it accommodate two smaller doors. With a simulated center stile fastened to one of the doors, original hinges can be used without reframing the opening and setting the hardware in new locations.

Prepare the exposed surfaces of the cabinet frames by washing with a household cleaner (or a mild solution of household ammonia and warm water). Then fill any cracks with a wood filler such as Durham's Rock Hard Water Putty and sand all exposed surfaces with a 120- to 150-grit sandpaper. This scuffs up glossy surfaces and helps the veneer bond.

Peel-and-stick wood veneer is then applied to the cabinet frame faces and end panels. Measure and cut individual pieces with a sharp scissors or razor knife allowing a ⅛- to ¼-inch overlap. To join horizontal and vertical veneer strips use this procedure:

- Install the vertical strip.
- Leave the paper backing on the end of the horizontal strip where the two strips overlap.
- Carefully draw a thin pencil line with a straightedge where the horizontal strip crosses the vertical strip.
- Cut the line with a razor knife or scissors.
- Peel away the tape and press the end into place. For best results, use a veneer roller to firmly press the thin wood strips into place.

After removing hardware, trim existing drawer fronts flush with the drawer. This way it will slide into the opening and the new front will overlap the cabinet frame. Apply the new solid-wood drawer fronts so that they evenly overlap the existing drawer. Secure them with glue and screws applied from the inside of the drawer through the old drawer front.

To finish, apply stain or a clear sealer, such as polyurethane, or both. This work can be done before the drawer fronts and cabinet doors are set in place. In most cases, the new panels can be drilled so that old handles can be reattached. Of course, you may want to buy new hardware to match your resurfaced, if not completely new, kitchen cabinets.

TOP: Masonite, which makes wood resurfacing kits, estimates the job will take from 16 to 24 hours and save up to 70 percent of the cost of installing all new cabinets. LEFT: Solid wood doors, drawer fronts and matching veneers provide a completely new surface.

Paint Colors on Ceiling Moldings

Q. Our apartment has high ceilings (almost 10 feet) and substantial moldings on the wall about a foot from the ceiling. What is the best way to strike a balance between featuring them too much (won't that make the ceiling seem lower), and still highlighting them?

A. In rooms with high ceilings (at least a foot or two over the standard 8-foot height), almost any color and finish combination can be used without overwhelming the room's generous proportions. But, as a rule, ceilings painted lighter shades than walls seem higher; those painted darker seem lower. The effect mirrors the difference outside between a low dark overcast and a light, bright blue sky that seems endless.

Using starkly contrasting colors on cornice moldings, though, will visually chop up a room into segments—not a good idea in smaller rooms with 8-foot ceilings. A more reasonable option would be to paint the cornice in a light pastel shade that complements the color used on the walls. Even a more subtle effect is possible by switching surface finish and color intensity. For example, use flat paint (with no sheen) on walls and ceilings, and slightly brighter semigloss on molding.

Moldings painted with white semigloss would pop just a bit from walls coated in a more off-white flat paint. That seems like the effect you want—a little visual oomph, but not too much.

Painting Over Nails

Q. Looking over the outside of the house before repainting, I'm concerned about the slightly rusty-looking nail heads showing through the paint. A few are protruding from the siding. How can I prevent this problem from reoccurring?

A. There are two, not necessarily related, parts to this problem. First, popping nails may indicate trouble within the wall frame, particularly if the popping is concentrated in one area or one piece of siding. Condensation or a leak could be causing one or more of the wall studs to twist, or the piece of siding to expand, or both. In cases where siding is actually pulling away from the wall it may be necessary to remove the nails and use countersunk wood screws to pull the wood back into position.

Assuming that only the occasional nail is popping, simply drive it slightly below the wood surface (about ⅛ inch should do), apply caulk or putty, then prime the spot before repainting. But if the nail is popped well above the siding surface, and seems to slide back into its hole without any resistance, pull it, and secure the siding with a wood screw. It should be either a little longer, or a little thicker than the original nail to gain holding power.

Conceal the old, discolored nail heads (or new screws) by sanding, then coating with a rust-inhibitive primer before repainting the house. Note that while box nails should be used on siding, sometimes larger, common nails are used, which cannot be countersunk properly. Remove these if possible before repainting.

Old Paint Adhesion

Q. After years of neglecting the ceiling, I recently tried to roll on a fresh coat of latex paint. But patches of old paint kept peeling off on the roller. Is there a solution other than starting from scratch with new drywall?

A. Ceilings in older homes may have many layers of paint, all with what's called a low binder content. Calsomine, whitewash, and other old-fashioned, soft-skinned finishes can be partially dissolved by the solvents in fresh paint. This can soften the old surface so it sticks to the roller and peels away. You can see that, with such a finish in place, the more you tried to improve the appearance by repainting, the more of a mess you would get.

Short of resurfacing, try scraping off the loose paint, and applying hot water on stubborn spots. When dry, spackle where necessary, sand thoroughly and apply an oil-base primer/sealer. Finish with a coat of latex or oil-base ceiling paint.

Differences Between Varnish and Lacquer

Q. What is the difference between varnish, polyurethane, and lacquer, and which will work best over a wood coffee table?

A. Varnish is a clear coating of oils and resins, available in water-base and oil-base blends. Polyurethane is just one type of oil-base varnish, popular because of its hardness and resistance to scratches and wear, and because it is available in three surface finishes: high gloss, semigloss, and a low luster satin finish that resembles the finish provided by paste wax. Lacquer is a completely different, solvent-based finish commonly used by manufacturers on wood furniture. It leaves a thin protective film over wood as the solvents evaporate.

For a home application, try polyurethane in the gloss you like best. It is easier and safer to use than lacquer, which dries very fast and easily shows brush strokes. Polyurethane takes longer to dry but is more self-leveling (settles more evenly) so that it hides imperfections from a do-it-yourself application.

Improvements
and
Repairs Outside

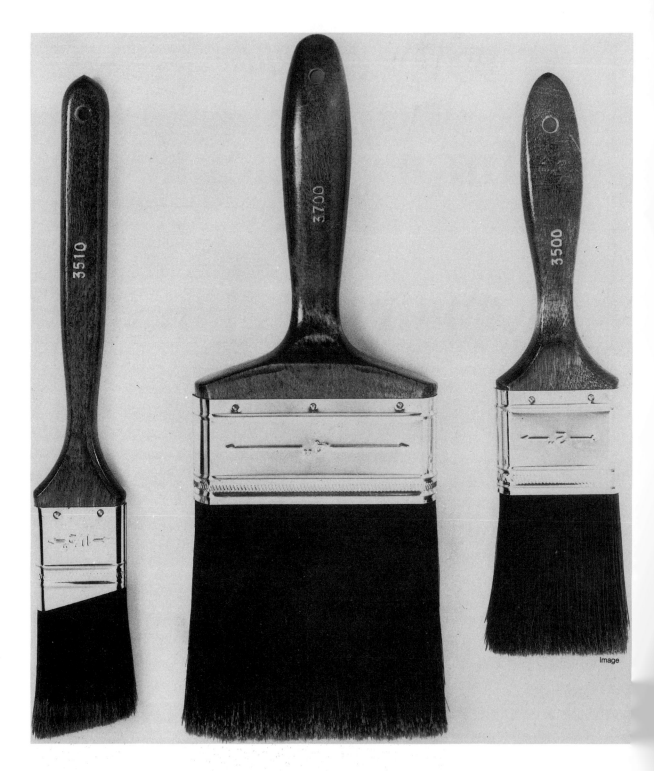

Image

Eighteen

EXTERIOR WALLS

Evaluating Brick Buildings
Discovering Limits and Remedies for Brick Walls

Throughout history, important buildings that were built to last were built of masonry. Although a row of brick houses with iron railings and granite steps out front seems indestructible, no material or building system, not even the pyramids, can withstand the elements indefinitely. Brick and mortar are subject to deterioration from changes in temperature, humidity, wind, dirt, chemicals, and also from structural settling.

There are three basic elements in a brick wall: the bricks, the mortar joints, and the overall structure combining the two materials. Each component has different characteristics, and therefore reacts differently to environmental and structural stresses.

To evaluate a brick wall each component must be considered. Large cracks, called faults, in the overall structure are usually the most obvious problems, also the most severe and costly to repair. Usually, faults can be traced to uneven settling, a phenomenon normally associated with new houses built on excavated earth that compacts gradually under the great weight of building materials. If the earth settles uniformly, so does the house. But when soil under one corner compacts more than another, the foundation and the brick wall above it can crack apart from the strain.

Sometimes activity near the house such as road construction, sewer or well installations, house building—any activity that disturbs the subsoil—can trigger new settling in an old and supposedly stabilized building.

A few years ago in the Back Bay area of Boston, for example, engineers found that seepage through an old, closed-up tunnel dug beneath the water had lowered the water table, which in turn caused the tops of pilings supporting the foundations of several town houses nearby to begin to rot. Undermining of a foundation can also be caused by something as simple as rainwater released from a downspout next to the house that washes down, and eventually under, the foundation.

The telltale signs of fundamental structural problems are staircase-pattern cracking along many courses of brick, and either large scale convex or concave cupping of the walls. This curving, which can be difficult to detect over a large surface, can be checked by placing a block of wood at each corner of the wall, tying a string over the blocks, then checking to see if the string maintains an equal distance from the wall (equal to

Opposite: Big, 4-inch-wide brushes are a lot to handle when loaded up with paint. Most do-it-yourselfers substitute a roller. But a 2-inch trim brush is invaluable. Use it to "cut-in" trim, and edges where one color meets another. The angled sash brush makes trim paintings even easier.

the thickness of the blocks) along its length. (Masons use blocks and strings to build straight walls.)

Don't write off a building just because it has some cracks. They may be only cosmetic, or from settling that occurred long ago. Old, stable cracks can be patched and sealed against the weather. New, unstable cracks indicate that the building is still in motion.

Although the best policy by far is to have an experienced home inspector, or preferably a structural engineer, check such problems, a close look into the cracks is revealing. Old, stable cracks usually are somewhat weathered, dirty, and may contain bits of leaves, insects eggs, or spider webs—all evidence that the cracks have been there for a while in their present state. On the other hand, new, unstable cracks are usually clean. The masonry inside the crack is often a lighter color than on the surrounding wall.

Repointing cracked and deteriorated mortar between bricks helps keep a wall in place. It is just as important to caulk seams where water could get in behind the wall and rot, or warp wood sheathing and studs, which could eventually disrupt the wall and damage the house frame.

Scranton Photo Studio

Continue the evaluation by checking the mortar joints, the other weak link in a brick wall. Any mortar that is loose, spongy, and easily scraped away needs to be repointed. Typically, this process includes excavating the mortar to a depth between two and three times the width of the joint, cleaning away all loose dust and debris, then refilling the joints with mortar.

Without repointing, the process of deterioration accelerates, particularly in winter. As water seeps into the joints freeze-thaw cycles can exert immense pressures on brick and mortar, further opening the seams, which lets in even more water, which exerts more pressure when it freezes, and so on.

Expect to repoint brick homes built before 1900, not due to age alone, but because mortar commonly used until that time was lime-based, making it softer and more porous than later mixes which include portland cement to 3 or 4 parts hydrated lime and 12 parts sand.

Even in old walls, the bricks are more durable than the surrounding mortar, although leaks and condensation can harm bricks in an unexpected way. When wood lintels (horizontal supports over door and window openings) have been built into brick walls, leaks and condensation can eventually cause them to rot. As they weaken, the structural load they carried is transferred to the surrounding masonry, which can split off the exterior faces of bricks—a condition called *spalling*.

Like early mortars, early brick that is prized for its subtle gradations of texture and color is softer and more porous than modern brick. That makes it more easily damaged by freeze-thaw cycles, gradual chemical attack (most commonly from sulfur), and deterioration from organic substance such as mildew, moss, and ivy.

While repointing, patching, and applying sealers can help preserve a brick wall, cleaning old brick walls by sand- or water-blasting can do far more harm than good. Stresses from high-pressure cleaning at 10,000 psi or more would seriously erode if not shatter nineteenth-century brick, which may not tolerate more than 100 psi.

Sandblasting can also produce unexpected results. While sand hits the brick at a uniform rate and pressure, old brick is anything but uniform. This mismatch can lead to pitting and channeling that produces a ragged, blemished surface. If an old brick building has made it through most of the twentieth century intact, be very cautious about turning modern technology loose against its walls.

Stone Masonry Maintenance
Preserving the Eternal Building Material

Stone is the building material for the ages. Egyptian pyramids, Greek temples, and Roman aqueducts are made of stone and still standing, though softened a bit by centuries of exposure. Your stone house, or wall, or patio, or barbecue, or fireplace may last a long time, too. In the meantime, you may want to clear away some of the dirt, smoke stains, grime, and other elements that can make the stone less attractive and cause deterioration. Here's how.

Large areas of stone such as the side of a house, can be cleaned by sandblasting, with chemicals, with water, or steam. Sandblasting, though very thorough and fast, may remove more than the dirt, leaving a coarse and pitted surface in softer stonework. It's risky. You should have a small, unobtrusive area test-cleaned before continuing.

Chemical cleaning (there are many different treatments depending on conditions), is less risky for the stone but potentially hazardous because of fumes and caustic liquids. Protection during careful application, and thorough cleanup should be handled by an experienced professional firm.

Selecting the right stones for each part of the wall is the part of stone masonry calling for a lot of experience. Construction is straightforward, and involves using a level and following string lines tied to stakes at each end of the wall.

Washing with water is effective on run-of-the-mill dirt, depending on the water you use. Hard water may leave mineral deposits and cause staining, while excessive washing can waterlog the wall and deteriorate mortar joints and interior plaster. Steam cleaning, handled by professionals, is often the best alternative since it is a potent, one-shot method that is not mechanically abrasive or chemically hazardous.

Now for the more mundane problems.

Although ivy-covered walls look wonderful, plant life can be very destructive to stone walls. When ivy roots start growing into cracks in mortar between stones, you should cut the roots as close to the wall as possible and treat the ends with a plant killer such as ammonium phosphate paste.

It may be possible to maintain the beautiful effect of an ivy-covered wall by installing a trellis, or even wires for the vines to cling to. But unless you prune on a regular basis, the plant is likely to reroot between the stones.

Mold and mildew also may take hold on stone that is not exposed to enough fresh air and sunshine. To test whether or not the discoloration is mildew or just dirt, drop a small amount of household bleach on the area. It will whiten mildew but have no effect on dirt. To clear the mildew, wash the area with a soft scrub brush using a solution of up to 50 percent household bleach in warm water, then rinse.

Stains from hardware such as iron hinges on shutters or steel brackets holding up gutters and leaders can be removed with a solution of oxalic acid. Mix approximately 1 pound of the crystals in a gallon of water, brush the mix over the stained area, then rinse off.

Stone walls are also likely to be stained with asphalt and tar from the roof. Trying to wipe these stains away can be frustrating, since you are likely to spread the tar over a wider area. (The same goes for many types of caulking.) The best approach is to remove as much tar as possible in bulk, by sliding a sharp putty knife, chisel, or straight razor blade under the goo and slicing it off the wall.

The remaining stain can be thinned and cleaned with benzene flushed with a mild detergent. Unfortunately, some of the asphalt is likely to remain ingrained in the stone.

To remove it, or at least most of it, make a poultice by mixing a paste of benzene and a binder such as fullers earth or sawdust, and pat it over the stained area. The poultice will draw asphalt traces out of the wall.

Re-Siding Questions and Options
Labor May Loom Larger Than Materials

People can shed moisture through pores in their skin. This flexible, washable, durable exterior layer even lets perspiration out without letting rain in. There is no such miraculous skin for buildings.

Moisture from cooking, washing, and other normal household operations moves through walls until it reaches the building skin. On many homes the outermost skin is paint. It is applied to beautify and protect the house on the outside. But it can be cracked, bubbled, and peeled by moisture breaking through from the inside.

Painting is still popular. Nearly half a billion gallons of paint and other architectural coatings are sold every year. But periodic repainting can become a tiresome and expensive chore. To avoid this job, which never seems to make the house look quite as good as it did after the first painting, many homeowners opt for re-siding.

Although the job seems straightforward, it raises many questions. Here are answers to a few of the most common concerns.

☞ *What type of siding is best for re-siding jobs, aluminum or vinyl?* This is by far the most common question about re-siding. But there is no unequivocal answer. For one thing, there are several other material options: wood clapboards, wood shakes, exterior plywood paneling such as Texture-1-11, steel (used more for commercial jobs than for residential projects), and others. But vinyl is the most popular choice, in part because it is less expensive than aluminum. Aluminum is second.

There are pros and cons to both materials. But opinions vary widely. Some contractors say vinyl is easier to work with, which saves labor costs. Others say it is more likely than aluminum to fade or crack in very cold weather. Some say aluminum is structurally more durable than vinyl, but that even small dents and scratches are difficult to conceal. Others say neither one holds a candle to real wood, which can be stained instead of painted to avoid peeling and cracking. There is no best choice.

☞ *Are re-siding jobs for specialty contractors, or carpenters, and are they do-it-yourself projects?* There is so much demand for re-siding work that many contractors who might also do general carpentry, for example, don't bother. But a general contractor or carpenter with a successful remodeling track record should be able to do the job. On most homes, at least some scaffolding is required. That, plus the experience needed to tailor new materials to the peculiar twists and turns on an older house, usually makes this a project for professionals.

☞ *What are the best reasons for re-siding, and when is re-siding unnecessary?* Too often homeowners confuse surface dirt on paint with more permanent deterioration. Washing the siding with soap and water can sometimes make a dramatic difference.

Use ⅓ cup of liquid detergent to a gallon of water. If mildew spots have discolored walls, use 1 quart bleach to 3 quarts water. (Do not combine bleach and ammonia, which produces dangerous fumes.)

Re-siding is often most appropriate on older homes with chronic exterior paint problems, or high energy bills due to minimal insulation, or both problems. Typically, peeling and chipping paint is caused by an excessively thick buildup of paint layers, inadequate insulation, or inadequate vapor barriers.

These large, Masonite Superside panels demonstrate the variety of composite siding materials. In addition to building in joints to simulate narrower, individual clapboards, wood grain imprints can be manufactured into the surface.

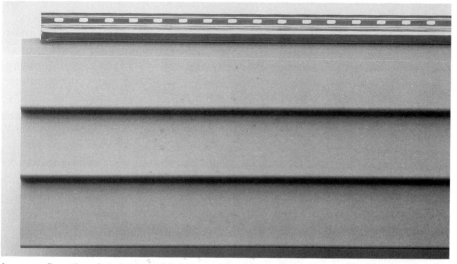

A new configuration of vinyl siding, called Flotrac, uses an aluminum nailing strip that interlocks with a corresponding flange on the next extruded vinyl panel on the wall. The manufacturer, Wolverine Technologies (1650 Howard St., Lincoln Park, MI 48146), says the Flotrac system is stiff enough to span dips in existing walls.

After 20 or 30 years, many houses have been repainted several times. Their multilayer skins are the most likely to crack, particularly in a pattern resembling an alligator's skin. This condition can quickly resurface in a fresh layer of paint. Scraping clean an entire exterior down to bare wood is often too costly, if not impossible.

Older homes are also likely to have minimal insulation. Re-siding provides an opportunity to improve the insulating value of walls. Without new siding, extra insulation must be blown through holes cut in existing walls. This job may produce inconclusive results. Blown-in insulation tends to settle 5 to 10 percent, which leaves a portion of the wall unprotected. Also, some wall sections, blocked off by pipes, wires, and bracing, for example, may never fill with insulation. Under new siding, however, the entire wall surface can be covered and adequately protected.

Older homes also may be missing a vapor barrier. This is a layer of plastic or foil just beneath the interior wall surface. It prevents interior moisture from traveling into the wall cavity, and through to the outside where it breaks through the paint film.

However, contrary to advice given by some contractors, adding such a barrier outside, just beneath the new siding, will not help prevent moisture and condensation problems. But new siding will cover over the damage these problems produce.

☞ *Should a foil moisture barrier be applied outside under the new siding?* Wrapping a house in foil can create problems with paint and wallpaper on interior walls, cause bad odors, mold and mildew formations, soak insulation batts in wall cavities, and foster wood rot. It's a bad idea. Many of the contractors who still use foil-faced foam board on re-siding jobs use a type that is purposefully perforated to let the moisture escape. So why use foil at all? Good question.

Engineers have come up with one situation where the reflective quality of foil can be beneficial. To have a positive effect on energy saving, however, the foil must be on a uniform surface with a uniform dead air space between the foil and the siding. These and other stringent restrictions are virtually impossible to achieve on re-siding projects over existing walls.

☞ *Should extra insulation be built into the siding, or added in sheets beneath it?* Many siding estimates include an insulation option. Since both aluminum and vinyl are sheet materials in the shape of clapboards (not solid like wood), the idea is to fill the space with molded panels of insulation. These individual sections of insulation are often called "backer boards."

Adding backer boards is a marginal way to improve the thermal value of a wall. But if existing walls are underinsulated, adding an inch of rigid foam board with an R-value (a measure of insulating value), up to 6.5 per inch is much more effective. (Typical fiberglass insulation has an R-value of about 3.5 per inch by comparison.) And if existing walls are reasonably well insulated, adding backer boards is not worth the extra cost.

In older homes where moisture will continue to work its way through the walls, backer boards may even get in the way. Re-siding systems are designed with tiny holes and other openings to allow moisture that condenses against the siding to run off. Backer boards might soak up the moisture or block the holes.

Adding large tongue-and-groove panels of foam increases R-value, but also wall thickness. Before starting it is very important to determine exactly how any extra thickness will be accommodated around windows and doors. Ask contractors bidding on the job to bring sample materials, and hold them up in place on the wall. This way you can see how trim pieces will be used to make room for the insulation and siding, and cover their exposed edges.

Most contractors can do a reasonable job laying siding over a flat wall. Good trim work often is the difference between a skilled, conscientious contractor, and one who is taking the shortest route to the final payment.

House Washing
The Benefits of ''New, Improved,'' Plain Old Soap and Water

Conventional methods of sprucing up building exteriors include restaining, repainting, and re-siding with wood or low-maintenance aluminum or vinyl. Somehow, the low-cost alternative of simply washing a house has not caught on with consumers, even though the appearance of brick, wood, aluminum and vinyl siding, and trim can be greatly improved by a straightforward washing. Just think what it does for your face and hands after a few hours working in the garden.

Even in extreme cases, for example, where a stucco surface has become a chronic maintenance problem due to peeling paint, washing with chemicals more potent than a mild detergent can be a sensible alternative to more costly re-siding.

Buildings, like cars or work shirts or the back of your neck, eventually become dirty. But the time-honored solution to these problems—a good washing—may seem too simple and too low-tech for a house. The urge to apply some form of new exterior skin is often the first response when a house becomes dirty. Old, dingy paint gets repainted or buried out of sight and out of mind under new siding with other cosmetic and possibly more serious structural problems.

Cleaning is also a crucial but often overlooked step in the renovation process. Paint won't adhere well to a surface that is coated with a fine layer of grime from years of exposure to the elements. Most paints will last longer and require less maintenance when applied over a clean wall.

According to many building professionals the best all-purpose cleaner for many types of exteriors is no more exotic than soap and water. The advice offered by several prominent trade associations in the siding industry is simply, ''wash with warm water, a nonabrasive household detergent, and a soft brush.'' A typical formula is ⅓ cup liquid detergent to a gallon of water.

Bleach can be added to combat mold and mildew formations in a proportion of up to 25 percent household bleach (1 quart bleach to 3 quarts water). However, care must be taken to avoid combining bleach and ammonia, which produces dangerous fumes. If you are unsure about the contents of a liquid detergent that may contain some ammonia, check the label.

Although it is possible to do the job by hand, equipment is available that can make the job of washing easier, extending your reach, which can eliminate trips up and down a ladder. These exterior cleaners attach to a garden hose, and provide a way to mix detergent with the domestic water supply.

One such tool, called the Gardena Clean System,[1] repackages the basic components of warm water, soap, and brush into a single, adjustable unit. The Clean System kit contains a 4-foot handle, click-on hose connectors, a 3-foot knee-joint extension, a brush attachment, and 9 ''shampoo'' tablets, which the company describes as a mild, nonabrasive cleaner. (Stronger tablets, extra brushes, and a second extension handle are available as options.)

To use the system, cleaning tablets are inserted in the handle where they are dissolved with the water stream to produce a steady flow of cleaning solution through the extension wands to a brush. Like ''power-painters'' that connect directly to the paint can and eliminate trips back to the bucket, these cleaners provide a steady stream of soap and water inside a scrub brush, even if it's 6 or 7 feet above your shoulder.

Other systems, such as the Gilmour Hose-end Sprayer,[2] work on the same principle but provide a canister for cleaning fluid attached to a nozzle that attaches to a standard garden hose. In this way they are similar to paint sprayers, except that normal water flow through a hose replaces compressed air used to propel paint particles.

Instead of using specially manufactured cleaning tablets, you can mix different cleaning solutions for different jobs. (The manufacturer reports that many consumers use the tool for spraying insecticides, washing cars, and other jobs using a variety of liquids.)

To use hose-end sprayers, you pour the desired cleaning mixture into the canister, then connect a water supply hose to the tool handle. As the trigger is depressed, cleaning mixture and water are combined and sprayed onto the house.

Gilmour also makes an all-purpose hose-end sprayer, which has a 1-quart canister. An adjusting dial on the handle makes it possible to alter the combination rate (mixing cleaner and water), from 1 to 10 tablespoons of cleaner per gallon of water. The company says this unit, and the heavy-duty version, which has an insulated handle but no combination rate adjustment, both provide a 25-foot water stream, given average water pressure (between 40 and 60 psi) and piping. These systems do not boost water pressure. They simply direct the flow into a concentrated stream.

Hose-extension cleaners can make it easier to apply cleaning solution. But elbow-grease will still be needed to dislodge some built-up dirt and mold. There is no magic solvent for every discoloration that dissolves dirt, grease, grime, tree sap, nail head rust, mold, bird droppings, grit from industrial pollution, and every other material that may be deposited on a building.

Also, washing cannot substitute for thoroughly preparing a damaged wall with buckling layers of paint before repainting or restaining. Peeling paint that is not removed by the water stream must still be scraped off; bare spots must still be primed.

A heavier-duty option is to pay a professional cleaning company to do the job. This may be a bit of a luxury when simple surface washing is called for. But it is a sensible alternative on jobs where accumulated grit and grime is rooted in the paint film, and where several layers of deteriorated paint must be removed from a building

---

[1]Gardena Inc., 6031 Culligan Way, Minnetonka, MN 55435
[2]Gilmour Manufacturing Co., P.O. Box 838, Somerset, PA 15501

exterior. Such projects generally require handling pressurized water or sand systems, or large volumes of potent cleaning chemicals.

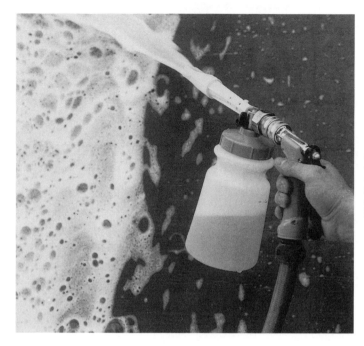

Hose-end washers provide an efficient way of combining a cleaning solution with a stream of water from a garden hose connected to your plumbing system. This unit, made by Gilmour Manufacturing Co. (P.O. Box 838, Somerset, PA 15501), puts out a 25-foot stream of water given household water pressure of 40 to 60 psi.

There are two ways to approach these projects: sandblasting and chemical cleaning. Each has advantages and disadvantages. But chemical treatment is somewhat easier to control—to tailor to the material being cleaned. Sandblasting tends to take more of the siding away with the dirt—a case of throwing the baby out with the bath water. Very high pressures, pushing steam or water or sand, can have a devastating effect on some brick, and on most types of wood.

Before opting for such a drastic face-lift, test wash a small patch of siding. Plain soap and water may provide surprising improvement. And don't forget to wash behind the ears, I mean shutters.

Exterior Painting
Planning and Preparation are the Keys

Painting is one of the most popular do-it-yourself jobs because everyone knows how easy the job is: Just dip the brush in the can and start painting. Actually, that's the easy part. Preparing the job—cleaning and sanding siding and trim, for instance—is likely to take the most time and be the key to a durable job. Here are some tips that should make the hard part, and the painting, a little easier.

Preparatory cleaning. Before painting siding speckled with the dots and blotches of gray-green mold and mildew, wash and disinfect the walls. Use a proprietary mix, or about 1 quart of household bleach to 3 quarts of water and a dash of nonabrasive household detergent with a stiff scrub brush. Remove droplets of resin with mineral spirits or turpentine. If traces of stains or blemishes remain, apply a coat of pigmented white shellac, which prevents stains from bleeding through the surface coating.

Scraping and sanding. Don't scrape, spackle, and sand as you go. Too much debris will stick to the paint. Even if it means moving your ladder twice along a wall, make one pass to scrape away loose paint, sand down the edges of adhering paint, and brush the wall free of dust, and another to apply the paint. Take the time to sink protruding nail heads, and to caulk small cracks in siding, seams between siding and trim, and nail or screw hole punctures.

Older homes suffer from peeling that can be produced from leaks inside and out. Uncaulked seams between siding and trim is one problem. But peeling also can be caused as moisture inside the house works through walls that do not have a vapor barrier.

Brushes. While a nylon brush is the best choice for latex paints, a natural bristle brush provides the best results for oil-base and alkyd paints and stains. A top-quality brush is "tipped," which means the ends of the bristles are pointed, and "flagged," which means the ends of the bristles are split, which helps the brush hold more paint and spread it more evenly.

Rollers. Rollers are normally used inside on flat walls and ceilings. But they can be a help outside, applying paint or stain to siding, since they hold more material and spread it out more quickly than a brush. One good system is to use the roller to move paint from a pan or 2-gallon bucket to the siding, spread it out, and then use a brush to fill in cracks and seams.

Paint base. The choice between oil- and water-based paint is a toss-up. It's a lot easier to clean up with latex than with oil paint. But many painters still say you should use oil outside and water inside. To minimize deterioration, the best policy is to stick with the type of paint that's already on the wall. In general, paints with the same bases adhere best to each other.

When to paint. Don't paint over wet walls. To hold paint effectively, a wall should be dry, smooth, and clean. If humid weather is making walls damp, it's best to wait for more favorable conditions. Also, avoid direct, midday sunlight, which can cause paint blistering. Try to follow the sun around the house, letting the sun burn off morning dew, and dry out the siding before you get there.

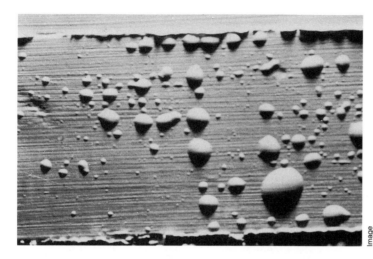

This test panel shows the results of spreading a thin layer of paint over a hot surface. Avoid blistering by following the sun around the house.

Sealing and priming. Prime raw surfaces and clean stains and blemishes on adhering paint. Priming makes the absorptive quality and appearance of the wall more uniform before the top coat is applied. Otherwise, dull, flat spots will show over raw, sanded wood. If blemishes begin to show through a thin first coat, resist the temptation to load on extra paint, in effect, applying two coats at once. A single, thick layer is likely to dry unevenly, droop in spots leaving lap lines, and wrinkle.

Wet edges. Lap marks are created when the wet edge of paint on an upper clapboard, for instance, dries before you finish the section of wall below and move your ladder. To keep a wet edge, tackle small sections of wall at one time, ideally, between natural architectural borders such as window and door casings. Where this is impossible, feather the wet edge by lightly brushing toward the unpainted surface with a dry brush. The idea is that this thin, feathery layer of paint will blend in with similar coating from the opposite direction once you move over a few feet.

Re-Siding With Wood Over Wood

Q. Several of our neighbors have put a second layer of Texture 1-11 siding on their houses with tar paper between layers. Aside from improving appearance, the motivation has been to keep out rain and moisture, which may be a problem because the first layer of siding is nailed directly to the framing with no sheathing. Is this project worth the cost, and what material should go between layers?

A. Texture 1-11 is a very durable plywood panel siding, normally applied in 4-by-8-foot or larger sheets with a vertical surface groove every 4 or 6 inches, simulating individual boards in a shiplap application. I have used it directly over framing where permitted by code, and over ½-inch sheathing, which always struck me as redundant since well-nailed, nearly ⅝-inch thick Texture 1-11 ties the frame together as well as, if not better than, ½-inch sheathing.

Like most siding it weathers, discolors, and becomes worn and dull looking. Also, it may warp or twist on the framing (or be twisted by movement in the frame itself), which can open seams to the weather. This is not so much a drawback of the material but the fault of the installer who may not have used enough or the right type of nails.

Adding a second layer is probably the most expensive and complicated way to improve the situation. It may even do more harm than good. At best it is overkill unless the existing siding is rotting or severely warped or otherwise structurally damaged, which is unlikely with Texture 1-11. And if the existing sheets are that bad it would be wiser to remove them, not bury them under tar paper, plastic, or foil. Such a step is akin to putting your house in a plastic bag.

Many homeowners have found that after re-siding over a weather barrier like tar paper or foil, they encounter a new set of problems inside the house such as peeling paint and wallpaper, bad odors, and mildew growth. That's the plastic-bag effect, which can make a house nearly hermetically sealed.

A vapor barrier outside (just beneath new siding) bottles up an average of 7 gallons of moisture per day produced inside a typical house (by cooking, washing, and such), as it seeps past the vapor barrier just under the inside wall surface (if you have one at all) and heads outside. In winter, that moisture is likely to condense against the cold tar paper and soak the buried layer of wood siding.

So work on the siding you have instead of adding another layer. Keep out the weather by caulking seams between panels, and at all window and door openings. Add flashing at horizontal joints on high walls where one panel sits on another.

Improve appearance and help to seal out moisture by refinishing the wood. First, wash the siding with a proprietary mildewcide cleaner or a home brew made in a proportion of approximately 1 cup of household bleach (without ammonia) to a gallon of warm water. Second, cut down raised grain and rough spots with a light sanding.

Finally, apply a full-strength coat of full-bodied, oil-base, pigmented, penetrating stain—costly stain with enough pigment to have the consistency of pea soup.

For best effect select a color close to the one already on the house. If patches of the siding are extremely worn (down to the bare wood, for instance) you may have to apply a slightly thinned prime coat to avoid flat spots in the final application created as stain is soaked up like a sponge by the dry wood.

Staining Over Paint

Q. I wish the original owners of our old clapboard house had stained instead of painted. But I am stuck with peeling and cracking. To avoid applying more paint that will crack and peel in turn, can I stain over paint?

A. I face much the same situation with my house, and find myself wishing that the remaining paint that has not flaked or peeled would let go already. Ideally, we both would spend endless weekends or pay a professional painter a lot of money to scrape the siding completely down to the wood, then start with two fresh coats of a pigmented, oil-base exterior stain. Instead of these imposing options, I started staining over paint.

First, I scrape off loose paint. Where patches of bare wood are surrounded by thick layers of paint, I sand down the paint edges to minimize the ragged appearance. Then, to keep the house white, I mix a quart of boiled linseed oil per two gallons of white-pigmented, oil-base stain, add about a cup of turpentine since the linseed oil thickens the brew. Then, I box the paint to make sure the proportions are evenly distributed in each gallon—the painting equivalent of shuffling cards.

This brew seems to last for about 4 or 5 years. Then, instead of peeling or cracking like paint, it starts to fade gradually. That I can live with—until I get organized enough to do it all again.

Sagging Door Sill

Q. How can I raise the sill beneath a pair of aluminum sliding glass doors? The dip in the middle has made the door scrape against the frame, even though I have raised the wheels on the door to their full height.

A. There are two possible solutions, depending on what you find beneath the door frame. First, lift out the door (they are quite heavy so you may need help), raising them in the frame, then tilting the bottom off the track. Next, back out the screws holding the frame in place on the sill to get a look at the support beneath the aluminum.

If you discover severely rotted wood, you will have to remove the entire frame and replace the rotted section. (Since the frame sections are screwed together through the faces toward the house frame, it is impossible to remove only the sill.) But if you remove the sill screws, pry the sill up a bit, and discover solid wood, you should be able to get by with shims. These are thin sections of wood that should be inserted only a few inches apart, and set with construction adhesive. Judging their thicknesses will take some trial and error, since shims in the middle of the depression must be thicker than those at the ends of the dip to create a level support for the aluminum sill.

If you have access to the sill from a full cellar or crawl space, inspect the area to see if some structural weakening below the sill is causing the depression. But sometimes buildings just settle a bit—unevenly and not in the best locations—then take hold, in which case the shims should last for years and solve your scraping problem.

Replacing Cornice Molding

Q. What is the best way to patch and replace a section of the wooden cornice overhanging the facade of our row house?

A. Unfortunately, deterioration in overhanging cornices is highly visible but very hard to get at. Minor repairs may be made by professionals from extension ladders. But larger-scale, heavier-duty repair work such as replacing rotted sections may call for more elaborate scaffolding.

Wood can be used to fabricate replacement parts of ornamental dental block and other molding shapes. But several firms now offer period molding in lightweight synthetic materials.

Although purists may scoff at these low-maintenance, synthetic replacements, it is almost impossible to spot them, particularly when the one-piece, painted synthetic cornice is three floors up. You could contact a company such as Fibertech,[3] which makes both stock parts and custom sections of cornices, balustrades, and other house parts in reinforced fiberglass. The fiberglass material does not rot, and is available in a wide variety of colors and finishes.

Securing Porch Lattice

Q. What can I use in place of lattice work between a porch and the ground to keep animals out? I have replaced strips of lattice snapped away, I think, by raccoons. But they always seem to find another way in.

A. You can keep the attractive, airy appearance of lattice skirting by beefing it up on the inside and securing it to a grade board set into the ground.

For instance, if the lattice is set in frames, which is a common design, you could dig a narrow trench about 1 foot deep directly below the frame, and set a pressure-treated 2-by-12 on edge in the trench backed up by 1-by-2 or 1-by-3 pressure-treated stakes. Drive the stakes, which should be pointed and about 2 feet long, into the ground, then nail through the backs of the stakes into the 2 by 12. When dirt is repacked around the 2 by 12, you will have a neat and solid base that should prevent burrowing. Also, you will be able to nail, hinge, or bolt the lattice frames securely against this grade board.

If the critters are rambunctious enough to punch through the middle of the lattice, remove the panels and staple or nail across the backs layers of dense chicken wire—the heavy-duty, galvanized variety with openings of only about half an inch. Unless you look closely, even this dense mesh should not be visible from the yard.

---

[3]Fibertech, P.O. Box 9, Clemson, SC 29633

Nineteen

ROOFING

Asphalt Shingle Roofs
Decisions That Lead to a Durable Roof

If you are standing out in the yard with a pair of binoculars at the ready, passersby might mistake you for a bird-watcher. How could they know that you are only following the advice of the Asphalt Roofing Manufacturers Association and inspecting your shingles.

If your knees get a little wobbly when you climb a ladder, using binoculars is not a bad idea. Of course, you could ask two or three roofing contractors to take a look instead. But it is a good idea to know something about the condition of your roof and at least some guidelines about installing a new roof before asking for estimates to make repairs or add a new layer of shingles.

Here are some of the options to consider, and answers to the most fundamental questions.

☞ *When do you need a new roof?* Most shingles should last without leaking for 15 to 20 years. Some last longer, even 25 or 30 years. After about 15 years, however, you might start checking for signs of wear. But don't jump the gun. There is no advantage in reroofing a building ahead of time—before the shingles have started to deteriorate and years before they are ready to spring a leak.

Before asphalt shingles let go completely they usually give two warnings. One is an accumulation of surface granules at the bottom of the downspouts. The other is curling. Exposed tabs on this roof are starting to crack. When the tabs break off, nail heads will be exposed, and leaks will result.

Here are the four progressive stages of shingle wear to look for. First, you may notice the tiny chips embedded in the surface of asphalt shingles, called granules, accumulating in gutters and at downspout outlets. Second, you see bare patches of black tar appearing as more granules are lost. This is hard to see on a dark roof, even with binoculars, but obvious on shingles with white or gray surface granules. Roofs at this stage probably will not leak—not yet. But in a year or two they probably will.

In the third stage, exposed sections of the shingles, called tabs, that have lost most of their surface granules start to become brittle. You have to touch the tabs to detect this condition. Within a few seasons, however, the tabs will start to curl noticeably. Even then, the roof may not leak. But now is a good time to reroof—before the curling becomes excessive and gets in the way of new shingles.

In the fourth stage, brittle shingle tabs crack and break. Bare, black patches that appear as the tabs break off are unmistakable. You also may see nail heads holding down the shingles beneath the broken tabs. At this point, you are likely to have small leaks that may start to rot the wooden roof deck and rafters even if you do not see large water stains on the ceiling. After all, nails put holes in the shingles, and are placed so that they will be covered by the next highest row of shingles on the roof.

☑ *What type of shingle should you use?* Four out of five residential roofs are made of asphalt shingles or continuous sheets of asphalt called roll roofing, which is usually reserved for low-slope roofs not visible from the ground.

Although you will probably want individual shingles, not roll roofing, for your house, you may be asked to choose between asphalt or fiberglass shingles. Actually, both asphalt and fiberglass types are basically asphalt shingles. The only difference is in the bottom layer of the shingle, called the *base mat*. In all-asphalt shingles both the mat and upper layers are asphalt. In so-called fiberglass shingles the mat is a synthetic fiberglass mesh that is lighter, stronger, and longer lasting than an asphalt mat.

In practical terms, this means that you can match the fire resistance and durability of a heavy, all-asphalt shingle with a somewhat lighter asphalt-fiberglass shingle. This makes fiberglass-mat shingles a good choice for reroofing over existing roofs, and reduces the load carried by the roof rafters without giving up durability.

By now, however, about 80 percent of all shingles sold for new homes and for reroofing jobs are the fiberglass-mat variety, including almost all the heavyweight, overlay-type shingles carrying 25-year warranties. You are likely to get this type of shingle no matter what you ask for.

☑ *What shingle weight should you use?* Shingle weight is an important factor on new roofs and on reroofing jobs because heavier shingles last longer, carry a longer warranty, and generally offer a better fire rating. Of course, that means they are more expensive than lighter shingles.

The weight rating, 240 pounds for a standard shingle, for instance, denotes the total weight of shingles needed to cover 100 square feet of roof, which is called a "square" in roofing parlance.

The heavyweights are over the 240-pound rating and generally rated 300 pounds per square or more. Individual shingles in this category often are configured in layers—like a shingle on a shingle—that simulate a dense pattern of slate or wood shakes. The heavyweights are a good choice for new homes and additions, but a questionable choice for reroofing jobs where their great weight can overload the roof structure.

If their textured appearance is irresistible, chances are you will have to remove the existing shingles to start the job, while a lighter shingle could be applied directly over the existing roof. Although some roof frames are a lot stronger than others, as a rule you should never add more than three layers of light to medium-weight shingles. And adding a third layer is questionable, even if the roof can hold it. In most cases the third layer will not lie flat, but waffle over the deteriorating shingles below. Also, nails driven through the third layer of shingles are likely to break apart brittle shingles below and may never attach to the house frame at all.

On sloped roofs, shingles at the top of a vent or plumbing stack are set in roof tar over flashing. On the low side, flashing should extend onto the next course of shingles, which redirects water near the vent back onto the roof, and on towards the gutter.

What color should the shingles be? Not often do you see a bright green or a vibrant red roof, even though asphalt shingles are available with surface granules in those colors. Color is a matter of personal taste. But bold blues, greens, and reds can become a bit oppressive after a few seasons—even though it would be easy to spot your house from the air.

In general, off-white or light grey shingles make a house look larger, the way white paint makes a ceiling seem higher. Light colors will mar more easily than dark shingles and show wear sooner, even though they will not wear out any faster than dark shingles. But light colors on the roof can reflect more sunlight than dark shingles, which will keep the house cooler in summer and reduce air conditioning costs.

If gaining heat in winter is more important than reducing heat in summer—in a house in Maine, for instance—a dark shingle would be the most energy-efficient choice. If cooling is more important, a lighter roof is more sensible.

Roof Coatings
The Benefits and Traps of Thin-Skinned Protection

Liquid coatings applied over an existing roof may add protection against the weather, increase fire resistance or energy efficiency, or simply alter the color. However, these coatings are relatively temporary compared to longer-lasting and more permanent roofing materials such as shingles. And contrary to the advertising claims of some firms, they are not imbued with almost magical properties that seal all leaks and eliminate normal wear and tear.

If such a coating did exist roofing manufacturers would be hard-pressed to hide it from consumers for a decade or two until their shingles or built-up roofs started to deteriorate. There is simply no all-purpose weather barrier that lasts indefinitely.

Yet roof coating, along with driveway surfacing, continues to be a staple of fly-by-night home improvement contractors. (For more about consumer rip-offs, see Chapter 8.) Unsuspecting consumers, swayed by a low-cost, unsolicited estimate—often some "special" deal that seems too good to pass up—may receive slapdash treatment with bogus roof coatings made of virtually worthless, and sometimes potentially damaging materials.

Concoctions ranging from extremely thinned asphalt to old automotive crankcase oil may be rolled or brushed onto decaying roof surfaces. At first glance, such a slick, uniform coating will hide obvious blemishes. But the beauty may be only skin-deep and very temporary. Thinned down or oily coatings may begin to drip into the gutters under a hot sun, or wash away in the rain, spilling oil out of downspouts onto nearby walkways and shrubbery.

Though the buyer of roof coatings must beware, there are some applications that can be used. Generally, they are designed to serve three legitimate purposes: to increase weather resistance, change color, or impart some special quality to a particular roof covering, such as increasing the fire rating or resistance to ultraviolet decay.

There are many variations of asphalt-, aluminum-, and acrylic-based roof coatings, each offering particular advantages and disadvantages under different conditions with different roofing materials. There is no pat answer to choosing the right coating. But several guidelines apply to all recoating jobs.

❖ The coating must be compatible with the roofing material. For example, common asphalt coatings cannot be applied successfully over a wood shingle roof, and aluminum coatings cannot be applied over coal tar roofs or tar coatings. If in doubt, check application instructions for the coating or consult a roofer.

❖ Roof coatings should not be applied on flat roofs over a gravel ballast (a layer of gravel on top of the roofing). While heavy tar may seep between embedded gravel to stop some leaks temporarily, it can make the inevitable job of reroofing much more complicated and expensive.

❖ Do not use roof coatings instead of reroofing. Thin-skinned surface applications cannot substitute for more durable roofing, such as a new layer of tab shingles on a sloped roof, or a new layer of modified bitumen (an elastic, rubbery, material applied in sheets and sealed to itself by heating with a propane torch), or flat roofs.

❖ Do not expect roof coatings to stay intact or bridge gaps over a deteriorated base. For example, no coating can prevent brittle, cracked shingle tabs from breaking if they are about to break.

❖ When choosing a contractor to coat a roof, follow standard selection procedures even though the job seems very simple and straightforward. In brief, check references, including other recent clients, local consumer protection agencies and the Better Business Bureau; ask for proof of insurance and local home improvement licenses where required; ask for a written estimate from two or more contractors who inspect the roof before quoting a price; sign a written contract for the job that specifies details of materials, costs, and a warranty. (For more details, see ''Home Improvement Contractors'' in Chapter 8.)

❖ Use roof coatings before serious deterioration occurs, as part of a regular maintenance program.

❖ Be on guard against unsolicited estimates for roof coating jobs, for ''on-the-spot'' specials, for example, where you may be given a supposedly reduced price on materials left over from another job, or a mark down because you are the first in your neighborhood to use the contractor.

One of the most successful roof treatments for aging, low-slope and nearly flat roofs common on row houses, uses a combination of a new roofing skin and an aluminum pigment coating.

On a typical job, flashing that seals seams between the roof skin and protrusions such as chimneys, skylights, and bordering parapet walls is checked and reset where

Too many reroofing jobs include this kind of slapdash flashing—aluminum tucked against a chimney with tar. New flashing should be folded back into the mortar between bricks. On this chimney, temperature changes will soon open the temporary tar joint, letting in water.

necessary. Simply coating exposed seams of metal flashing with tar is an inferior solution. The correct procedure is to scrape some mortar from joints between brick, then fold the top edge of flashing into the seam before remortaring.

If settling of the building has caused low spots to form in the roof which puddle (a relatively common occurrence), sheets of modified bitumen can be cemented in place to build up the depressions. Then the rubbery sheets are "torched" together, a tricky process not for inexperienced do-it-yourselfers, in which the roofing is heated almost to the point of combustion, so the surface is boiling hot and sticky. With this process the roofing acts as its own adhesive and becomes a single elastic covering capable of bridging minor irregularities.

Although not required, a surface application of pigmented aluminum can be rolled on to protect the roof from decay caused by ultraviolet light, and to make the surface reflective. The extra cost of this coating is generally paid back in only a few years of reduced costs for air conditioning.

Flat Roof Repairs

Q. Once a flat roof has started to leak, can it be reroofed like a conventional shingle roof?

A. Tracking down the leak can be difficult, and most repairs should be considered temporary. Generally, roof cement or roof tar is used to seal any seams that have opened. This is most likely to happen around the roof edges, and any place the roof is pierced, for instance, by a plumbing vent pipe or chimney. On vent pipes and other protrusions, consider new, elastic flashing—a piece of metal that is embedded in the roof with an elastic rubber neck that grips the pipe and seals out water. Sometimes, a section of the roof can be cut away and a patch made of layers of roofing paper and tar can be woven into the surrounding material.

Reroofing is possible, but only under two conditions. First, any surface stone (pebbles that protect the roof surface, called ballast in the trade) are removed. Second, the surface must be flat and firm. Spongy or raised areas are likely to reappear in the new surface. Removing the old roof and starting from scratch is generally a better idea.

Many roofers still insist on redoing flat roofs with a traditional five-ply roof built up with hot-mopped tar between layers. But another material, called modified bitumen, is an interesting alternative. It is very pliable, rubbery, and installed by roofers using a propane torch to almost liquefy the edges of the material where layers overlap. This makes them bond together, becoming one, large, rubbery sheet.

Ice Dam Solutions

Q. Now that the damage from recent snows and resulting ice damming on the roof edges has been done, what is the best way to dry out a wet ceiling? Does the wallboard have to be replaced, and wet rafters, too? Also, what is the best way to make sure the same kind of weather won't do the damage again next year?

A. Short-term soaking is not likely to do long-term damage to rafters, ceiling joists, or other structural parts of the building, as long as the frame is uncovered and allowed to dry thoroughly. Leaks can weaken gypsum wallboard or plaster, however.

As a rule, spongy, waterlogged gypsum panels should be pulled down and replaced after the frame has dried. This also offers an opportunity to inspect the damaged area in detail.

Without disturbing existing shingles, you can prevent ice dams from forming two ways: install a continuous strip of sheet metal over the four or five courses of shingles covering the eaves (the part of the roof that overhangs the walls of the building), or install heat cables in a zigzag pattern over the same area. Sheet metal, used widely in the Northeast but often considered substandard in appearance elsewhere, encourages the ice and snow to slide off the eaves. Heat cables keep the coldest part of the roof warm to prevent freeze-ups and ice dams.

If the shingles must be repaired or replaced, take the opportunity to install a rubberized ice and snow shield membrane directly on the roof deck below the new shingles. It offers "worst case" protection by keeping any ice or water that does back up under shingles from dripping into the house.

A last defense against leaks caused by ice dams is provided by Ice and Snow Shield, made by W.R. Grace & Co., Construction Products Division (62 Whittemore Ave., Cambridge, MA 02140). The rubberized sheets are installed beneath the last rows of shingles along the freeze-prone eaves.

Roof Flashing Seams

Q. How can I prevent a roof leak that I have traced to the seam between a piece of metal flashing and the edge of my flat roof? I have covered the seam with tar several times, but it keeps opening.

A. To help secure problem seams between different materials (part of the problem is that, in extremes of temperature, they expand and contract at different rates), try this sequence. First, if the flashing rises more than just a fraction of an inch above the roof, push a coating of roof tar in under the flashing, then nail it down into place with wide-headed roofing nails. (Nailing is not necessary if the flashing rises just enough off the roofing to let water in.)

Then coat the nails and flashing with roof tar. Embed in the tar a layer of fiberglass roof tape. A 3- or 4-inch-wide strip of this mesh material, covered with a final layer of roof tar, binds the seam together, and helps to prevent the flashing and the roofing material from separating.

Reroofing With Dimensional Shingles

Q. We are getting bids for reroofing our house with heavyweight dimensional shingles. One contractor wants to remove the existing shingles, which are just starting to curl. (A few broke away when the T.V. repairman went up to check the antenna.) But another contractor says the weight of the new shingles will keep them in place, and that any ridges will just add to the "dimensional" look. Who's right?

A. When in doubt, observe this cardinal rule of remodeling: Don't bury problems. If you do, at some point they will rise to the surface again and cause more problems. So take off the curling shingles before you reroof.

There are three good reasons for making the extra effort. First, you won't risk overloading the roof structure (if not with this layer, with the next one). Second, you'll

Dimensional shingles get the name from their multilayer look. The heavyweight shingles (often 300 pounds or more per square), have extra, small sections attached to the base shingles, which, to some, simulates the appearance of slate—a considerably more expensive alternative.

have a chance to repair the roof deck and metal flashing that may have been damaged by leaks. Third, the shingle manufacturer and the roofer will not be able to blame any future problems on the old shingles.

Heavy, "dimensional" shingles, which have extra surface layers to create the effect of thicker roofing such as slate, may compress some of the spongy trouble spots on your existing roof. But I don't think the manufacturer would agree with the contractor that a few extra bumps and lumps here and there would make the dimensional effect even more desirable. That's hype.

The contractor has bent the word "dimensional" in a slick attempt to turn a disadvantage into an advantage and close the sale. Give him credit for effort and imagination. But give the reroofing job to someone else.

Twenty

OPENINGS

Replacement Windows
A Project Where Methods Loom Larger Than Materials

Many consumers start thinking about the job of replacing old, leaky windows with modern, energy-efficient substitutes by asking, "Which kind of window is best: wood, aluminum, or vinyl?"

There are two problems with this seemingly fundamental question: there is no definitive answer, and, even if there were, choice of material is one of the least important considerations when you're thinking about replacement windows.

There is no good answer because no one of the three most common replacement window materials is inherently much better than the others. A nod could go to solid wood, the traditional choice, because it is a better natural insulator than solid plastic or metal. However, since aluminum and vinyl frames are made of specially molded shapes and not solid blocks, even this kind of basic comparison is pointless.

Even if there were a clear choice, good material cannot guarantee a good finished product. For instance, some cars perform better and last longer than others not because they are made of metal but because they are designed and built well. It's the same with replacement windows. The quality of construction and, even more so, the installation are the most important factors.

You may not receive this kind of appraisal from a firm that makes or installs only one type of window. This means you should discount rave reviews from suppliers and installers with an obvious vested interest in one material (the one they handle) over others.

It is also wise to downplay the importance of, and distinctions between, different types of insulated, energy-saving glass, which is commonly built into replacement windows. Too often, a confusing energy numbers game of R-values and U-factors takes the place of a straightforward, commonsense explanation of overall quality.

To put it simply, any reasonably well-made window with double-glazing (typically two panes of glass with an insulating layer of dead air in between), is much more energy efficient than the same window with only one pane of glass. Double-glazing is a good idea that saves heat in winter and air conditioning costs in summer. It also cuts sound transmission by about half, a very beneficial by-product if the replacement windows face a noisy street. Triple glazing is needlessly extravagant in all but the coldest climates.

But once the improvement from single to double panes is made, the difference between the insulated glass in one window and the insulated glass with a special tinting, or even with a high-tech, low-emissivity (called low-E) coating in another window is relatively marginal. (See "Low-E Glazing" in Chapter 25.)

You are also unlikely to receive this appraisal from many replacement window dealers. They may ballyhoo their particular type of double glazing as much as they push the importance of their framing material. But providing windows with double glazing is the easy part of the job.

When comparison shopping, put the issues of frame material and double glazing aside and concentrate instead on three key areas: general consumer checkups, thermal break construction, and installation details.

General consumer checkups include asking the window firm for the names of clients you can contact, and checking for a home improvement license, insurance, and any

Combinations of windows that create distinctive patterns are possible with new units such as Andersen's quarter-round clearstory window. It's 6 feet across. The curved shape opens up a room that faces such an inviting vista—reflected in the mirror-glass surface.

other information you can use to evaluate them. Also, make inquiries at your local Better Business Bureau and consumer protection agency. Check for a record of complaints, which can warn you of fly-by-nighters and others with a bad track record.

''Thermal break,'' the second key subject, is the general term for some type of foam strip, airspace, vinyl tube, or other insulating barrier that interrupts temperature transfer from the outside to the inside of the frame.

This is why many homeowners buy replacement windows—not because it saves energy, although two panes are more energy efficient than single glazing—but to stop condensation. The insulated air buffer between double panes keeps the inside surface warm and minimizes condensation.

It's an important feature because in winter a metal frame without a thermal break can be almost as cold on its inside surface as on the outside. This fosters condensation, drafts, and other problems. Without an effective thermal break even a triple-glazed window with bone-dry glass can flood the sill with condensation dripping off a freezing cold frame.

Don't be misled or put off by high-tech, energy-saving mumbo jumbo. Keep it simple. Ask the replacement window dealer or installer to trace the path of temperature transfer through the frame. Start on the outside surface of a cross-section drawing of the frame or an actual window sample. Follow the temperature flow, waiting for an explanation of the thermal break that interrupts the flow and keeps the inside surface of the frame close to room temperature and free of condensation.

Next, zero in on the third key area—the installation. The best policy again is to stand with the installer outside your home and get a close-up explanation and view of exactly what will go where. Ask to see where the window will fit, how it will be trimmed, how its frame will butt against existing siding, and how the frame will be flashed and caulked.

Beware of a problem called downsizing. This is the term for replacing an existing window with a smaller unit—sometimes surprisingly smaller. Minor adjustments may be unavoidable, particularly when the nearest stock size offered by the window firm doesn't match your old window. But some installers pack out your existing window opening with 2 by 4s, stick a much smaller window into the new opening, then add wide, gawky-looking pieces of trim between the small new window and old siding.

In many cases, this kind of oversize trim makes the new windows a heavy-handed addition to the building facade. The corner-cutting practice can change the architectural scale enough to make a formerly attractive building look silly, or, worse yet, plain ugly.

Sliding Glass Doors
Planning a View with the Room

Windows are an afterthought in many homes, small glitches in the solid walls of siding and drywall that define building style and layout. That's okay, if there is nothing worth seeing outside. But what about your rock garden, redwood deck, rose bush, or even a single, scraggly but green tree?

To bring some of the outdoors inside, make a room seem larger, increase natural light and ventilation, the solution is obvious: build a bigger opening. You could install a larger window. But the planning and construction work required for that project can, on a somewhat larger scale, provide the ultimate in wall openings—a sliding glass door.

In this beach house, two stories of sliding glass doors will provide a see-through living space. On the first floor, sliders will open onto an entry deck between the two wings of the building. Above, a small balcony will cover the entry and provide a small deck for the sleeping loft.

"Sliders," either aluminum or wood frames enclosing large glass panels, are available in many widths, and standard door height of 6 feet, 8 inches. Taller panels are available on special order. Manufacturers also offer sliding screen panels. You can imagine the increase in ventilation when almost 23 square feet of solid wall (the area of one, 4-foot-wide sliding panel) is replaced by a screen.

Sliders such as this three-part unit (one door slides open, while doors to each side are fixed), are one of the easiest and most efficient ways to open a room. Wide, unobstructed glazing can make the deck feel like part of the room inside, dramatically increasing the sense of space.

There are several key points in the project—possible pitfalls for contractors and, even more so, for do-it-yourselfers. For instance, in almost all localities, you will need a building permit, which means a small fee, and inevitable bureaucratic entanglements. These may be annoying to your contractor, but protect you from building in a hazard or structural weakness—a particularly valuable service if you tackle the job yourself.

If you make a basic, dimensioned, scale drawing of the wall, showing the location and size of surrounding timbers, doors width, and such, an inspector may be able to grant you a permit after drawing in a 2-by-10 header instead of the 2 by 8 you thought would suffice.

One crucial decision is where to locate the slider. The choice may seem obvious if you have only one view worth capturing. Still, the location—sometimes only a few feet one way or the other—can make quite a difference. It depends on what's buried beneath the plaster or drywall. It could be a jungle of electrical cables, plumbing pipes, low-voltage intercom and speaker wires. Rerouting them could cost more than installing the door. Moving a radiator or baseboard convector also can complicate the job, although a floor register from a hot-air furnace won't intrude.

The best choice is a location in a purely structural wall, filled only with insulation. Surface switches and outlets can provide clues to circuit wiring in the wall. Finding plumbing pipes can be more difficult, although you can take a hint from exposed plumbing pipes in the cellar or crawl space.

Another important step in planning the job is to make provision for the debris. A compact, 8-foot length of wall can turn into a surprisingly large pile of rubble. If you work with a contractor, include removal in the contract.

Also, be sure that you have the door on-site before demolition begins. A contractor should have no trouble completing the job in 1 day—if the door is there, ready to install.

Although wallboard and siding can be torn down easily enough, remember that brick, concrete block, or wooden studs are part of a unified system that holds up the house. If roof rafters over the opening sag as you remove the wall, which is likely, it can be difficult to nudge them back in place as you frame the new door.

Collapse is unlikely, since houses are constructed more securely than a pyramid of soup cans at the supermarket. In fact, it is difficult to make a house fall down by pulling out only a few of its many legs.

Nevertheless, you will need a temporary structure to support loads carried by the exterior wall during construction. This framework should be placed before you begin demolition. Typically, a 2-by-4 wall frame set between 2 by 6s across the ceiling and floor a few feet inside the exterior wall to allow for working room, will serve the purpose. But special loads or circumstances may require beefier support.

The final key to installation is the size of the beam, called the *header*, that spans the opening. Since the beam carries all the structural loads that were carried by the wall, it must be much larger than standard 2-by-4 wall studs.

As a general guide, an opening for a 5-foot door consisting of two, 2-foot, 6-inch panels requires at least two 2 by 8s spiked together and set on edge, while a larger 8-foot opening may call for two 2 by 12s. Fortunately, header size, which depends on door width, the type of building construction, and the load from materials above the opening, is controlled by local codes.

Unsticking Windows
Breaking the Seal on Ventilation

After a long winter closed up inside the house, you may want to do something that you haven't done for a while: open all the windows all the way and let in some fresh air. But you may discover that your trusty double-hungs have been locked in place by layers of paint or excessive swelling caused by condensation dripping off the glass.

Don't break your back pushing them open. Start small. Just try to get the windows cracked. If the frame is swollen, or if seams between the window sash and the surrounding frame are sealed by paint, you could be in for a wrestling match. Sometimes the window wins. Sometimes the trim, called stop, holding a double hung window in place, must be pried off the frame before the window will move.

If a double-hung window won't move, first try a sharp push with the heel of your hand on the sash at the center of the window, right by the window lock. A good crack may break a thin paint bond. It's not a good idea to hit the frame with a block of wood, or to brace something like a 2 by 4 against the frame and hit it with a hammer. This will provide more force than the heel of your hand—maybe enough to break the window.

Before you go too far, make sure the window lock is unlocked, and that no one has set a finishing nail through the sash or installed some other security device. It's embarrassing to curse at a window that won't move when it's locked and not supposed to move.

Usually, the trick is to slice apart the painted seams between the window sash (the framed glass section that is supposed to move up and down) and the stop that makes a track for the sash. You can slice the paint with a utility knife, although rolling the wheel of a sharp pizza cutter along the joint also works well and is somewhat safer because it is easier to control.

If the window has been painted on the outside, cut through those seams as well. Then try another shot with the heel of your hand. If the window still won't move, try slipping the thin, metal-cutting blade from a jigsaw—just the blade, which you must hold carefully in your hand—between the sash and the frame.

Finally, you can force the window with a thin pry bar, called a flat bar, set between the window sill and the bottom of the sash. This is one step short of beating the window with a stick. But it should provide more than enough leverage. However, the tool will probably dig into the sill and the sash.

Minimize the scarring by laying a wooden shingle under the flat bar across the sill. This spreads out the downward prying force and reduces gouging. If there is enough room, slip a piece of aluminum flashing between the sill and the window sash so that the flat bar will be pushing against the aluminum instead of the wooden sash. This can prevent some gouging on the frame. In the end, though, the window is likely to show some traces of this heavy-duty approach.

In the worst scenario, you may have to pry away the stop, working gently and gradually to avoid splitting the wood. This is a major production.

If none or only some of these steps are necessary to crack the window but it still won't open and close freely, you may have to make some other adjustments.

On a painted wooden window, for instance, built-up paint layers can simply make the sash too big for the sliding track. The solution is to scrape or sand off enough paint so that, even with a fresh coat, the sash will be a hair thinner.

An easier but less elegant way to make the sash move more freely is to cut some traveling room between the sash and stop. Increase the clearance by tracing the sash perimeter with a utility knife, then a metal-cutting jigsaw blade, and, if need be, a slightly thicker wood-cutting blade between the sash and surrounding trim also will help.

On many windows, tension that holds the sash in place is supplied by some type of spring clip, usually in a tight, V-shape, that is built into the window frame. It presses against the sash. To decrease the tension, place a 1 by 2 over the spring clip and give it a few shots with a hammer. You may find that you have to use some really firm blows before noticing any difference.

If you happen to suffer from the opposite malady and the window sash is too loose in the track, you can increase the tension by slipping a screwdriver into the V-clip and prying it open a bit. In this case, only a little pressure tends to increase the tension a lot.

To minimize the effects of swelling as the weather gets warmer and the humidity increases, make sure that wooden window sashs are protected with paint or a coat of clear sealer.

OLD WINDOW WEATHERSTRIPPING

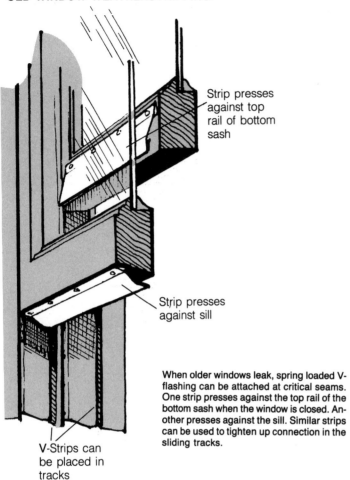

Strip presses against top rail of bottom sash

Strip presses against sill

V-Strips can be placed in tracks

When older windows leak, spring loaded V-flashing can be attached at critical seams. One strip presses against the top rail of the bottom sash when the window is closed. Another presses against the sill. Similar strips can be used to tighten up connection in the sliding tracks.

Sticking Sliding Door Track

Q. One of my sliding glass doors scrapes along the metal track. It has gotten to the point where I have to lift the door a little in order to make it close completely so I can lock it. How can I fix this problem?

A. Look down near the bottom of each end of the sliding panel, and you should see a small slot or hole. Inside there should be a screw that can be turned to raise or lower the wheel inside the door frame. By lowering the wheel in relation to the door frame, the frame will ride a bit higher and clear the track.

Before you turn the adjusting screw, however, lift the end of the door with a crowbar, for instance, and insert a small block of wood between the frame and the track. Then get down on the ground when you turn the screw so you can see for sure that you are lowering the wheel, not raising it. After a few turns (lowering it only ¼ of an inch might be enough to provide clearance) pry up the door slightly, remove the block, and give it a test slide. You might find that the other end still catches, in which case you simply repeat the procedure on the wheel at the other end of the door.

Dust, dirt, leaves, and other debris is supposed to be swept away by brushes at the bottom of the door. If need be, raise the door slightly to clean off and realign the brush. The innermost door has a slot near the base, providing access to a concealed screw that raises and lowers the gliding wheels.

Twenty One

YARD

Planter Design and Construction
Bringing the Landscape up off the Ground

Almost any patch of ground is a potential planter. Border it in redwood, fence it in with mini pickets, box it in with railroad ties, and a common, ordinary piece of sod is transformed. Of course, it helps to plant something attractive inside the box.

There are two possible obstacles to building a planter in practically any shape or size you desire, from a huge raised bed inside railroad ties to a small window box or patio planter. The first is rot, which stems from putting wood in contact with wet dirt. The second is poor drainage, which stems from encasing soil and plants in a solid box.

On stand-alone designs, the temptation is to build a box like a bureau drawer—tight and secure. But if you do, excess water has nowhere to go. Even small, circular, clay planters (flower pots) have a hole in the bottom.

Although some water and mud probably will seep out, stand-alone planters should have a few holes drilled in the bottom. In a typical design, the bottom of the planter should have a series of ⅜- to ½-inch-diameter holes distributed approximately a foot apart. To keep the dirt in, staple galvanized or plastic insect screening over the holes.

To aid drainage and prevent the bottom board of the planter from rotting, add "feet," such as 1-by-2-inch pressure-treated slats. In a short box, only a foot or two long, one slat at each end will do. On longer boxes, you should add more slats to prevent sagging. This keeps the bottom board slightly off the deck or patio, out of the damp.

Even then, rot can take hold from the inside out. Adequate drainage helps. But choice of materials is also important. For instance, you could use a naturally rot-resistant wood such as kiln-dried redwood. Most vegetation also seems to survive in planters built of pressure-treated wood—lumber that is injected throughout with wood-preserving chemicals. Few types of vegetation can survive inside a planter when caustic, wood-preserving chemicals are painted over the wood surfaces. If you ever have spilled some deck sealer on the grass or flowers nearby, you know from experience how potent it is.

But you can build a planter box out of soft, untreated wood, such as pine, if you line the inside (aside from the screened holes) with a liquid asphaltum or aluminum sheeting (the thin, easily bent variety commonly used for roof flashing).

On planter boxes built with 1 ½-inch-thick wood, such as 2 by 6s or 2 by 8s, predrill holes before nailing to avoid splitting the wood at the corner joints. This also is a good idea on boxes made with thinner, ¾-inch-thick wood. Even then, it can be difficult for novices to drive nails through the face of one board into the end grain of another without running off center. This may split the board, or cause the nail point to poke through the wood surface.

If this kind of nailing poses problems for you, cut the boards to fit, clamp or tie them in position, then secure the corners with screws through predrilled holes in angled brackets: decorative types outside or plain, galvanized mending plated inside the box.

To construct a larger, in-ground planter, for instance, a 2-by-6-foot raised bed, start by laying out the area with small stakes and string. Sink the stakes about a foot beyond the actual planter area, two at each corner, so the strings between stakes overlap, and the stakes are not in your way. Then, following the string line, or one of the planter boards laid on the ground, cut through the sod in a neat line with a sharp shovel, and remove the grass inside the planter area.

To build a structurally sound planter box, out of 2 by 8s, for instance, nail the box together on a flat surface, and check your layout by comparing diagonal dimensions.

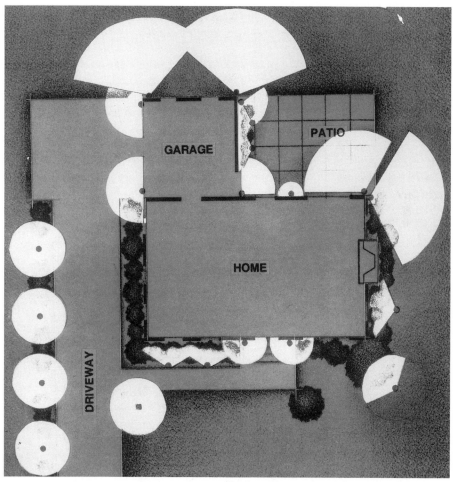

Raised planting beds (accentuated by landscape lighting in this diagram), can help the house fit the site. In many developments, where buildings look as though they were dropped out of a plane, a raised bed that mirrors the house line can "attach" the building to the site.

When the diagonals are equal, the corners are square. Then nail a 1 by 2 or other brace along the diagonal to keep the box rigid while you move it into the excavated area.

You may have to do a little digging and filling to make the box level—until it centers the bubble in a level, or until your eye is satisfied. Then you can drive a series of pointed, 1-by-2, pressure-treated stakes into the ground that rest against the inside of the box frame. One near each corner should be enough to secure a 2-by-6-foot box, for instance.

Drive the stakes deep enough so their tops are hidden below the edge of the planter frame. Then clamp the stake to the box, or brace the box at that point with a board, or a heavy tool such as a sledge hammer, and nail the stake to the box frame. If you do not brace the box while nailing, you may disrupt the corners. The same embedding process can be used with railroad ties. It makes a neat edge between the surrounding ground and the planter.

To encourage consumers to build outdoor projects such as a planter box, one manufacturer of pressure-treated lumber, the Osmose Wood Preserving Company of America, offers project brochures that include a building plan, instructions, and a list of needed materials through home centers and lumberyards.

Redirecting Surface Water

Q. The floor of my storage and garden shed is directly in the way of a small stream that appears during heavy rains. Moving or raising the shed is not a possibility, since there is only one place it can sit. How can I divert the water?

A. The safest approach is to interrupt the flow before it gets anywhere near the shed. Water diverters have two basic parts, which may be configured in many ways and sizes: one part, a drainage basin or trench, gathers the water; the other, a drain pipe, redirects its flow.

For instance, you might dig a small trench—about 2 or 3 feet deep and a foot wide— perpendicular to the flow. One end of the trench should be extended. It will contain the pipe.

Line the trench with heavy, black plastic to help contain the water. Then add a few inches of gravel. Next, lay some form of drain tile (sections of foundation-type tile or lengths of perforated plastic pipe) sloping at least slightly downhill to a release point. Depending on the lay of the land, this point might be only a few feet away from the original water stream, or well across the yard. Obviously, the release point must be located where the stream cannot flow back to its original course.

Finally, fill the trench with gravel. If this strikes you as unsightly, you could cover the gravel with a ground filter fabric—a heavy gauze carried by some home centers and, more likely, by landscape suppliers. The fabric, which can be covered with sod, lets in water but keeps out dirt that could clog the drainage basin.

Here's how the system should work. The stream of water drops into the extremely porous, gravel trench, where it filters into the drain tile or perforated drain pipe and flows to its release point.

If the water does not form into a controllable stream until it nears the shed, you can create the same basin and pipe system next to the building.

Sealing Redwood Decking

Q. Does redwood decking and siding need a sealer to prevent weathering, and does the wood really turn black without it?

A. Although redwood has a high natural resistance to rot and to pests, like other woods it will weather without protection, and, although much more gradually, even with protection.

Unprotected redwood eventually becomes a silvery gray tinged with a light tan—an elegant finish. But during the weathering process, unprotected redwood loses the original pinkish tone, darkens, and may turn almost black before lightening to the final gray-tan stage. Adding a sealer eliminates this ugly step. It also slows the weathering process in general.

Several types of coatings can be used. Clear sealers, for example, cause the least amount of alteration in the wood's appearance. Two coats should be applied on raw wood. A single recoating should be added every year after that for best results.

Nails were driven too close to the ends of these deck boards, which encouraged splitting. Moving them back a bit and predrilling the holes would have helped. Also, regularly recoating the deck with a weather-resistant sealer could have minimized checking and splitting by keeping water and ice out of the grain.

Some clear sealers use paraffin as the water repellent in a mineral spirit base, others use an oil base. The California Redwood Association[1] doesn't specify one over another. (The association does supply numerous pamphlets on redwood applications and sealing to consumers on request.) But their technical services division does recommend clear sealers with an ultraviolet light (UV) inhibitor. It blocks some of the sun's rays that fade the wood.

Semitransparent, redwood-colored stains also retard weathering. But the pigment they add to the wood is subject to noticeable wear. For instance, after a few years, traffic paths will lighten much more than surrounding areas. This problem can be

---

[1]Calif. Redwood Association, 591 Redwood Highway, Suite 3100, Mill Valley, CA 94941

minimized by diluting the coating even further, mixing equal parts of semitransparent stain and a compatible clear sealer.

On an existing deck that has already started to weather, the original tone can be "renewed" with one of several proprietary chemical restorers, or, with caution in handling, with this home-brewed formula: 4 ounces of oxalic acid crystals in 1 gallon of warm water (mixed in a plastic bucket). Brush the mix on the deck, let dry, then hose off. This solution is caustic to nearby vegetation. But it can bring up the original pinkish tone of redwood before a surface sealer is applied.

Cleaning Up After Insects

Q. Every few years there seems to be an infestation of bugs that inevitably cause a mess on our wood deck. This year it was cicadas. What can I use to clean up their debris and remains, which have left dark blotchy stains all over the wood deck?

A. The not very exotic cicada juice remover is soap and water, if the stains are, in fact, from cicadas. Dr. George Rambo, technical director of the National Pest Control Association (NPCA) suggests that such dark, blotchy stains are most likely due to other insects, particularly aphids, which leave black sooty deposits that quickly grow fungus in a warm and humid environment. For stubborn stains add a little bleach, which helps to kill fungus growth.

If you happen to catch one of the blotch producers in the act, you can identify it by using a unique service provided by the NPCA. Seal one of the bugs in a pillbox or plastic bag, send it to the NPCA[2] with your name, address and phone number, and they will identify the bug, then call or write to tell you the results. The NPCA does not charge consumers for this exceedingly helpful service.

If the problem is from the bizarre species of 17-year cicadas at least you will not have to worry about cleanup again until May or June, 2004.

Hose Fittings

Q. The first time I tried to water the flowers this spring I got sprayed instead because the garden hose leaks. Is there some way to mend leaks right at the coupling (I've tried electrician's tape), or must I buy a new hose?

A. Most home centers and hardware stores carry coupling replacement kits (also handy if the threads are damaged). Start by cutting off the old coupling, then insert a tapered bushing into the open end of the hose. Next, fit a new coupling onto the hose and bushing. The three-piece assembly (bushing covered by hose covered by coupling) is connected by turning down the bushing with a T-shaped tool supplied in the kit.

To make the job a little easier, dip the end of the hose in very hot water before inserting the bushing. This softens the plastic and makes the edges pliable, so a tight connection is made between bushing and coupling.

---

[2]NPCA, 8100 Oak Street, Dunn Loring, VA 22027

Twenty Two

SEASONAL MAINTENANCE

Spring Projects Outside
Spring Spruce Up for the House Exterior

When winter weather fades, it is time to start thinking about exterior improvement and repair projects—without worrying that you will be driven back inside by snow, sleet, and freezing winds. If you have been procrastinating, standing by the window, looking at the deck that needs sealing and the drain that needs clearing, the jig is up.

Here are some tips on handling some of the most common spring repairs and improvements.

Exterior wood. Wood decks, steps, and railings exposed to the elements year-round must have weather resistance built in or brushed on. Even then, a piece of wood may twist enough to loosen a nail or two, and rise up from a deck or step to create a hazard. You can refasten loose boards with either a wood screw or a nail slightly longer than the one that became loose.

If you must replace damaged deck boards, you can use pressure-treated timber that is injected with preservatives, or construction-grade fir that can be stained to match the surrounding surface, or sealed with a clear wood preservative to resist deterioration, or both (stain first). It's a good idea to renew these coatings every 2 or 3 years, particularly along traffic paths.

Although it is an elegant touch of carpentry, mitered clapboards at outside corners can lead to leaks and deterioration, since it is difficult to keep the corners closed. Caulking will help, but nails may have to be replaced with wood screws for a long-term solution.

For more money (sometimes half again the cost of fir), more exotic species such as redwood or cedar can be used. They are more naturally resistant to the elements, and more beautiful, at least when you first nail them down. Many people who spend extra for redwood or cedar are disappointed when the elegant wood hues fade in the weather after a few seasons.

Exterior cleaning. If you're planning to paint this spring to brighten up the exterior, try washing a small section of wall first. Cleaning alone may make a surprising difference. And even if you decide to paint, cleaning will help. Most paints last longer and require less maintenance when applied over a clean wall.

The best all-purpose house cleaner is the same stuff that has been working so well on your hands and face—soap and water. If your siding is so dull you are considering re-siding the house, also consider the much less expensive option of washing the building with warm water, a nonabrasive household detergent, and a soft brush. A typical formula is ⅓ cup liquid detergent to a gallon of water.

Bleach can be added to combat mold and mildew formations in a proportion of up to 25 percent household bleach—1 quart bleach to 3 quarts water. (For more on house cleaning, see "House Washing" in Chapter 18.)

Exterior drains. Improving spring weather is also likely to include spring rains, which can test gutters and downspouts, and the site drainage around the house.

You can flush the gutter system to make sure it's clear and free-flowing. If it is sluggish, check for obstructions at the offset fittings in downspouts just below gutters—the most likely bottlenecks. In the worst case, you may have to take the fitting apart to pry out a tangle of twigs and leaves.

Lighten the burden on foundation drains by connecting the downspout to a pipe that will deposit water from the roof away from the house. At a minimum, add a few feet of pipe to the bottom of the downspout, angled away from the foundation. Regrading around the house, creating a slope in the soil away from the foundation, also helps.

Area drains, which range from natural, water-carrying gullies in the yard, to man-made trenches filled with gravel and pipe, should be cleared of leaves and fallen branches. In heavy rains, one branch in the path of surface water can trap leaves and other debris to create a dam that may divert water towards the house instead of around it.

Screens. Spring is also a good time to repair screens that will keep houses and porches and sun rooms bug-free during the summer. If wooden-frame screens come out of winter storage with a wobble, you can strengthen them with long wood screws, corrugated miter joint fasteners driven across the seams at the corners, wooden dowels, or, if you're not too particular about their appearance, metal surface brackets, called mending plates, secured across the frame joints with screws.

If you have to replace screening in a wooden frame, avoid wrinkling and a loose fit by stapling the sides first, working from the center toward the top and bottom. Staple across the center divider (a common, stiffening feature on wood frames) last.

If your screen frames are old and warped, you may want to try this little trick to get a tight fit. Create a temporary concave dip in the frame by inserting blocks of wood under each end, and weighting the center divider or clamping it to the surface you're working on. When the bow is released after stapling, energy stored in the slightly bent frame works to tighten the screen for a neat fit.

If the screens have only a tiny, bug-sized puncture or two, you can seal them with clear waterproof glue (on metal screens) or an acetone-type glue (on plastic screens). Larger holes on metal screens can be sealed with small sections of screen. Bend the end wires of the patch piece down, like table legs, so they go through the screening surrounding the hole. Then rebend the end wires flat to hold the patch in place. Plastic patches can be sewn or glued in place.

<hr/>

Summer Maintenance Checks
Some Unexciting "Status Quo" Summer Projects

Home improvements get most of the attention. New decks, and snappy, remodeled kitchens and baths are obvious positive additions to your home and its value. But once in a while you've got to get down there in the trenches and maintain the status quo. It's not a pretty sight. But someone's got to do it. Here are several candidates for your attention this summer.

Up on the roof. There may be several jobs that need doing in order to keep the house dry inside. Start by planning for an early morning foray, before the shingles heat up and become so gooey that you leave footprints in the tar. Then start at the weakest link in the roofing system: the flashing.

Flashing can open up along the roof edge, between the roof and masonry parapets, and around protrusions such as chimneys and vent pipes. The metal strips, normally made of aluminum, are designed to seal seams between different materials—asphalt shingles and a brick chimney, for instance. Naturally, this is a tough job, since aluminum expands and contracts in the weather far more than asphalt.

Along the edge of a flat or gently-sloped roof, the best solution is to spread roofing tar under the raised portion of flashing with a trowel, then secure with roofing nails. That will keep the flashing in place but create more potential leaks. So a really thorough job involves a few finishing steps. First, coat the flashing surface and an inch or so of the adjacent roof with roof tar. Then embed into the tar a layer of fiberglass roofing tape (it's strong enough to hold the seam in place) that covers the flashing and the seam to the roofing material. Finally, spread another thin layer of tar over the fiberglass tape.

Around small protrusions in the roof such as plumbing vent pipes, use a special, rubber-necked piece of flashing available at home centers, lumberyards, and roofing supply houses. These fittings, available in several sizes to fit different types of vents, come with an aluminum sheet that is set in roof tar and covered by shingles on the high side of the pipe, and lapped over shingles on the low side. A rubberized ring attached to the sheet forms a tight, long-lasting, seal around the pipe.

Guarding the gutters. Instead of waiting for leaves to fall and clog the gutters, now is a good time to install leaf guards. Although there are slight variations in style, a typical strip of guard—a few feet long and 4 or 6 inches wide—consists of a coarse screen section that rests on top of the gutter, and a thin frame with nailing tabs that extends under the first coarse of roof shingles. The idea is simple: the screen lets water into the gutter but keeps leaves out.

Getting the most from your air conditioner. You can improve the efficiency of a room air conditioner by following instructions in the owner's manual for the following jobs. Clean dust and dirt off the condenser coil (the tubing facing outside the house) with a soft brush. Clean the water tray along the bottom of the unit with a disinfectant. Some manufacturers offer cleaning mixtures through factory-authorized dealers that disinfect and deodorize the pan. Many suggest cleaning with a disinfectant such as Lysol, followed by a thorough rinsing. Also, clean the interior air filter. Most thin, foam types can be washed and reinstalled, but some must be replaced.

Cooling down the attic. On a hot day, air in poorly ventilated attics might reach 140 degrees Fahrenheit. This warms the living space below and burdens air conditioners. Insulating the attic floor will help, but ventilation is more important. Usually, small triangular grills, called gable-end vents, are installed near the roof peak at each end of the attic to provide ventilation. But without additional inlets at the eaves where the roof overhangs the house, cross-ventilation is limited to the center of the attic. Adding plug vents (small, screen-covered air inlets) between each pair of rafters along the roof overhang will keep attic temperatures only moderately above outside air temperature.

Skylights and roof windows flood a room with sunshine, and drive up summer cooling costs. One versatile solution is to install a shaded, automated window. This Andersen unit opens and closes electronically. It even includes a rain sensor, which will close the hatch if you're away.

Cooling hot windows. Shades, drapes, and blinds can keep out the sun, but also any view you might have. To let in light but minimize heat gain, add storm windows or a temporary, interior layer of clear plastic. Heat-shrink plastic, applied to the interior window frame with double-faced tape and shrunk with heat from a hair dryer to eliminate wrinkles, provides a clear, distortion-free surface that acts like a double-glazed window, trapping a layer of dead air.

Cleaning mold and mildew. Gray and green dots forming on wall surfaces from excessive summer dampness are unsightly and can eat through a fresh layer of paint. You can clean the spots before they combine into large blotches with one of the many proprietary mold and mildew cleaners, or a basic home brew of warm water and approximately 25 percent household bleach (1 part bleach to 3 parts water). Also, you should wear gloves and a long-sleeved shirt to protect against possible skin irritation.

Scrub with a stiff brush to dislodge the greenish dots, and let the area dry thoroughly. If stains remain, spot prime with a coat of pigmented white shellac, which will prevent any traces of the discoloration from bleeding through a new coat of paint.

Rescuing a retaining wall. Concrete and masonry block retaining walls often start to tilt in time from the hydrostatic pressure of ground water, which can eventually tip them over. The solution is to release the pressure by providing an outlet for the water—a series of small openings called weep holes.

When such walls are built, small drainage channels are normally made by building in pieces of galvanized pipe every few feet along the bottom of the wall. They are supposed to have screening on the dirt side of the wall, and a bed of gravel to let groundwater flow freely into the drain holes. But in time, this system—if it was ever there—can become clogged.

You could try threading a plumber's snake or a steel rod through the wall to clear the hole. If that doesn't work, you'll have to excavate a trench along the dirt side of the wall, and install the gravel and screens.

Fall Maintenance Survey
Early Preparation for a Change in the Weather

Even if you relish home maintenance about as much as an IRS audit, fall is one time when it really makes sense to overcome your fear and loathing of checking up on that ever-deteriorating place you call home.

Certainly, home maintenance is not all fun and games. Its purpose is not to transform or add to the living space, but simply to maintain the status quo—not a thrilling concept. But to spur yourself into action, consider the difference between sweeping some leaves out of the gutters now, and some frigid winter evening dealing with leaks caused by ice and snow piled up behind leaves you didn't remove.

Not every item on this checklist is a must. And not every area that should be checked, particularly on an old house, is on the list. No list is long enough.

Windows and doors. Check the seam across the top of windows and doors, which is normally protected by a piece of metal flashing tucked up beneath the siding. If the flashing is rusted through or bent out of place, water may be funneled into the wall. If new flashing must be installed, cover the joint with a flexible silicone or polyurethane caulk first, then pry the siding away from the house just enough to slip new flashing beneath it. Caulking should be sufficient on the three other window seams.

The weakest link at door openings is along the bottom, where rain and snow collect. On wood doors, this edge may be roughened by opening and closing so the door soaks up water and swells. After sanding, apply several coats of wood preservative along the bottom edge to seal out water.

Siding. Check for openings where nails have popped up. Replace them with slightly longer nails for more holding power or wood screws for even more holding power on twisted or bowed clapboards. For security, insert a bead of flexible caulking in joints before closing them.

Skylights. Short of installing new flashing around a leaking skylight, roof tar is the best cure for leaking seams. Use a small trowel to spread a coat of roof cement against the skylight frame, working the tar underneath surrounding shingles.

Gutters and downspouts. Blockages, even from a handful of leaves, are the biggest problem. Sometimes these roadblocks are hidden in the S-shaped offset fitting between the gutter and the downspout. After sweeping leaves from the gutters, pour in some water from a garden hose to make sure the entire drain system is open. If not, take the downspout apart and dislodge any twigs or leaves that have become wedged in place.

Roofing. You can prevent ice from forming along the eaves and in the gutters by installing electric heat tapes (cables that look like extension cords but give off some heat), along the lower courses of the shingles. Several configurations of snow clips (twists of wire that tuck under shingles along the eaves) can prevent a pile of snow from dropping off the roof—above a doorway, for instance.

Masonry chimneys and foundations. Loose mortar between bricks or concrete blocks leaves gaps where water can enter and exert tremendous pressure against the masonry if the water freezes at night. Prevent this deterioration by scraping away loose mortar and applying a fresh layer. A coating of clear silicone-based sealer provides more general protection over the entire surface.

Fireplace and wood stove flues. Check soot and ash dumps at the bases of furnace and chimney flues. Accumulations may signal inefficient combustion and potential dangers of puff-backs as oil-laden soot near the furnace combustion chamber is ignited. Flue pipes on furnaces and wood or coal stoves can be disassembled and brushed clean.

If you don't call in a professional cleaning service, save yourself a grimy cleanup indoors by working on the flue pipes outdoors. To work on a masonry fireplace flue, first cover the fireplace opening to prevent airborne soot from sifting into every nook and cranny of the house. Raising and lowering a sand-filled, heavy canvas bag through the flue provides a cursory cleaning. Naturally, a professional chimney sweep can do better, using special steel brushes to dislodge creosote buildup.

Variations in temperature between the warm flue tile and surrounding masonry exposed to ice and snow, have cracked the cement wash on this chimney. A dense, hydraulic cement will help keep out water. But such problem seams should still be checked once a year.

Condensation. The best way to avoid condensation problems as warm indoor air hits cold window panes is to install two layers of glass. Factory-made double glazing is available in new windows. But you can create an effective double barrier simply by adding a storm window, either a framed unit applied outside, or a more simple plastic panel or even clear, heat-shrink plastic installed inside.

Furnace. Tuning up the heating plant is perhaps the most important piece of home maintenance to attend to now, when a constant flow of heat is not as crucial as it soon will be.

Any heating plant that is close to a decade old should be checked annually, even though the rule of thumb is to clean and tune new oil furnaces annually, but new gas furnaces only every 3 years. Typical maintenance steps found in owner's manuals include only a few do-it-yourself jobs such as changing air filters, before suggesting that you call in a professional. That's good advice.

Professionals should not only clean blowers, fans, and grills, but adjust the rate of combustion and analyze furnace operation with a series of instruments do-it-yourselfers don't have. The tune-up can be performed by a plumbing and heating contractor, by the furnace manufacturer's personnel or local contractors fulfilling the manufacturer's service agreement, and sometimes by selected contractors as a follow-up service to a utility company's energy audit. Many oil and gas utility companies employ a service staff to care for the equipment they supply with fuel. If your utility company does not supply service, chances are it will be able to recommend a reliable service contractor.

Winter Exterior Maintenance
Keeping the Exterior Closed to the Weather

Winter weather is not likely to do in your home in one fell swoop. But it can cut an unexpected chink in the armor that separates the cold, snowy, windy weather outside from the people trying to stay warm and cozy inside.

Most problems are likely to be slow-developing—the kind of deterioration that will require some maintenance and repair work in the spring. For instance, the combination of temperature variations on siding and trim (from warm sunlight to subzero wind chill) plus rain, sleet, and snow, can cause shrinking and swelling. As wood siding (or the wood sheathing or furring strips beneath vinyl and aluminum siding) moves with the weather, nails can pop loose and siding seams can open. That lets in moisture and water, and cold air that can freeze pipes.

But a violent winter storm might cause some exterior problems that would require more immediate solutions. For instance, many houses no longer carry the extra protection offered by shutters. And on many homes that do have shutters they are purely decorative, screwed down to the siding instead of mounted on hardware that allows them to be swiveled over windows.

If an icicle or tree branch does crash through a window (a serious problem during a power outage when you need to conserve heat), you can make a temporary cover from the inside, even on a large window, by securing plastic sheeting to the window frame with duct tape, then tacking spare blankets, towels or other insulating material over the plastic.

Heavy plastic sheeting (or a camping tarp, a painter's drop cloth, or a small rug, in a pinch) can be tacked over the window from the outside to help keep out snow and rain. But in gusty winds there is not much point in trying to install an exterior cover unless the entire perimeter is held by trim such as strips of lath.

Another temporary solution is to duct tape a spare storm window or storm door insert over the opening. If you have all the storms in place providing double glazing, shift one to the broken window. If you have screen inserts, wrap them in plastic—even multiple layers of plastic garbage bags or something like Saran Wrap taped down to the screening.

When freeze-thaw weather cycles produce icicles you should carefully dislodge them from gutters, roof eaves, and elsewhere, even though they provide a sparkling show in the sunlight. Eventually, their weight may pull gutters and downspouts off the house. (That's aside from terrifying your dog or cat who happens to be in the vicinity when one lets go and crashes to the ground.)

Before heavy winter weather hits, you may want to tackle a few of the several projects that will prepare the outside of a building for winter's worst.

Siding. One of the most basic preventive measures is caulking exterior seams. Even if you do not take the time now to pull loose nails from bowed clapboards and set them back in position with longer nails or wood screws, at least cover the gaps left in siding with a water-repellent caulk. Silicone and polyurethane caulks (both of which are available as clear gels and in several colors) are well-suited to this job since they are flexible. If a clapboard continues to move a bit in the weather, for instance, a pliable, self-adhering caulk may have enough flexibility to keep the seam closed.

On brick siding, mortar joints are the weak link. When small cracks appear, water begins to enter, which hastens deterioration. The solution is called *repointing*—scraping out the old mortar and adding fresh material. You can increase the wall's weather resistance with a protective coating such as clear silicon sealer. (It will darken concrete, block, brick, and stone a shade or two but leave the natural texture and color gradations of the material intact.)

Paint. When a paint film is the outermost protective layer on a building, its condition often determines the amount of deterioration below. Of course, you can leave cracking, splitting, or peeling patches for warm-weather repairs. In the meantime, even a quick scraping to dislodge the loosest material, a brief sanding with rough sandpaper, and a quick, two-coat touch-up will help preserve the siding or trim beneath the paint.

Masonry steps and patios. Open seams between concrete steps, porches, patios, walks, and driveways abutting the house should be closed to prevent the powerful force of freezing water from lifting and cracking the masonry.

Close small gaps, say about ½ inch wide or less, with hydraulic cement—a dense mixture that swells as it hardens. On problem seams that continually reopen a liberal bead of flexible, waterproof caulking such as silicone or polyurethane may stand the best chance of keeping the seam sealed. Scrape out any loose material and brush away any dirt before applying a filler or sealer.

Water that enters through cracks in concrete will freeze in the ground during winter. This frost action produces "heaving"—like water expanding in ice cube trays as it freezes—with enough force to lift and break the slab. Patch now, or replace the entire slab later.

Windows and doors. Freezing rain and melting snow can clog gutters and disrupt shingles on the roof. They also can cause problems at the seams around windows and doors. The most exposed seam across the top of a window or door should be protected by a strip of metal or rubber known as cap flashing. Caulking the seam will help.

For a more complete fix, push the flashing back in place and cover any exposed edges with caulking. A complete repair requires that you first clean and dry the seam between window and house, and cover the joint with a flexible silicone or polyurethane caulk. Then pry the siding above the window or door away from the house, enough to insert new flashing beneath it.

Foundations. One common trouble spot on many types of buildings is the seam where a lot of different layers and materials come together—at the joint between foundation and wall. In many houses where the siding runs to near ground level, the transition between a masonry foundation and a wood-framed and sided wall is covered with only a slight overhang of siding.

Unfortunately, many houses have plumbing pipes or heat ducts or both located just inside this seam. Adding caulking may help some. But there are more complete solutions for this trouble spot.

In the Northeast many homeowners wrap exposed masonry foundations and a few courses of clapboards or shakes above in heavy-duty clear plastic. The top edge is secured to the house with lath or furring strips. Some lay batts of insulation beneath the plastic or pack in sawdust or some other insulator. Close up it's an unsightly solution, but it sure does work. The critical seam stays closed to the weather. And drifting snow, ice, and water produced in the drifts on warmer days do not contact the house.

Several types of products are designed to provide less complete but similar protection. For instance, Insul-Guard, manufactured by Trend Products,[1] is a relatively new system for covering and insulating this weak link. Kits are sold in 8- to 24-inch widths and include rigid foam insulating panels that are covered with light gray, hard fiberglass panels, flashing, and trim.

[1]Trend Products, P.O. Box 650, Keshena, WI 54135

You could fashion your own version of this two-stage covering by attaching rigid panels of insulating foam board over the exposed foundation and straight down the foundation wall. Above ground level, nail it to the house studs or wooden sill. Over masonry block walls use galvanized concrete nails and either a galvanized or nylon washer (about 1½ inch diameter placed approximately 16 inches on center in all directions). The washer grabs more surface area and increases holding power.

Below grade and over poured concrete foundations, use either a water-based adhesive or petroleum-based adhesive marked ''polystyrene-compatible.'' That means it won't dissolve the petroleum-based foam panels. Don't risk puncturing and disrupting the foundation waterproofing barrier by nailing below ground level.

Set the panels in place with dabs of the adhesive and set nails and washers added above-grade just slightly into the foam surface. Since foam board is not very attractive you will probably want to cover it with some type of stucco-like coating. A typical surface coating consists of liquid latex, cement, sand, and chopped fiberglass for reinforcement.

Winter Survival Kit
Tool and Materials to Have On Hand

You may know someone who is held in awe by neighbors because he is always prepared for every emergency. Faced with frozen pipes, power outages, sputtering furnaces, and virtually any type of lifeless home appliance, this former Boy Scout (their motto is ''Be prepared,'' after all) produces a small bag of spare parts and specialized tools. Implausible events follow, as the quintessential do-it-yourselfer examines your dead furnace and says something like, ''What this little baby needs is a new timer relay, a 1959 XYZ type, which I just happen to have in my bag.''

If only life's little winter emergencies could be solved so easily.

Unfortunately, preparing a special box of spare furnace belts, fuses, pipe solder—even a working flashlight—is the kind of foresight most do-it-yourselfers exhibit only in hindsight, after the emergency.

The following emergency kit is by no means complete. Experience dictates that a house combined with the natural forces of winter can produce a nearly infinite variety of problems. Also, too long a list can produce do-it-yourself inertia—a common syndrome in which no part of a job is done if the entire job seems too overwhelming.

But even if you put aside only one or two simple, inexpensive items, they just could be the ones that become invaluable at 2:00 A.M. some winter night when the furnace belt rips, the lights go out, or the pipes freeze.

☞ *Flashlights.* This is probably the most basic but elusive item in any winter emergency kit. It's basic because, of course, your emergencies inevitably take place at night. No one knows for sure why homes that practically sink into the ground under the weight of working flashlights during the day cannot produce a single working flashlight after dark.

Having lived through this paradox once too often, I finally found the paradox-proof tool. It's a rechargeable flashlight (that solves the dead battery problem), which stays plugged into a standard wall outlet. When the power is on, its light is off, and the battery charges. When the power fails the light comes on automatically using the battery power. It makes sense to keep it in an outlet near stairs for safety or near your bedroom. Once found, you can remove the unit from the outlet and use it as a portable light. Many such units, which cost about $15 to $20 in hardware stores, home centers, and mail-order catalogs such as Brookstone Hard-To-Find Tools, keep a charge for about an hour.

☑ *Nonelectric light.* For prolonged power outages there is no substitute for candles—for psychological comfort as well as light. Glass-globed hurricane lamps throw even more light, particularly if they have a metal reflector behind the wick. In a pinch, dig through your camping equipment. Kerosene lamps are bright enough to light an entire room temporarily.

☑ *Pipe equipment.* To resolder copper pipes in an emergency you'll need the following items: three or four elbow and tee fittings, a foot or two of pipe, a pipe cutter (although a hacksaw will work if you're careful), solder, flux (a paste that draws the solder into the pipe joint), and a propane torch. One common pitfall is running out of propane, a problem easily solved by acquiring a spare tank.

Short of soldering, there are a few things you can do to stem a small pipe leak until the plumber arrives. Tiny pin holes can sometimes be plugged with a lead pencil point. Leaks through split pipes can be stemmed by wrapping a piece of rubber or almost any firm but pliable material over the leak and clamping the patch in place. Try a few short lengths of automotive radiator hose (sliced apart to make a patch piece) held by adjustable band clamps that are used on car engine hoses.

☑ *Fire extinguishers.* Basic emergency equipment for every home should include an ABC-rated fire extinguisher. It can be used against any type of small fire (while someone else calls the fire department). Fires concealed in chimneys call for special equipment. Chimfex canisters (sold in many wood stove and fireplace outlets and mail-order catalogs for about $10) are about the size of a large road flare. Each one releases a massive volume of gas into the flue that will not support combustion. The advantage of Chimfex over liquid extinguishers is that its gases can follow the fire into the flue to reach inaccessible hot spots.

☑ *Generators.* A portable generator offers comprehensive backup for power failures. Generating capacity varies greatly (along with cost). But you should be able to find a unit rated approximately 2,000 watts and 5 horsepower that will run for a few hours without a fuel refill for about $600 or $700. Such a unit should make enough electricity to run a small heater, refrigerator, a few lights, and a few small appliances, depending on their specific wattage ratings.

☑ *Spare parts.* Extra pieces for crucial systems in the home also can be handy. In this category the key is to assemble in advance of a winter emergency the crucial cogs in the mechanical wheels that make your home habitable.

The most obvious spare parts are fuses. (Circuit breakers can be reset and do not require new parts when they trip.) Other valuable spares include furnace fan belts, which will put the main blower back into action, even though some heat will rise through the ducts anyway. Don't forget batteries for a portable radio so that you can tune in to find out about widespread power failures and the weather forecast.

☞ *Water.* If you have enough of warning, increase your supply from a gallon in the refrigerator to a bathtub full. With an adequate supply you'll be able to keep cooking and washing and refill toilet tanks to keep the drainage system active.

☞ *Wood heat supplies.* If you have to rely for emergency heat on your wood supply, remember that it may rely on an operating chainsaw, plus a modest supply of gas and oil fuel.

☞ *Salt.* Eventually, corrosive salt may pit masonry steps and walks. However, that future maintenance problem is a small price to pay for secure footing gained as salt eats through ice that can make for treacherous footing.

☞ *Caulk.* A tube or two of silicone or polyurethane caulk is handy to seal leaks around windows and doors and to serve as emergency putty when setting plastic into a window with broken glass.

☞ *Plastic film.* If winter storm damage breaks windows and you don't happen to have spare panes on hand (Is anyone that prepared?) heat-shrink plastic (or any plastic sheeting) is the next best thing. Heat-shrink kits sold for about $10 to $15 include double-face adhesive tape to set the film in place around the window frame. Applying heat from a hair dryer removes the wrinkles and shrinks the plastic to a tight fit.

☞ *Basics.* It almost goes without saying that it will be a lot easier to make temporary repairs from storm and ice damage if you have an assortment of nails, screws, bolts, and such on hand. Also, consider adding a roll of duct tape (the wide, very strong gray tape), which can hold broken glass together, seal drafts, and serve many other purposes.

Safety
and
Security

Twenty Three

SECURITY AND FIRE PROTECTION

Camouflaged Home Security
Securing Your Home When You're Away

Burglars who think nothing of helping themselves to everything of value in your home may be low-life, mean-spirited misfits. If only they were all as stupid as they are crooked.

When there is a pile of daily newspapers by the front door, overgrown grass in the yard, empty garbage cans, no car in the driveway, and no lights on at night, even a real idiot of a burglar will get the message that you're away from home. And then, even beefy, expensive locks might not be able to keep out a thief who can leisurely unhinge a door or cut out a window pane without fear of interruption.

Of course, it is important to protect your possessions, even though insurance may help you avoid a financial loss. But it can be even more important to protect your sense of privacy. That's not covered by any policy.

Whether you live in a mansion behind security fences or in a tiny apartment behind a single, deadbolt lock, at least it's your place, where you can stroll around in your underwear, eat cold pizza for breakfast, and impersonate Sinatra's voice in the shower.

That unique, secure privacy may be your greatest loss in a burglary. Somehow, the antique bureau from your grandmother's house—the one where you store wonderful, secret things from your childhood—may never seem quite as wonderful or private after its contents have been tossed about by a burglar. Even if you own little of great financial value, you have something precious to protect.

It is easiest to preserve privacy and security in an active home, buzzing with lights and radios and people coming and going. That kind of activity makes the home a poor risk for burglars. But if you are able to take a few days of vacation now and again, the empty home you leave behind will become a prime target for burglars. And the longer you're away, the more obvious your absence is likely to become.

So here are some suggestions for creating a lived-in image in an empty home.

Closing the house. It's a mistake to hide away every common sign of daily life. Certainly, you should lock up before leaving. But if there is usually a rake leaning against the garage, or a sprinkler in the front yard, leave them there. Don't pull down all the shades. If the house looks obviously closed up as you pull away, it will look obviously unoccupied to a burglar.

Opposite: In case you don't carry around the automatic garage door transmitter, or if you lock it in the car, this unit, made by Genie Home Products (3040 W. Market St., Akron, OH 44313), can be mounted by the garage, and programmed to operate any brand of door—without the portable transmitter.

House-sitters. The most realistic lived-in look is made by trusted friends who stay in your home while you're away. Most home burglars don't operate like street muggers. They tend to avoid confrontations. So if your home is occupied, they are likely to search for an easier target.

House-watchers. Neighbors can help by simulating at least some of your activities. Aside from walking over and physically checking the doors and windows once in a while, they could park a car in your driveway, put garbage in your trash cans, pick up your mail. Maybe one of the neighbor's kids could mow your lawn. The point is for your friends to do some of the things you would do if you were home—particularly things that are obvious from the outside.

Police-watchers. Some local police departments have the capacity to increase the frequency at which a patrol car travels past your home, if you let them know when you are going away. But aside from police and trusted friends, you should not advertise your absence.

Light timers. You can handle after-dark simulations with a few inexpensive 24-hour timers. The small units are timed switches that plug into wall outlets. Lights, radios, and televisions plugged into the timers then can be programmed to turn on and off according to your normal schedule—lights out downstairs at eleven, for instance, while bedroom lights upstairs go on at the same time.

Phone call diverters. A clever thief can bypass your attempts at subterfuge by dialing your phone number. If the phone rings and rings, day or night, he can confirm that no one is home. You can break a burglar's direct line inside the home by installing an answering machine. The burglar may never reach you in-person. But he can't be sure that no one is home. Call forwarding, a phone company service available for a monthly charge in most areas, can have the same effect by transferring incoming calls

This compact box can be built into the house wall to accept deliveries when no one is home. The Sears Package Minder tips out to provide a box for mail or packages without providing access to the house—whether you happen to be there or not.

from your line to another number, for instance, a neighbor who might agree to answer your calls for a few days. Another obvious option is to have an unlisted phone number.

Locks. Strong locking hardware is an important safeguard—for appearance sake, and to make entry more difficult. Dead bolts for doors, reinforced door jambs, locks for sliding glass doors, screws to join the top and bottom sash of double-hung windows, all can present time-consuming obstacle's to burglars.

Safeguarding obvious targets. In most cases, burglars are looking for portable goods that can be easily sold—items such as VCRs, televisions, stereo equipment, cameras, and home computers. At a minimum, make sure you have recorded serial numbers from such equipment. This can help the police to recover the items if they are stolen, and may be important in settling an insurance claim.

Although many homeowners think they can find a perfect hiding place for valuables, too often, they can't. It's a burglar's business to know about those places, after all. Jewelry and other small, precious items might be best protected in a safe deposit box at your bank.

Professional help. Most police forces, even in small towns, now have a crime prevention unit. On a small force it may be one particular officer who can offer expert generic advice on security systems, locks, and other burglary prevention methods. Since crime also is their business, it pays to seek their advice.

Smoke Detector Checks
Reliable Warnings From the First Signs of Fire

For about $15 you can buy the most effective, reliable long-term protection against one of the most lethal threats to life and property. Fifteen dollars is the average cost of a smoke detector, a modest price for the key to residential fire safety, and about $10 less than the average cost when smoke detectors were introduced in the early 1970s.

Most consumers know how important this protection is. Close to 75 percent of American homes already have at least one smoke detector. But the U.S. Fire Administration (USFA) and other groups estimate that one-third to one-half do not work. Some units may be worn out or clogged with dust. Others may have dead batteries. Many have purposely been disabled to stop the occasional shrill blast brought on by a piece of burned toast or a brief puff-back from the fireplace.

Whatever the cause, such gaps in residential fire safety are partly responsible for about 6,000 deaths (more than three-quarters in the home), 100,000 injuries, and $7 billion of property damage from fires every year. (The United States has the highest fire death rate per capita of all industrialized Western countries, according to the USFA.)

Typical smoke detectors are simple to install, requiring only a screwdriver and about 5 minutes for the job. They are simple to maintain, requiring only a push on the test button once a month and a battery check once a year. But easy installation and easy maintenance may be part of the problem: Smoke detectors are also easy to forget about.

FIRESTOP FRAMING

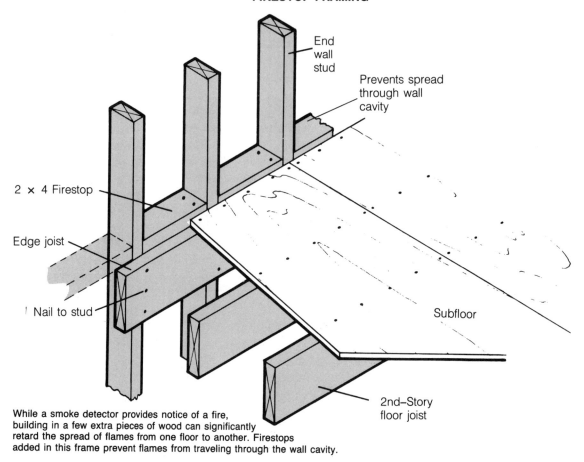

End wall stud

Prevents spread through wall cavity

2 × 4 Firestop

Edge joist

Nail to stud

Subfloor

2nd–Story floor joist

While a smoke detector provides notice of a fire, building in a few extra pieces of wood can significantly retard the spread of flames from one floor to another. Firestops added in this frame prevent flames from traveling through the wall cavity.

But even the $60 cost of buying four brand new detectors (enough to protect most homes thoroughly), pales next to the cost of replacing the average house. And detectors also protect lives that cannot be replaced. A number of studies by the USFA, the National Fire Protection Agency (NFPA), and other groups have shown that smoke detectors are one of the best ways to prevent fire deaths.

In fact, many states and countries now require that all housing include smoke detectors. But if you are in the minority and still do not have smoke detectors, consider this fact from a NFPA study: People in homes without smoke detectors are twice as likely to die in a home fire than people in similar circumstances who have them.

If you have one or more operating smoke detectors, the ear-splitting sounds they emit are likely to be the first and most important warning of a fire. The International Association of Fire Chiefs (IAFC) reports that detectors provide the first warning of a fire 60 percent of the time when a fire erupts at night. Night fires tend to be the most deadly, since these blazes are often slow developing, smoldering fires that break out after everyone is asleep.

Early warning is crucial because the longer the delay in discovering a fire, the more deadly the consequences. One NFPA study shows that 63 percent of overnight fire fatalities occur when it takes more than 20 minutes to discover the fire. And two-thirds of those fatalities occur when it takes more than 40 minutes to discover the fire.

Smoke detectors have another built-in benefit. Of the three consequences of a home fire—loss of life, loss of property, and personal injury—detectors are best at saving lives. (Sprinkler systems, which are about 20 times more costly than smoke detector systems, are best at protecting property.) The NFPA has found that smoke detectors cut property loss by only 20 percent and reduce the risk of injury by only 5 percent. This small risk reduction seems to be the only shortcoming of early warning, which also provides occupants with a chance to fight the fire, a potentially dangerous activity that increases the chance of injury.

But the lifesaving potential of smoke detectors can be short-circuited by mechanical problems and old age. Like everything else, smoke detectors can simply wear out. The NFPA reports a failure rate of between 16 and 30 percent of detectors bought since 1974. Many units can be tested by pushing a button mounted on the detector surface. Some may have to be triggered by holding a candle nearby, for instance. It is easy enough to find out if detectors are working. But the percentage of owners who test their detectors monthly has dropped from 48 percent in 1977 to under 40 percent in the most recent NFPA surveys.

A fresh battery may bring a dead detector back to life. But after 5 or 10 years of service, springing for a new $15 detector is not an extravagant investment.

New smoke detectors should bear the label of a testing lab such as Underwriters Laboratories. "Hard-wired" detectors may be powered by the house electrical system with battery back up. "Stand-alone" units that do not require wiring are powered by batteries alone.

Detectors should be installed on every level of a home, high on the walls or on ceilings in centralized, open areas such as hallways where smoke is more likely to spread from floor to floor. Since most fatal fires occur at night, it is important to locate detectors in halls just outside bedroom doors.

Although smoke detectors are easy to install, it can be more difficult to plan an efficient but effective network of detectors throughout the house. In many areas the best source of fire prevention and safety information, your local fire department, can offer practical installation advice. Some departments even have personnel who make house calls.

This is why home insurance policies cover 80 percent of your home's value—because when everything else goes, the masonry foundation remains. The site is a stark reminder of the importance of installing an inexpensive smoke detector.

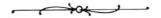

Electrical Safety
Easing the Worries of Wiring

A surprising number of adults who think nothing of zipping down a highway at 65 miles an hour about 2 feet away from complete strangers doing the same thing in the opposite direction are apprehensive about changing light bulbs. They are completely paranoid about electricity.

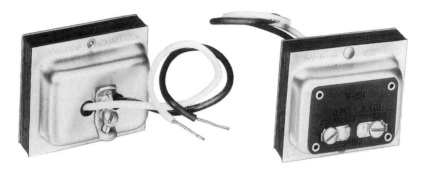

Installing bell systems is one of the projects most consumers can handle. The electrical power is stepped down to a low voltage with a transformer such as this Nutone model.

These people do have a point, even if they take it to extremes. Unlike painting, refinishing furniture, and other cosmetic home improvement projects, electrical work has a very small margin for error. Painting mistakes, for example, may be a little messy and increase your cleanup time. But electrical mistakes can be dangerous—even lethal. So some apprehension is healthy.

But an exaggerated fear of electrical shock keeps many do-it-yourselfers from making basic electrical repairs, outlined and illustrated in detail in many how-to books, such as the ''Basic Wiring'' entry in the Time-Life series. Pictures do help. But the biggest roadblock is fear, even though this work is probably less dangerous than driving a car. It's safer as long as you follow the most basic rule of turning off the power before you start. The damage is also lessened by the stringent, code-controlled safeguards built into modern home electrical systems.

Before you tackle any basic electrical project you should have at least a basic understanding of how residential electricity works. It can be a little confusing because you don't see electricity in your home the way you see paneling or paint or water coming out of a tap. You see the results of what electrical power can do—lighting lights and powering blenders.

But the house electrical system is, in a broad way, like the plumbing system. Wires in the wall carry power through the house the way plumbing pipes carry water. Big pipes carry more water than little pipes, and thick wires carry more power than thin wires.

Just as water is fed to fixtures under pressure (if not, it might never arrive), electrical force, called voltage, feeds electricity to appliances and lamps. Generally, the power is pushed along "hot" wires, normally covered by black-colored insulation. The power is like a stream of water that shoots out of a tap. But once you use the power to light a light or run an appliance motor it loses its "pressure" the same way water does in the sink.

Water completes its circuit (back to the ground where it came from) through drain lines. It no longer has any pressure. Electricity completes its circuit along "neutral" wires, normally white-colored. Normal household voltage that feeds outlets, lamps, and most appliances is rated at 120. A more powerful 220 line may be used (along with very heavy wiring and special plugs and outlets) to feed appliances such as electric furnaces and stoves that use a lot of power.

An ampere (usually shortened to "amp") is the unit of measure for the amount of electricity flowing along the wires, like the number of gallons of water in the sink, regardless of pressure. Circuits, circuit breakers, and fuses all are rated in amps, for instance, a 15-amp circuit protected by a 15-amp fuse. It can help to think of amperage as a measure of capacity. There are only so many lights and appliances that you can run on any one circuit. So if you have wiring in a circuit rated at 15-amps, don't re-place a blown 15-amp fuse with a spare 20-amp fuse. It would let more power into the circuit than the circuit could handle safely.

With some sense of all the activity behind the outlets and switches, you should realize how important it is to observe the most obvious wiring rule: Turn off the power before you begin. This is easy to do with a lamp; just unplug it. To turn off the power at a wall outlet, though, you have to trip the right circuit breaker or unscrew the right fuse—the one protecting that circuit. Even though many fuse boxes have "maps" or "keys" on the door showing which circuit feeds what part of the house, there is always room for confusion. Do the hall outlets near the kitchen go on and off with the circuit breaker marked "kitchen" or with the breaker marked "dining"? Was the hall wiring added after the house was built, or included on a different circuit altogether?

To be sure it is safe to proceed—absolutely safe and sure—do two things. First, plug a lamp or a radio into the outlet and turn it on. When the light goes off or the music stops as you work through the rows of circuit breakers, you'll get positive feedback that you have tripped the correct breaker. Even then, you should touch bare wires with a voltage tester before touching with your hand.

Voltage testers are simple, inexpensive tools consisting of two insulated wire leads with metal points and a small neon bulb. On an outlet or switch, for instance, touch one tester lead to the terminal screw holding the black wire, and the other lead to the screw holding the white wire. (If there are two sets of black and white wires you should test both of them.) If the tester bulb lights when both tester leads are contacting the black and white wires, the wiring is still "hot." You'll have to check the breakers or fuses again.

Killing the power supply by unscrewing fuses and tripping breakers, and then double-checking with a voltage tester, should ease your wiring worries and provide the peace of mind you need to proceed.

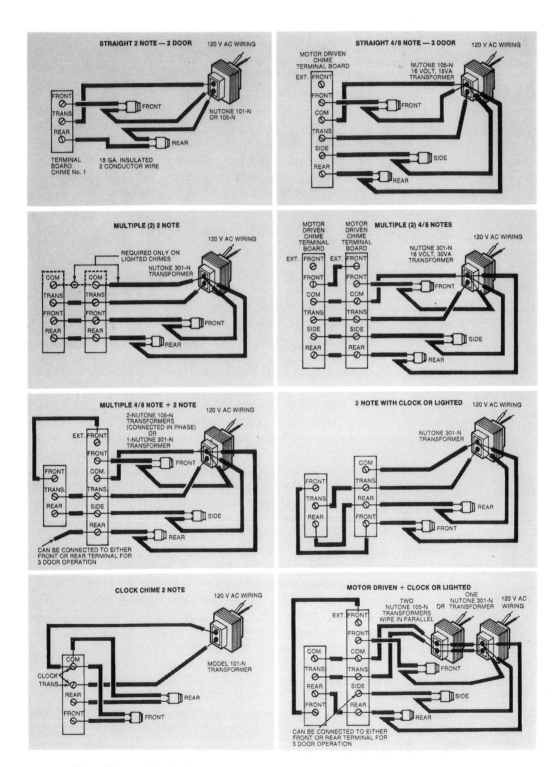

Internal house wiring for low-voltage bell systems can be installed to ring one or many bells. Nutone

Electrical Power Fluctuations
Regulating the Flow of Power

Electricity appears to be an all or nothing proposition. Either the lights and appliances go on, or they don't. And since they respond to a flip of the switch almost all of the time, most of us take electricity for granted. But power can be supplied in several different ways and at different costs. To manage the flow of power effectively, most utility companies have taken steps to organize themselves in cooperative groups and to offer their customers several ways to save money and restrict power use during peak use periods.

Power fluctuations rarely are severe enough to blow fuses or trip circuit breakers. But when work on one part of the electrical system is required, it is helpful to have a house wiring diagram, or even simple tags saying which circuits control different rooms of the home.

Demand for electricity normally increases during the summer as people turn on their air conditioners. During the peak use period from noon until 8:00 P.M. Monday through Friday, the combined demand from homes, businesses, government agencies, and other electric users can put a strain on the generating capacity of some utility companies.

But blackouts (total losses of power) and brownouts (purposeful power reductions to prevent blackouts) are unusual events these days. One reason is that utility companies have learned that standing alone may invite disaster, such as the widespread power failure of November 1966 dubbed "The Great Blackout." It darkened most of the Northeast and two Canadian provinces. Many areas were without power a day or more.

Now, utilities such as Potomac Electric Power Company (PEPCO), which serves almost two million people in and around Washington, DC, are part of power pools—groups of utility companies that routinely shuttle power among themselves to meet extraordinary demands.

That's what happened during PEPCO's last 5-percent voltage reduction, which occurred in January 1985. Unusually cold weather through the mid-Atlantic and southern states caused a surge in demand by electric resistance heaters. Also, several of the eight utility companies who, with PEPCO, are part of the Pennsylvania, New Jersey, Maryland (PJM) Interconnection, were caught short with generating equipment out of service undergoing routine maintenance. In order to stabilize the system, PEPCO sent power to other utilities in the PJM power pool, and had to cut power by 5 percent to its own customers.

Such cutbacks worry many consumers who attribute (usually incorrectly) a wide variety of household electrical problems to voltage reductions. These include fluttering or dimming lights, a slightly shrunken television picture, unpredictable behavior by home computers, and various glitches in electronic phones, microwave oven clocks, and many other appliances that use sensitive microprocessors.

Utility companies, appliance manufacturers, and electrical engineers say voltage reductions are not normally the cause of these ghosts in the machines. A recent survey of utility customer service reports in Ohio found that 80 percent of the glitches were due to problems in house wiring. For instance, any appliance with an induction motor (refrigerators, washers, dryers, air conditioners, and others) draws the most power when it starts. These power peaks can cause power valleys elsewhere in the house.

Electrical engineers at General Electric (GE) say that 5-percent voltage reductions do not harm appliance motors, and, in fact, probably go unnoticed by consumers. A 5-percent reduction on a standard 120-volt appliance is only 6 volts, leaving 114 volts for operation. Problems do not occur until voltage on a 120-volt machine drops to 105 volts, almost a 13 percent reduction, according to GE engineers.

While appliance motors may not be damaged, Joe Vandenberg, of the Edison Electric Institute says, "Problems with the increasing number of appliances controlled by microprocessors are becoming more noticeable." The problems arise because sensitive microprocessor computer chips can be adversely affected by the normal amount of very small peaks and valleys in power supplied to homes by utilities. However, such variations generally create no more than an inconvenience, jolting a microwave clock timer from A.M. to P.M. for instance.

Without buying expensive, whole-house electric backup systems consisting of standby generators and other equipment, there is not much you can do to prevent about half of these microprocessor problems—those caused by power valleys. Such backup systems are employed by large computer firms, hospitals, and other groups that cannot afford even minor power drops which in a household might do no more than occasionally microwave a T.V. dinner into oblivion.

On the other hand, small power surges, or peaks, in homes can be handled by relatively simple devices generally called surge suppressers. Typically, such devices are built into independently fused outlet strips that are routinely sold with home computer systems.

While utility companies control the flow of power to your home that may occasionally jolt a microprocessor, consumers can, to some extent, control how that power is used and how much they pay for it. Generally, these plans involve financial benefits for customers who agree to restrict power use during peak periods.

PEPCO, for instance, has three such programs. Your utility may as well. The most unusual is a new program called PEPCO Kilowatchers Club in which the utility places a radio-controlled switch on customer's air conditioners. Customers in the program agree to allow PEPCO to broadcast a signal to their air conditioners that automatically turns off the compressor. (The air conditioner fan remains on.) The computer-controlled radio signal turns off the compressor for 13 minutes each half hour over the 8 hour peak period (noon to 8:00 P.M.), Monday through Friday excluding holidays. The signals are sent on no more than 15 days of high electrical demand during 5 summer months.

Consumers receive a $7 per month credit above the normal savings for using less electricity. Approximately 30,000 PEPCO customers have signed up for the program, which the utility plans to expand to 100,000 customers.

Many customers of PEPCO and most other utilities can also save money with a much milder form of energy cycling by switching to special electric meters and time-of-use rates. Although the particulars vary from one utility to another, the basic idea is that you are charged less for power used during off-peak periods.

Residential customers don't participate in, but do benefit from, another type of power management program offered by many utilities. Currently, about 100 high-volume commercial customers, such as hospitals and large businesses who have backup generating equipment, have voluntary agreements with PEPCO to restrict power use during peak periods.

For instance, on a very hot afternoon when demand for electricity grows, PEPCO can order a curtailment period during which large-volume customers cut back their power use. This reduces the overall demand on generating capacity. (Last summer demand once reached 4,700 megawatts out of PEPCO's total generating capacity of 5,375 megawatts.)

Some of the high-volume commercial users even shut off all power from PEPCO for 4 to 6 hours, substituting their own generating equipment. They receive a financial credit for the curtailment while bringing their crucial backup equipment on line, which allows testing and fine tuning.

"The combined electric savings of all these power management programs will eventually save about 400 megawatts a year," says Nancy Moses of PEPCO, "approximately the capacity of a new generating plant, which PEPCO will not have to build."

Twenty Four

ENVIRONMENTAL CONCERNS

Building a Nontoxic House
Designs and Materials to Make a Healthful Home

A healthy home environment can be threatened by asbestos, radon, formaldehyde outgassing from plywood, and other sources. This cumulative threat from a growing number of pollutants poses a significant health risk to a broad spectrum of the population.

Yet pollutants have been uncovered, publicized, and dealt with gradually, one at a time. But now some architects and home builders are thinking about home designs that avoid built-in pollution problems and make their houses healthy places to live.

Most of the research on air quality to date has concentrated on industrial and outdoor pollutants. In fact, the American Council for an Energy-Efficient Economy reported recently that for every three dollars of federal research expenditures on outdoor pollution, one cent is spent on indoor pollution research.

While no one would argue that outdoor air quality issues such as acid rain are not worthy of investigation, there is growing concern over research priorities. For example, some environmental researchers say that in the mid 1980s the Environmental Protection Agency (EPA) missed the boat on radon, a naturally occurring gas that seeps into homes and may cause as many as 20,000 cancer-related deaths per year. (It took from 1984, when radon in residences surfaced as a major threat, until September 1988 when a seven-state EPA survey finally led to a national health advisory recommending radon tests in all homes.)

At a conference of groups particularly interested in indoor air quality, such as the American Lung Association (ALA), Dr. Thomas J. Godar, Chairman of the ALA's National Air Conservation Commission, described the "sick building" syndrome that is often most noticeable in office buildings.

Dr. Godar said widespread problems including nasal congestion, sneezing, coughing, headache, fatigue, nausea, eye irritation, and more serious ailments have been attributed to contaminants that have been present in the workplace for a long time. "They have become a greater problem in recent years because newer buildings are sealed and do not have windows that may be opened,", he said.

At the conference, sponsored in large part by a grant from Honeywell Corporation, the ALA announced that it will urge Congress to specifically designate the Environmental Protection Agency, which already administers the Clean Air Act covering outdoor air pollution, as the agency with primary jurisdiction for research on the health effects of indoor air pollution. Currently, almost 20 government agencies participate to varying degrees in different types of indoor air quality work through an interagency task force.

Stated simply, indoor air quality is important because most people spend most of their time indoors. The ALA reports that the average American is inside 90 percent of the time, and more than half that time at home. While many office buildings are completely sealed, insulation, vapor barriers, and other features necessary to keep costly heating and cooling inside residences also trap pollutants, for example, by-products of the 45 different aerosol products found in the average household.

It matters what you bring into the house. But it also matters what the builder brought in to build the house. At The Masters Corporation, a small architecture and construction firm in New Canaan, Connecticut, the staff has adopted a whole-house approach to improving the indoor environment. They are reexamining every major residential building component. Now, before asking whether or not it is strong enough, or energy-efficient enough, or durable enough, or good-looking enough, they ask a more fundamental question: is it a polluter? They have identified hundreds of materials and products that are, and found many nonpolluting substitutes.

Paul Lytle, principal architect and cofounder of the firm, acknowledges that some of the alternatives do add to the cost of construction. "Going all-out from the ground up on new house nontoxic construction might add 20 to 25 percent to job costs," says Lytle, "and 10 to 15 percent on remodeling projects and additions." His rationale for the additional expense is simple: It's worth it. Apparently, buyers agree with him.

Since the firm devoted itself solely to nontoxic design and construction several years ago, their business has quadrupled, their staff has tripled, and they are booked almost 3 years in advance.

Lytle says, "Frankly, I'm surprised that with all the attention being given to indoor air quality—front-page stores on radon, formaldehyde outgassing in many building products, and other subjects—that there aren't more firms in this field."

Some consumers are under the mistaken impression that nontoxic, healthful homes have to look like hospitals. This design by Paul Lytle, an architect at the Masters Corp., a Connecticut firm specializing in healthful house design, incorporates nontoxic building materials to provide a clean indoor environment.

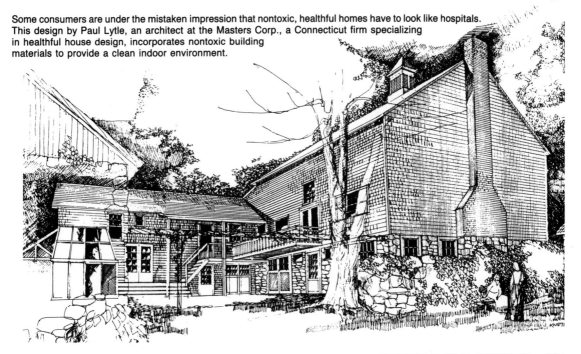

And the firm's houses do not look like antiseptic hospitals. The work of Mr. Lytle, the principal designer who has a Masters of Architecture from Yale, ranges from updated colonial townhouse projects to distinctive, modern houses that have been published in *Architectural Record Houses of the Year, Architectural Digest*, and elsewhere.

The firm now incorporates many nontoxic features in its designs that are workable in most types of residential construction. For instance, to reduce formaldehyde outgassing from composite board, and, to a lesser degree, from plywood used in wood frame sheathing, the firm uses diagonal, tongue-and-groove pine planking. (This material and application predates plywood and is commonly found under siding and finished floors in older homes.)

To prevent infiltration of soil gas containing radon and other contaminants, a ground sheet, called Soilflex, is laid. Foundation walls are covered with a wire mesh, called Enkadrain, that relieves hydrostatic pressure. In addition to providing the conventional advantage of a sound foundation free of water damage, this product is selected because it helps to keep cellars and crawl spaces dry, eliminating a breeding ground for biological contaminants, including mold and mildew. Other measures include installing advanced air filters, capable of removing 99.9 percent of airborne particulates, and applying air and acoustic barriers between house and garage to seal off combustion emissions.

Indoor Air Quality
Clean Air Behind Windows and Doors
Closed for Winter

When someone says, "Let's get a breath of fresh air," it is likely that they mean to go outdoors, not from one room of the house to another. That is the obvious thing to do, particularly in winter when houses are sealed up to conserve heat and indoor air is most stagnant.

Unlike a good bottle of wine, indoor air does not improve with age. As contaminants trapped indoors accumulate, the air can become unhealthy enough to trigger or complicate medical problems such as allergies, headaches, dizziness, nausea, rashes, eye and throat irritation, and other symptoms. Long-term exposure to some forms of unhealthy indoor air (with elevated levels of radon over time, for instance), can even be lethal.

There are two general components to the potentially harmful quality of your indoor environment (both at home and at work): the number of contaminants and the time of exposure. Contamination is a complex issue due to the great variety of building materials, floor plans, building locations, heating systems and other variables in homes and home life—plus the large number of potentially dangerous products we use there. For instance, the American Lung Association (ALA) reports that average households contain 45 different aerosol products.

A case of sneezing and watery eyes might be traced to a particular combination of household cleaners, for instance, or to fungus breeding in a humidifier, or to one of hundreds of other indoor sources of contaminants.

The second component, time of exposure, has a way of magnifying the effects of even a modest amount of dust, mold, formaldehyde gas from the glue in plywood and particleboard, or some other irritant. Exposure is a key factor because the average American is inside 90 percent of the time, and more than half that time at home, according to ALA studies.

Indoor air quality can be improved. But the improvements can take many forms, from simple do-it-yourself projects to professional installations of complex and expensive equipment. At home, your senses are usually the best indicators of most indoor pollution. Trust them. For instance, when mold and mildew start to trigger watery eyes and sneezing and coughing, it doesn't much matter exactly how much mold is present.

Another possible red flag is sweating windows. Excess condensation could be produced if a humidifier on a hot-air furnace, for instance, is set too high, or if you do not exhaust steamy air produced by hot showers or cooking. But wet windows are likely to indicate that your house or apartment is pretty tight. This is good news financially, since a tight building conserves heat. But it may be bad news environmentally, if contaminants that might be exhausted or at least diffused in summer when windows and doors are opened, are trapped inside along with the heat.

However, two of the most dangerous indoor pollutants are also the most insidious just because they do not trigger early warning signals in your body.

Radon. Unsafe levels of this odorless, colorless, naturally-occurring, cancer-causing gas seep from the ground into as many as 8 million American homes, according to estimates by the Environmental Protection Agency. To determine if you have elevated levels of radon indoors, buy a radon test kit, place the small canister in your home for a few days, then send it back to the manufacturer for analysis. These kits sell for $10 to $15.

If a short-term screening test uncovers clearly unsafe or even questionable results it is wise to buy a long-term test canister (about $25) that is left in place for a month or more. A longer exposure period may provide a better indication of the overall radon level.

Reducing or eliminating indoor radon can be a complicated business. It may involve simple, inexpensive projects, such as sealing cracks in foundations, or elaborate installations of foundation vacuum and vent systems costing from several hundred to several thousand dollars. Given that financial risk (and the potentially lethal health risk) you just shouldn't move into a home without first making a radon test. (See ''Radon Pollution'' and ''Radon Testing Business'' in this chapter.)

Asbestos. This fibrous material can be found in many roofing and flooring products. But its most common and troublesome residential use is as pipe and furnace insulation. Actually, it does the job very well. A health threat arises only when wrapping around heating pipes, for example, becomes loose and torn so that asbestos fibers are released into the air. The fibers do not deteriorate. They can become lodged in lung tissue, which may eventually lead to serious or deadly disease.

While simply sweeping up the loose fibers seems to make sense, disturbing the material in any way is, in fact, the worst thing you can do. Vacuuming, for instance, can spread fibers into carpets and drapes, to be released back into the air years later. Unfortunately, their lethal potential does not deteriorate with age.

HOW INDOOR AIR POLLUTANTS AFFECT THE BODY

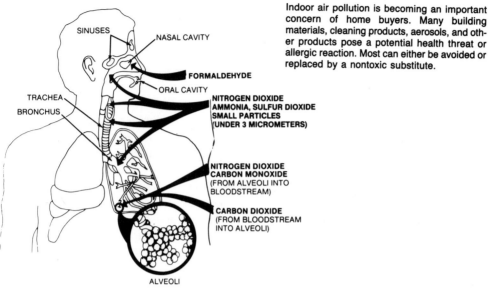

Indoor air pollution is becoming an important concern of home buyers. Many building materials, cleaning products, aerosols, and other products pose a potential health threat or allergic reaction. Most can either be avoided or replaced by a nontoxic substitute.

SINUSES
NASAL CAVITY
FORMALDEHYDE
ORAL CAVITY
TRACHEA
BRONCHUS
NITROGEN DIOXIDE
AMMONIA, SULFUR DIOXIDE
SMALL PARTICLES
(UNDER 3 MICROMETERS)
NITROGEN DIOXIDE
CARBON MONOXIDE
(FROM ALVEOLI INTO
BLOODSTREAM)
CARBON DIOXIDE
(FROM BLOODSTREAM
INTO ALVEOLI)
ALVEOLI

Sulfur dioxide, ammonia, acrolein (in tobacco smoke), formaldehyde	Sensory irritants
Sulfur dioxide, ammonia and allergens	Bronchial constrictors
Nitrogen dioxide and small particles	Pulmonary irritants
Carbon monoxide	Asphyxiant
Carbon dioxide	Discomfort indicator

The most thorough and safest removal method is to hire specialized asbestos removal contractors. But if the cost of this exercise is prohibitive (and it could amount to thousands of dollars in some cases), loose, ragged asbestos insulation can, as a stop-gap measure, be sealed in heavy, spiral-wrapped tin foil with seams sealed by duct tape.

Carbon monoxide. This by-product of combustion is regulated outdoors where it exists as a pollutant coming from vehicle exhaust pipes. Indoors, it is produced by unvented kerosene heaters, tobacco smoke, improperly vented gas appliances, wood stoves, and other sources.

Although pollution is one reason consumers might choose to avoid kerosene heaters, which do offer relatively low-cost supplemental heat, an even greater concern is the hazard of fire. According to the Consumer Product Safety Commission (CPSC), which continues to study the emissions and fire safety of kerosene heaters, 1985 fire statistics for kerosene heaters shows that 2,800 fires and 140 deaths were directly linked to the heaters. Despite technical improvements, such as tip-over safety switches and wrap-around grills, many localities have banned completely the use of any liquid-fueled heaters.

Formaldehyde. Health problems resulting from improperly balanced installations of urea formaldehyde foam insulation (UFFI) eventually put an end to the pumped-in urea foam insulation industry. But formaldehyde gas can leach out of the glue in many building materials, including some types of plywood and particleboard, which are used for sheathing, rough flooring, furniture, and cabinets.

This process, called *outgassing*, does become less troublesome with time as building materials give off less and less of the gas. To avoid the problem on new construction projects, buy plywood and particleboard a few months before building starts and let it outgas in a shed, for instance. Or, you can buy specially-graded, low-formaldehyde plywood that was developed to meet U.S. Department of Housing and Urban Development emission standards for manufactured homes. Grade stamps on these panels include specifications such as, "formaldehyde emission 0.2ppm," or a statement referring to the emission standard itself, such as "conforms to HUD 24 CFR Part 3280."

Microbes and fungi. Although certain viruses and bacteria are a common, even inevitable, component of indoor air, excesses can cause problems ranging from bad odors to serious health problems. Often, the problem can be traced to a breeding ground of stagnant air and water, for instance, improperly maintained air conditioners, humidifiers, dehumidifiers, and furnaces. Change filters in such appliances regularly (or clean washable filters). Each heating season it is wise to take apart, scrub, and disinfect the parts of a humidifier that add moisture through a hot-air furnace system.

There are preliminary indications that fiberglass heating and air-conditioning ducts (they have replaced more expensive metal ducts in some new homes) are also a breeding ground, since their rough interior surfaces can trap dust and debris.

Although many contaminants exist, there are basically two general approaches to dealing with the nonlethal varieties. One is to crack a few windows once in a while, run exhaust fans in kitchen and baths, and generally let the house "breathe" a little—even if you have to turn up the heat on occasion. Decent indoor air is well worth the price of a few extra gallons of fuel oil, cubic feet of gas, or kilowatts of electricity.

The other approach, which is finding less favor as memories of the energy crisis fade, is to keep the house closed, caulked, weatherstripped, and sealed as tightly as possible, then manage the exchange and cleaning of indoor air mechanically. This is a high-tech, generally high-cost approach.

In slightly leaky older homes, the air-exchange rate (the time it takes the volume of air inside to be replaced with a fresh supply) might be one full air exchange per hour. In more modern, tightly constructed homes the rate may be only 0.3 or 0.2 air changes per hour. Too much moisture is a common problem in tight homes. Occupants may even have to run dehumidifiers (extra appliance number one). To remove impurities that cannot flow out of open windows, an electrostatic air cleaner may be necessary (extra appliance number two).

A typical machine attaches to the air-supply ducts of a furnace. Impurities in the air are forced against a sieve of electrically charged metal plates, then washed off the plates and out of the air-supply system. If you have a specific medical problem, such as an allergic reaction to excessive dust or mold, ask the air cleaner manufacturer for a fact sheet describing exactly what percentage of various impurities are removed by the equipment. You can ask your doctor if removing that percentage will help or even eliminate your symptoms, which would make the equipment a very worthwhile investment.

To provide a continuous supply of fresh air in a very tight building, some form of heat exchange ventilator may be needed as well (extra appliance number three). Generally, these machines are designed to capture some heat from warm stale air being exhausted, and transfer it to cold fresh air entering from the outside.

But these systems have some drawbacks. For instance, they don't function during a power outage. In winter, the moisture in warm air may freeze at the exit point, clogging the system. Also, cross-flow leakage of warm air exhaust, seeping into the cold air intake, may reach 25 to even 40 percent on some units, defeating the purpose of the system.

Two years ago, Consumer Reports even compared the costs of the low-tech and high-tech approaches. They calculated that the cost of warming 20 degree Fahrenheit air entering through an open window (enough to get a minimal 0.3 air exchange rate per hour), to 70 degrees Fahrenheit, and compared this to the cost of using an efficient exchanger, plus the cost of warming the exchanged air to 70 degrees Fahrenheit. The window method cost $19 per month: the exchanger $14 a month. The report concluded that even with the most efficient heat exchangers, it could take from 20 to 40 years of energy saving before you would finally break even on your air exchanger investment (not including air cleaners and other equipment).

Compared to simply cracking a window, spending a thousand dollars or more and running three or four appliances to maintain air quality in a tight building, all for the sake of saving a modest amount of fuel, may not make much sense.

Pesticides Report
Evaluating the Risks and Regulations

Before a pesticide can be sold it is tested and evaluated, a process that may take several years. After it has proven to meet standards for effectiveness and safety it is approved for use by the Environmental Protection Agency (EPA), and given an EPA registration number. But what seems like an effective safety screen is, in many cases, providing consumers with a false sense of security about pesticide safety.

Since the pesticide registration process was formalized in 1947, there has been a fundamental change in our understanding of how pesticides work. This has led to a complete revamping of the tests and standards used to determine pesticide safety. At the end of 1988 Congress again wrestled with this issue: that hundreds of untested pesticide chemicals remain on the market.

Most pesticides bearing an EPA registration number and used widely by homeowners, private firms, government agencies, and others, were registered before the modern testing standards went into effect. Most were never tested for long-term effects on people and the environment.

The EPA is now faced with the job of reassessing the health risks of about 600 chemicals used as the active ingredients in 50,000 pesticides. (Pesticides, according to EPA terminology, includes household disinfectants, wood preservers, and many other products in addition to those that control pests.)

Once it has served as breakfast, lunch, and dinner for termites, this beam won't have much, if any, strength left. Before opting for chemical treatments, make sure the PCO (pest control operator) is using an EPA-approved and registered chemical.

This project was described in a report on nonagricultural pesticide risk and regulation by the General Accounting Office as ''an enormous task that will continue into the twenty-first century.'' Fewer than 5 percent of the 600 active ingredients have been reevaluated and reregistered so far.

In the meantime, consumers who use pesticides (and buy a wide variety of products containing pesticides, ranging from treated lumber to insecticides), will have no apparent way of knowing whether the product was evaluated according to old or new standards. There is a dramatic difference.

In 1947, the Federal Insecticide, Fungicide, and Rodenticide Act (FIFRA), based federal registration primarily on effectiveness and immediate health risk. The Department of Agriculture, which administered the registration program before the EPA assumed responsibility in 1970, sought to screen out products and chemicals that caused acute damage—immediate health problems such as nausea and dizziness during or shortly after application.

In the 1960s, spurred in large part by Rachel Carson's book about chemical pollution *Silent Spring*, consumers and regulators became increasingly aware that chemicals in pesticides could have significant long-term effects. This concern took legislative form in 1972 in a series of amendments to the 1947 Act.

The amendments directed a complete reevaluation of all existing pesticides. This complex process, which can involve years of testing for a single product, takes advantage of scientific techniques not available when many pesticides first came to market. Also, the new evaluation process is designed to detect fundamentally different problems: long-term effects on the environment, and chronic, long-range health effects on people.

When the amendments became law in 1972, Congress and the EPA apparently believed the reevaluation could be completed in only a few years. But in 1975, Congress extended the reregistration deadline from 1976 to 1977; then in 1978, removed it altogether. Instead, the EPA was directed to complete reregistration "in the most expeditious manner practicable." The EPA is now on a schedule of reregistering old chemicals at the rate of only 25 per year.

To evaluate the EPA reregistration effort, the General Accounting Office (GAO) examined a sample of 50 pesticide chemicals. They found that as of October 1985, 32 of the 50 had not yet received even a preliminary assessment. Of the 18 that had, some portion of the data needed to investigate chronic toxicity was lacking on 17. The amount of missing information (known in the EPA as "holes in the data base"), can vary widely. A chemical registered 35 years ago may be missing only one type of test, while a chemical registered 10 years ago may be missing most of the data needed for reevaluation.

The GAO report paints a bleak picture for consumers interested in balancing the benefits of pesticides against the potential health risks of exposure. It summarizes the issue this way. "Neither the nature, frequency, amount, or extent of these exposures, nor the potential chronic toxicity of these chemicals is well known."

Amid the inconclusive data on Trichlorfon, Piperonyl Butoxide, and a seemingly endless list of other tongue-twisting chemicals, the GAO did discover one conclusive trend. Consumers don't know about the problem. In fact, a major section of the comprehensive report has this ominous title: "The General Public Receives Limited and Misleading Information on Pesticide Hazards."

The GAO investigated this particular subject in a number of ways. They reviewed product label information and application literature. They surveyed product advertising in 20 magazines ranging from trade-oriented publications such as *Garden Supply Retailer* and *American Fruit Grower*, to general interest publications such as *Popular Mechanics* and *Reader's Digest*. They also wrote to pesticide manufacturers in the guise of consumers requesting safety information.

None of the literature, advertisements, or written responses they analyzed specifically mentioned chronic (long-term) health effects. The GAO reports, "In general, manufacturers/distributors' discussions of health and safety were limited to assurances that products are safe or have low toxicity."

While general information about pesticide safety was found to be inadequate at best and misleading at worst, a more obvious defect in consumer information was summed up this way: "Pesticide labels provide no indication that the chemicals in pesticide products sold in supermarkets, garden supply stores, etc., have not been assessed for chronic health risks."

The general consensus at the EPA Office of Policy and Special Projects of the Pesticides Program seems to be that any kind of label distinction would, by inference, suggest that the approximately 500 chemicals registered prior to 1977, when the new standards took effect, are harmful to some degree. That suggestion might be incorrect. But maybe not. That's the problem.

No one knows for sure how many of the active ingredient chemicals will prove to be too great a health risk under the new standards. But EPA officials acknowledge that some products on the market now will almost certainly pose problems.

As the issue of informing consumers is debated, EPA estimates indicate that almost 1.5 billion pounds of pesticide active ingredients will be used each year by homeowners, pest-control firms, and others for nonagricultural purposes. The bulk are used as wood preservatives, disinfectants, herbicides, and insecticides.

Until there is a plan to differentiate between pesticide chemicals evaluated by old and new standards, weighing safety risks will be a difficult task for consumers. Theoretically, any pesticide registered after 1977, when the new evaluation standards took effect, should be safe. But Karen Flagstaff of the EPA's Office of Pesticide Programs advises against using this yardstick. Since the registration process can take several years, some chemicals may have been in the registration pipeline prior to the enforcement of new standards. Another EPA official suggests that 1978 would be a reliable cutoff date.

To distinguish between chemicals tested under old and new standards, consumers now must read the active chemical ingredient from the product label, then call the EPA in Washington, and confer with a product manager to determine if that chemical has, in fact, been reevaluated and reregistered, or if it is a newer chemical registered after 1978. Of course, this will be difficult with many products such as treated lumber that contain some amount of chemicals but do not bear either an EPA registration number or a label listing ingredients.

Currently, that convoluted and impractical route is the only one available to consumers. Expanded label information appears to be a dead issue at the EPA. So until some label notification method is adopted, or until the reevaluation process is completed sometime in the twenty-first century, hundreds of old pesticide chemicals not tested for chronic health effects, will bear EPA registration numbers and be sold side-by-side with new products evaluated by modern standards.

Reregistration will also produce an interesting paradox. During the reevaluation process, the EPA expects several older pesticides to be voluntarily dropped. For example, if the EPA requires a pesticide manufacturer to supply several long-term and expensive tests on a product to meet the new standards, a marginally profitable chemical might be retired by the manufacturer.

In such a case, and the EPA expects several, a pesticide may come and go, possibly staying on the market for decades, without ever being tested for long-term health effects.

Finally, in late 1988 Congress reentered the picture in establishing a 9-year deadline for retesting the chemicals. This time around they have taken a more realistic approach and supported the EPA's effort by mandating, for example, that manufacturers pick up testing costs.

Water Quality and Lead Levels
Taking Steps to Reduce Lead in Your Drinking Water

What most people think of as lead, a heavy, malleable, gray metal, would clank against the sides of a glass of water and sink quickly to the bottom. If there was lead like that in your water supply, surely you would know about it, avoid the water, and have the problem fixed. Unfortunately, you cannot see, taste, or smell lead that is dissolved in drinking water and delivered at unhealthy levels to over 40 million of the 220 million Americans served by public water supply systems.

Many of the harmful health effects of lead have been known for over a century. More recent problems, such as the severe health risks, including brain damage to young children who eat lead-based paint chips, are well documented. But the widespread problem of lead in drinking water has received increasing attention since the EPA released a report on the subject in December, 1986.

The EPA report attributed increased risks of hypertension, heart attacks, blood disorders, even small but measurable IQ losses in 250,000 children, and a variety of other health problems to elevated lead levels in drinking water.

But not all houses and apartment buildings have a lead problem. It depends on when they were built, what kind of plumbing pipes they have, and what types of water mains connect the building to the public supply system. The significant dose of lead doesn't come from water in underground aquifers and reservoirs, but from pipes, both lead pipes and lead solder used to connect copper pipes, that carry water.

Contamination can start with a corrosive reaction between lead and water in the large lead pipes of municipal water-delivery systems and in smaller lead pipes, called service connections, that link large mains to the pipes in buildings. Through the early 1900s it was common practice to use lead pipes for interior plumbing as well.

So it is possible that people in some older buildings drink water that has traveled exclusively through lead pipes. But, in general, you are most likely to find lead pipes in systems installed prior to 1930. However, the EPA regards the lead in solder used to seal connections between copper pipes (the most common residential plumbing material), as the major cause of lead contamination in household water today.

The threat posed by lead solder is greatest in new homes. It decreases with age and is generally considered an insignificant threat after 5 years when mineral deposits in the water have formed a coating inside the copper pipes that seals off the solder. EPA literature says, "More likely than not, water in buildings less than 5 years old has high levels of lead contamination."

Currently, the EPA has a two-part standard for lead in drinking water: a theoretical, health-based goal and a legally enforceable standard. Both are currently 50 parts of lead per billion parts of water, although the EPA report was based on a more stringent standard of 20 parts per billion (ppb).

New proposals are expected to create a health-based goal of zero ppb and an enforceable standard of 5 or 10 ppb. The lower numbers seem to indicate a more stringent standard. But possible changes in statistical methodology (basically, averaging in high lead levels that otherwise might violate even the 50 ppb limit used in the EPA report) make it unclear whether or not new standards would be an improvement.

In any case, the relatively small percentage of consumers with lead pipes should consider replacing them with copper or, where permitted by code, plastic. Consumers with copper pipes in systems less than 5 years old are advised by the EPA to avoid using water that has been in contact with the solder at pipe connections for more than 6 hours. Always run water from the tap before using it for drinking or cooking.

Hard water full of minerals may taste good. But it can severely corrode the plumbing gradually building up on the walls of pipes. If soap forms a low curd when mixed with water (instead of airy bubbles), you may need water softening equipment.

It may take 15 to 30 seconds to flush water that has been standing in the pipes overnight or while you're at work. One approach is to run the cold water until it gets as cold as it can get. This usually means you have cleared water warmed up by sitting in pipes inside the building. Running water for another 15 seconds is likely to clear water standing in the service connector as well. Unfortunately, flushing is usually ineffective for high-rise apartment dwellers due to the volume of water standing in large-diameter supply pipes.

The EPA also advises consumers not to cook with water from the hot tap since hot water dissolves lead more quickly than cold water. This is particularly important when preparing baby formula for three reasons. First, lead deposits are proportionally a much larger and potentially more damaging part of a baby's body than an adult's. Second, health problems limit development most severely in babies with so much of their lives ahead of them. And third, of course, babies drink a lot of formula. Although it may be convenient to mix formula with warm water so that bottles need not be heated, it should be mixed with cold water from a thoroughly flushed line, then heated.

Consumers also may wish to have their water tested for lead, which may cost from $20 to $100, and to install a tap filter system such as a reverse-osmosis or distillation device. Several common forms of water-treatment appliances, such as carbon and sand filters, often sold with replaceable cartridges, may filter out many contaminants. But, according to the EPA, they do not remove lead and do not reduce corrosion in pipes. Your local health department and water company should be able to provide help in locating testing firms and treatment devices.

One other note. Additions to or repairs on copper pipes, even in a house over 5 years old, should not be made with lead solder. Although there are several substitutes, the material of choice seems to be tin antimony solder. This lead-free substitute is slightly more expensive than lead solder, but adds only about $2 to the cost of a complete plumbing system in a new home.

Radon Pollution
The EPA Says Almost Every Home Should Be Tested

Most people have no trouble recognizing an obvious threat to their health and safety—a speeding car swerving over the double line, or a howling hurricane.

But many were puzzled, even panicked, when a national public health advisory was issued in late 1988 that cited a national threat from radon, and recommended that almost every home be tested for its presence.

The subject is puzzling, in part, because radon is not an obvious threat. It is an odorless, invisible, naturally occurring, radioactive gas that seeps up from the ground into homes across the country. Any home could have a radon problem—even a severe problem—and the occupants would be unaware of the threat.

For decades, scientists have known from tests on uranium miners that radon gas can cause lung cancer. But until 1984 and 1985 when the EPA broadened its investigations, that problem was seen as an isolated, occupational health threat. The miners were endangered only because they breathed in a concentrated dose, day after day, surrounded by rocks containing uranium that emitted radon.

However, after tests in recent years by scientists, private labs, and government agencies, a new consensus emerged: Radon was seeping into homes, and in some cases, reaching levels well above the health threshold established by the EPA of 4 picocuries per liter of air (pCi/1). (Picocuries are a standard measure of radiation.)

Living in a home at that level of exposure presents approximately the same health risk as smoking half a pack of cigarettes a day. Standing anywhere outdoors, you would be exposed to the ambient, or average background level of radon—0.2 pCi/1, a harmless amount.

For smokers the radon threat is considerably more severe, since radioactive decay particles of the gas that become attached to microscopic dust particles in the air, also attach to particles in smoke. This "piggy-backed" radon is then breathed deeply into the lungs where the radioactive particles lodge, decay, and damage lung tissue.

Although it is unusual, some homes have levels of 100, and even 200 pCi/1, or more. In a notorious case that triggered widespread interest in radon, a Pennsylvania home investigated in 1984 registered radon levels approaching 300 pCi/1—a staggering health risk equated to smoking over 200 packs of cigarettes a day.

But after a seven-state survey conducted by the EPA to determine radon levels in homes that led to the Public Health Service advisory, radon emerged as a more serious and widespread threat than many suspected.

As a result, the EPA has recommended tests to detect and measure radon in all houses, first and second story apartments (those closest to the ground from which radon gas rises), and every time a house changes hands.

The EPA findings were based on short-term tests taken in 11,000 homes during the heating season last year. The EPA claims that the data supports its previous estimates that elevated radon levels are present in at least 8 million homes across the country, and that radon causes as many as 20,000 lung-cancer deaths per year.

Some scientists have commented that radon is not as serious a threat as new EPA data suggests. An EPA spokesperson acknowledged that the tests were expected "to capture worst case measurements." They are screening tests—a first step akin to a jogger checking his pulse for only a few seconds instead of waiting for a full, 60-second sample at the end of his run.

Against that background, consumers are faced with three crucial tasks: testing for radon in their own homes, making decisions about retesting based on laboratory reports, and, if an elevated level is confirmed, taking remedial action.

Fortunately, testing is a simple, inexpensive and, if consumers observe a few sensible safeguards, highly reliable process. If needed, remedial action can be taken to seal off radon entry points—caulking foundation cracks, and sealing an open sump pump pit, for example. However, in homes with high radon levels more elaborate and expensive remedies may be needed. The EPA estimates that the national average cost for radon remediation is $1,000 per house. Yours could be more. Most remediation jobs cost considerably less.

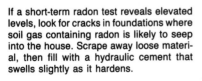

If a short-term radon test reveals elevated levels, look for cracks in foundations where soil gas containing radon is likely to seep into the house. Scrape away loose material, then fill with a hydraulic cement that swells slightly as it hardens.

Scranton Photo Studio

Here is the information you need to proceed with the key task—testing to detect the presence and level of radon in your home.

Who should use short-term tests. Most real estate transactions do not allow enough time for a buyer to make a long-term test that samples indoor air over 1 to 4 months. Home buyers must make short-term tests, most of which take 3 or 4 days. Insist on it, even if your real estate agent and mortgage banker do not.

Homeowners and renters also can use short-term screening tests—the fastest, least expensive way to find out if you have a radon problem. These tests reliably indicate whether or not there is a problem. However, long-term tests are considered more accurate in pinpointing the level of radon. Also, long-term tests more closely reflect the overall, changing quality of indoor air you breath.

How short-term tests work. Most devices consist of absorbent charcoal sealed in a metal canister or fiber envelope, and packaged in a foil pouch about the size of a small, thin paperback book. When you buy the package you pay for a future laboratory analysis and report at the same time, in one total price, typically between $10 and $20.

You should follow the manufacturer's instructions. In most cases, this means opening a package, and simply placing the charcoal canister in your home—not a job requiring the expensive services of a radon "expert."

After the specified testing period, you return the canister to the manufacturer who analyzes the sample and sends you a report. Although many firms also send along information about radon levels and remediation, there is one key number to look for: the radon level in picocuries per liter of air (pCi/1).

Who should use long-term tests. Although most owners and renters can afford to take from 1 to 4 months for a radon test, long-term detectors may be most useful as a backup to a short-term screening test. Here's the logic.

If your home has a very low level of radon, a short-term test will confirm it, and the process is concluded. If your home has a high radon level, it helps to know about it as soon as possible with a short-term test. But unless the level is alarmingly high and demands immediate action, it makes sense to conduct a longer, follow-up test before proceeding with remedial action. It's just like getting a second surgical opinion before an appendectomy—unless the diagnosis is acute appendicitis.

How long-term tests work. These small canisters also are sold with future analysis and reporting included in the cost, typically between $25 and $50.

This type of device is generically called an "alpha-track" detector because a small sheet of plastic in the canister records the tracks left by alpha particles in radon gas. Following manufacturer's instructions, you expose the canister in your home, repackage it, return the canister for analysis, and receive a lab report containing the critical picocurie level.

Where to buy test kits. Test kits are widely available in hardware stores, home centers—even supermarkets. If, for some reason, you can't locate one, contact your town, county, state department of health, or department of consumer affairs for help.

However, before buying any testing device or hiring any radon-testing firm, verify that the manufacturer or firm is listed on the EPA's Radon Measurement Proficiency Report, which also is available from all state and most county departments of health or consumer affairs.

A firm is listed only after its test results are certified by the EPA as being accurate to a degree of plus-or-minus 25 percent. This margin, which could, in theory, allow for a 49 percent error, underscores the wisdom of making follow-up tests.

Where to place testing devices. You should follow manufacturer's instructions. But some people don't. Since radon may be seeping thorough the sump hole in the cellar, they reason, why not set the canister down in the hole and find out how much is getting through? But no one lives in the sump hole. It is only reasonable to place detectors in the rooms you use, surrounded by the air you breathe.

Cautions about radon reduction methods. If your radon level is elevated, remediation is the next step. There are many ways to reduce radon levels—some simple and inexpensive, some extremely complex and costly. There is no single, correct method. The EPA has concentrated on one approach: preventing radon gas from seeping into the house. But even the agency's mediation booklet, *Radon Reduction Methods: A Homeowner's Guide*, presents many possibilities.

There is no magic radon filter, no radon-dispersing light bulb. (Many consumers already have been bilked by unscrupulous contractors installing useless devices.) Consumers whose tests reveal elevated radon levels should exercise the utmost caution in selecting a remediation contractor.

Some members of Congress familiar with the radon problem are considering measures that would establish training programs and some form of evaluation system for radon mediation contractors.

Basic guidelines about picocurie levels. The EPA has recommended four "action guidelines" at various radon levels.

- At 200 pCi/1 and above, immediate remedial action is called for "within several weeks."
- From 20 pCi/1 to 200 pCi/1, remedial action should be planned "within several months." Common sense suggests that you should act more quickly at levels approaching the somewhat arbitrary 200 pCi/1 guideline.
- From 4 pCi/1 to 20 pCi/1, the EPA suggests remedial action "within a few years," but sooner if the levels are near 20 pCi/1.
- From 0.2 pCi/1, the ambient level of radon, to 4 pCi/1, the current EPA health threshold, the EPA makes no recommendation for action, noting that it may be "difficult and sometimes impossible" to reduce radon levels any further.

Consumers should know that there is no such thing as a good amount of radon. The 4 pCi/1 threshold is simply an efficient guideline—a point above which the health threat becomes serious, and effective remedial action becomes both possible and practical.

This somewhat arbitrary and cold-blooded threshold, and its health risk equal to smoking half a pack of cigarettes a day, got a reaction from many consumers, and a few members of Congress. In late 1988, as the House was reconsidering The State Radon Program Development Act of 1987, which passed the Senate in 1987, members included a provision to do away with the artificial 4 pCi/1 level, and mandate that the EPA make recommendations to consumers all the way down to the ambient radon level of 0.2 pCi/1. Additionally, the bill provided $30 million to state radon programs over three years, and mandated an EPA radon survey of schools.

Where to find out more about radon. Some town, most county, and all state health or consumer affairs departments can provide the following information.

- Help locating a radon testing device.
- The EPA Radon Measurement Proficiency Report that certifies the accuracy of radon testing devices and firms.
- Copies of two EPA booklets: *A Citizen's Guide to Radon: What It Is and What*

SEASONAL INDOOR RADON VARIATIONS
Fairfax County, VA

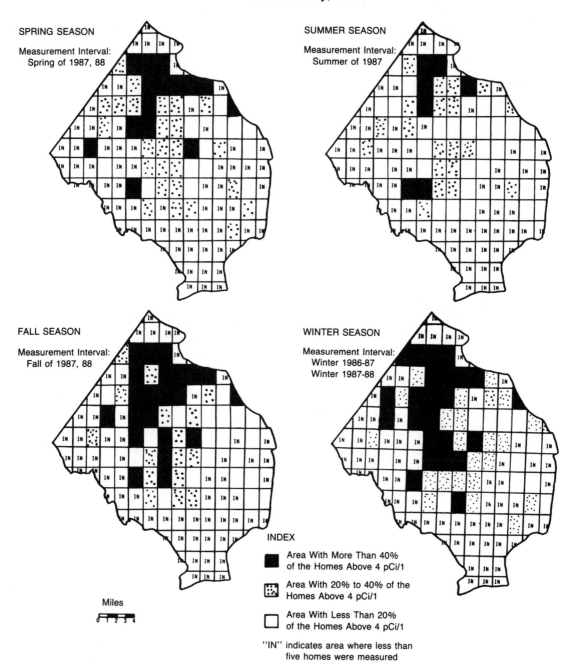

SPRING SEASON

Measurement Interval:
Spring of 1987, 88

SUMMER SEASON

Measurement Interval:
Summer of 1987

FALL SEASON

Measurement Interval:
Fall of 1987, 88

WINTER SEASON

Measurement Interval:
Winter 1986-87
Winter 1987-88

Miles

INDEX

Area With More Than 40%
of the Homes Above 4 pCi/1

Area With 20% to 40% of the
Homes Above 4 pCi/1

Area With Less Than 20%
of the Homes Above 4 pCi/1

"IN" indicates area where less than
five homes were measured

While national maps showing radon concentrations can be misleading, this study of one county in Virginia shows that radon levels can vary significantly season to season. The long-term study was conducted by Dr. Douglas Mose, a radon expert, and geology professor at George Mason University in Fairfax, Virginia.

to Do About It (scheduled for an update under the new radon legislation), and *Radon Reduction Methods: A Homeowner's Guide.*

Radon Testing Business
The Business Side of a Consumer Health Issue

The business of testing homes for radon underwent explosive growth in 1988. Unfortunately, the growth brought an increasing number of inexperienced companies and unscrupulous operators into the field of testing homes for radon.

When the EPA, which administers a voluntary certification program for radon testing firms, first measured the testing accuracy of radon firms several years ago, it examined the results of 35 participating companies. In mid 1987, they were analyzing the testing accuracy of approximately 350 firms. According to several industry experts there are at least another 4,000 firms in line for future EPA test programs.

Passing the EPA's accuracy tests, which allow for errors of plus or minus 25 percent, is important to radon testers. The EPA lists firms certified as accurate in the Radon Measurement Proficiency Report, which is sent to state agencies that make the names available to consumers. Naturally, many consumers are likely to select a certified tester over a firm that either failed or did not participate in the EPA program.

But as the number of firms in this field increases exponentially, so do the abuses. Major manufacturers of radon testing kits report that unscrupulous middleman operators are gouging consumers by charging over $100 for short-term test kits (requiring 3 or 4 days of air sampling) that are commonly used as preliminary screening tests during real estate transactions. Such kits include a measuring device, laboratory analysis, and a report of the test findings, and are widely available in hardware stores, home centers, supermarkets, and directly from manufacturers for approximately $10 to $15.

Dr. H. Ward Alter, a senior consultant at Terradex Corporation, the largest manufacturer of long-term (3 months of air sampling exposure) radon testing kits that cost $25 says, "Some fly-by-nighters are charging up to $180 for placing our container in a home—a job that anyone can do by reading the simple directions, opening the package, and placing the container on a shelf."

Reputable testing firms may charge more than the face value of a radon test kit to cover other services, for example, taking repetitive air samples or tracking down radon entry points through a foundation. But some firms simply act as middlemen, passing on a manufacturer's kit complete with laboratory analysis at an inflated price.

Major test kit manufacturers also report that some firms with little or no experience in the field have started these middleman operations. Bernard Alvarez, president of Air Chek, which manufactures short-term test devices, says, "One small shop that specializes in sewing machine repair is now also offering home radon testing."

Mike Mardis, chief of the EPA's radon mitigation, prevention and quality control branch, says that several unlikely firms are going into the radon-testing business, including a carpet cleaning company that will start a radon test while shampooing your rugs. "Actually, if they use proper procedures and a certified testing device, there's no reason why you wouldn't get an accurate report," says Mardis.

However, inexperienced firms may have problems attempting to do more than simply passing on another manufacturer's testing device. Several established firms in this field have conducted between 100,000 and 150,000 tests. This volume allows them to calibrate their findings, accounting for seasonal and other variations, based on information in an extensive data base of test results.

Despite their inexperience, thousands of firms want to become radon testers. It's an easy business to get into. Unlike pest control operators, electricians, real estate agents, home improvement contractors, and other home professionals who routinely undergo some type of mandatory registration or licensing procedure, almost anybody can become a radon tester. Only a few states have a certification program for testers.

Middleman radon testing also imposes few start-up costs because a firm need not buy expensive analysis equipment or spend for research and development of existing kits. And since elevated radon levels have been recorded in many areas throughout the United States, there is a very large, critically interested, nationwide market of potential test kit buyers.

Interest is critical because radon can be lethal. There are several structural and mechanical improvements that can reduce radon infiltration into a home to a level considered acceptable by the EPA. But these mitigation methods may cost from several hundred to several thousand dollars. And some homeowners and buyers are uneasy about buying or living in homes sitting on a life-threatening problem that is being diverted from living spaces by control systems that are still somewhat experimental.

Long-term health risks can be complicated by financial risks. Radon contamination can undermine the resale potential of a home, even after radon mitigation improvements have been made. Given a choice between two similar homes, one radon-free, and one in which potentially lethal levels of radon gas are being diverted, buyers are quite likely to choose the radon-free home.

Mike Mardis, of the EPA, says, "Eventually testing may be controlled by the lender, handled more like a termite inspection as a standard part of the transaction." About 25 percent of Air Chek's sales are for contingency real estate testing. In late 1988, the EPA recommended that anyone buying a home make a radon test.

Pressure-Treated Chemicals

Q. Is it necessary to paint or stain green-colored, pressure-treated wood used on decks and outdoor furniture? I have two concerns: that the wood last as long as possible without rotting, and that chemicals used in the wood stay sealed in so they will not present a hazard.

A. If you were using raw, untreated lumber, applying two coats of a penetrating sealer or stain, which lies at the top of the lumber, would be necessary to keep out the weather. But pressure-treated lumber is injected throughout with preserving chemicals, and does not require a surface coating.

The most common chemical treatment for residential uses is Chromated Copper Arsenate (CCA). Wood pressure-treated with CCA is sometimes called "salt-treated" or "waterborne preserved." In addition to being a strong deterrent to termites, this chemical should make properly installed decks, planters, gazebos, and other outdoor structures last at least 25 years, and probably longer.

The main environmental concerns for consumers using pressure-treated wood— there are special concerns for workers involved in producing the material—are in site selection, handling, and disposal.

Pressure-treated lumber is injected with wood-preserving chemicals in a giant kiln. Since the chemicals reach through the entire piece of lumber, cutting—particularly with a power, circular saw—can spray chemical-laden sawdust. Wear goggles and a respirator mask during cutting operations.

Although, when dust and debris is carefully controlled, CCA-treated lumber can be use inside—not that there is a good reason to do so—almost all uses are exterior. Here is a checklist of precautions.

☑ Wear a dust mask when cutting the wood, and goggles if you're using a power saw.
☑ Do not burn scrap wood or sawdust in a fireplace or wood store.
☑ After working with the wood, wash before eating, drinking, or smoking.
☑ Do not use treated wood in applications where the chemicals can become a component of food. Use it for a picnic table, but not for a countertop or cutting board.

Although it certainly is sensible to exercise these precautions, they amount to a stringently safe approach. Obviously, you would not want to grind up CCA-wood to use as a meat loaf extender. On the other hand, you should feel free to walk around on your deck in bare feet for the next 30 years or so.

Household Chemicals

Q. Is there some central clearinghouse for information on the nature of chemicals used in household products; some place that can offer expert advice on safe use, storage, and similar questions?

A. Although it is a referral service, the Chemical Referral Center is a good place to contact for nonemergency information about the proper use and effects of chemical ingredients in pesticides, cleaners, fuels, and countless other household products.

The service is provided nationwide at no cost through toll-free lines by the Chemical Manufacturers Association (800-262-8200). The service was started, in part as an industry response to the chemical accident in Bopal, India in December, 1984. (Toxic fumes of methyl isocyanate gas used in pesticides leaked from a Union Carbide plant killed over 2,000 and injured approximately 50,000.)

Operators at the center, on duty from 8 A.M. to 9 P.M. eastern standard time Monday through Friday, can refer consumers to the most appropriate source of information, for example, a government agency or manufacturer. The center has some 2,000 products computer-indexed by company, trade name, and ingredients. They can provide the name and number of manufacturers' representatives at over 100 chemical companies who can explain the effects and proper use of company products.

Many of the calls to this underpublicized center (they have been handling about 50 calls per day), are about pesticides: which ones to use inside or outside; how to apply them; potential dangers to humans, plants, and animals; and more. But operators also handle calls about product labeling, disposing of caustic cleaners, and requests for information and safety literature on specific chemicals.

Cellar Drain Closer

Q. In literature I have read about preventing radon gas from seeping into the cellar, I have yet to come across a solution for the center basement drain that empties into the gravel bed beneath the concrete floor. Since the basement is not finished living space and does get wet every once in a while, I don't want to close it up. Is there a way around this problem?

A. With some excavation and plumbing work you could build a nearly airtight cover for the drain with a trap below, similar to traps on sinks and other plumbing fixtures that connect to waste lines. Traps are U- or S-shaped pipes that seal the drain line by maintaining a water level across the U- or S-bend of the trap. On a sink, for instance, some water that drains out of the basin remains in the trap to prevent gases in the sewer line from seeping back into the house. However, in a basement drain, where water is not flushed through on a regular basis, standing water could create a breeding ground for mold and bacteria.

A similar trap system is designed into a product called Dranjer, made by Dranjer Corporation[1] The firm's retrofit model to use against radon infiltration in existing

---

[1] 1441 Pembina Highway, Winnipeg, Manitoba, Canada R3T 2C4

homes consists of a flexible rubber flange that seats into the drain catch basin. The flange can be trimmed to fit drain basins from 4 3/4- to 11-inch diameters. A floating ball in the U-shaped pipe beneath the flange lifts to allow water to drain through but drops into the pipe to prevent air from seeping up through the pipe.

The drain (suggested retail is $25.95) can be ordered direct from the manufacturer, which sends product information on sizes and suitability (the product will not work in all types of cellar drains) on request.

Safe Drain Cleaners

Q. What kind of drain cleaners can be used to unblock sink and bathtub lines safely, without eating away the plumbing pipes, or risking chemicals burns from splashes and spills? And if there is a safe product, does it clear the drains?

A. The main active ingredient in many drain uncloggers is lye. Some contain sulfuric acid and other caustic or poisonous chemicals. That's why most drain cleaner product labels carry the skull and crossbones poison symbol and many other warnings and precautions.

Although various homeowners may swear by one particular chemical product or another, it may be wise (and safe) to consider chemical drain cleaners a last resort. One reason is that they often do not work with one dose. Caustic chemicals may be diluted only slightly in water sitting in the tub or sink drain. If you then attempt to clear the obstruction with a plumber's snake or plunger you can stir up a dangerous but innocent looking liquid.

Here is a reasonable sequence of repair techniques. First, try a plunger. If that fails, try a snake, either a hand-fed metal coil or a powered version (a snake attached to a power drill). Also, before using any chemicals, try unscrewing the clean-out plug found at the base of many S-trap fittings. This often allows more direct access to the obstruction.

Another nonchemical alternative is to use a compressed air unclogger. These devices use a small compressed air canister (similar to the type used in soda water bottles), to set off shock waves in water standing in a drain line. The plan is for the shock wave to dislodge any debris.

Restrictions on Pressure-Treated Lumber

Q. I have read warnings about pressure-treated wood that advise against applications where the chemicals can become a component of food. Is it safe to use these timbers in raised garden beds, where toxic chemicals could leach into soil and contaminate carrots, beets, lettuce, and such that will be eaten?

A. Yes, it's safe. The potent, wood-preserving chemical does not leach out of the wood. In order to ingest it you have to ingest the wood.

The warning was intended to discourage the few consumers who might assume that if chemically-injected, pressure-treated wood won't rot outside on the deck, it would be a good choice for a kitchen counter, which also gets wet.

There are many preposterous examples that can illustrate the error in making such leaps of logic, for instance, throwing a few burning embers into bed on a cold night, since the coals work so well producing heat in the fireplace.

But you are right to be concerned. And there is one gray area: pressure-treated picnic tables. You can rest your arms on them, take a nap on them—anything except chop up your salad ingredients. If you did, there is a small possibility that an extremely small amount of chemical dug up in a few, tiny wood splinters would become part of the salad and be ingested. But if someone's hot dog rolls off the plate, and, for some reason, they happen to cut it on the table, don't throw it out. Of course, using a plate or cutting board eliminates even the most marginal threat.

It is immeasurably more important that if you build your own table, you wear goggles and a respirator mask when making repeated cuts on pressure-treated wood with a circular saw that creates toxic sawdust.

Energy *and* Mechanical Systems

Twenty Five

ENERGY EFFICIENCY

Energy Efficiency vs Air Quality
Must You Have One at the Expense of the Other?

The relationship between energy efficiency and indoor air quality has been a paradox. Traditionally, you could only improve one at the expense of the other.

Concerns about energy efficiency surfaced first, spawned by the 1973 oil embargo and steadily rising oil prices. Remember the energy crisis? Now, as energy costs have moderated, the quality of indoor air is receiving more attention.

In modern construction, buildings are tightly sealed to preserve costly warm air in winter and cool air in summer. But they also trap stale air and pollutants.

In winter, opening a few windows quickly clears lingering cooking odors, smoke spilling from the fireplace, or just stuffy, stale air. It also makes the room cold. This contradicts the most basic energy-saving idea of separating the air inside a house from the weather outside.

In the 1970s, saving energy dollars became a prime concern of homeowners and buyers. Builders and remodelers responded with techniques to tighten up buildings. During the same period indoor pollution didn't get much publicity. The subject paled next to record-high prices for heating oil, and wartime-like gasoline rationing.

Interest in air quality was focused on outdoor, environmental pollution. Industrial smokestacks manufacturing the ingredients of smog and acid rain were obvious culprits. They still are. But the quality of air indoors may have more telling health effects, particularly since most people spend 90 percent of the time indoors, and more than half that time at home. The indoor environment is at least as important as the larger one outside.

Dealing with the two issues independently has lead to some one-sided solutions, and caused a lot of confusion. Four misconceptions seem to cause the most trouble.

Myth 1. *It's always better to build tight houses.* When energy was inexpensive (home heating oil cost less than 25 cents a gallon through the early 70s) little cracks around windows and doors hardly mattered. A reasonable amount of ''natural'' ventilation (the tactful term for a leak), was expected, even built-in on purpose.

Only 15 years ago that was considered good building practice. Leaving small gaps between panels of plywood sheathing, for instance, provided an escape route for excess

---

Opposite: Photovoltaic cells, which convert the sun's rays directly into electricity, may be the wave of the future. The system does neatly bypass the utility companies. However, since the conversion is not very efficient yet, panels such as these units made by Arco Solar, Inc., are mainly used on very remote sites.

Passive solar design features such as this sunspace require no mechanical equipment or ongoing expense. Heat collected from the sun can be absorbed by building materials (masonry holds the most heat for the longest time), then radiated back into the living space overnight.

moisture that can cause mold, mildew, and other problems in tight houses. Small gaps helped to exchange stale air at the minor cost of a few gallons of fuel oil.

Then came the energy crisis, and houses became tighter to save money, not to improve indoor air quality. In fact, more recent investigations into residential air quality (and common sense), suggest that tight construction contributes to air quality problems by trapping pollutants.

Myth 2. *Building tightness doesn't effect air quality.* Some designers and builders argue that tight buildings aren't polluters. Certain chemicals and substances inside the buildings are the problem. But there are flaws in this reasoning.

First, several building materials do contribute to indoor pollution. Formaldehyde in some plywood glues, for instance, can cause severe health problems for some people. Second, the effects of pollution in a tight house can be magnified when contaminants are trapped by nearly airtight barriers.

The American Lung Association's National Air Conservation Commission reported that the "sick building" syndrome (described in Chapter 24) is often most noticeable in office buildings. Problems including nasal congestion, sneezing, coughing, headache, fatigue, nausea, eye irritation, and more serious ailments, have been attributed to contaminants in the work place. Some experts think they have become a greater problem in recent years because newer buildings are sealed and do not have windows that may be opened.

Myth 3. *Stale air is inevitable in tight houses.* In St. Paul, Honeywell environmental scientists were called in by the Minnesota Department of Energy and Economic Development to work on an energy-retrofitted house. Alterations to heating, ventilating, and air-conditioning systems had reduced energy consumption 50 percent. That was the good news.

But the occupants were complaining about bad odors and various discomforts from stale air. Dr. James Woods, Honeywell scientist in charge of the investigation, found that several pollutants were being trapped by the tight-house improvements.

Honeywell modifications to the retrofitted house included reducing relative humidity, adding return air ducts, relocating an exterior air intake for the home's air-to-air heat exchanger away from a nearby source of car exhaust, and replacing the kitchen range hood with an electronic air cleaner. The air quality was improved without sacrificing energy efficiency.

Myth 4. *Air exchangers are the answer to indoor air problems.* The justification for an air exchanger (whole-house models cost between $600 and $1,000), as opposed to simply cracking a window, is their ability to rescue heat from the exhausted air. In it's most basic form this exchange is made by channeling the cold air next to the warm air with a thin wall in between.

The idea is disarmingly simple. As warm but stale indoor air travels along one side of the wall, the exhaust side, it gives off heat through the wall to a flow of cool but fresh air entering the home.

But an efficiency study conducted by *Consumer Reports* (check the October 1985 issue), found that the most effective units are only about 55 percent efficient. And many have a cross-flow problem—they leak stale outgoing air through the heat exchanging surfaces into the fresh incoming air.

A comparison of cost-effectiveness in *Consumer Reports* calculated that letting some fresh air in through a window (and losing some heat) compares surprisingly well to the costs of operating most air exchangers. The primitive window method of fresh air exchange cost about $19 per month; the high-tech air exchanger about $14 a month. The magazine concluded that even the efficient units could have a 20 to 40 year payback period.

Some heat exchangers may be able to improve indoor air quality just because they do bring in fresh air. But it makes sense to use such a machine only as part of a whole-house approach to improving indoor air quality.

Insulation R-Values
The Energy-Saving Language of Insulation

Every time you go outside into the cold you could first wolf down a bowl of hot soup and bounce through a hundred jumping jacks in the front hall. Or you could do something a little easier on the digestion that might keep you even warmer—something basic, like putting on a coat.

The sensible idea of preserving heat instead of making more and more also works pretty well on your house. There, the equivalent of a puffy down parka is insulation. It helps to keep in the heat so your furnace doesn't run to replenish lost heat 24 hours a day. And even though we are not in the middle of an energy crisis (at least not in the short-term), insulation is still a good investment. Unlike fuel, which is a pay as you go proposition, you pay for insulation only once, although it works to preserve heat every day of every winter as long as your house remains standing. It helps in summer, too.

Like clothing, insulation comes in all sorts of shapes and sizes. Picking one item over another can be difficult. But at least some of the confusion is eliminated by relating every type of insulation with a common denominator. It's called an R-value; the measure of a material's resistance to heat flow.

In general, lightweight, air-filled materials such as fiberglass insulation batts have high R-values per inch of thickness and are good insulators. Fiberglass is rated at about R-3.5 per inch. Heavy, dense materials such as brick (R-0.2) and plaster (R-0.3) have R-values so low it's difficult even to think of them as insulators.

Every type of insulation has an R-value. It is stamped on the insulation itself and displayed in all written insulation advertising. It is the only reliable way to determine how effective the insulation will be, and the only way to compare one type to another. (Recommended R-levels for different parts of the country are available from insulation manufacturers, and local building departments.)

For instance, you might be unsure which one of these three alternatives offered the most thermal protection: 1½-inch-thick rigid urethane board (one type of foam board), 3½-inch-thick fiberglass batts, (the itchy stuff that looks like cotton candy), or 4 inches of loose fill Vermiculite (the dusty, cork-like material that looks a bit like kitty litter). This particular case is one of those College Boards nightmares—a trick question—because each example is rated at R-11.

But you can see that it would be a mistake to pick one type of insulation over another based only on thickness. For example, 5 inches of a traditional, pour-in insulation such as Vermiculite or Perlite rated at about R-14 would provide only about 60 percent of the thermal protection offered by an inch less (4 inches) of urethane board rated at about R-23.

So in order to reach an insulation rating of R-11 in walls, R-19 in floors and R-30 in ceilings (a reasonable amount in many areas, though each climate zone calls for different levels of protection), you would need different amounts of commonly used insulation materials.

To reach R-11 you would need about 3½-inch-thick fiberglass batts, 3 inches of poured-in cellulose fiber, 1½ inches of urethane board, or 2¼ inches of styrene board. To reach R-19 you would need about 6-inch-thick fiberglass batts, 5 inches of poured-in cellulose fiber, 2¾ inches of urethane board, or 4½ inches of styrene board. To reach R-30 you would need about 9½-inch-thick fiberglass batts, 8 inches of poured-in cellulose fiber, 4½ inches of urethane board, or 6½ inches of styrene board.

Despite all the evident precision, I can tell you something that none of your math teachers ever could: don't worry about the fractions. R-values are useful comparative tools. But an odd "R" here or there is hardly significant when you remember that we are talking about a house where people live, not a laboratory. Chances are that someone in your house will forget to close the fireplace damper, or leave the kitchen vent fan on overnight, or spend 10 minutes standing in the open doorway, shivering, saying good bye to the last folks to leave the party. A few "Rs" of insulating value can very easily get lost in that kind of real-life shuffle.

Comparing R-values without splitting hairs should show which one of several insulation alternatives will provide the most resistance to heat loss. But some types are best suited to certain kinds of installations. That means you must consider other insulation characteristics in addition to the R-value. Generally, this is the kind of on-the-job judgment supplied by a contractor.

But do-it-yourselfers should bear in mind that foam boards generally offer the most insulating value in the least amount of space. That makes them a good choice if you want to insulate a cold exterior wall in a closet and still have room for a coat on a hanger. Foam boards also do not rot or compress when wet. They are commonly used to insulate concrete foundations, tacked directly to the outside wall and buried in the dirt.

Light, fluffy, foil- or paper-faced fiberglass batts might be best in an exposed attic floor, and in walls and in ceilings between rafters. Batts or rolls of fiberglass insulation cut to batt size are ideal for insulating the spaces between framing timbers in exterior walls, floors, ceilings, and roofs.

Another important characteristic common to all types of insulation is the law of diminishing returns. This means that the first inch offers the greatest benefit, while the second inch offers a bit less, and so on. Adding even a minimal amount of insulation to an uninsulated wall makes a radical difference. You get to take off the sweater and save a lot of money on fuel costs. Adding a bit more makes a more modest improvement.

But while each successive inch saves less and less heat (although each one does save some), the tenth inch of fiberglass costs exactly what the first inch costs. The first inch is a bargain one-time investment. But the tenth inch of the second, 10-inch layer of fiberglass in the attic floor (and several inches beneath it) are pure overkill.

R-38 ceilings, which you would get with about 12 inches of fiberglass batts, is about right for northern Maine and Minnesota. Buying much more than the high-end limit designated for your area amounts to making a charitable donation to some insulation company.

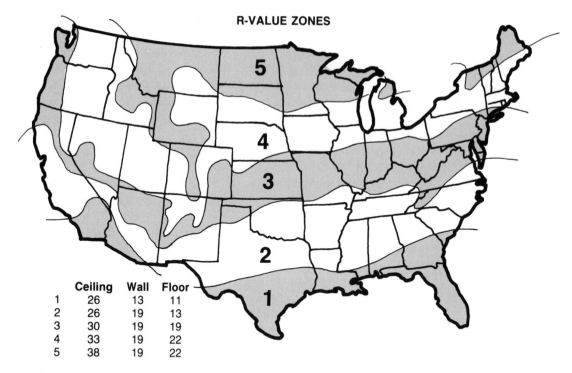

R-VALUE ZONES

	Ceiling	Wall	Floor
1	26	13	11
2	26	19	13
3	30	19	19
4	33	19	22
5	38	19	22

Although individual sites may call for specialized solutions, this map gives a general indication of the amount of insulation you need. For each region, the ratings in R-values are given for ceilings, walls, and floors. Thermal protection increases as the R-value rises.

Radiant Reflective Insulators
Thin, Foil-Faced "Bubble Pack" For Your House

In March of 1988, near the end of the ski season in Maine, sheets of a¼-inch-thick reflective insulation called Foil-Ray were laid over an 800-foot-long ski run at Sugarloaf Mountain. When the sheets were removed five months later, 200 skiers made the trip north from as far away as New Jersey for a unique experience. Dressed in T-shirts and bathing suits, they shushed down the mountain on natural snow in August.

A snow-saving system using Foil-Ray has been patented by an avid skier who owns a local logging company. Sugarloaf owners are examining the possibility of using the system to save large amounts of snow over the summer. This would allow them to open ski runs in October, extending their season by 4 or 5 weeks. Radiant insulators also are being used in homes.

Thin, reflective insulators have been used in other exotic applications, such as NASA space vehicles, making Foil-Ray a true "space-age" product. But it is readily available, offered, for example, in the Sears catalog where it is recommended as a space-saving insulator in mobile homes.

Reflective insulators are available in several configurations. The most basic form is a polyethylene bubble sheet (like "bubble pack" used to cushion fragile items during shipping), covered on both sides with a sheet of aluminum foil. The material is flexible (it comes in rolls), tear-resistant, nontoxic, and only ¼ inch thick.

Here's how it works. Insulators like Foil-Ray reflect approximately 95 percent of radiant heat rays back into the living space. To visualize how radiant heat works, think of radiant heat rays from the sun passing through space as rays of energy. The rays do not produce heat until they hit an object such as your house.

Some of the heat inside your house is in the form of radiant heat rays emanating from wood stoves, floors, couches, and other objects. Radiant insulators reflect most of these rays. But the thin, foil-faced sheets do absorb some heat, which would be lost without a backup of conventional insulation, such as cellulose or fiberglass. Radiant insulators are not designed to replace conventional insulation.

These skiers had the unusual chance to ski in summer—on a hill of snow preserved for weeks under a blanket of reflective foil insulation. By packing the sides of the snow with sawdust, and covering it with foil, temperatures were kept cool enough to allow skiing in August.

Although it is difficult to calculate energy savings with reflective insulators as a dollar amount, they can be measured in R-values. (Remember: R-value is the standard measure of thermal efficiency, the higher the better.)

A standard 2-by-4-inch stud wall contains R-11 insulation. Instead of using 2-by-6 studs to make room for more fiberglass or cellulose insulation, adding ½-inch Foil-Ray brings a 2-by-4-inch, R-11 wall up to R-19.

In its most common application, Foil-Ray is applied across the face of framing timbers (over standard insulating batts), inside the house. When seams between sheets are sealed with foil tape, Foil-Ray does more than reflect radiant heat.

Since foil is impermeable to moisture, the sheets also provide a vapor barrier and an air-infiltration barrier. Moisture produced inside the house can't seep into the wall cavity. And air leaking in from outside around windows and doors can't reach the living space—if the foil seams are sealed. The foil-faced material has other useful properties, too.

Unlike rigid styrene insulation, which must be covered with gypsum board for fire safety, Foil-Ray can be left uncovered over floor joists in cellars and crawl spaces. Since the material is only ¼ inch thick it is also a sensible, space-saving way to increase energy efficiency when remodeling. Sheets can be stapled onto existing walls under new wallboard or paneling.

Foil-Ray is also being used to isolate potentially dangerous air in garages from living space. Some studies have traced abnormally high levels of carbon monoxide inside homes to exhaust from cars started or warmed up in attached garages. Common walls and ceilings between garage space and living space can be sealed with Foil-Ray. All joints, including cutouts around electrical outlet boxes, must also be sealed with foil tape.

Foil-Ray and a series of similar reflective materials are imported from Holland by Energy Saver Imports, Incorporated.[1] One of the firm's instruction sheets, titled "Recommended Installation For Foil-Ray Products," illustrates and explains a variety of applications, and shows how the flexible material works well as an insulated pipe wrap and water heater blanket. It has also been used as a carpet pad over cold floors, and as a night time window insulator stitched to the back of fabric shades.

Low-E Glazing
Low-E Glass Does More Than Cut Energy Costs

Several major window manufacturers report that between 20 and 30 percent of their sales are for windows with Low-E glass. Low-E, which stands for low-emissivity, is the name for invisible metallic coatings applied directly to the glass or suspended on thin films between panes. The very thin coatings filter certain types of light and heat emissions. The result is a dramatic improvement in insulating value and comfort.

---

[1]Energy Saver Imports, Incorporated, P.O. Box 387, Broomfield, CO 80020

Low-E glass became widely available in the mid 1980s. Despite moderating energy costs, it continues to sell strongly, generally as an upgrade option on new homes. According to a survey of builders by Builder Magazine, most home buyers, though impressed by the long-term, energy-saving efficiency of Low-E glazing, spend the extra 10 or 15 percent above the cost of double glazing because Low-E glass cuts drafts, reduces cold spots near windows, and makes a house noticeably more comfortable.

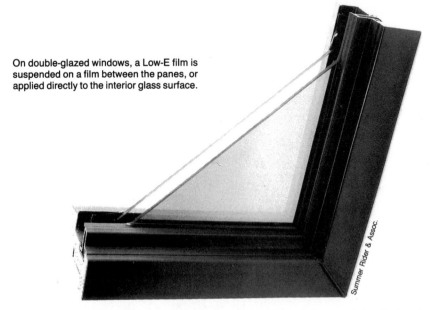

On double-glazed windows, a Low-E film is suspended on a film between the panes, or applied directly to the interior glass surface.

Conventional double glazing has two panes of glass with a sealed, insulating airspace between them. It has an R-value of approximately R-2. Single glazing is rated less than R-1. Low-E glazing is rated from about R-3 to R-4.5, depending on window configuration.

Here's how the different glazing options compare. Single glass is the least expensive and the worst insulator. Double glazing is more costly and more energy efficient. Low-E glazing is about 10 to 15 percent more expensive than double glazing, and even more energy efficient. Low-E is generally less costly and more energy efficient than triple glazing.

Spending for a few additional points of R-value may seem like splitting hairs. But any increase is important on windows because they are the weak link in a building's energy envelope. Heat passes through glass 10 to 12 times faster than through an insulated wall.

More efficient glazing is also responsible for halting the trend to less window area in residences. While great improvements were being made in the thermal efficiency of walls, windows remained thermally porous. Many designers found that the only way to maintain efficient energy envelopes was to reduce the amount of glass. While that approach does work, it can also make homes a bit claustrophobic.

Two panes of glass helped. The 1973 oil embargo and ensuing energy crisis triggered a dramatic increase in the sale of double-glazed units. Dead air, which itself has an

WINDOW STYLES

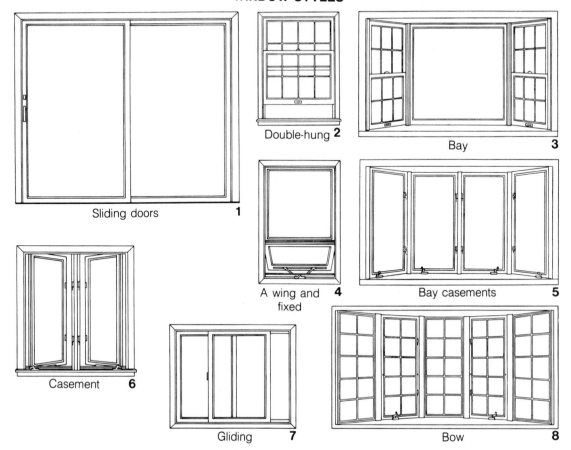

Sliding doors   **1**

Double-hung **2**

Bay   **3**

A wing and fixed   **4**

Bay casements   **5**

Casement   **6**

Gliding   **7**

Bow   **8**

Low-E glazing is available on the full range of window styles and is a good way to improve energy efficiency without adding the weight of yet another pane of glass.

R-rating of just less than R-1 per inch, serves as the thermal buffer. The interior pane of double glazed windows remains close to room temperature. This saves energy, and reduces or eliminates condensation problems.

Working on the premise that more is better, the next step was triple-glazed windows. But triple glazing has some problems. First, the windows are costly and very heavy. They are difficult to install. They may sag on hinges, shifting enough to move locking hardware out of alignment.

Instead of adding a third pane, Low-E glazing modifies a standard, double-glazed window. There are two basic types of applications. On one, an incredibly thin metallic film (about the thickness of 200 atoms) is applied directly to the exterior face of the interior pane. The application method is called "sputtering," a process of bombarding metals with electrons that knocks off an ultra-thin, uniform "mist" of atoms. The technique was developed for the semiconductor industry to apply thin, even metallic coatings on computer chips.

Another Low-E manufacturing system also uses the sputtering technique, but draws a thin polyester film through the metallic mist. This film is then suspended in the dead airspace between two panes of glass. This system is sold under the trademark of Heat Mirror, and available in windows from several manufacturers.

The coating acts like a filter. While not visually reflective, it screens out radiant energy flow (long-wave and ultraviolet rays), while allowing shorter-wave, visible light to enter.

Both conventional and Low-E glass let in sunlight. In winter, radiant heat from inside the house is absorbed by conventional glass and reradiated from both its surfaces. Heat radiated outside is lost. Low-E glass reflects more of the radiant heat back into the house. The saving can be dramatic because approximately two-thirds of the heat lost through double-glazing is radiant heat.

In summer, Low-E glass reflects heat radiating from driveways, patios, and other surfaces outside. Conventional glass does not. This reduces the cooling load and air conditioning costs.

Low-E glazing is the only significant improvement in window efficiency since double-glazing. Surprisingly, the process that caught on after an energy crisis in the 1970s was patented in 1865. But even more exotic improvements already have a toehold in the window industry. A few manufacturers have tested and now sell a limited selection of gas-filled, double-glazed windows. Some that also incorporate Low-E coatings have a thermal rating above R-5.

The idea is to fill the dead air space between panes with an inert gas, typically argon, that is heavier and less conductive than air. Many window manufacturers appear to be waiting for further long-term tests to ensure that the gas will remain sealed in the window.

If experiments with, believe it or not, krypton gas prove successful, window efficiency will have reached superhuman proportions, capable of deflecting heat, if not leaping tall buildings, in a single bound.

Storm Windows
On Windows Two Panes are Better Than One

If someone ever invents a clear, see-through insulation, problems with cold, drafty, energy-leaking windows, skylights, and sliding glass doors will be eliminated. But until that miracle product arrives, the only effective way to make cold windows warmer (and still see through them) is to add an extra layer of glass or plastic.

The idea is to trap dead air between sheets of glazing. The air acts as a buffer between cold air outside and warm air inside, adding an R-value of only .92 per inch, compared to typical fiberglass insulation at about 3.5 per inch. Dead air is not a terrific insulator, but you can see through it.

There are many ways to add at least one layer of glazing. The most expensive is to replace existing, single-pane windows with new, double-glazed units. These factory-sealed units have two panes of glass sandwiching a sealed airspace.

This design may keep the inside glass surface close to room temperature, which also cuts down condensation problems. But double-glazing has no effect on temperature transfer through the frame, and no effect on leaks through seams between window sash and frames. Some homeowners overlook these facts and opt unnecessarily for replacement, paying for double glazing, a new frame, and the installation when their existing frames are in reasonably good condition.

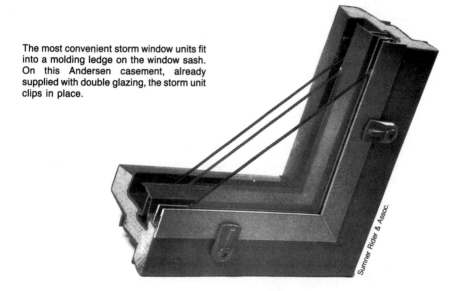

The most convenient storm window units fit into a molding ledge on the window sash. On this Andersen casement, already supplied with double glazing, the storm unit clips in place.

One of the least expensive ways to add a second layer of glazing is to install heat-shrink, optically clear, plastic film trapping air over the inside of the window. Window kits of clear plastic sheeting and adhesive tape cost only $5 or $10 per window, depending on size. They work very well, although thin plastic film is, by nature, temporary.

The most traditional solution to cold, sweating, drafty windows is to add exterior storm units. There are many types, from aluminum-frame, triple-track units that include two storm sash and a screen, to simple, wood-framed units holding a single sheet of glass.

Here are some of the decisive factors to consider when you spend money to save energy, cut down on drafts, reduce condensation and make your home more comfortable in cold weather by double-glazing windows.

Buying double or triple glazing. Resist sales pressure to save even more energy with triple-glazed windows. Such an investment may be worthwhile in the most northern states where winter temperatures are regularly frigid. In most of the country, triple glazing is overkill.

Replacement window frames. Too often a decision is based on the frame material: wood, vinyl, or aluminum. The truth is, it doesn't make such of a difference, so long as the aluminum and vinyl frames have a thermal break built in. That's a strip of insulation that interrupts the flow of temperature straight through the frame. Concentrate instead on the firm's reputation for good business practices and thorough installations that do not dramatically alter the style or appearance of your house. Some firms reduce the size of a window opening in order to match the next smallest stock-size unit they offer. The result may be energy efficient but ugly.

Mounting exterior storms. The key to successful installation of exterior storms with a permanent frame is continuous caulking between the storm frame and existing window frame. Instead of installing the unit, then caulking the edges of the frame, apply a continuous bed of silicone, polyurethane or other flexible caulking on the window frame where the storm frame will rest. Then tighten the screws so that the caulk seals the joint thoroughly.

On seasonal storm windows, such as wood-frame units that are hung on clips above the window, you can improve weather tightness by adding self-stick foam adhesive or tubular weather stripping on the frame where it meets the window frame.

Homemade, interior storms. Handy do-it-yourselfers can make storm units custom fit to almost any window size. Many hardware stores and home centers sell U-shaped plastic or aluminum trim that can be cut and bent to make 90-degree corners. The U-shape channel holds ⅛-inch-thick plastic. Some trim pieces are mitered (cut at 45 degrees) and joined with small clips that fit into the channel in each piece.

Temporary plastic storms. Although a sheet of plastic stuck in place with adhesive tape may sound tacky (sorry; bad pun), heat-shrink plastic is unobtrusive, inexpensive, easy to install, and effective. It's a great deal.

Several firms now make heat-shrink plastic that is optically clear, once you get the wrinkles out. And that's the fun part of the job—using a hair dryer to shrink the plastic in place. It takes some experimentation to get the knack of how much heat to apply. But holding the dryer nozzle very close to the plastic (closer than the directions may indicate) and at a 45-degree angle seems to work well.

If you already have a storm window of one kind or another, but still have drafts and condensation problems, either the house window or the storm window is leaking and needs caulking or weatherstripping or both. Here's how you can tell which window to seal.

If the inside surface of the interior window is fogging and sweating, the exterior storm window is leaking cold air into the dead air space. But if the inside surface of the exterior storm window is fogging and sweating, the interior house window is leaking warm air out of the house into the dead air space.

Foamboard Foundation Insulation

Q. How should I attach foam panels to the masonry foundation outside my house? This seems to be the best way to insulate the crawl space (and the first floor above it), since there is really only room enough to "crawl" around down there.

A. Rigid panels of insulating foamboard can be applied over the building frame, and straight down the foundation wall to the footing. Above ground level, nail it to the house studs. It can also be nailed over masonry block walls with galvanized concrete nails and either a galvanized or nylon washer (about 1½ inch diameter placed approximately 16 inches on center in all directions). The washer grabs more surface area than the nail head and increases holding power.

Below grade and over poured concrete foundations, use either a water-based adhesive or petroleum-based adhesive marked "polystyrene-compatible." That means it won't dissolve the petroleum-based foam panels. Don't risk puncturing and disrupting the foundation waterproofing barrier by nailing below ground level.

Set the panels in place with dabs of the adhesive and set nails and washers added above ground just slightly into the foam surface. Since foamboard is not very attractive, it is usually covered with some type of stucco-like coating.

A typical surface coating is like a very thick paint, consisting of liquid latex, cement, sand, and chopped fiberglass for reinforcement. Some surfacing systems require seams between boards and nail perforations to be taped before the surface mix is applied.

Foamboard insulation also can pay for itself by preventing cold air infiltration along the foundation or between frame sill and concrete slab that can freeze pipes.

Attic Insulations

Q. To install extra insulation in the attic, should we use batts, rolls, or loose fill? And should the insulation have a plastic or foil vapor barrier installed at the same time?

A. The only place to put the vapor barrier is beneath all the insulation (the layer you add, and the existing layer), directly above the ceiling of the rooms below the attic.

The idea is to prevent warm, moist air in the living space from seeping into the insulation where it could encounter cool temperatures and condense. This would make the insulation wet, decrease it's insulating value, and possibly do damage to surrounding floor joists.

There is nothing inherently better about batts, or rolls, or loose-fill insulation. The three configurations are simply for convenience. Batts work well in outside walls because they are precut to fit. Rolls can be most convenient for long stretches, such as the space between floor joists in attic floors.

But if your attic is under a low-slope roof, and several feet under the sloping eaves are inaccessible, loose fill may be easier to place. You can do this yourself, buying loose-fill insulation in large bags, or hire a contractor who pumps the material in place through a large air hose.

Crawl Space Insulation

Q. Insulation batts exposed between floor joists over a dirt crawl space beneath the house have become torn, bunched up and damp. The insulation smells very musty, too. Do I have to start from scratch with new insulation, and what can I do to prevent these problems?

A. Before the cold weather arrives pull down the old insulation and let the floor framing air out thoroughly. You may find greenish blotches of mold growing on the wood (accounting for the musty odor), which should be scrubbed off with a solution of one part household bleach to three parts warm water.

Staple up new batts of insulation with a foil face upwards. (The foil vapor barrier should face the heat source.) Then, to protect the insulation, nail or staple either rigid foam insulating boards across the floor joists, or use sheets of a reinforced foil.

With foam boards, you'll get protection and increased insulating value. With reinforced radiant foil barriers such as Miofoil, distributed by Energy Saver Imports, Incorporated,[2] you also get increased insulating value by reflecting radiant energy lost through the floor insulation back toward the living space.

To help with the moisture problem, cover the dirt floor with overlapped layers of heavy roofing felt (tar paper) or sheets of heavy plastic. Also, don't close off foundation vents into the crawl space, even though cold winter air will be entering. With the additional insulation the floor will stay warm, and the vents will allow any moisture that does seep up into the space to find its way out through the vents instead of up into the house.

Installing Radiant Foil Barriers

Q. I am interested in installing one of the radiant foil barriers (the foil sheets enclosing a thin, air bubble material), over an existing wall in a room we are remodeling. But as I start to nail up a new gypsum drywall panel it seems spongy over the foil barrier. How is this problem solved?

A. Manufacturers of the radiant barriers you described (two sheets of foil sandwiching a thin layer of polyethylene bubble pack material) recommend screwing gypsum sheets to wall studs instead of nailing. Most hardware stores and lumberyards sell fasteners called drive screws that have flat Phillips heads, a very sharp starter point, and wide sharp threads to provide exceptional holding power. Drive screws will stabilize the sheets, even over the bubble pack.

On new walls this stability problem can be eliminated by applying the foil sheets, which are effective insulation and vapor barriers, as the first layer over the exterior surface of wall studs, followed by sheathing and siding.

---

[2]Energy Saver Imports, Incorporated, P.O. Box 387, Broomfield, CO 80020

Twenty Six

APPLIANCES, LIGHTS, PHONES

Energy Guide Labeling
Buying Appliances by the Numbers

Years ago consumers comparison shopped for refrigerators based on cubic feet of storage, and furnaces based on Btus of heating capacity. But it was almost impossible to buy these and other major appliances based on energy efficiency—even though efficiency determines operating cost and is more important than purchase price in the long run. For example, an $800 refrigerator is likely to use almost $2,000 worth of electricity over its useful life span.

Since the National Energy Conservation Policy Act of 1980, this crucial information has been available for several appliances through energy guide labeling, a consumer information program run by the Federal Trade Commission. The prominent yellow and black labels appear on major appliances that account for 75 percent of residential energy consumption, including air conditioners, clothes washers, dishwashers, refrigerators, freezers, furnaces, and water heaters.

Manufacturers may still stress "bell and whistle" convenience features. But now Energy Guide information makes it possible to consider energy efficiency as well as capacity, color, and the size of automatically frozen ice cubes.

The labels offer two types of information in addition to basics such as the appliance model number and capacity: relative energy efficiency and actual operating cost. To show relative efficiency, an estimated annual operating cost for the appliance in question is compared to the highest and lowest operating costs for appliances with similar capacities. The graphic display of this relationship is simply a line with the best and worst at each end and "This Model" somewhere in between.

Relative energy costs are listed in specific dollar amounts based on a national average cost for electricity. (This figure is likely to be 8 to 10 cents per kilowatt-hour.) However, since utility electric rates, measured in cents per kilowatt-hour (kwh) fluctuate and vary from one utility company to another, consumers must use the label formulas with their local utility rate to compute actual annual operating costs.

While operating costs are important, crunching numbers to arrive at a reliable estimate can be downright boring. For instance, some consumer groups insist on accounting for the inflation rate, which economists often find difficult to pinpoint for 1 year, much less the 10- or 15-year life span of an appliance. Other groups treat energy-saving computations like major financial investments, discounting the value of dollars saved by an efficient appliance toward the end of its useful life because those dollars have not been invested and earned interest the way dollars saved earlier on might have.

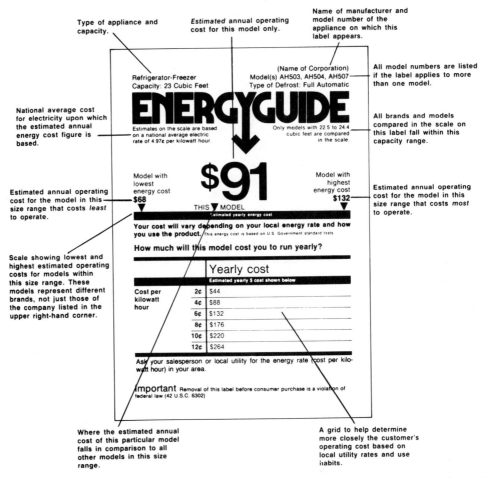

Type of appliance and capacity.

Estimated annual operating cost for this model only.

Name of manufacturer and model number of the appliance on which this label appears.

Refrigerator-Freezer
Capacity: 23 Cubic Feet

(Name of Corporation)
Model(s) AH503, AH504, AH507
Type of Defrost: Full Automatic

All model numbers are listed if the label applies to more than one model.

National average cost for electricity upon which the estimated annual energy cost figure is based.

ENERGYGUIDE

Estimates on the scale are based on a national average electric rate of 4.97¢ per kilowatt hour.

Only models with 22.5 to 24.4 cubic feet are compared in the scale.

All brands and models compared in the scale on this label fall within this capacity range.

$91

Model with lowest energy cost
$68

THIS ▼ MODEL
Estimated yearly energy cost

Model with highest energy cost
$132

Estimated annual operating cost for the model in this size range that costs *least* to operate.

Estimated annual operating cost for the model in this size range that costs *most* to operate.

Your cost will vary depending on your local energy rate and how you use the product. This energy cost is based on U.S Government standard tests

Scale showing lowest and highest estimated operating costs for models within this size range. These models represent different brands, not just those of the company listed in the upper right-hand corner.

How much will this model cost you to run yearly?

Yearly cost		
		Estimated yearly $ cost shown below
Cost per kilowatt hour	2¢	$44
	4¢	$88
	6¢	$132
	8¢	$176
	10¢	$220
	12¢	$264

Ask your salesperson or local utility for the energy rate (cost per kilowatt hour) in your area.

important Removal of this label before consumer purchase is a violation of federal law (42 U.S.C. 6302)

Where the estimated annual cost of this particular model falls in comparison to all other models in this size range.

A grid to help determine more closely the customer's operating cost based on local utility rates and use habits.

The "EnergyGuide" labels on major appliances provide a wealth of information, including the range of operating costs for products in a given general capacity range, and the estimated annual expense of operating the appliance in question.

Sometimes the professional number crunchers forget that buying a refrigerator is not the most important thing you have planned this year—it's only a step to get a place to put some of your food.

Striving for that kind of accuracy is all well and good. But for the purpose of comparison shopping, simply use the estimated annual cost listed on the "EnergyGuide" label next to the 8 or 10 cents per kwh figure. If you know your utility rate, and it is more or less than the listed average figure, use that figure instead. (A range of rates is listed on the label.) While the difference between a rate of 6 and 8 cents per kwh could alter annual operating costs by about $35 on a typical refrigerator, a comparison between two appliances can be made with any reasonable kwh rate, as long as the same rate is applied to both units.

To gauge the full impact of operating costs, multiply annual costs by the predicted appliance life span. These statistical averages may not mirror the operation of your appliance, but again, they can clarify a choice between similar models. The American Council for an Energy-Efficient Economy uses these averages: 11 years for dishwashers and clothes dryers, 13 years for water heaters, 19 years for refrigerators, and 21 years for refrigerator freezers. So if one manufacturer's 20-cubic foot refrigerator-freezer has an estimated annual operating cost of $100, while another's is $135, the difference over the machine's life span is about $665 worth of electricity.

The Council offers another means of short-circuiting the mathematics of energy-saving. In their booklet, *The Most Energy-Efficient Appliances* (available for $2 from the Council),[1] the highest-rated appliances are listed by manufacturer and model number without regard to price. In the refrigerator section, for example, eight different categories are listed including top freezer and side-by-side types, grouped with other models of similar capacity ranging from 10 to 24 cubic feet.

The source of some of the information used to prepare the Council's booklet is also available to consumers. The Association of Home Appliance Manufacturers (AHAM) produces two booklets (each costs $1), one covering refrigerators and freezers, published annually in late January, the other covering room air conditioners, published annually in mid March. Both booklets include all available models, the most and least efficient. For copies, write to AHAM.[2] The booklet titles are: *Directory of Certified Refrigerators and Freezers*, and *Directory of Certified Room Air Conditioners*.

Lighting With Lamps
Illuminating Options with Lamps and Fixtures

Nothing makes the importance of lighting hit home like accidentally walking into the edge of a door in a dark room. "Ouch! Where did that come from?" Like any other object made invisible by the absence of light, it "came" out of the dark.

Lighting can focus attention on stair treads, patches of ice on a driveway, and other potential obstacles. But cleverly designed lighting also can put the best possible face on a room, make a small space seem larger, and a cavernous space seem cozy.

On the other hand, inadequate or poorly planned lighting causes all kinds of problems. It can be dangerous, in some cases; in others, just a nuisance. Bad lighting can give you a headache from eye strain, or more directly, from the edge of an invisible door. It can cancel the soothing effect of a subtle color scheme. It can also make you look your worst—an unnaturally gaunt, shadowy face in the bathroom mirror.

On the most basic level, light lets us see what's there. Light rays reflect from surfaces into the eye. There, a lens focuses the illuminated shape upside down on the retina. A central area of the retina, called the *fovea*, handles small details. Less distinct, but equally important peripheral vision is handled by the surrounding area. If enough light is shed on the subject, the brain makes sense of it all.

---

[1] The American Council for an Energy-Efficient Economy, 1001 Connecticut Avenue NW, Suite 535, Washington, DC 20036
[2] AHAM, 20 North Wacker Drive, Chicago, IL 60606

There is no single "correct" amount of light. Every situation is different. And the eye can accommodate a wide range of light, adjusting from a dark movie theater to bright sunshine in about a minute. Successful lighting matches the right kind and amount of light to the task at hand.

The pupil of the eye functions like a camera, closing to accommodate bright light and opening to accommodate dim light. Uneven lighting forces the pupil to open and close, to adjust to different light levels. This is distracting and uncomfortable.

Generally, the eye works best when everything in the visual field before it is equally bright. If the task is reading, the correct task lighting lights the pages uniformly. If the task is pulling a car into the garage, good task lighting illuminates the nearby walls of rakes and shovels, not just the middle of the floor. Planning uniform brightness is one of the most basic keys to good task lighting. Here are guildelines for many tasks developed by General Electric lighting engineers.

As a general rule, a table lamp should be positioned so the bottom of the shade is at the eye level of anyone seated nearby, generally 38 to 42 inches above the floor. The most efficient and comfortable lighting is provided by open top, white or neutral colored translucent shades. Vinyl, parchment, fabric laminates, and lined dense fabric shades provide the best combination of task lighting, say, for reading, and general area lighting.

A new line of light bulbs from General Electric carries wattages in the 150 to 200 range. New studies by GE indicate that your mother probably was right when she said you would ruin your eyes (or at least strain them), by reading in a dim light.

Reading. Table lamps should be placed to cast light on the field of visions (the book or magazine), with a shade to block direct light from your face. The best placement is 16 to 20 inches directly right or left of the reading material. The shade should have an open top and be moderately luminous. For intermittent use, a 100-watt bulb is recommended. A 150- or 200-watt bulb is recommended for prolonged use to reduce eye fatigue. To cover all situations a three-way lamp is ideal.

Grooming. The best lighting by a dresser or bathroom mirror comes from two lamps (one on each side of the mirror) at eye level. Highly translucent shades covering 100-watt bulbs provide even light that eliminates shadows.

Desk work. Desk lamps should be placed on the left side of right-handers, and on the right side of left-handers. The lamp should be about 15 inches to the side of the work area and 12 inches in from the front edge of the desk. The bottom of the shade should be 15 inches above the work surface. For intermittent use a 150-watt bulb is recommended; 200 watt for prolonged use.

Another option is down-lighting, locating lamps beneath a shelf overhanging the work area. Fluorescent shelf lights (30 watt bulbs for 36-inch runs and 40-watt bulbs for 48-inch runs), should be placed about 15 inches off the work surface, and shielded along the front edge.

Workbench. A small, portable, high-intensity light is useful to fully illuminate small details common to tasks such as model building. For general lighting, center a fixture over the front edge of the workbench, 48 inches off the surface. Fixtures should hold 2, 40-watt fluorescent tubes or 2, 150-watt silver bowl bulbs.

Area lighting. Recommendations for general area lighting can be provided by suspended ceiling fixtures, by wall lighting, or by recessed ceiling fixtures. General Electric lighting engineers make the following recommendations based on room size.

For small rooms (under 150 square feet), ceiling fixtures should have 3 to 5 sockets totaling 150 to 200 watts; wall lighting should use 4, 50-watt reflector bulbs; recessed lighting should use 4, 75-watt bulbs.

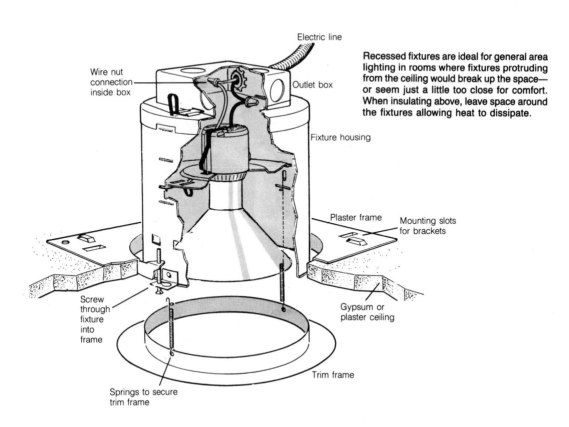

Electric line

Wire nut connection inside box

Outlet box

Recessed fixtures are ideal for general area lighting in rooms where fixtures protruding from the ceiling would break up the space—or seem just a little too close for comfort. When insulating above, leave space around the fixtures allowing heat to dissipate.

Fixture housing

Plaster frame

Mounting slots for brackets

Screw through fixture into frame

Gypsum or plaster ceiling

Trim frame

Springs to secure trim frame

Average-size rooms (185-250 square feet, should have 4 to 6 sockets in ceiling fixtures totaling 200 to 300 watts; wall lighting should use 5 to 8, 75-watt reflector bulbs; recessed lighting should use 4, 100-watt bulbs. For large rooms (over 250 square feet), one ceiling fixture should be used every 125 square feet to provide light at the rate of 1 watt per square foot; wall lighting should use one 75-watt reflector bulb per 25 square feet; recessed lighting should use one 100 to 150 watt bulb per 40 to 50 square feet.)

Installing Telephones

Decisions about Wiring, Fixtures,
and Maintenance

Before a ruling by the Federal Communications Commission (FCC) in July, 1977, it was illegal to buy and install your own telephones. The phone company was responsible for every part of the system. But consumers now have a lot more leeway and many more options, some of which cause confusion and could lead to unnecessary charges.

Before the ruling, many people illegally bought their own phones and installed their own wiring to save the one-time installation cost and ongoing rental of an extra extension or two. But the phone company could detect these attempts to beat the system by calling the customer's number and registering the electrical resistance caused by the ringing. Ma Bell even could figure out how many phones those customers had connected.

If they detected any unrented extras, they had the legal right to go into the home and remove them. And, if called into a home for other service, installers would remove (or at least clip the wires of) any illegal extras they came across. But the FCC reports that no violators were ever prosecuted, though some customers did lose their illegal equipment, which was confiscated without reimbursement.

Now you can install all the phones you want to without the slightest fear of spending time behind bars. Because of the FCC ruling, the phone business is now operated like other businesses in which a service is provided to consumers in their homes, while leaving it up to the consumers to decide how they wish to use the service.

For instance, your utility company sends electricity to the main box on the side of your house, or in the cellar of your apartment building. But you don't have to rent a radio, a television, and other electrical appliances from the utility company just because they send you the power. Similarly, you don't have to rent your furnace from the oil company or your sink from the water company.

When you think about it this way, AT&T had a good thing going before 1977: consumers paid for telephone service, and paid for each phone, month after month, year after year.

Even though we have been freed from this limited and not very capitalistic situation, some consumers were not happy about the FCC ruling, or the breakup of AT&T into many smaller companies. It did lead to confusion over long-distance calls, buying versus renting, and making repairs. Some consumers preferred simpler times when a call to the monopoly would cure any problem in the phone, in the line, outside on the pole—anywhere.

I made the switch from renting AT&T equipment to buying and installing my own after I discovered that I had been paying $5.28 per month for a short piece of extension cable. I discovered that the convenience of having a phone extend a little further into the office had been costing $63.36 a year. When a service representative suggested that I might want to buy the piece of cable (about $40), I suggested that they might want to come take everything away and I would buy my own, thank you (at a fraction of the cost at Radio Shack).

There are now two basic options for consumers. First, you can have the phone company install and take responsibility for the entire wiring system up to and including the modular phone jacks screwed onto baseboards throughout the home. Second, you can install and take responsibility for the phone system inside the home—from the point, called the interface, or connecting block, on the side of, or just inside, the building where incoming wires from the phone company terminate.

Surprisingly, few consumers take the second option. Only 15 percent of Chesapeake & Potomac's (C&P) 1.3 million District of Columbia area customers have installed their own phone systems, for example. Eighty-five percent still pay for what's called "inside wire maintenance." For about $6 a year in Maryland and Virginia, C&P will be responsible for all the wires and boxes inside the house—every part of the system except the phones.

For most people, $6 a year seems to be a reasonable price for maintaining most of the old status quo. If your dog chews through an extension line, or you crash the vacuum cleaner into a modular jack, it's the phone company's problem, not yours.

In one common circumstance you would be moving into a home that already has wires and modular jacks. You would buy a few phones with the features you want from the vast selection, plug them in and you're done. If you pay for inside wire maintenance, the phone company moves the modular jacks and installs any new jacks you want. Generally, though there are exceptions, a small move, say, placing a jack on one side of the bed instead of the other, is billed by time and materials. It might cost $30 or $40.

If you do not pay for inside wire maintenance, any changes to the existing system are up to you. You can run a line for a modular jack into the broom closet if you like. But if the system doesn't work when you're done, it's your fault, your problem.

That's where most of the confusion occurs. If you install your own wires and jacks and there is a problem, chances are that you made a mistake somewhere. But maybe not. All sorts of things can go wrong with phone lines outside the building. But if you call the phone company and their service call reveals that the trouble is in your part of the system, not theirs, they won't fix it, and you'll still be charged for a visit.

So before you call, plug one of your phones into the jack on the main connector block, or interface. This phone is then plugged directly into the phone company lines, bypassing your wiring inside the building. If you still encounter the problem, it is being fed into your system from the outside. Call the phone company; it's their fault. But if the trouble disappears when you plug into the interface, the bug is somewhere past the interface in the system you wired—the one you have to troubleshoot and fix.

To inquire directly about these installation and service options, check the consumer guide pages in the front of your directory, which include instructions about where you should call for different types of service.

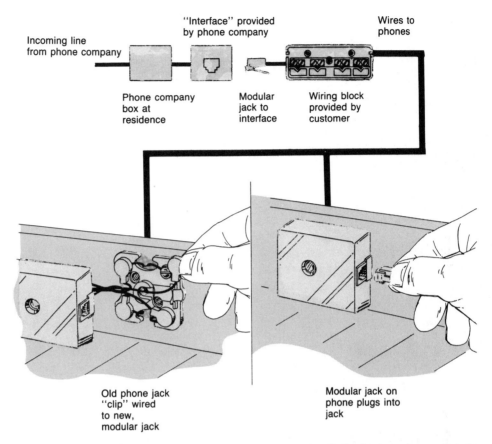

Once old-style wiring is connected to modern, modular phone jacks, clipping in phones is easy. But when consumers take on this job, they are responsible for any trouble in the internal house wiring. Phone company responsibility stops at the interface.

Electronic House Tenders
Electronic Living in the Programmable House

A new generation of electronic devices now makes it possible to control and program many household functions previously handled by more specialized, single-purpose appliances. The specter of "1984" mindless automation has passed. But some of these new machines are just a little creepy.

The new devices can communicate a great variety of information through household wiring already in the walls. And they may be only the first course offered by home consumer electronic manufacturers to their customers who appear to have a limitless appetite for sophisticated, programmable machines that are unquestionably "smart."

On a small scale "smart" means the capability to understand and communicate with a limited number of other similar machines. For example, an infrared remote control device made by General Electric, called Control Central, can store and use the infrared codes of remote controls made by other manufacturers.

On a grand scale "smart" means a single appliance, typified by GE's Homeminder, communicating with and controlling any electronic appliance in the house, registering phone messages, remembering the dates and times of appointments and displaying them on your television screen, and more. (More information on the product is available through GE's toll-free information service: 800-626-2000.)

This kind of electronic home management was what many marketing experts foresaw as the role for home computers—bringing the space-age kitchen and every other room in the house under pushbutton control at a central console. But while the diverse operations of a small business can often be conducted conveniently and efficiently at a single work station (that's a computer on a table), most households run more haphazardly, with different tasks relegated to different rooms at different times.

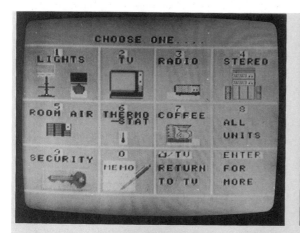
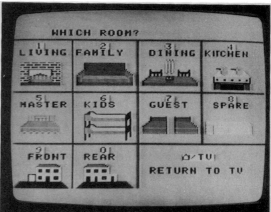
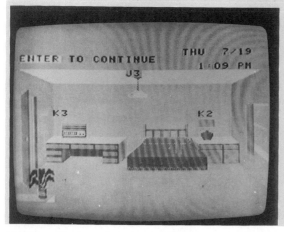
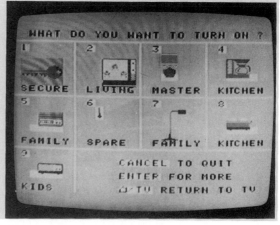

The Homeminder, made by General Electric, can monitor lights and outlets, even turn them on and off, by working through the house wiring. Status of appliances, lights, and other electrical fixtures are displayed on your television screen.

It's convenient to control television channels when you're in front of the television; handy to time a 3-minute egg when you're in the kitchen. Other specialized devices around the house do a good job on such individual tasks as automatically turning down the thermostat, or taking phone messages. Such devices are normally installed "on site," attached to the thermostat, or sitting next to the phone. Another factor that favors single-purpose appliances is ease of operation. When appliances become complex enough to handle many tasks, controlling them can seem like an additional job that needs doing before you get to the job at hand.

These two factors—the location and complexity of a control device—figured heavily in the planning of the Homeminder unit, which is as high but about half as wide as most VCRs with rows of connecting jacks on its back panel. The Homeminder is attached to the house wiring system, phone line, and television, through which the unit is programmed and controlled. Richard B. Williams of GE says, "We selected the television because it usually occupies a central location in the home. And people are already accustomed to programming video cassette recorders from their T.V."

Location is limited only by the length of phone wires and connecting cables. But since the unit does so much it would be difficult to remember what appliance you were programming in what room, and for what time periods, without the help of pictorials (complete with choice of furnishings in a stylized house) that accompany the programming menus. Your T.V. must be on to program the unit. But once programmed, the unit's memory will carry out commands such as turning off lights at bedtime—even dimming them to an exact percentage of the bulb wattage—whether the T.V. is on or off.

The Homeminder console, which retails for approximately $500, works with small control boxes (between $20 and $40 each) that must be plugged in between an appliance, such as a lamp or a coffee percolator, and its wall outlet. Pictorial programming menus first display the house, then offer a choice of rooms, then appliances in the rooms you select and place on the screen to resemble the real thing.

Once installed, the program will turn on and turn off any electric appliance. The unit also cycles light and appliances on and off according to a schedule, and can change the schedule slightly each day if you're away on vacation to simulate the inexact routines of a lived-in house.

The system also displays a memo pad screen on which the dates and times of appointments can be recorded. (A warning lamp glows on the appointed day whether the T.V. is on or off.) Also, a limited number of preselected messages (and programmable phone numbers) can be sent to the screen over the phone. In fact, the random timing of appliances for security, and any connected appliance, can be activated over the phone. So, if you stay at work later than expected, you can call home before leaving to reset the microwave "on" switch, and turn on the outside lights.

To some, this kind of electronic control leads to a bizarre and sterile existence not as comical as the one depicted in the Jacque Tati movie *Mon Oncle*, a 1958 French view into the electronic future where commuters driving home on Friday had to race out of the garage before the automatic door closer locked them in for the weekend.

But devices such as Homeminder are only the first wave of "smart" multitask machines that link appliances and lights and phones into a single, controllable system.

In many cases, simply turning a switch by hand is still more sensible and more economical than turning on a T.V. and flipping through a few menus to get to the picture of the switch. But, inevitably, software will become faster and more versatile, leading, perhaps in the next decade, to voice control that will make computer control of many household operations as easy as saying "on" and "off."

Fixing Simple Machines
Mind Over Matter and Manufacturer's Instructions

The five o'clock shadow had grown into full-fledged stubble. I growled at the rechargeable razor, then clicked the switch on and off another five times to confirm what I had known the day before. It was still dead as a doornail.

 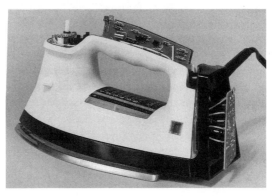

Remember when things used to be simple—like the ultimate simple car. The first Volkswagon "bug" built in 1952 was almost as easy to maintain as a lawn mower. Today's appliances, like this Sunbeam iron, have "smart" circuitry built in. This iron will even shut itself off if you walk away for too long, or if it tips over.

But last week, on top of a burned-out relay in the well pump, it just seemed like one breakdown too many. It wouldn't recharge, buzz, hum—nothing. I thought about popping it with a hammer or sending it back to the manufacturer for repairs, even though it had outlived its warranty.

I've done that before with other dead machines. For all the letter writing, packing, and postage (some fun with a 125-pound television) the response has never been very good. In fact, I know the drill well enough to contemplate sending a multiple choice, return-addressed postcard along with the razor—to get the bad news a little faster. I could allow for the four basic possibilities, and ask them to check one, please.

☐ Letter arrived without razor; don't know where razor is; please don't write to us again; have a good day.

☐ Razor arrived in 200 pieces and cannot be repaired; could have been hit by truck.

☐ Special parts on order for razor; parts expected to arrive in 3 years.

☐ Razor here; parts here; please forward check for twice the cost of brand new razor to fix old razor.

You can tell that I've been through this before. That's why I decided to take the plunge, try to open up the lifeless little box and fix it myself. I succeeded. The razor works very nicely.

This is not earth-shattering news. And the exact details of repair are not very important. All kinds of little machines go on the blink. Each may need a one-of-a-kind repair. But even in this insignificant venture, there are some underlying principles that could be instructive.

Deciding to crack the shell. There must be a dozen reasons not to try to open up a simple machine and fix it yourself. Just look at the manufacturer's instructions for anything from an electric pepper mill to an auto-focus camera. The do-it-yourself troubleshooting section may have only two entries. One says you can clean the item, if you work carefully with a soft cloth. The other says DON'T TOUCH ANYTHING ELSE, YOU FUMBLE-HANDED BLOCKHEAD (well, not in exactly those words), just send it back for authorized repairs.

Last week I authorized myself. If the razor had still been under warranty, of course, voiding the protection with unauthorized repairs could have been a bad decision. But the razor job was a last ditch effort. Without help, I knew it would become a permanent fixture in the sock drawer, lying there stone cold.

Disassembly disinformation. It happens to everyone—maybe with a troublesome flashlight. You unscrew the lens cap, remove the reflector, the reflector retainer spring, and the bulb in about a minute. Then it takes an hour to put the pieces back together again.

The trick is to treat yourself like a real dope during disassembly: take notes, make a sketch, set the pieces down in an orderly row as you remove them. With those little tricks you won't feel like a dope trying to put the pieces back together.

Safecracking the shell. Manufacturers can make it difficult to open a simple case. It's as if they don't want you to see just how simple that $40 machine really is—or the internal components of their "American-made" product with motors labeled "Taiwan."

You may encounter tiny allen screws too small for any of your allen wrenches. You may have to track down the right-sized tool in a good hardware store, or a specialty supplier such as Brookstone's Hard-To-Find Tools. My razor casing is held together with slightly hidden spring clips. Pretty sneaky. There are special removal tools for spring clips. But I've found that a small, high-quality, needle-nose pliers is handy for almost any small-scale mechanical surgery.

Deciphering the innards. Since the manufacturer doesn't want anyone mucking about in the razor, there is no road map or wiring diagram. You have to follow your common sense. And in many cases, it is easy to see what's wrong. On the razor, a wire from one of the recharging batteries had disconnected from the soldered connection on the motor.

First I shaved off a little wire insulation, then wrapped the copper around the motor terminal, and secured the connection with solder using a simple soldering tool.

Granted, an officially authorized repairman might have had an easier time, tackling the small-scale repair work in a brightly lit razor factory with specialized tools. But, after working my way in reverse order through the desktop of disassembled parts, it was very satisfying when the formerly dead-as-a-doornail razor buzzed back to life.

Furnace Efficiency

Q. Is there much difference between the energy efficiency and resulting utility costs of gas and oil furnaces? We will need to install a new unit rated at about 100,000 Btus per hour, and already have both gas and oil lines nearby in the basement.

A. The American Council for an Energy-Efficient Economy, which annually issues a publication called, "The Most Energy-Efficient Appliances," lists 18 high-efficiency gas furnaces in the capacity range you need. The highest has an efficiency rating, called the Annual Fuel Utilization Efficiency (AFUE) percentage, of 96 percent. The lowest is rated 91.4 percent. The list includes such manufacturers as Clare Brothers, Lennox, Amana, Dayton Electric, Duo-matic/Olsen, Sears, Heil-Quaker, Whirlpool, and others.

In comparison, the 5 high-efficiency oil furnaces on the list with approximately the capacity you require have AFUE ratings ranging from 87.0 to 86.1. This list includes such manufacturers as Williamson Company, Duo-matic/Olsen, and Thermo-Products. While this favors gas furnaces on paper, differences in fuel costs from one area to another can alter the equation.

But you could do a quick study as follows. Suppose your heating fuel fill is $1,000. Buying a 96-percent efficient gas furnace instead of an 86-percent efficient oil furnace should make about a 10-percent difference in fuel costs—about $100 per year. And if the gas unit cost $1,000 more than the oil unit, it would take you about 10 years to break even on the extra investment.

The 18-page booklet, which includes similar efficiency listings for refrigerators, freezers, dishwashers, air conditioners, and other major appliances, is available for $2 from the American Council for an Energy-Efficient Economy.[3]

Cleaning Furnace Humidifiers

Q. Do furnace-mounted humidifiers require regular cleaning? If so, how often should the job be done and how do you do it?

A. When water is in motion through the humidifier system, mold and mildew growth associated with standing, stagnant water (a problem during summer months), is not likely.

But it is a good idea to clean the humidifier holding tank, and on many types of humidifiers, the sponge pad that dips into the water, before and after each heating season. Normal soap and water does the trick unless you have very hard water with a high mineral content, for instance, from a private well.

---

[3]The American Council for an Energy-Efficient Economy, 1001 Connecticut Avenue NW, Suite 535, Washington, DC 20036

In this case, you have to soak the deposits overnight (some home owners use a vinegar solution), then attack the crusty deposits with a stiff brush.

Refrigerator Frost

Q. Even though I have a frostless refrigerator-freezer, the floor and lower back wall of the freezer compartment is icing up. I have emptied the freezer and defrosted manually once, but the ice returned. What is the problem?

A. There are two likely problems. First, is a broken freezer fan or a broken freezer fan switch. To check, open the freezer door, and look for a small switch on the face of the freezer wall—where it would be compressed as the door closes. With the door open, depress the switch by hand to see if the fan runs. If it doesn't, you'll need a service call to replace the fan or switch, or both. But ask the service representative to check the switch first, since it is less expensive to replace than the fan. Sometimes, the switch becomes fouled with a little melting ice cream or water and just stops working.

If the fan is working, check for the second problem—a clogged drain line. On many models, water produced by automatic defrosting collects at the base of the freezer and runs through a hose or metal tube leading from the freezer compartment floor to a drain pan beneath the refrigerator. There, it is gradually evaporated in the stream of warm air produced by another fan that blows air over the compressor to keep it from overheating.

Defrost manually once more to clear the ice. Then, after unplugging the refrigerator, flush the freezer drain line with hot water. A squeeze-top baster works well, and can provide enough pressure to dislodge bits of food or paper packaging that cause the clog.

Clogged Dryer Vent

Q. I have a gas clothes dryer that is taking longer and longer to dry clothes from the washer, yet the dryer seems to be operating normally. It just takes longer for the bell to ring. What could the problem be?

A. My guess is a partially clogged exhaust vent. Although most modern machines have some type of lint filter (often a fine screen mounted on a removable frame somewhere around the dryer door), inevitably, some lint gets by the filter. It often is blown out with the hot air through a duct to an exterior vent.

But since the lint is usually still damp, it can catch on the side of the duct, typically at one of several potential bottlenecks, such as an elbow fitting where the duct turns into the wall, or at the exterior face of the vent line. Many exterior fittings have a hinged flap over the duct to keep cold winter air from flowing in. The flap is designed to rise when pushed by the flow of warm exhaust air from the machine. But it may be clogged with lint.

First, clean out the lint filter on the machine. Then check for built-up lint at the exterior vent. If you cannot detect an increase in the rate at which warm air shoots out of the duct and the problem persists, take the duct apart. Chances are it's clogged at one of the fittings, or at one of the twists in a single-piece, flexible duct.

Fluorescent Lighting Ballast

Q. Fluorescent lights under the kitchen cabinets have started buzzing. Although the bulbs seem to last a lot longer than incandescent bulbs, when I replaced them, I got more buzzing and no light. Do I need new fixtures?

A. Depending on the type of fluorescent fixture you have, the problem may be in the fixture ballast, which is concealed in the fixture housing, or in the starter, which looks like a small, silvery button usually located near the end of the fluorescent tube. If the fixture has a separate starter, replace it first, since it is less costly than the ballast and more accessible. If that doesn't work, and the buzzing sound is quite distinct, replace the ballast.

You may have to replace an old fixture since suitable ballast may be unavailable or costly enough to be most of the price of new fixture.

But there could be another problem. In some recessed fixtures, heat buildup will cause an automatic shut-down. The solution, in this case, would be to provide more ventilation—drilling holes through surrounding ceiling joists, for instance.

Conditioning Indoor Air

Twenty Seven

MOISTURE AND VENTILATION CONTROL

House Ventilation
Sensible, "Breathing," Energy-Efficiency Homes

Remember when you first discovered just how heavy a sweater you needed to stay warm when the thermostat was lowered from 72 down to 68 degrees Fahrenheit? Starting with the energy crisis in 1973, our concerns about energy-efficiency grew along with the price per barrel of oil. Years after odd-even gas days, after double-wall, double-insulated houses wrapped in plastic and foil like a piece of chicken in the refrigerator, many consumers, and builders, are still paranoid about energy.

Of course you should think about energy costs when you buy a house or plan major renovations. But you don't have to go to extremes and calculate degree days and solar angles. Just use your common sense, and some of the following guidelines.

For instance, it is okay for a house to breath—even desirable. New England is dotted with century-old houses that have been breathing like crazy from the day they were built.

It's okay for houses to breath out some cool, conditioned air in summer, and some warm, heated air in winter. Yes, air you pay to condition will escape. But it will take some of the 7- to 10-gallons of moisture produced inside a typical home along with it.

You may picture insulation company ads of dollar bills flying out leaky windows. But those ads don't show all the dollar bills that must fly back in to pay for a vent fan in the stagnant kitchen, new tile to replace the buckled floor in the bath, new paint or wallboard to replace the mold-encrusted walls in the cellar—only some of the problems caused by trapping moisture inside.

If you're looking at a new house, check the attic, which can heat up under the sun like an oven. The best venting combination is a large grill at each end of the attic, high on the gable wall since heat rises, plus venting along the eaves where the roof overhangs the side walls of the building.

The space between joists (commonly 2-by-6 or larger timbers) in the attic floor should be nearly filled with insulation, separating living space from dead space in the attic. In a dead space attic not used for living, the spaces between rafters in the attic ceiling should not be insulated—not unless there is ample room provided for ventilation between the top of the insulation and the bottom of the roof.

Beware of these telltale indicators of poor ventilation: water stains on exposed rafters, and rusty ends on protruding roof nails. Water on nails or rafters could have

---

Opposite: Like the more traditional fireplace, a woodstove tends to be a focal point and natural gathering place in a home. For this reason, many people choose mid-wall locations in the den, family room, or living room.

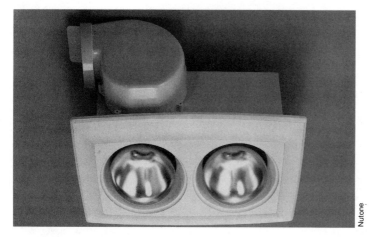

Bathroom moisture can be evacuated with a fan, combined, in this Heat-A-Vent unit made by Nutone, with a small heater. Ask an electrician about wiring the fan component to a timer switch. This way you can turn on the heat lamps without creating a draft with the fan. Before leaving the room, set the fan switch on for five minutes to pump out excess moisture, and turn the unit off.

Nutone

come from a leak. If so, you should see a thin dark line around the edge of the water stain, which are traces of asphalt from the roof.

Whole-house vent fans—those monster machines mounted in stairwell ceilings— also can cause problems with ventilation unless provision is made to conduct the large volume of air out of the attic. Instead of costly air conditioning, whole-house fans can cool off a house quickly. In the evening, simply open first floor windows, turn on the fan, and pull fresh air into, up through, and out of the house.

Unless new, large, gable-end vents are installed (vents matched by the installer to the cubic volume of air moved by the fan) the process will be self-defeating. One good option is to install the fan in place of one of the gable-end vents. In a typical system, a motorized grill in the ceiling of a central area such as a stairwell is triggered by a thermostat that also starts the fan.

Poor ventilation is also obvious in bathrooms. Too often, a costly tile job is ruined by excessive moisture that erodes the grout between tiles, then sweeps down to break the adhesive bond between tile and subfloor, which, in severe cases, may rot and warp.

Natural ventilation should be added in small baths, that can reach mist-filled, nearly tropical conditions when someone takes a long, hot shower. The best bet is a vent fan in an exterior wall. Hop out of the shower, dry off, then turn on the fan to evacuate the mist. Yes, warm air escapes. No, your tile will not buckle years ahead of schedule.

There is a practical drawback to this system, however. In winter, naked, wet people do not like a cool breeze, so they don't turn on the fan until they're ready to leave the room. And then, being paranoid about energy efficiency, they may decide against turning on the fan at all since they will be going to work soon, or know that they will probably forget to turn the fan off later on. This is the kind of energy efficiency that saves you 88 cents of electricity at the expense of an $880 tile job.

The solution is to install (or consult an electrician about installing) a timer switch for the fan—the kind used on saunas to make sure you don't dehydrate. When you leave the room, set the switch for 5 or 10 minutes—enough time to evacuate the excessive moisture, close the door to minimize the loss of warm, household air in winter, or cool, conditioned air in summer, and forget about energy altogether.

SOFFIT VENTS

Overhanging eaves can be vented by installing plug vents, or stapling screening (to keep out insects and birds) over a channel in the soffit. Aluminum strip grill vents, with flanges that tuck under the plywood, are durable and easy to install. Ceiling insulation should cover the stud wall without blocking the vent or air flow below the roof deck.

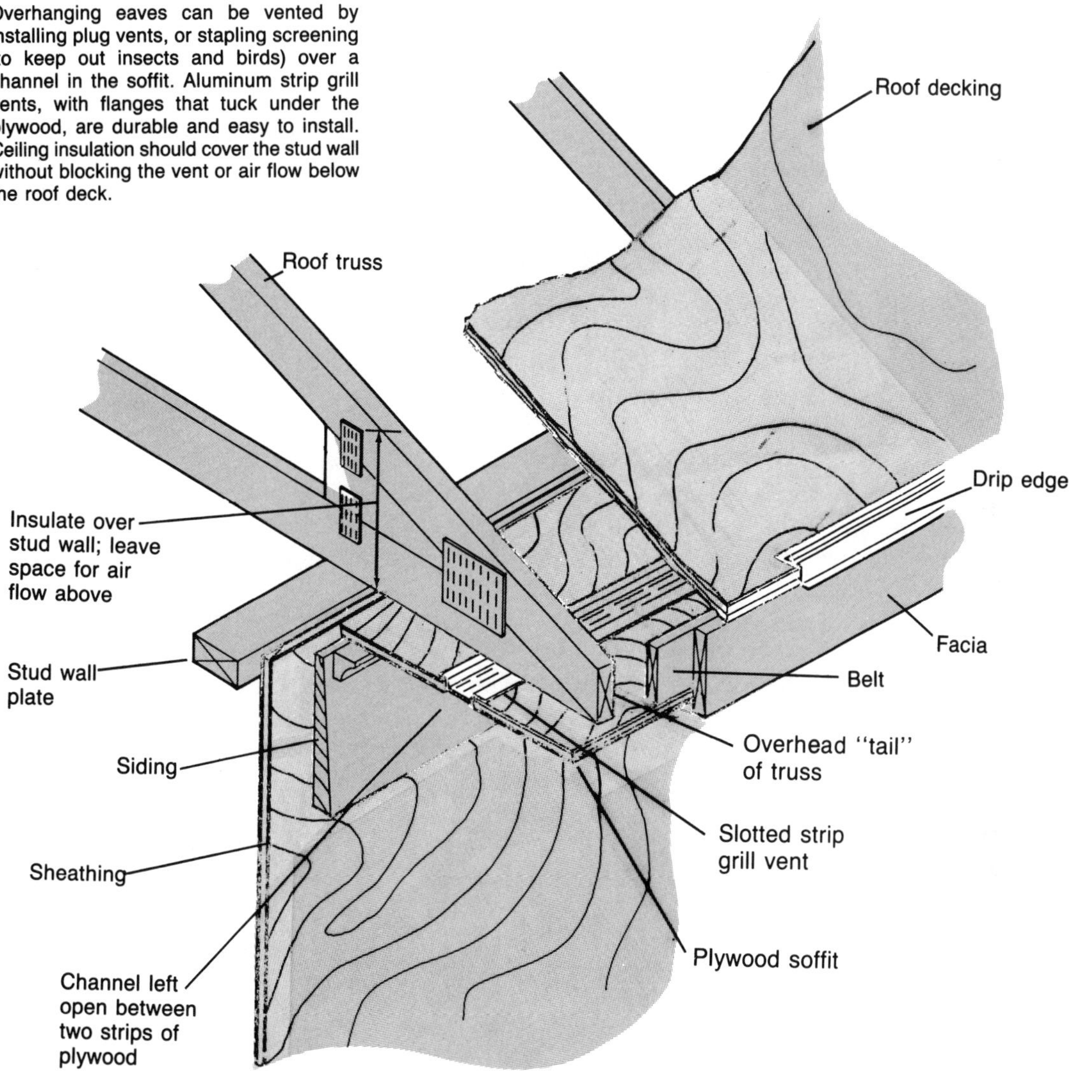

Roof decking

Roof truss

Drip edge

Insulate over stud wall; leave space for air flow above

Stud wall plate

Facia

Belt

Siding

Overhead "tail" of truss

Sheathing

Slotted strip grill vent

Plywood soffit

Channel left open between two strips of plywood

Dampness Control
Dealing with the Damp Dog Days of Summer

Who needs to hear a meteorologist analyze the relative humidity rating and temperature-humidity index when there are so many obvious indicators of excessive dampness—sticking to the furniture, for instance. If you find yourself shedding clothes the minute you're inside the door, running out of towels, and lingering in front of an open refrigerator, it's time to make your home less like a steam bath.

If sweating windows and moldy walls are the main problem (more so than temperature alone), dehumidifying the air can be very effective because dry air feels cooler than humid air at the same temperature. If you run an air conditioner to keep cool, it will help dry out the air but may not solve the dampness problem completely—especially if you run only a room unit, in the bedroom, for instance.

There is a drawback to running a dehumidifier. While it complements air conditioning, it may be oppressive in a very small area. A dehumidifier has a compressor that produces heat just like an air conditioner. But the hot side of a room or central air conditioner is outside the house, while heat from a portable dehumidifier stays in the room.

The effectiveness of a dehumidifier is measured by how much moisture it removes from the air in a rating termed "pints per day." These ratings permit comparisons of units, which are manufactured with capacities ranging from 13 to more than 50 pints per day. Variations in operating coasts among units of different capacities are marginal.

The Association of Home Appliance Manufacturers recommends different capacities depending on how big and how damp the area is. In a moderately damp, 500 square foot area, for instance, a 10-pints-per-day dehumidifier is recommended. In an extremely wet area the same size, capacity is recommended at 16 pints per day. In a large, 2,500 square foot area, the Association recommends a unit rated at 26 pints per day for moderately damp conditions, and 44 pints per day for extremely wet conditions. But these are only guidelines.

In addition to reducing moisture with a dehumidifier, other common-sense measures can help.

Venting "wet" areas. Installing vent fans to the exterior in kitchens, baths, and laundry areas where moisture is produced can remove most of the 7 to 10 gallons of moisture generated daily by normal household operations such as taking showers.

Ventilating dead spaces. Supply at least 1 square foot of vent per 300 square feet of attic floor to release heat and humidity. This also decreases the air conditioning load by decreasing the oven effect of hot air trapped in the attic. Use a combination of vents at two locations for the most efficiency: either round, plug-type, or continuous-strip vents along the eaves where the roof overhangs the walls of the house, and larger grills called gable-end vents at the end walls of the attic just under the peak of the roof.

Double-glazing windows. Double glazing is a good investment in summer as well as winter, reducing air conditioning costs and removing surfaces prone to condensation. A buffer of dead air between two panes of glass—even a thin layer—keeps the inside pane close to room temperature so that moisture in cooler inside air is less likely to condense on the glass.

You can simulate the effect of double glazing for about $10 for an average-sized window by applying a layer of heat-shrink plastic film. The thin, optically clear film is applied on double-faced adhesive tape. It also is effective in winter, but won't last as long as a second pane of glass.

Insulating masonry walls. Basement walls and foundations, kept cool by sheltering earth on the outside, can become covered on the inside with condensation as moisture in warm interior air condenses on their surfaces. One thorough solution is to build an insulated wall just inside the masonry, using 2-by-2 inch studs, and styrene-type insulating board, which resists damage from moisture. The wall is covered with a plastic or foil vapor barrier, then surfaced with drywall or paneling for appearance.

Bath fixtures. Another chronic site of condensation problems is any cool ceramic surface, particularly the surface of a water closet because it holds a regularly replenished supply of cool water. These tanks can "sweat" enough to puddle the floor and disrupt grout and tile adhesive, which eventually can dislodge the tile and rot the wood floor underneath.

Between boiling, frying, and steaming, the stove is a prime source of interior moisture. The best way to control moisture is to evacuate it at the point of production—with a range hood ducted to an exterior vent. Many units have built-in grease filters to reduce clogging and general grubbiness in the ducts and fan.

Improving bathroom ventilation with a vent fan to the exterior will help. You can also apply a ½-inch-thick foam rubber lining to the inside vertical walls of the tank with waterproof resin glue, staying clear of the valves and flushing mechanism. A more expensive solution involves running a hot water pipe to a special mixing valve that replaces the standard, cold water cutoff valve. The mixer feeds a blend of room-temperature water from cold and hot water pipes to the tank.

CRAWL SPACE VENTING

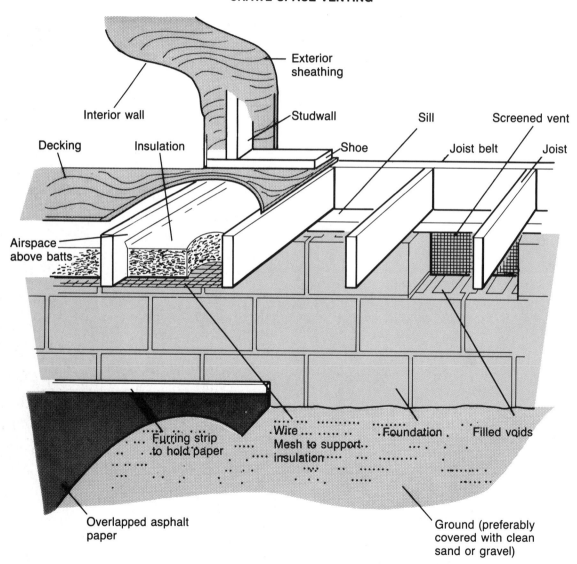

In crawl spaces, suppress ground moisture by pouring concrete, gravel, or clean sand over the dirt, and covering with overlapped sheets of asphalt paper, rolled up onto the foundation wall. Also, vents should be provided to evacuate moisture that would seep up into the living space.

Wet Walls
Solutions for Summer Sweats

One of the most common complaints about houses, new or old, is downstairs dampness: wet walls in cellars, basements and finished rooms partially or completely below ground level. Even if foundation walls keep out groundwater and periodic deluges from gutters and downspouts, condensation inside the house can produce as much water as serious, widespread leaking.

The wetness is certainly unpleasant, for instance, at night, in bare feet, going from a wooden stair tread to a cold, swamp-like concrete floor. But the mildew, bad odors, possible allergic reactions, deterioration of building materials and furnishings it produces are the real problems. And in many cases mildew and bad odors linger despite stringent preventive measures.

The amount and frequency of condensation depends on things such as wall mass, depth below grade, room temperature, and the dew point at different percentages of relative humidity. Feel free to skip the next paragraph if a simple explanation—when its hot and humid your walls are likely to sweat—will suffice.

Wall design is based on data from engineering tables displaying different dew points for a range of temperatures. A table would show, for instance, that at 70 degrees Fahrenheit and 40 percent relative humidity, the dew point (the temperature to which air must be cooled to form dew) is 45 degrees Fahrenheit. Next, the difference between inside and outside temperatures (70 outside, 10 inside, say, or 80) is compared on a U-factor (total thermal value of a wall), calculation chart to the difference between the inside air temperature and dew point (say, 70 inside, 45 dew point, or 25). The chart displays both temperature ranges and shows the minimum U-factor required to prevent sweating. It's a matter of finding where two curves intersect on a graph. But for consumers, it can be a puzzling business.

However, it points up the most effective way to prevent wall sweating: Minimize the temperature difference between the cool foundation wall and the warm, humid air inside the house.

Another complementary approach is to reduce the inside air temperature (air conditioning) or the inside air humidity level, or both. Air conditioning does both jobs. A dehumidifier only removes moisture from the air (and actually produces some heat from the compressor motor). Vent fans at key locations where moisture is produced (above stoves, in bathrooms and laundry areas, for example) can reduce the load on both appliances.

The first step in altering existing basement walls to prevent sweating is to clean away the mildew and moss and potato patches thriving in the dark, damp corners. In most cases a cup of bleach to a gallon of hot water, applied vigorously with a stiff scrub brush, then rinsed, will kill the fungus and odors. Any leaks must be stopped before adding materials and closing in the wall. If there are small, thin cracks that let in some water during heavy rains, patch them with hydraulic cement after scraping out and thoroughly drying the crevices.

In most cases there are two components of the anti-sweat project: first, some form of insulation to minimize temperature differences at the wall surface; second, some form of frame to support wallboard or paneling to cover the insulating material. (To leave a brick facade intact it is necessary to insulate outside, which may involve some excavation work, while scraping and sealing the brick inside.)

The typical, do-it-yourself cellar renovation—you can find it illustrated in ancient *Popular Mechanics* and *Popular Science* magazines—calls for 1-by-2 furring strips secured with cut or concrete nails directly to the concrete or block walls every 16 inches, in rows parallel to the floor. (Furring strips are usually an inferior grade of spruce with a lot of knots, twists and bows.)

The next step is to add insulation between or over the furring strips—¾-inch thick foamboard, for instance. It's light, easily cut, shaped, and placed with a spot or two of construction adhesive.

That part of the job takes care of temperature variation against the wall. Adding a vapor barrier before wallboard or paneling prevents moisture at any temperature from reaching the masonry surface. Without a barrier, moisture would work its way through wallboard and insulation, then condense on the masonry and rot the furring strips. The most effective barrier is foil. It is impervious, but more expensive and more difficult to work with without tearing than the very inexpensive alternative, plastic sheeting.

After the frame and insulation (thin batts of fiberglass work well, too) are in place a continuous sheet of plastic (4- or 6-mil thick) is draped over the wall. Attach it temporarily with only a few staples, since even small punctures will let moisture into the insulated space. The sheets will be punctured as you nail the finished wall panels in place. But those punctures will be sealed by pressure between the panel and furring strip beneath.

This simple renovation project does have a few drawbacks, though. Even with special nails designed for masonry, sometimes the darn things just won't go in. They snap, which can be dangerous and demands eye protection. Also, they can put a crack in the furring strip.

You try a nail. It snaps. You try another a few inches away. Maybe that one goes in; maybe not. Sometimes this sequence starts to split the furring strip in two, which means you have a row of nails firmly embedded in concrete that must be removed so you can install a new strip. It can get frustrating.

Also, the nails can create a fault line in the masonry wall. If you had a dry wall, and, for some reason, wanted to make it leak, what better way then to drive a line of nails into it, like driving splitting wedges into a log to make fencing.

Substituting independent 2 by 2s for 1 by 2s solves these problems. It costs more, but not a lot more. And it's worth it. First, the extra depth lets you add more insulation, which better separates the cool masonry wall from the warm and humid interior air. Second, the larger framing is strong enough to be built like a house wall—studs every 16 inches on center held between 2 by 2s top and bottom parallel to the floor. It can be assembled on the floor after careful measuring, then tipped up into position.

Set the bottom of the frame on the concrete floor next to the wall in a bed of construction adhesive. (One or two nails can lock the frame in position.)

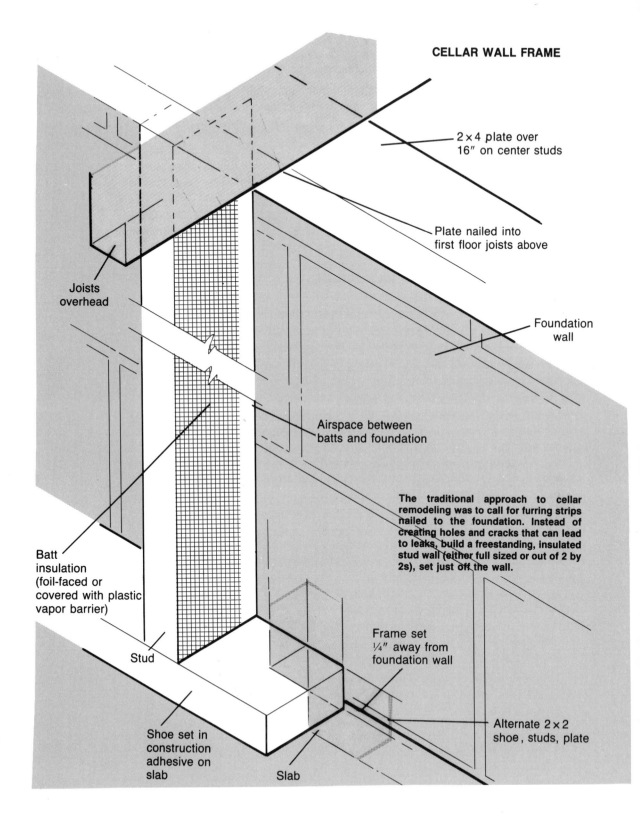

CELLAR WALL FRAME

2 x 4 plate over
16" on center studs

Plate nailed into
first floor joists above

Joists
overhead

Foundation
wall

Airspace between
batts and foundation

The traditional approach to cellar
remodeling was to call for furring strips
nailed to the foundation. Instead of
creating holes and cracks that can lead
to leaks, build a freestanding, insulated
stud wall (either full sized or out of 2 by
2s), set just off the wall.

Batt
insulation
(foil-faced or
covered with plastic
vapor barrier)

Frame set
¼" away from
foundation wall

Stud

Alternate 2 x 2
shoe , studs, plate

Shoe set in
construction
adhesive on
slab

Slab

Nail through the top horizontal 2 by 2 into the ceiling joists. If you have measured for a snug fit this will be more than adequate. Remember, these are not bearing walls carrying structural loads from the roof. They support some wallboard, period. This method eliminates all nails into masonry, increases insulation protection, and makes the work easier too, since there is simply more wood to work with, and less chance of splits and bent nails.

Mildew Smells

Q. Once mold and mildew deposits from summer condensation have been cleaned off walls, what's the best way to get rid of the lingering, musty aroma? I expected cold weather would do the trick, but when the furnace runs the smell seems even more pungent.

A. Deposits removed with soap, or even a more powerful detergent, may only temporarily solve the problem. To remove lingering odors, first try washing the area again with one of a proprietary disinfectants such as Lysol, or a homemade solution of 1 cup household bleach to 1 gallon of water. For tough problems, increase bleach.)

Once the area is clean there are three ways to deal with remaining odors. First, let them dissipate naturally, providing as much ventilation as you can manage given the colder weather. Second, try a chemical air cleaner. One company specializing in this field is Mateson Chemical.[1] They manufacture many specialized cleaners, deodorizers, and disinfectants, including a general purpose, synthetic charcoal filtering material called Bad Air Sponge, and a liquid designed to inhibit mold and mildew growth in damp areas that can be "spritzed" on wall surfaces, insulation, and other materials, called Blue Vitriol 13.

If trace odors remain despite all attempts to clean the surface, try sealing in the problem. Apply multiple coats of oil-base paint, varnish, or similar finish. In some areas it may also be necessary to coat normally unfinished surfaces such as the raw plywood inside kitchen cabinets and bathroom vanities.

Mold Stains

Q. Dark streaks have begun to show along the edges of the ceiling above a shower in a second floor bath. How can I tell if they come from a roof leak, and if not, what else might cause them?

A. If the streaks were pale with dark edges you could assume that they were from a roof leak. (A dark ring results from traces of asphalt migrating toward the edges

[1]Mateson Chemical, 1025 East Montgomery Street, Philadelphia, PA 19125

of the wet area.) If you do not see that telltale indicator, assume that the streaking is mold and mildew growth—a common occurrence in that location.

Fix the problem by scrubbing vigorously with warm water and household bleach (half and half is a potent mix that should be used with care). After the area dries, apply at least one coat of pigmented white shellac to prevent any remaining discoloration from bleeding through a finish coat of paint.

Attic Condensation

Q. I have noticed drops of water forming on nails protruding through the roof into the attic. Do I need more insulation on the attic floor? Should I crack the windows at each end of the attic for more ventilation, or is there another solution that will stop the dripping?

A. Two improvements will help: keeping warm, moist air from the heated living space below out of the attic, and increasing attic ventilation to get rid of any moisture that does get in.

To stop moisture, install a vapor barrier (normally 6-mil thick plastic sheeting), beneath the attic insulation. Vapor barriers are placed between the heat source (your furnace) and the insulation. To improve ventilation, simply open the windows at each end of the attic an inch or so. This may seem crazy in winter, but it will help.

Opening the attic to winter weather will make the attic colder, and the attic floor, too. This may translate into slightly cooler temperatures in the rooms below unless you have a floor filled with insulation. Of course, this also depends on how cold it gets where you live.

In buildings without operating windows (that's the trade phrase for windows you can open), vents serve the same purpose. In an attic with a vapor barrier provide at least 1 square foot of vent inlet and 1 square foot of vent outlet per 500 or 600 square feet of attic floor space. (You should have about twice as much vent space in an attic without a vapor barrier.)

For thorough ventilation the best plan is to provide vents on the end walls of the attic, and along the eaves where the roof overhangs the walls of the house. I don't favor roof-top ventilators when eave and gable end venting is possible on the principle that the fewer holes in the roof the better.

Winter Humidity Level

Q. How can I maintain a comfortable level of humidity (without causing windows to sweat) while running a forced hot-air heating system backed up with a wood stove during the winter?

A. Install an automatic humidifier on the hot-air furnace. Most humidifiers, which connect to a water pipe and feed moisture into the warm air supply, include some form of sensor and adjustment that monitors the relative humidity of air returning to the furnace.

You can add more moisture on very cold days when the furnace runs a lot, and reduce the setting on warmer days that may be humid enough without any help.

Most people feel comfortable in 30 to 40 percent relative humidity. Air much drier than that can cause sore throats and discomfort from dry skin, not to mention problems in your house, such as shrinking floorboards.

The trick is to strike a balance, adding enough humidity to feel comfortable just up to the point where the warm, moist air condenses on windows. You'll have to fiddle with the controls to get the balance right.

And the balance will change when you light the wood stove. In that room the air will be much drier than elsewhere. Compensate for this extra dryness by setting a cast-iron kettle or heat-tempered crockery pot filled with water on top of a wood stove. It will add moisture gradually, and, if you drop in a few peels of lemon or lime, a few drops of vanilla flavoring, or some other aromatic, the air around the stove will smell nice, too.

Vapor Barriers and House Wraps

Q. What is the difference between a house wrap barrier and a vapor barrier, and, if there is a difference, where is the proper location for these barriers on an exterior wall?

A. They are two related but different animals. A vapor barrier is placed on the interior wall face, directly over wall studs, just beneath the drywall. It can be made of plastic (6-mil-thick polyethylene is a common choice) or foil. It is intended to prevent moisture produced inside the house from seeping into the wall cavity.

Without a vapor barrier, warm moist air moving through the wall eventually would meet a cold surface—probably exterior sheathing or siding. Then the water vapor would condense, soaking insulation, fostering mold, mildew, and rot in the wood frame. Another problem is that moisture can travel completely through the wall, and disrupt paint on the exterior siding.

House wrap, referred to as an air-infiltration barrier, is placed outside the house, over plywood sheathing, just before siding is installed. It is a thin, rugged, paper-like fabric that keeps wind from blowing in, while allowing moisture to get out.

Normally, the entire wall from foundation to roof is wrapped, which seems a bit silly. Granted, you may have energy-robbing leaks around windows and doors, and where the floor frame joins the foundation. But these crucial seams can be thoroughly sealed with insulation and multiple layers of caulking. It is difficult to imagine air blowing in through expanses of solid siding between windows and doors, which is nailed directly to ½-inch-thick, solid plywood sheathing.

Interior vapor barriers are essential. But house wraps are an extra—something to buy after you allow for a few pieces of new furniture, an increase in the utility bill, braces for the kids, and a quart of milk.

Attic Ventilation Options

Q. My attic overheats on warm days, which makes the second floor bedrooms too warm in the evening. I have small, triangular vents at each end of the roof, but no fans, ventilators, or vents at the roof overhangs. Each type of vent has been suggested as the answer by various contractors. Which one is the most effective?

A. Each suggestion has merit. But the weakest link in your existing system is the lack of any eave vents at the soffits (the portion of the roof overhang facing and parallel to the ground just outside the house wall). Without such vents you probably have a small, lazy stream of air wandering along the ridge line from one end of the attic to the other. This leaves most of the attic unventilated.

Adding plug vents (small, grill-covered, screened vents) in the soffits between rafters on both sides of the house will introduce many small airstreams along the attic perimeter. These vents are the easiest to install for do-it-yourselfers; simply drill a hole and pop in the vent. Strip grill vents provide the same function but are long, narrow aluminum grills that run the length of the soffit. Obviously, a correspondingly wide strip of soffit has to be cut away (not the easiest job working with a power saw over your head) before such vents could be installed.

Add eave vents first. Then increase the size of your small gable-end vents. Chances are this will do the job, and you won't have to install fans or put a hole in your roof for a ventilator.

While this attic vent louver might be large enough to evacuate built up heat and moisture, vines growing outside have shut the vent by using the slats as a trellis. To ventilate the complete attic space, gable-end vents should be combined with eave venting.

Twenty Eight

HEATING SYSTEMS

House Warming Alternatives
Six Ways to Make a House Warmer Without Turning Up the Heat

You may have missed Energy Awareness Month, designated as October by the Department of Energy (DOE), since that is when many furnaces are turned on for the first time in the heating season. But for many people, energy awareness starts a good while after the furnace rumbles into action—when the first bills for oil or gas or electricity arrive. While the DOE's publicity program may have escaped your attention, those bills will not.

But if you neglected to make a lot of energy-saving home improvements before the heating season began, there are still several steps you can take to make your house warmer in winter—without turning up the heat. Here are six of them.

Limit the flow of heated air out of the house. Although built-up condensation can cause problems, particularly in kitchens and baths, use exhaust fans in those rooms sparingly.

A dormant fireplace also can funnel warm air out of the house—up to 8 percent of your heat, according to DOE estimates—unless the damper is closed tightly. As burning embers smolder and the damper must remain open, reduce heat loss by closing off the fireplace opening with fireproof doors.

Reduce air leaks at windows and doors. To check if you need caulking and weather stripping hold a lighted candle near these openings. It's a primitive method of detection, but it works. If the flame dances there is probably too much air flow—a leak.

Seal exterior seams with caulking, and the joints around the moving parts of windows and doors with weather stripping. This should cost about $25 for an average house with 12 windows and 2 doors, according to DOE estimates. That modest investment could net a 10-percent saving in annual energy costs. And you still haven't touched the thermostat.

Install storm windows and doors. Although there are many types of storm windows, one of the most effective, least expensive, and easiest to install (an unusual combination) is clear, heat-shrink plastic. The optically clear film is applied over double-faced adhesive tape, then stretched free of wrinkles by applying heat from a hair dryer.

You can improve the weather tightness of seasonal storm windows, such as wood-frame units that are hung on clips above the window, by adding self-stick foam adhesive or tubular weather stripping around the storm window frame where it meets the window frame. The DOE estimates that sealing these intentional holes in the house can save up to 15 percent of your annual energy costs.

On some oil-burning furnaces, problems stem from the photoelectric cell, shown here turned out of position toward the camera. Normally, it faces into the combustion chamber to detect the presence or absence of a flame. Soot clouding the face can hinder combustion, and is sometimes overlooked in routine servicing.

Insulate the attic floor. If there is no insulation in the attic floor, the DOE estimates that your energy costs could drop by as much as 30 percent after you add insulation. In most homes, which have some insulation in the attic floor, the question is whether or not to add more. Some insulation advertisements seem to indicate that you couldn't have too much insulation.

There is no fast rule. But if you have minimal attic floor joists (2 by 6s or smaller) and the spaces between them are not completely filled, it is probably cost-effective to add another 3 or 4 inches. If you already have more than 6 inches of insulation in the attic floor you should probably tend to other energy-saving improvements before adding another layer that will cover the joists completely.

Ask your local utility company about an energy audit, which can provide a more detailed analysis of this question, and pin down how much energy this job will save, which will help you to decide if the project is worth the investment.

Tune up the heating equipment. This is the job you should do before you need the furnace. Any furnace that is a decade old should be checked annually, even though the heating industry rule-of-thumb is to clean and tune new oil furnaces annually, and new gas furnaces every 3 years. Professionals should clean blowers, burners, and adjust the rate of combustion. The tune-up can be performed by a plumbing and heating contractor you deal with already, or contractors who provide this service as a follow-up to a utility company's energy audit.

Lower the thermostat. Of course, this is the easiest way to save energy. It's called using less. Without spending a cent you can reduce your heating bill by about 3 percent for every degree of heat you do without. For instance, if the last person to bed lowers the thermostat from 68 to 59 degrees, and the setting is not raised for eight hours, you'll save about 9 percent of your heating costs. (The 9-degree reduction is for 8 hours, or one-third of a day, which is like turning the thermostat down 3 degrees for 24 hours.)

To avoid waking up in a cold house you can manipulate some thermostats automatically, programming a rise in temperature 15 minutes or so before the alarm rings. Automatic setback thermostats cost between $50 and $150, depending on

Typical setback thermostats, such as this Honeywell Fuel Saver can be programmed in advance to raise and lower the thermostat setting at least two times during a 24-hour cycle. Such units can be wired and fitted in place in the same location as old thermostats, which avoids rewiring.

complexity. Most units in the $100 range automatically lower and raise thermostat settings for at least two separate and adjustable blocks of time during a 24-hour time period.

They are particularly effective in households where everybody works or goes to school, so you can reduce the setting during the day and at night. For instance, you could set the heat back from 68 degrees to 53 degrees (15 degrees) for 8 hours during the day and eight hours overnight. This way you would be saving two-thirds of the 3 percent per degree proportion (by reducing the setting two-thirds of the day), which would be 2 percent for every degree of reduction, or, for this 15-degree reduction, a total of up to 30 percent of heating costs.

Of course, you might have to blow some of the savings on a sweater.

<hr />

Heat Pump Basics
Two Sides of the Heating and Cooling System

The first time I heard an explanation of a heat pump, I thought someone might be pulling my leg. The part about "a reversible air conditioner" made some sense. Air conditioners are cool inside and warm outside. Flipping the machine around might add heat to a house.

The really comical part of the explanation had to do with "rescuing heat from winter air." Sure, I thought, along with rescuing some cheese from the moon. I had been outside in cold winter weather before, and it had never seemed the least bit warm.

Although it defies experience, the idea of a heat pump is alluring, a magic bullet for highly efficient home heating—at least in moderate climates with balanced heating and cooling requirements. One machine produces cool air in summer and warm air in winter. It's so alluring that people started making the machines 30 years ago when heating oil was less than 15 cents a gallon. (It's almost 6 times that now.)

Millions of heat pumps are in use today. Some are room units, resembling a room air conditioner. Most are larger, whole-house systems. All consist of a closed loop of pipes through which a refrigerant, such as Freon, is passed. On most systems, temperature gathered and given off by the refrigerant at different points on the loop warms or cools the air directly. On some, temperature changes are transferred to water flowing around the loop.

The bulk of a typical, air-source heat pump normally sits just outside the house, in a unit about the size of a central air conditioner. Other, smaller parts of the system, mainly pipes and valves, are installed inside the house where they cool or warm air distributed through ducts.

In summer, the machine runs like a conventional air conditioner. The refrigerant passes through an expansion valve into a coil of pipes indoors where it changes from a liquid to a vapor. As the liquid evaporates into a cold gas it absorbs heat, which cools the air surrounding the coil of pipes. An indoor fan pushes the cool air through ducts.

Then the vaporized refrigerant is compressed, which raises its temperature and pressure. This high-pressure, hot gas--hotter even than the air outside—then flows into

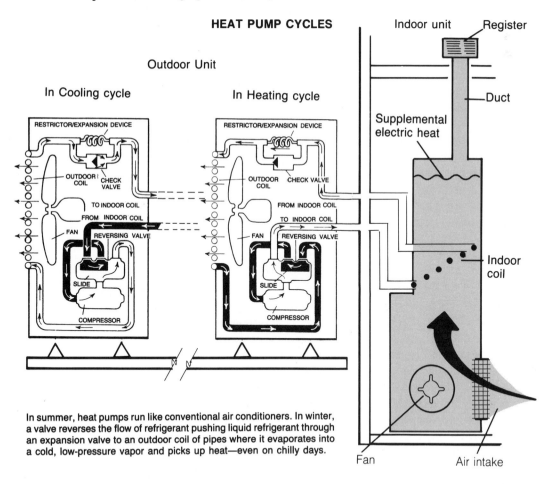

HEAT PUMP CYCLES

Indoor unit   Register

Outdoor Unit

In Cooling cycle   In Heating cycle

Duct

Supplemental electric heat

RESTRICTOR/EXPANSION DEVICE   RESTRICTOR/EXPANSION DEVICE

OUTDOOR COIL   CHECK VALVE   OUTDOOR COIL   CHECK VALVE

TO INDOOR COIL   FROM INDOOR COIL

FROM INDOOR COIL   TO INDOOR COIL

FAN   REVERSING VALVE   FAN   REVERSING VALVE

Indoor coil

SLIDE   SLIDE

COMPRESSOR   COMPRESSOR

In summer, heat pumps run like conventional air conditioners. In winter, a valve reverses the flow of refrigerant pushing liquid refrigerant through an expansion valve to an outdoor coil of pipes where it evaporates into a cold, low-pressure vapor and picks up heat—even on chilly days.

Fan   Air intake

an outdoor coil of pipes where it gives off heat, then condenses back to liquid form and starts the cycle again.

Now for the tricky part. In a heat pump, a valve is used to reverse the flow of refrigerant to provide the heating cycle. It begins as liquid refrigerant flows through an expansion valve to the outdoor coil of pipes. There, it evaporates into a cold, low-pressure vapor. If, for example, the gas became as cold as 30 degrees Fahrenheit and the temperature outside were 40 degrees Fahrenheit, the gas would gain heat. So it's not so much that a heat pump rescues ''heat'' from cold air, as that it makes a refrigerant so cold in comparison to the outside air, that the refrigerant becomes warmer.

Next, the warmed gas heads back inside to the compressor, which increases its temperature and pressure. The hot, high-pressure vapor travels through the inside coil of pipes where it gives off heat, which is pushed into the duct system with a fan. Finally, the warm, liquid refrigerant flows to the expansion valve again, and the cycle continues.

The theoretical beauty of this operation is that electricity is not used to make heat—at least not directly—only to push a refrigerant through the loop, run the compressor, and fans.

But as the weather gets colder, theory can collide with reality. Here's the problem. In general, the refrigerant in most heat pumps becomes too dense to flow efficiently through the expansion and compression cycles when the outdoor temperature drops to about 35 degrees Fahrenheit—a chilly, but certainly not frigid winter day in many areas. As the temperature falls, heat pumps lose their efficiency until a backup system takes over—standard, electric coils that work like a space heater built into the heat pump.

Since resistance electric heating is often the most expensive form of home heating, heat pumps are most suitable in areas where the backup system is not needed very much—areas that don't get too cold for too long.

Solar Energy Breakthroughs
Arctic Observations May Lead to
Solar Heating Advances

''Polar solar'' is one of the most unlikely, yet, potentially most fruitful avenues of state-of-the-art solar energy research. That's ''polar'' as in great big furry white bear.

Two scientists from Northeastern University in Boston inadvertently have discovered that the thick, shaggy coats of polar bears are capable of incredibly sophisticated and efficient solar energy conversion, changing light that hits the fur to heat that warms the body. The discoveries could be useful to homeowners.

So far, only the basics of these complex energy transfers are known. Detailed polar-solar research into the mechanics of these processes is just beginning. Yet dramatic increases of approximately 50 percent in residential solar collection efficiency have been measured in preliminary tests using basic polar-solar principles in simple, and relatively inexpensive, flat-plate collectors—the most basic type of solar heating equipment. Such improvements could signal a major change in the course of current solar research and eventually make solar heating a practical and attractive alternative for many more homeowners.

Over the last decade, solar energy research has gravitated away from simple, flat-plate collector technology to more exotic and expensive sun-focusing or concentrating systems. However, the new polar-solar principles may revitalize the flat-plate segment of the generally sagging solar energy industry, which recently lost a lot of steam with the end of tax credits for residential solar installations and the drop in oil prices.

Although there are many types of flat-plate collectors, these thin but large rectangular panels, normally mounted on roofs, typically consist of a translucent covering over an airspace in which heat from the sun's rays is trapped. The bottom panel of the collector is normally black, which helps absorb heat.

The heat gathered by this greenhouse effect can be cycled from the collector to the house and back again in a number of ways. Warm air can be blown by a fan directly from the roof collector into the building, or heat-absorbing fluid traveling through pipes coiled in the collector can be pumped into radiators in the living spaces.

The energy efficiency of typical flat-plate collectors (the rate at which they convert potential heat in the sun's rays on the roof to usable heat inside), is not very high—only 18 to 20 percent when it is 0 degrees Fahrenheit outside.

In many residential solar installations most of the roof must be covered by collectors in order to capture enough heat during the time the collectors are exposed to sunlight. The limitation imposed by collector size has led many researchers to investigate exotic booster systems using lenses, dish mirrors, tracking devices that follow the sun across the sky, and other means of concentrating or enhancing solar energy collection.

Polar bear fur may prove to collect and transfer solar energy more efficiently than any of these systems, according to Richard Grojean, Professor of Electrical and Computer Engineering at Northeastern University, and a technical director at the school's new Center for Electro-Magnetic Research.[1] He says that using the full range of polar-solar principles as effectively as polar bears do could eventually bring residential solar heating efficiency up to 90 percent. Currently, this kind of efficiency is available only in the most sophisticated and expensive furnaces.

The first insights into polar-solar technology came 5 years ago. At that time Grojean and colleague Gregory Kowalski, Professor of Mechanical Engineering at Northeastern, investigated reports by a Norwegian scientist who was part of a Canadian team counting arctic wildlife by photographing them from the air.

Since white-furred polar bears were almost impossible to spot in the bright white arctic environment, scientists switched from conventional cameras to infrared equipment, which displays subjects according to the heat they produce. The scientists were surprised when this system also failed to detect the warm-blooded bears.

However, when the scientists used ultraviolet equipment, which registers short-wave, invisible rays at the end of the light spectrum, the bears stood out dramatically, indicating an abundance of ultraviolet light on the bear's fur. These findings led Grojean and Kowalski to further investigations, which have revealed many unique properties of polar bear fur. Grojean describes it as a "one-way energy path" that gathers energy from the sun and transfers it to the body very efficiently.

---

[1] Northeastern University, Center for Electro-Magnetic Research, 360 Huntington Avenue, Boston, MA 02115

Grojean says that a single hair of white polar bear fur, viewed under a microscope, is actually transparent. The clear, smooth-surfaced hair has an opaque, hollow, but rough-surfaced core, called the medulla, that scatters light hitting the fur and somehow conducts 95 percent of the ultraviolet light down to the polar bear's black skin where it is converted into heat. Yes, under that white fur is heat-absorbing black skin.

The question arose, why does the bear need to use ultraviolet light rays, which are invisible, for heat? Why not the rest of the spectrum, the visible light rays? Grojean says that polar bears need the ultraviolet rays because they use up the visible rays making camouflage. Their fur reflects about 90 percent of visible light to make the transparent hairs appear white, in order to blend into the arctic environment.

Appearing white against a white background may be as crucial to the bear's survival as staying warm. In fact, Grojean says that while hunting and stalking prey when camouflage is most important, polar bears "hide" by lying on the snow, covering their noses (the only portion of their black skin that shows), with their paws.

In this incredibly practical and balanced system of energy use, the bear's fur uses almost all available visible light for camouflage to appear white, while converting into heat almost all invisible ultraviolet light not suited for camouflage. While many residential roof-top collectors could use a little camouflage just on an aesthetic basis, the addition of high-efficiency ultraviolet solar energy conversion alone could dramatically increase a collector's heating capacity.

Another unique quality of polar bear fur is that it absorbs light efficiently from all directions, including rays reflected from the ice and snow. Applying this property to residential solar heating could also increase efficiency.

Currently, flat-plate collectors work most effectively only when they are perfectly aligned with the sun. Since the sun moves and houses do not, this optimum efficiency is short-lived. Using polar-solar principles, residential collectors might remain highly efficient throughout the day, even under cloud cover, despite changes in the direction and angle of the sun.

The Northeastern scientists are now seeking long-term funding for more detailed research from several groups, including the Department of Energy. Grojean says the next step is to understand in detail exactly how the highly efficient solar conversions are handled in polar bear fur. Once the mechanics are known, models can be built, and from the models, prototypes of revolutionary new residential solar collectors. The new collectors may still have a translucent covering and a black base plate, simulating the natural system of translucent fur over black skin that works wo well for polar bears.

But the dead air space between the panels may be replaced by some form of synthetic, optical fiber "pelt" modeled after polar bear fur. With adequate funding for research and development, Grojean says such collectors could be available within 5 years, making rooftop-delivered, pollution-free solar heating much more efficient and affordable.

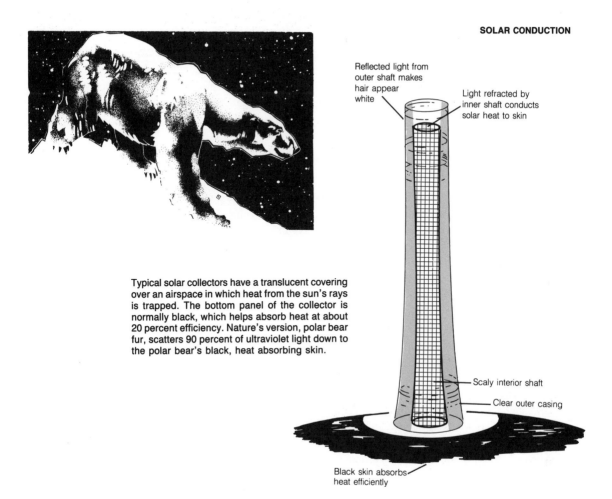

Reflected light from outer shaft makes hair appear white

Light refracted by inner shaft conducts solar heat to skin

Scaly interior shaft

Clear outer casing

Black skin absorbs heat efficiently

Typical solar collectors have a translucent covering over an airspace in which heat from the sun's rays is trapped. The bottom panel of the collector is normally black, which helps absorb heat at about 20 percent efficiency. Nature's version, polar bear fur, scatters 90 percent of ultraviolet light down to the polar bear's black, heat absorbing skin.

Heat Load Estimates

Q. Is there any way to gauge how much heat is needed in a given space? I've had four estimates on a large addition, all different.

A. Heating contractors should be using a detailed set of calculations that factor in many characteristics of the space to be heated such as cubic volume, exposure, and the type and amount of glazing and insulation. The result is called the heating load, which is matched to a corresponding furnace Btu capacity.

Theoretically, all the estimates should be close. But some heating contractors may be overestimating your needs. From their standpoint, you are likely to be dissatisfied if they estimate a smaller furnace that saves some money up front but can't maintain 68 or 70 degrees Fahrenheit during a cold snap when you most need the heat. But you are not likely to complain about paying more than necessary for a larger furnace if it always provides enough heat.

Of course, that puts the best possible light on an overestimation of your heating needs. Some contractors may overdo the estimate simply to sell you a bigger and more expensive furnace than you need.

Although heating load calculations are complex, you can attempt to arrive at your own estimate for comparison purposes with the help of Manual J, a combination of worksheets and tables produced by the Air Conditioning Contractors of America.[2] The manual costs $14. Also, ACCA will be producing Manual J on a floppy disc that takes numbers you type in and makes all the calculations to arrive at a heating load for a specific space.

Setback Thermostats

Q. Is an automatic setback thermostat (in the $125 range) a good investment, and will it save energy on an older, oil-fired furnace?

A. Progammable thermostats are cost-effective investments on new and old systems. Actually, a thermostat that drastically cuts running time on an old, inefficient furnace will pay for itself very quickly, although it is no substitute for tuning the furnace and, if need be, replacing it.

For instance, some old furnaces run at only 50-percent efficiency (50 cents of usable heat from a dollar of fuel), while many new oil furnaces are in the 80 to 85 percent range. By turning down the heat, you should expect to save approximately 3 percent of total heating costs per degree of setback on the thermostat over 24 hours.

---

[2]ACCA, 1228 17th Street, NW, Washington, DC 20038

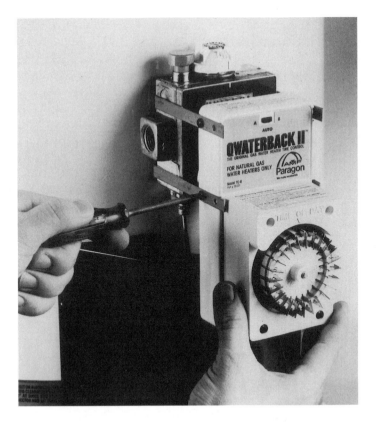

Specialized versions of setback thermostats also are made for water heaters. This Qwaterback unit, made by AMF Paragon, attaches over the thermostat control knob on an existing heater, allowing programmed temperature reductions. Units are made for gas and electric heaters.

Setback thermostats in the cost range you mention can automatically lower the thermostat for at least two separate and adjustable periods during a 24-hour cycle, which ought to be enough. You can have the heat turned down during the day, for instance, if the house is unoccupied, then back up shortly before you get home, then down again shortly after you go to bed, and back up again before your alarm rings.

A 15-degree setback for two-thirds of the day (8 hours during the day and 8 hours overnight) saves about 2 percent per degree of setback, or, in this case, 30 percent of heating costs. With an annual fuel bill of $1,000, this rate of saving will pay for a $100 clock thermostat in about 4 months.

Kerosene Heaters

Q. Are kerosene heaters a safe auxiliary heat source? We live in an all-electric house, and have no storage room for wood or coal.

A. First, be sure that portable kerosene heaters are allowed where you live. Check by calling your local fire department or building department. Then you have to decide if the attractive 99.6-percent energy efficiency of kerosene (it also humidifies indoor air at the rate of one gallon of water per gallon of kerosene burned), is worth the potential health and fire risk.

Although an improved generation of heaters promotes clean burning with double combustion chambers and other advances, the Consumer Product Safety Commission still recommends that units be operated only with the door of the room open to provide "sufficient dilution of pollutants." Even some manufacturers recommend leaving the room door open or the window cracked an inch during operation.

With this in mind, if you decide to purchase a heater, look for one of the newer models combining the benefits of radiant types that do the best job of burning off polluting nitrogen oxides, and convection types that do the best job with carbon monoxide. The double combustion heaters combine both types to produce significantly cleaner heat. Using the improved 1-k+ kerosene fuel is also a good idea. And manufacturers estimate that the new fuel will reduce maintenance by increasing the life span of kerosene wicks to 2 or 3 years.

Although the energy efficiency and portability of these heaters is attractive, overall I advise against them. Even though their combustion may be clean, the by-products are not vented. One study by *Consumer Reports* indicated a health risk from the pollutants that the magazine found unacceptable.

Also, enough local fire departments have outlawed heaters due to fire risk, so that if the pollutant argument doesn't make you search elsewhere for backup heat, the threat of a fire probably should.

Furnace Filter-Cleaner

Q. We need to change the filters in our hot-air furnace about every month because our house is so dusty. Is this too often, and, if so, what can we do to eliminate this annoying maintenance job.

A. In most houses changing the air filters every 2 months should be enough. Your place must be pretty dusty. But compared to walking around the house dragging a vacuum cleaner behind you, accumulating the dust in one place is a lot more convenient, even though changing the filters so often seems inconvenient.

Two improvements may help. One, a low-tech, low-cost solution, is to lay window screening over the return-air intake grill. This is the oversize grill, usually located in a central hallway or stairway, through which gradually cooling room air is sucked back into a return duct and fed into the furnace again. If the grill is in an obvious location you will see it accumulate dust and vacuum or wipe it off regularly.

This is a slightly flaky system. It simply relocates the dust trap from inside your furnace to out in the hall where you can see it and clean it more easily. The drawback is that if you forget to vacuum or wipe the dust off the screening the return duct won't be able to supply enough air to the furnace and air will be sucked in from other sources, which may create drafts and leaks where you never had them before.

The high-tech, higher-cost solution is to install an electrostatic air cleaner on the furnace. There are several designs for these machines. But one of the most basic draws return air through a vertical array of thin metal plates alternately charged with positive and negative current. This drives dust, pollen, and almost all airborne impurities against the plates. On some machines regular maintenance is reduced by an automatic washing cycle during which water flushes accumulations on the plates so they are clean to accumulate more dust.

CAC Furnace System

Q. On our old hot-air furnace there was always an initial cool draft of air from heating ducts when the furnace started up. Now, a contractor has suggested a continuous air circulation (CAC) unit. He says this will maintain a more even room temperature. But won't it cause the same problem?

A. You make a good point. The idea of CAC is to use a furnace blower with several speeds (which only some furnaces have) to shift automatically to a very low speed when the furnace is not making heat. This keeps some air circulating through the system all the time.

The advantage is that room temperature is more stable than it is when a hot-air furnace runs in a more conventional on-off cycle—kicking in to raise room temperature, then shutting down until the thermostat calls for heat again. This cycling can produce noticeable and uncomfortable temperature swings in some rooms in some houses.

But there are a few disadvantages to the continuous circulation system. The most obvious for home owners with relatively new furnaces is that you may have to replace a perfectly good, existing furnace blower with a multispeed fan. Sometimes, matching one manufacturer's furnace and thermostat with another's blower can be a problem.

Also, in a small house there is a welcome silence (particularly around bedtime) when the furnace and blower finally quit for the night. Theoretically, at that time of night you have reduced the thermostat setting enough so you can nod off in peace and quiet as the house cools, hopefully getting to sleep before the furnace and blower turn on again to maintain a lower, nighttime setting.

However, even modifying or replacing the powerful furnace fan, which pushes air throughout the house, may make more sense than installing several ceiling fans or area heaters to take the chill out of cool corners—if you can tolerate the constant machinery noise and constant flow of air through the house.

Hot-Air Heat Cycling

Q. Is there any way to raise the temperature of the air that comes out of the "hot" air ducts when the forced hot-air furnace starts up? After only a minute the air is very warm. But in one room that first blast is really cold.

A. You have hit on one of the drawbacks of forced-air systems, which is a tactful way of saying that there may not be much you can do about the problem. It's similar to what happens when you first turn on a hot-water tap. You don't immediately draw water from the hot-water heater. First, you get the tepid, room temperature water that is sitting in the pipes between the heater and the tap.

This problem is partially overcome by a built-in delay, after the burner starts making heat, before the fan starts pushing out warm air. The delay is supposed to provide enough time for air in the furnace to warm up before it enters the supply ducts. But that warm air has to push out the cooler air already in the ducts to get into the rooms. The problem is most troublesome in long ducts that feed rooms furthest away from the furnace.

One extreme remedy would be to install an electric assist heater just behind the duct spewing the coolest air. Installation would be a bit of a production, however. You'd need an electrician, maybe a plumbing and heating contractor, too, and, probably, several hundred dollars to pay the bill.

A more reasonable approach is to trace the route of the offending duct and insulate any exposed sections to keep the air sitting in the duct closer to room temperature. If the duct runs through an unheated area, say, a crawl space, or near an exterior wall, applying a thick layer of insulation (6-inch batts or more) may make a noticeable difference.

Furnace Ignition

Q. My 6-year-old oil furnace began the season by turning on and off a lot, a problem the furnace repairman who fixed it called short cycling. But lately the furnace has started to sputter and sometimes shuts down very soon after starting, although once it gets going it runs well and no longer short-cycles. What could be wrong this time?

A. Unfortunately, that type of symptom could be produced by a variety of problems that fit under the general heading of a mistuned furnace. For instance, such problems could arise if the mixture of air and fuel is not balanced properly, or pushed into the combustion chamber at the wrong pressure, or pushed through a clogged nozzle.

However, I am assuming that your furnace was tuned when it was fixed. That leaves two culprits that are often not attended to in a furnace tune-up. One is your fuel filter. The one on your furnace serves the same purpose as the one on your car. It prevents impurities in the oil from reaching (and then clogging or damaging) the furnace at the point of combustion.

And there are all kinds of impurities lying in the practically primordial muck at the bottom of your oil tank. Since they are disturbed when oil is delivered you should wait at least 15 minutes after a delivery before running the furnace. This gives the sludge time to settle. (Incidentally, the same holds true at gas stations. So avoid buying gas when you see the delivery truck filling the station's underground tanks.)

Most furnace oil filters are about the size of a big coffee cup, placed in the oil supply line, usually near but not in the furnace. These containers unscrew to reveal some form of mesh filter—the replaceable portion that traps the impurities. The filter may have become so clogged that it is interfering with the free flow of oil to the furnace, particularly as the oil flow begins. A clean filter may help, and it can't hurt.

Another possible culprit is the photoelectric cell. This is a small tube about the size of a stubby cigar positioned in line and adjacent to the opening where oil is sprayed into the furnace and ignited. The "photo" part looks for combustion, and, if it doesn't see it, sends a signal with the "electric" part to shut down the system. The sputtering problem could be caused by a dirty photoelectric cell, which "sees" combustion in fits and starts through sooty by-products of combustion stuck on its lens.

Once you or the serviceman locate the device (you'll have to check your owner's manual), simply wiping the cell surface with a soft cloth will clear its vision.

Ground-Source Heat Pumps

Q. A contractor has raised the possibility of installing what he calls a ground-source, water-cycle heat pump in our new house. He says that, although it is more expensive than a conventional heating and cooling system, it will save money in the end. Is this true, and are there disadvantages to such a system?

A. It's true. And the main drawback is initial cost. Although there are several variations, the basic design is very sensible. The idea is to pump water through a closed loop of piping in the ground, down where the earth shelters water in the pipe from seasonal temperature changes.

For instance, in the summer, a conventional air conditioning system would use a lot of electricity to cool outdoor air from 90 degrees Fahrenheit or more, down to a more comfortable 70 degrees Fahrenheit. But since water in the ground-source system stays as cool as 60 or 70 degrees Fahrenheit underground, using the water as a cooling medium costs less.

Conversely, since the earth stores solar energy and stays relatively warm in winter compared to the air above (that's why many animals hibernate underground in winter) the system can also save money when producing heat.

Although system costs can vary widely depending on size and the complexity of the installation, you might expect the ground system to cost 25 or 35 percent more than a conventional heating and air conditioning system. Why not ask the contractor for estimates on both types of systems. Then, ask the contractor, the equipment manufacturers, and your utility company to help you figure out the annual energy savings from a ground-source system to see if the extra investment makes sense.

Twenty Nine

FIREPLACES AND STOVES

Wood Stove Standards
*Designs That Increase Efficiency
and Decrease Pollution*

While diligent homeowners have been gathering logs for the wood-burning season, wood stove manufacturers and environmental groups have been burning the midnight oil. After sometimes intense negotiations, the groups have reached a consensus on the first national standard for wood stoves.

By 1990, after all proposed provisions of the standard are phased in, pollution from wood stoves in many of the 20 to 25 million households in this country that burn some wood will be cut in half. Stoves designed to meet these emission standards will burn wood more completely. This increase in combustion efficiency will also increase heat output.

Although wood is commonly thought of as an ecologically benign heat source (in part because it is a traditional, unprocessed, renewable fuel), its combustion by-products are an increasingly serious threat to air quality.

Wood burning produces potentially dangerous gases such as carbon monoxide. It also produces a variety of microscopic particles known collectively as *polycyclic organic matter* (POM). Many POM components have been characterized as carcinogenic by the Environmental Protection Agency (EPA).

Before the energy crisis of the 1970s spurred fuel costs causing a surge in wood stove use, the accumulation of emissions was insignificant. But wood stove sales have climbed to about 800,000 a year. On cold winter days many towns are now shrouded by a noticeable layer of wood stove smog.

In Denver, for example, wood stoves now produce almost half as much carbon monoxide pollution as cars and trucks. In Missoula, Montana, a light on a highly visible water tower is turned on when air-quality monitors indicate wood stove pollution is too high. When the light is on, inspectors can hand out tickets to homeowners who continue to feed their fires. In some states, selected municipalities have banned new wood stove installations altogether.

Colorado and Oregon already have set standards for wood stove emissions. In fact, the proposed national standard is modeled after, and considered even more stringent, than the Oregon standard.

Several other states, including Maine, Vermont, Massachusetts, Montana, and Washington, were considering similar action to control wood stove pollution. Townships may impose restrictions as well. The result is a morass of different regulations and stove certification procedures—a real problem for national stove manufacturers who, in theory, would have to build in different variations to satisfy rules in different regions.

Compared to this possibility, a uniform national standard, even if tougher than some of the state standards, became a desirable alternative. David Doniger, senior attorney at the Natural Resources Defense Council (NRDC), a citizens environmental group that initiated the negotiations on wood stove standards, said, "It was in everyone's interest to negotiate. That's why we succeeded."

In response to pressure from the NRDC, the EPA formed a committee to evaluate wood stove regulations. It consisted of manufacturers, the Wood Heating Alliance, an industry trade group, representatives from state environmental agencies, and others. An EPA spokesman said, "We didn't know what to expect because we haven't negotiated source performance regulations this way before." The Wood Heating Alliance noted that this is the first time regulatory negotiations have been used to formulate a federal standard.

Normally, it would take 4 to 5 years to bring such a regulation into existence. In this case, cooperative negotiations among interested parties will shorten the process to about 2 years. The EPA, which will officially propose the standard, served on the negotiating committee. The agency's main role was to gather and screen technical data, and prepare background papers on critical issues.

No party got everything it wanted. Joe Kowalczyk, from the Oregon Department of Environmental Quality, said, "We would like to have seen stove combustion efficiency included in the standard, the way energy efficiency ratings are provided on air conditioners. But the national standard is tough, and it closed some loopholes."

Dave Doniger reports the NRDC was willing to forgo some provisions of the standard in the interest of time. "By agreeing on a standard 2 years ahead of schedule, we will include over 1½ million wood stoves sold during the period that otherwise would not have been covered," he said. The standard will not be retroactive.

While each party grumbled halfheatedly about one provision or another it didn't get, all seem to agree that the standard is fair, and that it will significantly reduce pollution. All parties also agree that the formal EPA rule-making process, which includes a period for comments and alterations that is sometimes delayed by disagreements and litigation, will move ahead swiftly and smoothly.

The first phase of the standard imposed new emission criteria that many stoves already meet. And many manufacturers will bypass interim regulations, and go ahead with designs that will meet the final, 1990 national standard.

Many of the provisions are complex, involving particulate emissions measured in grams per hour. But it is significant that emission levels will be tested at all burn rates. In some stoves, vigorous combustion burns the wood thoroughly, and produces temperatures hot enough to burn off creosote and other combustion by-products. But low-level combustion, common when ventilation is retarded to maintain a fire overnight, may produce much dirtier exhaust.

Just as catalytic converters have been used to reduce exhaust emissions in cars and trucks, similar technology may help many stove manufacturers meet the new standard. Some models already include the wood stove version of a car's catalytic converter, called a catalytic combustor.

CATALYTIC STOVE OPERATION

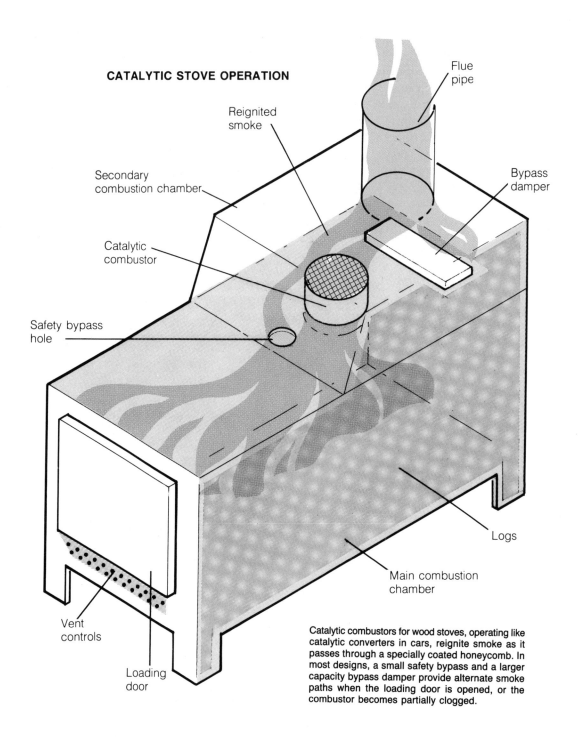

Flue pipe

Reignited smoke

Bypass damper

Secondary combustion chamber

Catalytic combustor

Safety bypass hole

Logs

Vent controls

Main combustion chamber

Loading door

Catalytic combustors for wood stoves, operating like catalytic converters in cars, reignite smoke as it passes through a specially coated honeycomb. In most designs, a small safety bypass and a larger capacity bypass damper provide alternate smoke paths when the loading door is opened, or the combustor becomes partially clogged.

Tests by Corning, the firm that developed the combustor, and independent labs, show that the honeycomb fixture built into a stove can reduce creosote by 90 percent, reduce many exhaust pollutants by 80 percent, while providing up to a 50 percent increase in heat output. The specially coated honeycomb acts like a supercharger, reburning exhaust gases. This burns wood more completely, producing more heat and cleaner exhaust.

If adopted 1990 national standard for wood stove emission limits will be 4.1 grams per hour for catalytic stoves, and 7.5 grams per hour for noncatalytic stoves.

In the meantime, consumers who want to buy stoves that will meet the new standard can write for an updated list of stoves certified under Oregon rules that modeled the national standard. The Oregon Department of Environmental Quality[1] will send, free upon request, their Wood Stove Certification List, which is updated regularly. Combustion efficiencies and heat output capacities of the stoves are included with emission rates.

Installing a Wood Stove
Selecting the Best Location and Installation Method

Shopping for a wood or coal stove is like shopping for clothes. They come in all shapes, sizes, and styles from mammoth, modern boxes with amber glass doors, to reproductions of petite Victorian parlor stoves with vine tracery metalwork as intricate as fine embroidery. There is at least one model (if not ten or more), to suit any taste and any situation. In most homes, however, it is much more difficult to select the best location and type of installation for a stove.

Several factors must be taken into account when choosing a location and type of installation: appearance from the inside and outside, convenience of use, energy efficiency, fire safety, and cost. Each factor should play a part in the decision, while no single factor need override all others.

Looking inside first, possible locations generally coincide with natural gathering points. Since a stove, like the more traditional fireplace, tends to be a focal point, the choices are often limited to mid-wall locations in dens, family rooms and living rooms.

Even with a heat shield mounted on the back of a stove, and a fire-safe material on adjacent walls, the front of the stove may wind up a surprising distance into the room. Freestanding stoves combined with a couch, a few arm chairs and at least minimal maneuvering room, can occupy a lot of floor space.

But a location that looks right and works conveniently inside may require an excessively expensive chimney that looks bizarre from the outside. As a rule, chimneys are most cumbersome on eave walls (the low walls of a house underneath extensions of the overhanging roof and gutters, typically the front and back). Rising well above the low roof edge for fire safety (and to create a reliable draft in the flue), masonry

---

[1]The Ore. Dept. of Environmental Quality, P.O. Box 1760, Portland, OR 97207

and prefabricated metal chimneys often look gangly, unstable, and out of place. Exposed chimneys usually look much better against a gable-end wall (the high walls, typically the sides of a house, over which the sloped roof forms an inverted V).

A central chimney that rises through the existing structure is another option. Central chimneys were the heart of early colonial homes. But adding a central flue after the fact will require ripping out at least some sections of walls, floors, and ceilings. The mess can be minimized by using prefabricated, insulated, stainless steel chimney pipe, with sections that can be easily screwed together in a small space.

The key to this type of installation is locating a vertical corridor in the building that can accommodate the pipe—like a stack of closets. Gentle bends (typically no more than 30-degree angles) can be incorporated into the flue so that even a rough vertical alignment of closets, cabinets, or other concealed spaces may suffice.

Older, existing chimneys should be thoroughly inspected before connecting a wood stove. But masonry or stainless steel lining systems may make it possible to use even an old, unlined flue. Either option is usually far less expensive than building a new one.

From the standpoint of energy efficiency a central location is best. The proverbial potbelly at the hub of a general store was in the best position to radiate heat for maximum effect. Surprisingly, small stoves in Shaker workshops were often located mid-wall at one end of the shop, while the flue pipe was sloped across the ceiling to exit at the opposite end. With typical Shaker efficiency, this installation milked the last dregs of heat from exhaust gases in the chimney pipe.

These lessons in efficiency can be applied on many modern stoves, most of which offer two possible exit points for exhaust: one at the back, and one on top. While a back exit hides the flue pipe, which may enter an existing masonry chimney, for example, directly behind the stove, a top exit that exposes a few feet of pipe is more energy efficient because heat radiates from the pipe before entering the chimney.

Costs of different stoves and installations vary widely, from under $1,000 to over $3,000. However, a cost analysis done by the Brick Institute of America, shows little difference between conventional masonry fireplaces and chimneys and their prefabricated metal counterparts. Given the source, that is not exactly astonishing. Total costs for labor and materials of a typical fireplace built of masonry were $2,172, and $2,025 for one built of prefabricated units. But while prefabricated fireplaces and chimney sections can be installed quickly in existing structures, masonry fireplaces require excavation to pour a foundation that supports the great weight.

Fire safety is another prime concern. Detailed standards in the field are set by the National Fire Protection Association. The standard, which is, in sections, technical and complex, is the basis for fire codes in many areas. To be sure your installation is safe and legal, call your local fire department and building department. (Fire codes govern, among other things, minimum distances between stove, stove pipe, and surrounding surfaces, chimney construction, and special connections through insulated pipe sections, called thimbles, where stove pipe enters a wall or ceiling.

A final, seemingly minor part of a stove installation is actually setting the stove in place. Recently, when installing an elegant, 500-pound Coalbrookdale stove, I used a system of homemade levers that allowed the stove to be lowered into place with a slight pressure from one finger, literally.

This strange-looking setup of counterbalanced 2-by-12 levers was necessary to raise the stove while inserting a stone slab hearth. The concrete blocks can be adjusted to counterbalance the stove exactly.

I cut the ends of two 2 by 12s so that they fit snugly between the stove legs and well under the main combustion chamber. A few feet away from the stove on each side, each board rested on a block of wood—the pivot of the lever, like the center of a seesaw. I set concrete blocks at the outer ends of the boards and adjusted them in and out to provide a perfect counterbalance to the stove. With the stove "levitating" so conveniently 4 inches off the floor, it was easy to position the hearthstone exactly, align the stove with the chimney connection, then lower it gingerly into place.

Wherever he is, the ninth-grade geometry teacher who told us, "Of course this is relevant. Just wait and see," has been proven absolutely right.

Heater and Stove Care
Safety Checks for Heating Systems Big and Small

Central heating systems should be capable of supplying enough heat, even during unusually cold weather, to keep living space at 68 degrees Fahrenheit. But inadequate insulation, air leaks, an inefficient furnace, and many other factors can create a need for more heat.

There are many sources, including a wide variety of auxiliary heaters and fuels. But supplementary heat sources are less automated than central systems and require more attention. Consequently, they are potentially more dangerous than a conventional central heating system.

When a wood stove, electric space heater, or other auxiliary unit is first installed, most consumers operate the new equipment carefully, and observe fire safety precautions. Familiarity with the equipment as the winter wears on may not breed contempt, but it can easily lead to a careless approach to handling the equipment, storing fuel, and other operations.

While local fire codes and manufacturer's instructions must be followed, sometimes they do not cover the fine points of almost casual, everyday operation. Here are some weak links in the complex chain of events that keep us warm in winter.

Fiddling with the furnace. In houses built before the 1973 oil embargo and ensuing energy crisis, many furnaces had more than enough heating capacity. But after 1973, all that changed, and furnaces were sized more carefully. Newer models may not have the extra capacity to carry you through the coldest days. But it is a mistake to attempt to squeeze more heat out of a furnace by fiddling with its components and settings.

A professional may be able to make some changes that increase efficiency. Aside from general cleaning and tuning, ask a service company about nozzle size on oil burners. Some furnaces are supplied with oversized nozzles, which spray more oil than necessary into the combustion chamber.

Also ask about fan-on and fan-off settings on a forced hot-air system. These settings control the fan that blows warm air through the ducts. By lowering the fan-on setting and raising the fan-off setting, it is often possible to deliver more of the heat produced in the furnace to the living spaces, although you may notice that the first air out of your registers is a bit cooler than it used to be.

Stirring up the sludge. One tried-and-true consumer truism is to avoid buying gasoline at stations when the gasoline truck is making a delivery. Why? The delivery stirs up sludge at the bottom of the tank, which may make its way into your car engine. The same goes for your furnace. It's an engine, too.

After an oil delivery at home, try turning down the thermostat (so it will not trigger the furnace to supply heat), for at least 15 to 20 minutes. This should be enough time for the sludge that accumulates over the years in most oil tanks to settle.

A chimney check. How often you should clean or at least inspect a chimney depends on many factors. An annual cleaning is sensible. But combustion from wood or coal stoves, particularly in older homes with older flue liners inside the chimneys, may produce enough creosote (a gummy by-product of wood combustion), or other deposits to require a mid-season cleaning.

Consider calling in a chimney sweep during a warm spell if you burn wood or coal almost every day, or if you use some softwoods such as pine, or green, unseasoned wood. Both tend to increase creosote deposits in the flue.

Boy Scout fire rules. As I remember it, one of the scouting guidelines for fire building was to separate the fire and the fuel source. This means don't store fuel, whether wood or coal or kerosene or anything else, near the point of combustion.

At home, apply this sensible rule by resisting the temptation to stack wood near the wood stove to dry it out. Also remember that coal should not be stored where its fumes can seep into living space. Safe separation also goes for igniters such as matches, "Cape Code lighters" (a soft, porous stone that rests in a bowl of liquid fuel), kindling, or other fire starters.

Live ashes that refuse to die. An unpleasant experience may teach wood and coal burners that a bucket of ashes with an innocent layer of cool gray dust on top can have live coals buried below. Eliminate dangerous surprises from a pile of supposedly dead ashes by designating a fire-safe deposit area at the beginning of the heating season.

Woodcutter's woes. If you take a hand in cutting or splitting some of your own wood, make regular safety checks of your wood cutting tools. Occasionally, everyone miss-hits a log. That can weaken or split an ax or maul handle. Once the handle head appears fractured or severely scarred, replace it. Wood replacement handles are sold at most hardware stores and home centers.

Deteriorating smoke detectors. Since no home can be made fireproof, every home should have an early warning system. Smoke detectors may provide the best chance to save people and possessions. (See Chapter 23, "Smoke Detector Checks.")

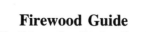

Firewood Guide
Striking the Right Cord

Just as hot dogs seem to taste better at the ballpark than they do at home, heat from a wood fire seems more penetrating, more relaxing and certainly more romantic than heat from a furnace.

Some of the more than 20 million wood-burning households in this country don't really need the extra heat. But many, particularly homeowners saddled with all-electric homes, burn wood in efficient, airtight stoves to supplement their central heating system. Modern stoves can make wood heat a cost-effective supplement to oil, gas, or electricity. But the type of wood you burn is just as important as what you burn it in.

Good firewood has a lot of potential heat. It lights easily, burns readily, and produces minimal amounts of creosote, a gummy residue that can build up and cause a fire in chimney and stove flues.

Whether you cut, haul, split, and stack your own, or pay someone else to do it, it's important to expend your resources on good wood. It will be the most expensive, naturally. But you can reduce the price, which can vary widely, by paying for a delivery of long logs, say 16 feet or so, and cutting short stove or fireplace lengths (plus splitting and stacking) yourself. Here are some of the most important characteristics of firewood.

Hardwoods are better than softwoods. They are heavier, denser, and provide more heat than softer, lighter woods of the same size. Softwoods have more air and fewer fibers, like fluffy, aerated bread that you can squash by spreading on some butter. Hardwoods are more like hearty brown bread that you can barely cut through.

Heating values of wood can be expressed in Btus (the same rating system used on furnaces). You can see on the following table of approximate Btu values of different woods that heavy, dense hardwoods have the most heating capacity. These representative ratings were compiled by M. Michaelson in the 1983 book *Firewood*. The ratings are for one cord of wood—a stack 8 feet long, 4 feet wide and 4 feet high.

Old flues without flue tile liners can be saved with one of several relining methods. The Ahrens Chimney Technique uses two masonry coatings that fill cracks and crevices. They are poured around a vibrating bell-shaped form raised through the refractory mix.

Btu Values of Different Woods

Wood	Btus/Cord (millions)	Weight/Cord (pounds)
Hickory	25	4,600
White Oak	23	4,400
Sugar Maple	21	3,900
Red Oak	21	3,900
Yellow Birch	21	3,900
Yellow Pine	21	3,700
White Ash	20	3,800
Douglas Fir	18	2,900
Red Spruce	15	2,600
Hemlock	15	2,600
White Pine	14	2,200
Aspen	13	2,200

Obviously, one cord of aspen is the same size as one cord of hickory. But expect the price to vary dramatically since a cord of hickory weighs about twice as much as a cord of aspen and delivers nearly twice the Btus. The message is clear: Don't buy firewood by the size of the pile.

Seasoned firewood provides more heat than green wood. Seasoning is the process during which most of the water in living wood gradually evaporates after it is cut. Recently cut green wood may contain more than one-third moisture by weight, which means you shouldn't buy firewood by weight, either.

Green wood is difficult to light and keep lit because it's loaded with water—not the most combustible material. Green wood loses as much as 15 percent of its potential heat vaporizing the excess moisture left inside. It's just like boiling a kettle of water. Btus of heat are literally boiled away up the chimney as steam.

Seasoning takes time. If trees are cut to log length and split in the spring, they may dry enough over the summer to burn well in the winter. But most species of unsplit logs won't burn efficiently until they are dried for 1 year. The best evidence of seasoning is radial cracking at the ends of the logs in a spider-web pattern. The more cracks, often referred to as "checking," the drier the wood.

If you burn wood only occasionally, cost is not terribly important. But if you intend to burn a serious amount of wood, say two cords or more, you may want to compare the cost of burning wood to the cost of leaving on your oil or gas or electric furnace.

It's important to compare these costs, but almost impossible. Not only do prices vary from fuel to fuel (and from one area to another even for the same fuel), but different fuels are divided up into different units with no easily compared common denominator. Also, different fuels are burned with different efficiencies in different appliances.

Nevertheless, you can make general comparisons three ways. First, you can ask competing fuel suppliers for estimates of operating costs.

Second, you can convert the standard measure of different fuels (cubic feet of gas, kilowatt-hours of electricity) to the common denominator of Btus. For natural gas the standard measure is cubic feet. To find the Btus per cubic foot of natural gas, multiply by 1,031. For electricity the standard measure is kilowatt-hours. To find the Btus per kilowatt hour, multiply by 3,412. You don't have to convert oil. Standard, No. 2 fuel oil is rated at 140,000 Btus per gallon.

Once you get a price for a cord of wood, say $200 for a cord of ash rated at about 20 million Btus, you can determine that $1 worth of wood will provide about 100,000 Btus. If, for example, your fuel oil costs $1 per gallon, which supplies 140,000 Btus, you can see that the wood will be more of a luxury than a cost-effective supplement.

Third, if all this gets too complicated, use the following very rough rule-of-thumb: one cord of hardwood equals the heat output of one ton of coal, or 200 gallons of oil, or 4,000 kilowatts of electricity.

Fireplace vs. Stove

Q. We want to add some type of fireplace to our 13-year-old, wood frame, slab floor contemporary. Is it better to build a brick and mortar fireplace or a prefab metal one? And if brick is best, should we include a ventilating system?

A. The answers depend on what you want most: a nice view of crackling logs, or an efficient supplemental heat source. The cozy, romantic, and highly inefficient custom-built masonry fireplace will likely be the most expensive option by far. And it will be so heavy that a section of the slab probably will have to be reexcavated and reinforced with a larger foundation—a tough job.

Prefab metal fireplaces are much lighter and much easier to install. You won't need to beef up the foundation, and the chimney can be built by simply screwing together sections of code-approved, multiwall, metal flue pipe. Compared to masonry, prefabs should cost about the same or more for materials, but much less for labor, and, therefore, less overall. Bear in mind that fireplaces, even with a built-in vent system to recapture some heat before it wafts up the chimney, are very inefficient. Generally, about half the heat produced in combustion is lost.

Freestanding wood and coal stoves are more efficient. And there is tremendous variety, for example, compact and elegant airtight wood and coal stoves in many styles that will maintain a fire for 24 hours unattended, and a basic Franklin stove with double-hinged doors that is more like a prefab fireplace.

It doesn't seem worthwhile to build a masonry fire column, or even a masonry chimney to operate anything except a full-blown masonry fireplace that requires such an expensive setup. Both prefabs and stoves work well with easily installed flue pipe.

Also, many wood and coal stoves can be operated with doors open for a bit of the fireplace effect, then closed down to provide heat much more efficiently. An airtight stove (the doors seal tight and combustion is controlled with a series of adjustable vents), with a large door opening, hooked into prefab flue pipe may be your best bet.

Fireplace Air Intake

Q. I need some help figuring out when to open and close the sliding vent on the outside of my fireplace, which is approximately 6 inches below the hearth. Also, when should I remove the brick in the hearth that, leads to the ash dump in the basement?

A. Fortunately, you have an energy-efficient version of a not very energy-efficient heat source. Since fireplaces need air to support combustion, they suck warm room air into the fire and up the chimney, in effect, reheating air that has already been heated by your furnace. This, in turn, can cause air leaks in other parts of the house as air is drawn in through cracks around windows and doors, for example, to replace the draft of air (and heat, unfortunately) shooting up the flue.

A very sensible way to avoid this is to supply the fireplace with its own source of outdoor air. That's what your exterior grill is for. To complete an energy-efficient design you should install fireproof doors that can be closed over the fireplace opening as the embers smolder and the damper in the flue must remain open. Even after you go to sleep, cool air that continues to filter in through the grill will simply head up the flue and back outside where it just came from. But warm air in the room won't be swept away.

The removable brick is another nice feature that minimizes the mess produced by cleaning ashes out of a fireplace without a built-in dump. Instead of shoveling up the ashes and carting them out of the house through the living space, you can simply push them into the hole in the hearth floor and directly into the ash dump below. Just remember that, periodically, you will have to clear the main dump in the cellar. You'll know when it's time for this job because the ash level will eventually rise up to the level of the hearth.

Chimney Flue Checks

Q. How can I tell if the chimney in our house, which we just bought, is safe? I'm not sure if there is a liner inside the bricks, or if there are cracks that could pose a fire hazard when I operate the wood stove.

A. The first step is to call a professional chimney sweep. If a wood stove has been used in the past, creosote, a gummy, brown by-product of incomplete wood combustion, may have built up on the bricks or the liner—that is, if you have a liner, some old chimneys don't. In either case, creosote deposits are a potential fire hazard and should be removed.

Another method of relining older flues uses Z-flex stainless steel, flexible tubing. It is snaked down the flue—even around obstructions and slight bends—to make a continuous, fire-safe connection between the damper and the chimney cap.

A professional sweep also should be able to tell you if the chimney has a liner, and if the flue is fire safe. This kind of inspection also can be made by a masonry contractor who builds chimneys.

The chimneys in many old houses may not have liners, but, for years, may have carried away soot, smoke, and occasional live ashes without incident. But it is safe to have a liner. The traditional material is clay flue tile, the term for lengths of rectangular pipe, stacked on top of each other inside the brick chimney as it is constructed. It is difficult to add these breakable flue tiles after the fact.

However, there are several methods of lining an existing flue. Snaking flexible stainless steel tubing down the chimney and pouring masonry mixes around a temporary form inside the bricks are two widely used methods.

Wood burners who use a lot of wood may tire of the tough, time-consuming process of splitting logs. Small-scale splitters such as this McCulloch Woodmate are rated to split about a cord of hardwood using an electrically activated ram in about 2 hours.

☰ *Thirty* ☰

COOLING

Air Conditioning Buying Guide
A Cool Head for Cooling Decisions

Before summer whether makes it too hot and humid, you should calmly collect your thoughts about keeping cool. Once a blanket of hot wet air arrives you may not want to hear about energy efficiency ratings, estimated operating costs and British thermal units of cooling capacity.

Those sensible issues will pale next to the basics: Will it fit in the window, keep you cool, and not sound so much like a bulldozer that you can't get to sleep? On a blistering July afternoon you're likely to say desperate things to an appliance salesperson like, "I don't care if it's much too big and much too expensive. It's the only one you've got left and it's going to be mine!"

Here are some cool, calm, and collected items that you should consider *before* the heavy-duty heat arrives.

Central versus room units. "Central air" has such a nice cool ring to it—a cool, expensive ring. Undoubtedly, it is an attractive feature in the resale market. So are saunas, swimming pools, and many other pricey options.

Of course, in many homes it is very difficult to install central air conditioning. A contractor may be able to set up machinery and ducts in an unused attic (after beefing up the attic floor joists in some cases). But in a two-story home you may have to give up some cabinet or closet space so that ductwork can be installed to carry cool air down to the first floor.

But the central question about central systems is if you really need cool halls and closets along with a cool bedroom or two. In most homes, on most warm summer days, one or two window or through-the-wall units can keep crucial rooms quite comfortable and spill enough cool, dry air to take the edge of heat and humidity off adjacent areas.

It's a question of preference and, of course, money.

Three capacity formulas. First, the most general rule-of-thumb is to buy 1 ton of cooling (12,000 Btus) per 500 square feet of floor space.

Second, the more complex "WHILE" formula takes into account several characteristics about your building. In this formula you substitute a characteristic for each letter in the formula as follows.

"W" stands for width of the room. "H" stands for room height. "I" stands for the amount of insulation. (Substitute 10 if the room is covered by an insulated, ventilated attic or another cool apartment, 18 for a top-floor apartment or room under an uninsulated attic.) "L" stands for length of the room. And "E" stands for exposure factor.

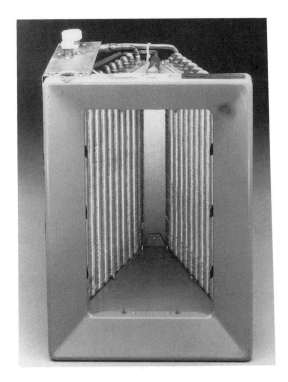

Research by Honeywell indicates that after only a few years, dirt accumulated on a central air conditioner coil increases operating costs 10 to 15 percent. By maintaining operating efficiency (an electronic air cleaner removes up to 95 percent of airborne impurities), you can reduce the capacity initially and ongoing operating costs.

(Substitute 16 if the longest wall faces north, 17 if it faces east, 18 for south, 20 for west.)

All substituted numbers are multiplied, and the subtotal is divided by 60 to show the required Btu capacity rating for the air conditioner. Here's how the formula works for a 15-by-20-foot room with 8-foot ceilings that is insulated and vented above, in which the longest wall is facing south.

$$W \times H \times I \times L \times E \text{ (subtotal)} \div 60 = \text{Btus needed}$$
$$15 \times 8 \times 10 \times 20 \times 18 \text{ (432,000)} \div 60 = 7,000$$

Third, the Cooling Load Estimate Form, available from the Association of Home Appliance Manufacturers, is considerably more lengthy and complicated, but also even more precise (see address on p. 407).

Energy efficiency. Although the average efficiency of air conditioners has improved greatly in the last several years, some units still produce significantly more cool air per dollar of electricity than others—enough so that it may pay to spend a little extra for a high-efficiency unit.

You can compare the efficiency of air conditioners by checking their "EnergyGuide" labels. (For more information see Chapter 26, "Energy Guide Labeling.") The yellow and black stickers explain annual electrical costs, compare efficiency among several unit, and list a specific Energy Efficiency Rating (EER) number. The EER is called a Seasonal Energy Efficiency Rating (SEER) on central-air systems.

This rating is the ratio of Btus used per hour of cooling to the watts of electricity used to produce those cool Btus. When fewer watts of electricity produce more Btus of cooling, efficiency increases. The higher the EER number, the more efficient the unit, and the less it will cost to run.

Here's an example of how what seems like a modest change in EER-ratings can alter your electric bill. On a 36,000 Btu central system with a cooling load of 1,500 hours and an electric rate of 5 cents per kilowatt hour, a system with a 7.0 SEER would

Freedman Advertising, Inc.

An awning to shade windows and sliding glass doors is another improvement directly related to air conditioner size and operating costs. This Pease Retractable Awning has hinged support arms allowing the canopy to fold back against the house.

cost $386 to operate for the season, while a system with a 9.1 SEER would cost $297, or about 30 percent less.

More information on estimating cooling can be found in the Cooling Load Estimate Form, published by the Association of Home Appliance Manufacturers.[1]

A 16-page planning guide called, "How to buy a Room Air Conditioner," available free from General Electric, provides guidance on estimating your cooling load, deciphering EER numbers, judging various air conditioner features, and other issues. Request a copy by calling the GE Answer Center toll-free: 800-626-2000.

A free fact sheet called, "Efficient Air Conditioning," is available from the Conservation and Renewable Energy Inquiry and Referral Service.[2] It includes purchasing guidelines for central systems and room units, heat pumps, fans, plus information on sizing, installation, operation and maintenance.

Installing a Room Air Conditioner
Tips for an Efficient, Practical Job

In the 1955 movie *The Seven Year Itch*, Marilyn Monroe revealed a unique way of beating the summer heat to Tom Ewell, whose family had departed for the cooler countryside, leaving him alone in a steamy New York apartment adjoining Monroe's. "You know, when it's hot like this—you know what I do?" she cooed, "I keep my undies in the icebox."

Most of us have to rely on a less exotic solution—a room air conditioner. This humdrum home appliance can transform suffocating heat and humidity into cool, dry air. The potential to make intolerable conditioners more than tolerable will trigger about 3 million room air conditioner sales this year.

Buying and installing an in-window or through-the-wall room unit raises many questions. Two of the best sources for buying information (about sizing, cooling capacity, energy efficiency and such) are: the Association of Home Appliance Manufacturers, and the American Council for an Energy-Efficient Economy.[3]

There are also many installation options. The most basic choice is between installing the unit in a window or in a wall. In-window units generally require less installation effort and expertise, even though many air conditioners weigh 100 pounds or more. Manufacturers commonly include metal and foam trim strips and panels to bridge gaps between the machine and the window frame.

One drawback is that you lose some of the view through the window and, since the machine is locked in place by the window itself, some natural ventilation on less blistering days. And you may not have a suitable window near an electrical outlet (most room air conditioners run on standard household current but should not be connected with extension cords), or one located where the machine will be at least partially shaded, which makes its operation cooler and more efficient.

---

[1]AHAM, 20 North Wacker Drive, Chicago, IL 60606
[2]CAREIRS, P.O. Box 8900, Silver Spring, MD 20907
[3]ACEEE, 1001 Connecticut Ave., NW, Washington, D.C. 20036.

On the plus side, in-window air conditioners do not permanently disfigure a building. They remain portable appliances that can be removed and used elsewhere leaving only a few telltale screw holes. However, such installations normally have no more aesthetic appeal than you could hope for when sticking a big metal box into a window.

There also are limitations on more permanent, through-the-wall installations; the job does involve cutting a hole in your house, after all. You could choose to turn over the job to a contractor. But installing a room air conditioner (even a through-the-wall model) is a reasonable, 1-day project for handy do-it-yourselfers. Here's a sample, case history installation. (Obviously, you should follow directions provided by the manufacturer on your own machine if they differ from this scenario.)

The machine. A Sears Kenmore Model 75087 combination air conditioner and heat pump; retail cost approximately $530. This machine is rated at 8,100 Btus. It also is rated to provide about 7,500 Btus of heat at exterior temperatures of 43 degrees. (The heating capacity of heat pumps declines with outdoor temperatures, in this case to about 3,300 Btus of heat at 32 degrees.) But with one installation you get a year-round appliance for supplemental cooling and heating. The machine's EER (Energy Efficiency Rating) is 8.7 (on a scale for models of this capacity of 5.7 to 9.8), with estimated annual operating costs of $94 based on use 8 hours every day over 4 months and a utility rate of 10 cents per kilowatt-hour of electricity.

The location. A through-the-wall installation about half way up the wall in a fully shaded exterior wall. The installation is eased by selecting a section of wall free of electrical cables that might have to be rerouted by an electrician, and free of plumbing pipes. Locating the machine above the standard height of wall outlets should avoid the bulk of in-wall electric lines in most homes.

The tools and materials. The job varies dramatically depending on the composition of the wall. Solid masonry walls (stuccoed block or brick veneer over block, for instance), pose the most problems. Making the hole is heavy-duty work without a reciprocating hammer tool (like a small jackhammer). Even then, it is easy to fracture a brick or block, and inadvertently make the opening larger and more ragged than necessary. Also, removing bricks or blocks undermines a masonry wall unless a concrete or steel lintel is inserted. This type of work starts to push the job out of the province of many do-it-yourselfers.

It is generally much easier to make the opening in a wood frame wall. That work is easiest with a reciprocating saw (commonly known by the Milwaukee Electric Tool Corporation trade name Sawzall), which is like an elongated jigsaw with a long blade. It can be used to cut through exterior siding and wall studs. Next best is either a jigsaw or circular saw to make neat exterior siding cuts, while wall stud sections are removed with a handsaw. Obviously, the entire opening can be made with hand tools; it just takes longer.

The plan. In a nutshell, the idea is to cut a certain-sized hole, referred to by installation guides as the rough opening, in the side of an exterior wall.

After marking the location it is wise to cut through wallboard or break through plaster carefully. Don't drill or saw into the wall cavity blindly before checking for

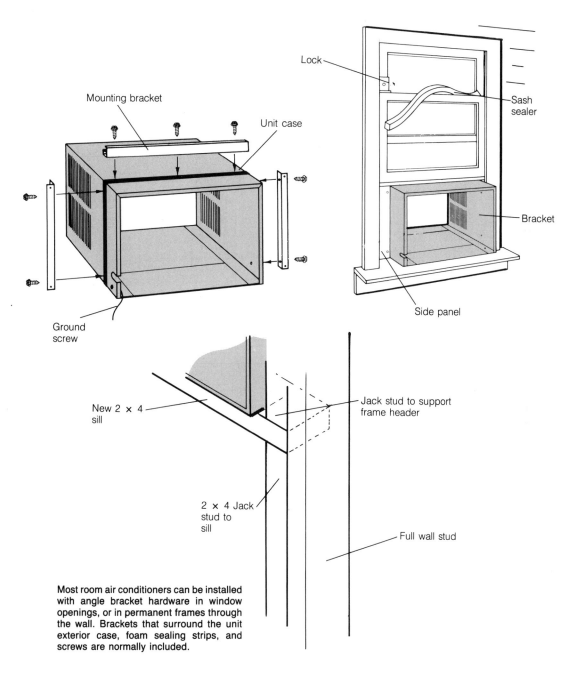

Mounting bracket

Unit case

Lock

Sash sealer

Bracket

Ground screw

Side panel

New 2 × 4 sill

Jack stud to support frame header

2 × 4 Jack stud to sill

Full wall stud

Most room air conditioners can be installed with angle bracket hardware in window openings, or in permanent frames through the wall. Brackets that surround the unit exterior case, foam sealing strips, and screws are normally included.

Through-the-Wall Frame

wires or pipes. With the interior wall surface removed, use a drill (or drive finishing nails) to transfer the position of the four corners through to the exterior wall.

To start a jig- or handsaw cut in exterior siding, first drill a hole large enough to accommodate a saw blade. (With a handsaw, which is considerably wider than a jigsaw blade, you will have to drill a series of connecting holes.) When siding is cut away, portions of one or two wall studs must be removed to make way for the air conditioner. The interrupted studs should be bridged by horizontal 2 by 4s, called headers. (All work must conform to local building codes.)

Some companies suggest building a box frame of a material such as ¾-inch-thick exterior-grade plywood, then nailing that box to surrounding studs. It is normally just as easy, and just as solid, to use the structural wall frame of 2 by 4s as the supporting frame for the air conditioner. This method saves a step, and some material, too. The framed opening is formed by headers top and bottom, and vertical studs placed to match opening width requirements provided in the installation manual.

When this opening is complete, the air conditioner housing can be set in place. Shims (typically pieces of tapered wood shakes) can be inserted on the room side of the unit to create a very slight, almost imperceptible slope down to the outside. This encourages proper cabinet drainage. However, the machine will drain adequately even if it is precisely level. The heaviest piece of work is fitting the machine, weighed down with compressor and piping, back into its metal housing.

Final steps include packing spaces between wall studs and finished frames with insulation, then trimming the opening inside and out. Because vibration will stress the seams between the machine and exterior trim, seal these exposed joints with a flexible material such as silicone caulk.

Overall, the job will run more smoothly if you take time to read and reread installation manuals before beginning, measure and remeasure the opening dimensions before cutting, and gather all tools and materials beforehand so you won't have to rush out to the hardware store or lumberyard in mid-project.

Fan Ventilation

Q. Is there a point at which natural ventilation through open windows with a fan assist, fails to provide enough cooling? We are trying to decide between some combination of ceiling fans and a whole-house fan in the attic, and central air conditioning, which is a lot more expensive. I would like to save the money, but not if the fans won't make much of a difference.

A. There are two many variables to make a valid comparison, personal tolerance of heat included. First, a breeze, even of muggy, 85 degree air, is better, and makes almost everyone feel cooler, than the same temperature without a breeze. The air evaporates sweat on your skin, the body's natural cooling system.

So if you invested in fans you would definitely feel an improvement. One of the most effective projects is to install a whole-house fan—typically mounted in a central location such as the ceiling in a central stairwell.

Although there are several installation variations, the plan is to close windows in the morning while the house is still cool, then, toward evening, after the house has been cooking in the sun all day, open the first floor windows and turn on the fan to exhaust hot air and pull cool, evening air up through the house.

If you opt for air conditioning, bear in mind that smaller fans can help you get the most out of conditioned air—either heated or cooled, for that matter—by moving the air where it is most needed. The ventilation can be provided by many types of fans: small and large portables, whole-house fans, attic fan ventilators, and ceiling fans.

To find out about relative costs, installations, and which type of fan will work most efficiently for you, request a free copy of the booklet "Fans for Space Cooling" from the Conservation and Renewable Energy Inquiry and Referral Service by writing CAREIRS.[4]

The efficiency of whole-house ceiling ventilator fans is greatly reduced when they push air into the attic faster than it can leave through typical gable-end louvers. Rooftop vents, such as this Nutone model, can add vent capacity, and vent eave storage areas partitioned off from the main attic.

[4]CAREIRS, P.O. Box 8900, Silver Spring, MD 20907

Air Conditioner Cycling

Q. Is there a break-even point, or some other way to calculate if it is more energy-efficient to leave an air conditioner on during the day, even at a low setting, or to leave it off until you come home?

A. There are too many variables for one rule to apply: the amount of glass area and direct sunlight, shade from trees, roof color, insulation in the walls, and, of course, personal preference.

When money is no object, obviously you will be most comfortable walking into a home that is at least moderately cool. However, since air conditioning is expensive, it is sensible to pay for cool, dry air when someone is around to feel its effect, and not when the home is empty.

But, and it's a big but, on a broiling day, even a powerful air conditioner with more than enough capacity—either a room unit or a central system—will take time to lower the temperature. It must cool the air, which must cool all the warm surfaces in the room that have stored heat during the day.

Unless you sit in front of the machine, it easily could take an hour before you began to feel some relief. But it won't take 8 or 9 hours. So a good compromise is to plug a room unit operating on standard household current into an automatic timer matched to the appliance electrical load, and program the timer to turn on the machine an hour or so before you come home.

With a central system operating on a temperature-sensitive thermostat, there are two options. First, you could raise the thermostat to a very high setting. With some fiddling, you probably could arrive at a setting that would keep the system dormant for most of the day, while still preventing the home from broiling. Or, you could ask a heating and cooling contractor about installing a programmable thermostat—the equivalent of a plug-in timer for a room unit.

Stated simply, the more you run an air conditioner, the more it costs. If the machine does not run at all for 8 hours, then works hard for an hour or so in the evening before leveling out to maintain a cooler temperature in cooler, evening conditions, you are likely to spend less than if you leave the machine on at moderate setting all the time.

Home Consumer Issues

Thirty One

HOME CONSUMER TRADITIONS

A Too Practical Christmas
"Oh, great! It's a hammer and saw," said the carpenter

The refrigerator is still packed with turkey left over from Thanksgiving, and already the signs are up and the pressure is on: buy, buy, buy—only about 30 days until Christmas. It's a common complaint these days. Christmas is just too darn commercial.

But buying a present or two is not a bad idea—as long as you can avoid becoming a practical Christmas Grinch. You have to watch out for these practical Grinches. They are likely to give very practical or, even worse, necessary presents. It's time this dastardly practice was brought out in the open.

I know about all this because I have been a target for Grinches. They single me out because my birthday is close to Christmas. One of the most flagrant examples of making the holiday season much too practical is combining such celebrations.

It may seem sensible, practical, and economical. But, at any age, it is disappointing whenever people you know take a killing-two-birds-with-one-stone approach to your birthday and Christmas.

Yet, this specialized form of Christmas practicality—the two-for-one combination present—confounds only that small segment of the population born near or on Christmas. But once a year, the deadly serious, necessary present may be a problem for millions more. You know about them: those presents you always dreamed about: a small container of subway tokens, a package of sensible underwear, a year's supply of odor-eater shoe inserts. Oh boy!

If you're a teacher, the Grinch might give you a terrifically practical present—something like a personalized box of chalk in case the supply at school runs out. Try pasting a sincere smile on your face when you unwrap that one.

If you're a bookkeeper, the necessary present might be something like an assortment of paper rolls for your calculating machine. A professional landscaper gets gardening gloves. Retired couples get books on how to be a retired couple. And so on.

Students may be the hardest hit. They are easy targets, too. And there are so many practical presents for them: book bags, shoe laces, packages of ballpoint pen refills, a subscription to *U.S. News & World Report*, toothpaste, and more.

Obviously, there is nothing inherently wrong with any of these items. They have

---

Opposite: M.I. Hummel figurines, based on drawings of Sister Maria Innocentia Hummel, were originated in 1935 by Bavarian porcelain maker, Franz Goebel. Now, the Goebel Collector's Club has 200,000 members in North America, and a gallery in Tarrytown, NY.

many diverse and positive applications. They are practical to a tee—too practical, in fact, for Christmas.

Of course, there are a few fuzzy areas. A little practicality is okay, sometimes. A practical pair of warm slippers, for instance, can be so emotionally comforting that they become a borderline case. If in doubt, you could easily push this selection into the wonderfully impractical category by choosing a pair with big gray and pink bunny ears flopping from the toes.

Grinches also give cost-effective presents. Maybe they worry about teaching the value of a dollar during the holidays—just the kind of lesson a nine-year-old is ready for, right? Grinches also shy away from giving too many presents. Try to imagine that nine-year-old pushing a few packages away and saying, "Oh no, Uncle Harry, that's definitely too many presents for me." Sure.

Kids don't know from too many presents. And many of them are not exactly connoisseurs of quality, either. "Quality" is not a hot topic of Christmas conversation with nine-year-olds. It's unlikely that they will be disappointed with your gift selection because it is not listed as a "Best Buy" in *Consumer Reports*.

Remembering that quantity does count, there are several ways around financial limitations imposed too often by practical Grinches. Presents can be slightly odd, homemade contraptions, or glued-down collages of vacation snapshots pulled out of a drawer, or something as frivolous as one of your spouse's favorite kind of cookie packed at the heart of a series of boxes. That's a great 10-cent present.

Louisa May Alcott pretty much laid this whole issue to rest in *Little Women*, writing, "Christmas won't be Christmas without any presents."

So here are a few guidelines that may help take some of the practicality and necessity out of the holiday season. If you know a too practical Grinch, send them a copy now, before they head for the stores.

Guidelines for Giving Impractical Presents

➠ Chances are you have stumbled upon a really good impractical present when you are only vaguely aware of what the item is, would be hard-pressed to describe what it does, and have a strong hunch the person you're giving it to knows less about it than you do.

➠ If you can picture the person buying the item on his own, don't buy it for them. If the item is just too good to pass up, buy it for someone else who wouldn't be caught dead buying it on his own.

➠ Immediately rule out any gift that the person could conceivably find useful on the job.

➠ Watch out if the word "appropriate" sneaks into your thoughts about the present. "Suitable," "need," and "really need," should also be considered red flags.

➠ Words and phrases that can be taken as green flags, indicating that you are on the right track, include "preposterous," "packed in natural feathers," and "Made in Botswana."

➠ Think twice about products that solve a problem. Granted, this is a tough category. A portable tire inflater that could be an important problem-solver on some dark and lonely highway is not a good choice; too serious. But a problem-solving, $3.95, nonspill, commuter coffee cup for your spouse's car inscribed, "See You Tonight Hot Stuff," is probably a fine choice.

➤ Don't select a present with the expectation of encouraging good study habits, or launching the recipient on a new career. This rule puts most educational gifts in a questionable light. For instance, it may not be wise to give the second year, high school Spanish student a Spanish comic book, hoping to put a "fun" slant on learning the vocabulary.

➤ Don't write a serious newspaper column about the potential dangers of tinsel near electrical outlets when the column appears on Christmas Day. Instead, write a Merry Christmas column.

➤ Generally avoid giving presents that add to collections. For instance, it is an impractical policy to give a cabinetmaker another Jorgensen hand-screw clamp, even though they could always use another one. However, I have come up with an exception.

M. I. Hummel painted porcelain figurines are popular collector's items, produced in many costumes and settings, including Christmas motifs. The first models were made in 1935 when a Bavarian porcelain manufacturer, Franz Goebel, translated the drawings on a Fransiscan nun, Sister Maria Innocentia Hummel, to three-dimensional figures.

Now, The Goebel Collectors' Club has 200,000 members in North America, and a gallery in Tarrytown, NY that attracted more than 25,000 visitors this year. But instead of giving a collector yet another little figurine, I'm thinking of making an offer on the showpiece of the center—a hand-crafted, 8-feet high, 3,300-pound replica of the "Merry Wanderer," the largest M. I. Hummel figurine in the world. But, even if I could buy the thing, it probably would not fit under the tree.

➤ When all else fails, and you find yourself gravitating to very sensible, very practical behavior, remember what Thomas Tusser wrote in 1557 in "A Hundred Points of Good Husbandry":

> At Christmas play and make good cheer,
> For Christmas comes but once a year.

New Year Resolutions and Wishes
Home Sense Resolutions, Revelations,
and Wishes for the New Year

Before resolutions and wishes can be properly made for the new year, loose ends from the past year must be attended to. This cleansing process may include some painful revelations about unfinished improvement projects. But it may help to make us more resolute about our resolutions, and make the wishes more likely to come true. So here goes.

I am a list maker. (That's not the revelation.) But several home-related items have been listed again and again this year. For instance, I have been planning to replace the clunky aluminum storm door to the redwood-framed greenhouse for quite a while now.

Expose 100 tons of copper and 125 tons of steel to a century of rain and salt sea air, and it's ready for the scrap heap. Repairs put off too long almost did irreparable damage to the Statue of Liberty. In 1986 workers shrouded in scaffolding had lowered the torch for complete reconstruction, necessary because of extensive corrosion.

Somehow, adding this project to a "to-do" list has the peculiar effect of relegating the task to the back burner. There are several ways to correct this. But which one will work best in the new year? The most obvious is simply to replace the door. Another solution would be to stop adding the job to my list.

A more subtle alternative is to make back burner projects part of much larger renovation projects. But that would probably cause the project to become hopelessly lost in a master plan that is perennially under development.

Revelations are the next item of business. Since I dispense information about home improvements, and spent years in business as a carpenter and general building contractor, one might think my house is as improved as a house can get. Well, not quite. In fact, not by a long shot.

But there are many good excuses for this state of affairs. First, I did not design or build this house. But I know who did. I live in an area that, at one time, was a haven for theater and movie personalities. One of the notables was Max Sennett, director of the Keystone Cops, king of slapstick pratfalls, car chases, and collapsing movie sets. His brother designed and built my house.

Comedy must have run in the family because Sennett's brother added some bizarre touches to the design of this flat-roofed, sort of Bauhaus style, 45-year-old modern house. Any time a repair or improvement project scratches the original surface. I know that, just like the hapless Keystone Cops, I am in for an unexpected surprise.

For instance, in my house the forced hot-air ducts are in the ceiling. What could the rationale have been? Hot air rises, so why not put the heat where it will wind up after a while anyway? It's nonsensical.

Another unique twist is the overly generous rim built around the edges of the flat roofs on both stories. It turns out this was designed to contain several inches of water (after the drains were stopped up), which would keep the house cool due to evaporation on hot summer days. On most houses, roofs are designed to shed water and prevent leaks. But not on my house.

Then there were the three wide bands of pastel green, blue, and tan striped horizontally around the living room, which was originally lit by a continuous border of thin fluorescent bulbs. Life here must have been very much like a cabaret, old chum—a prewar German nightclub at its most menacing.

There are too many weird little details to mention. If they had been obvious 17 years ago the house might still be on the market despite its isolated and incredibly peaceful wooded setting.

The final piece of year-end business is a series of wishes for the new year. My hopes cover a lot of consumer territory, including new products I wish someone would manufacture, and several sales practices I wish manufacturers would do away with.

• Someone please make a foam rubber-cased remote control. Extremely sensitive controls should not be housed in a hard plastic case. Drop it once or twice (my kids can do that easily every day), and the pressure-sensitive volume control button starts changing channels or simply goes dead.

• Instead of making smoke alarms that beep incessantly as the battery wears down, how about making one that releases a red flag. A modest-sized red flag would provide adequate warning, and be mercifully silent.

- How about an end to mold, mildew, tiles coming off the wall, cracked grout, and other problems with seamless, one-piece bathrooms. If manufacturers can produce one-piece fiberglass or acrylic tubs and spas, why not an entire seamless room, with molded sinks, shelves, toilets, and tubs built in?

- It's about time for a pour-on roof skin. Pour it over new tar paper or old shingles, and it becomes a rubbery, flexible, leakproof shield against the weather.

- I wish for more manufacturers to install toll-free, 800 information and troubleshooting phone lines, with real people to talk to instead of recorded messages. The flip side of this issue is a wish for retailers to dispense with automatically dialed, prerecorded sales pitches.

I do not respond well to a recorded message that says, "Hi, I'm a computer, and my boss has authorized me to offer you a unique opportunity to rent a meat storage locker." I wish his boss would pull the plug.

- I wish the supposedly serious home how-to magazines that purport to be on the cutting edge of consumer issues would drop ads they carry for positively lethal knives and similar "survivalist" gear. I wish they would do without the revenue from sponsors of spare time, get-rich-quick franchise opportunities that promise thousands of profits for practically no effort, and ads for "secret" business success plans. Frankly, I no longer take seriously the "serious" magazines who can't pass up a quick buck from such dubious advertisers.

If the nameless Florida millionaire really wants to "share the wealth," how come you have to read a full page of infinitesimal print to discover only that the secret is wonderful and amazing, and yours for a fee? This guy is no altruist.

- I wish for an end to "negative option" sales plans, used by many book and record clubs. They send you a book or record unless you send the club notice that you do not want the selection chosen for you.

Such plans often provide attractive incentives to get you to join. But selecting the negative option every month can be utter drudgery unless you are the ultimate consumer and like everything anybody sends you. If the selection happens to arrive when you're on vacation you unknowingly become the owner of a product you never ordered and may never have heard of. Pretty sneaky. Happily, more consumers have realized that they can simply not accept such unsolicited packages. That means the record club absorbs the returned record—and the postage, too.

- Could television and radio stations please end the endless repeats of financial success programs. If they can't find an old Three Stooges movie to fill these slots, I wish they would at least provide nearly continuous and very prominent notice to viewers that these programs are half-hour advertisements for the program's producers, and not educational programming provided by the station.

- I wish supermarket pricing labels about unit costs would include one more statistic that has nothing to do with quality or durability: the percentage of the price that goes to support product advertising.

- I wish companies would stop appropriating mythical figures, deceased heroes, and former presidents to hawk products. I don't think George Washington would have preferred the gifts offered by one bank over another, or that Santa has a favorite appliance store.

Homemade Christmas Traditions
From Ancient Rome to the Modern Post Office

If Julius Caesar had not crossed the Rubicon and the Roman Empire had somehow expired after that event in 49 B.C. we might not be celebrating Christmas each year. But thanks to Caesar, and even more so to his successor, Octavian, who ushered in 200 years of growth and peace known as the Pax Romana, the tradition has been preserved.

While the ancient Romans are well known for their majestic examples of architecture and engineering such as the Coliseum and the Pantheon (not to mention concrete, the semicircular arch, and a few other notable contributions to civilization), they are also credited with giving us something just as noble and long-lasting though far less tangible—Christmas.

However, there is no mention that I can find in books of Roman history about turkey, sweet potatoes and marshmallows, cranberry sauce, wild rice with peas, and pumpkin pie with vanilla ice cream, not to mention mistletoe, popcorn-and-cranberry garlands, snow angels, yule logs, and Christmas cards. These may not be majestic contributions to civilization. But they can be a lot of fun.

For instance, you may start (or cement) a relationship this Christmas by sitting under the Loranthaceae with someone. That's mistletoe, defined not very festively in a botanical guide I have as a family of parasitic herbs and shrubs with leathery leaves and waxy berries. Yuck.

The Druids, a not very festive bunch of Celts who once populated the British Isles, ascribed special powers to the sprigs of leaves and berries. Starting some time in the second century B.C., they burned mistletoe as a sacrifice to their gods, and invested the herb with many healing powers. The association with kissing may be linked more to the Scandinavians who associated the sprigs with Frigga, the goddess of love.

The Druids may have been the educated, upper crust of Celtic society a few thousand years ago. But it is only reasonable to question the collective intelligence of a group that preferred to use the sprigs for burning sacrifices instead of burning kisses.

Stringing cranberry-and-popcorn garlands for the Christmas tree is a tradition for which I have found no historical precedents. So far as I'm concerned, the practice started with my mother. Undoubtedly, this is not true.

However, historical background is not the main feature of stringing cranberry-and-popcorn garlands. The main feature is their tendency to become cranberry-and-cranberry garlands. The popcorn does tend to break as you poke a needle and thread through practically any location in the puffy kernel.

One could argue that trying to sew brittle popcorn is a job for witless idiots. Maybe. But, somehow, it's fun, certainly challenging, and made considerably less frustrating if you adopt the efficient system of eating all the pieces that break when you try to string them. No natural tree decoration is more beautiful or more functional.

And in case no one has passed on to you the secret of successful popcorn sewing, here it is. Make the popcorn a day early and leave it out on the counter. This way, by the time you start sewing, it will have gone a bit limp and stale, which makes the kernels less tasty, but also less breakable.

Another tradition that defies historical perspective is making snow angels. First, you get in a silly mood. Then, you run around outside in the snow for a while—preferably in circles or until you become thoroughly giddy from the cold air and exercise combined with some other stimulant. Finally, you select a pristine patch of sparkling, moonlit snow, collapse backwards into it and slowly drag your arms through the snow from your legs to above your head. That makes the wings.

There are two tricks to this practice: extricating yourself from the snow without disturbing the angel pattern, and arranging for a good snowfall on Christmas.

One of my favorite indoor Christmas traditions (bordering on a very ritualistic ritual) starts outside, early in the year, with a search for the yule log. In this year-long quest I am completely in-tune with history, since burning a yule log probably began in Scandinavia as a pagan Viking ritual that represented banishment of evil and, almost literally, a rekindling of the hearth from one year to the next. Ashes from the yule log were sometimes scattered outside the house to distribute the telltales of good fortune.

The significance of the custom, which was followed widely throughout Europe, varied from one region to the next, but generally signaled a reaffirmation of life. English twists on the yule log tradition included salting the fire with corn or wine in hope of a prosperous harvest. My own twist on the tradition is to find a hardwood log that will just barely fit over a shimmering bed of nearly white-hot coals in the wood stove, one that is beefy, knotty, and dry enough to burn and burn and burn.

But not all Christmas traditions are ancient. Although the ominous trend this year seems to be giving children talking, blinking, crawling, crying dolls and other fully automated toys that leave nothing to the imagination, some relatively recent Christmas traditions are considerably less complicated. For instance, sending printed Christmas cards is a practice that started in London in 1843.

But a tradition that was good news to parted friends was bad news to post office employees. A seasonal deluge of homemade Christmas cards taxed the U.S. Postal system as early as 1822 when the Superintendent of Mails in Washington complained that he would have to hire sixteen extra mailmen to cope with the extra cards.

Despite his protests, the practice of sending cards continued. And in 1843, one Sir Henry Cole, a British businessman who, among other things, ran a stylish precursor of Conran's on Bond Street, commissioned John Calcott Horsley, a London artist, to design a card. One thousand were printed. The tradition took hold in this country in 1875 when a Boston lithographer named Louis Prang began printing Christmas cards.

Now, the U.S. Postal Service has a slightly larger increase to deal with—a 24-percent jump in first class mail and a 40-percent increase in packages sent in the time from Thanksgiving to Christmas. Although the extra burden undoubtedly includes a few bills and other year-end communications, the extra load alone amounts to about 1.4 billion pieces of mail.

A small percent are children's letters to Santa Claus. Those including a return address get special treatment. In many areas, service volunteer groups are invited by the Postal Service to read the letters and make special, sometimes very tangible responses to ''needy'' letters.

But every letter with a return address is at least answered. In Washington, DC, for instance, Volunteers of the District of Columbia branch of the National Association of Letter Carriers hand-address envelopes in which a printed reply beginning "Dear Little Friend" is sent, courtesy of the U.S. Postal Service.

In addition to a cheery greeting, the note also includes an unusual line for Christmas cards—a plug for stamp collecting. But the message quickly retreats to more suitable seasonal prose, closing, "Christmas will be here and I'll soon be on my way. Have a merry merry Christmas on that wonderful day. Love, Santa."

New Year's Predictions
Past Prognostications and Pearls of Wisdom
That Missed the Mark

So far, the future hasn't been nearly as bad as a lot of people, past and present, said it would be. A good thing, too. What's the fun in making slightly outlandish New Year's resolutions and predicting great things in the coming year, if some cranky curmudgeon announces that this or that wondrous event can't possibly happen. Bah humbug to the savants!

Over the centuries there have been some mind-boggling leaps of logic and fogged-over forecasts about people, our homes, habits, inventions—even the world we live in. For instance, in 1633 (about 20 years after Galileo had discovered sunspots and understood that the earth rotated on its axis), a Professor of Philosophy and Mathematics at the University of Pisa, Scipio Chiaramonti, reasoned that, "Animals, which move, have limbs and muscles; the earth has no limbs and muscles, hence it does not move."

This statement may be the forerunner of "If all Thrells are Grulls and some Progs are Thrells" type of questions used on various intelligence tests. However, when you come to the kind of conclusion that the Professor came to, the Army decides you probably couldn't hack it in the motor pool after all and sends you packing.

On issues closer to home, there are many exceedingly common tools and machines of modern life that, according to some people, should never have been invented and certainly should never have caught on.

In 1946, Darryl F. Zanuck, who ran 20th Century Fox Studios, sounded the demise of television by saying, "People will soon get tired of staring at a plywood box every night." In 1865, an editorial in *The Boston Post* gave a double whammy to the telephone, telling readers, "Well-informed people know it is impossible to transmit the voice over wires and that were it possible to do so, the thing would be of no practical value."

Popular Mechanics predicted a rosy if somewhat inaccurate future for the computer in 1949. Comparing future equipment to the original ENIAC, which had 18,000 vacuum tubes and weighed 30 tons, the magazine predicted that "Computers in the future may have only 1,000 vacuum tubes and perhaps only weigh 1½ tons." Find a place for that little sucker in your home office.

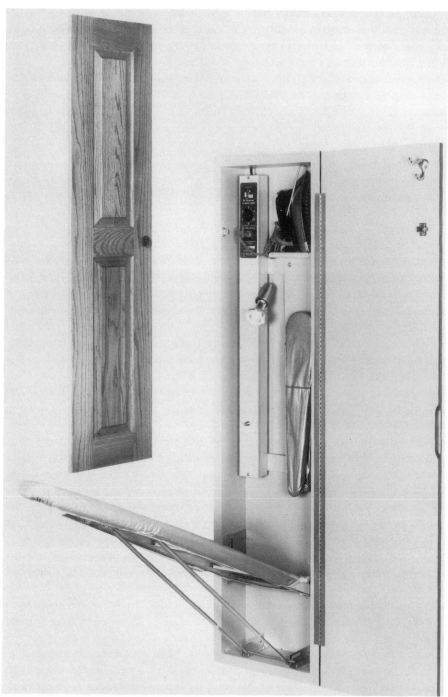

Who would have predicted ironing centers concealed in the wall? The In-Wall Ironing Center, made by SICO Inc., of Minneapolis, MN, includes a folddown ironing board that pivots 180 degrees parallel to the walls (useful in tight spots such as hallways), electrical outlets, light, and storage shelf, all tucked behind a door.

But the most confoundingly myopic view of engineering know-how and man's inventiveness was sounded in 1899 by Charles H. Duell, obviously the right man for the job of Commissioner of the U.S. Office of Patents. He said, "Everything that can be invented has been invented."

The next time you cozy up to the radiator (not to mention the next time you pay a utility bill) bear in mind what Henry Luce, the publisher of *Time, Life*, and *Fortune*, among other pursuits, wrote in 1956. "By 1980, all power (electric, atomic, solar) is likely to be virtually costless." Luce may have been listening to General David Sarnoff, Chairman of RCA, who said a year earlier that, "I do not hesitate to forecast that atomic batteries will be commonplace long before 1980." Of course, Sarnoff may have been prompted by Alex Lewyt, who ran the Lewyt Corporation, a vacuum cleaner manufacturer. In 1955, he said, "Nuclear-powered vacuum cleaners will probably be a reality within 10 years." Vroom, vroom.

Thinking of remodeling next year? One popular improvement in a climate with hot summers is air conditioning. However, you may not want to pin all your decorating changes to a metal box in the window, even though a 1960 *Audels Do-It-Yourself Encyclopedia* reported that, "An extensive recent survey indicates that changes, both interior and exterior, are beginning to appear in homes designed around air conditioning."

Your bath projects will certainly benefit from the wisdom of Charles James Fox (a Ph.D., no less) who wrote in a 1907 article for *House & Garden*, that the flooring material of choice for modern baths would be, "Tile that is absolutely nonabsorbent and germ-proof."

At the turn of the century many shelter magazines were full of predictions and new products for the next hundred years. A story in *Cosmopolitan* described the prototypical house of the future this way: "No wallpapers are used in the typical dwelling of the twentieth century here described. In fact, they have ceased to be employed in the houses of the well-to-do, largely because they assist the accumulation of dirt and disease-germs." The same story coined the forgotten phrase "liquid air" to praise the coming of some unexplained form of air conditioning. However, *Cosmopolitan* author Otis T. Mason was on track with his prediction of recessed lighting. He wrote that light bulbs would not be exposed, "avoiding dazzle."

Some prognosticators are like card counters at casinos—they like to have a system. For instance, an old issue of the *Farmer's Almanac* refers to cycles that portend to show, for instance, that the rate of precipitation in Philadelphia rises and falls in an 8-year cycle, along with cigarette production; that U.S. stock prices show a 4-year cycle, which coincides with field mouse abundance, and that real estate activity follows an 18.2-year cycle as does immigration into the U.S. Hey, why not.

If you are tempted to raise a glass of something alcoholic once in a while, bear in mind that you will be disproving the prediction of Henry Ford, who had a lot to say about matters other than automobiles. In 1929, having misunderstood completely the lessons of Prohibition, he forecast that "the abolition of the commercialized liquor trade in this country is as final as the abolition of slavery."

To browse among other mistaken or bizarre looks into the future, you may want to seek out these books: any edition of the *Old Farmer's Almanac, The Experts Speak* by Christopher Cerf and Victor Navasky (Pantheon Books, 1984), *The Portable Curmudgeon* by Jon Winokur (New American Library, 1987), and *The Third 637 Best Things Anybody Ever Said* by Robert Byrne (Atheneum, 1986). I have also taken advantage of my collection of old how-to books, including such dusty gems as a 1955 edition of *The Popular Science Do-It-Yourself Encyclopedia*. Its many volumes are filled with waves of the future (the selection on the effective use of linoleum as durable wallpaper springs to mind) that barely caused a ripple.

Prognostications can be alluring. But if you ever feel tempted to take too seriously the predictions of experts, even government experts, just remember that on December 31, 1929, 2 months after the stock market crash that ushered in the Depression, Secretary of the Treasury Andrew William Mellon said, ''I see nothing in the present situation that is either menacing or warrants pessimism.'' At the same time, the U.S. Dept. of Labor predicted in its New Year's Forecast that 1930 would be ''a splendid employment year.''

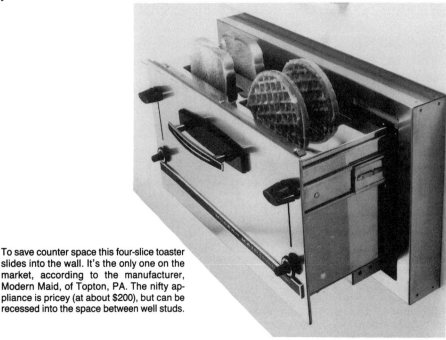

To save counter space this four-slice toaster slides into the wall. It's the only one on the market, according to the manufacturer, Modern Maid, of Topton, PA. The nifty appliance is pricey (at about $200), but can be recessed into the space between well studs.

Thirty Two

REAL ESTATE

Home Buying Checks
Some Top-Priority Deal-Breaking Issues

In the excitement of searching for a new place to live, there are so many things to see and check and attend to. There is a risk that buyers may become preoccupied with details and underestimate the importance of a few really crucial issues. That's understandable. But some can threaten your health, as well as your house.

Unfortunately, many housing professionals also become bogged down in details. The home inspector you hire may present a report filled with information about a cracked window screen frame, an open wallboard seam, and other obvious surface imperfections. Your builder may emphasize the low-maintenance kitchen floor and the efficient heating system. Your real estate agent may emphasize layout and storage space.

Many of these points are well worth considering. But they are not paramount and potentially deal-breaking issues. Most of the drawbacks you see in a walk-through, read in an inspector's report, and hear from a builder or real estate agent are part and parcel of owning a house. Most houses, even brand new ones, have many imperfections.

The potential problems that could be deal-breakers should get much more of your time and attention. Some are complex and may require the help (and expense) of yet another outside expert. Here is a rundown of several important issues that could make or break the deal.

Radon. Radon is one of the most potent potential threats to life and property value, therefore, it is foolish not to test for radon before buying—even if the lender and real estate agent don't insist that you do. (Imagine testing for termites that may weaken a few wall studs but not for radon.) Most houses can be retrofitted to prevent radon infiltration. But this sometimes expensive solution may leave owners with the uneasy feeling of living over a temporarily defused bomb.

UFFI. Shortly after the 1973 energy crisis, urea formaldehyde foam insulation (UFFI) was considered an ideal solution to rising energy costs in homes without insulation. The foam, in liquid form, could be pumped into walls where it hardened. But in some cases the material leached levels of formaldehyde gas that caused a variety of health problems, such as eye, nose and throat irritation. It made some houses uninhabitable.

A thorough house inspection should uncover UFFI. Look for traces of round patches at approximately 16-inch intervals on wall surfaces (between wall studs where the foam was pumped in). The material should be easy to see in exposed wall cavities in cellars, crawl spaces, and attics.

It's unlikely that you will find UFFI in a home built after 1982. But to be safe, preserve a few chunks of any hardened, foam-type wall insulation (like petrified shaving cream), in a plastic bag for testing. Ask local health department officials for referrals to several testing labs. There is no solution for UFFI in walls that are leaching unhealthy levels of formaldehyde gas. If you find it, UFFI could be a decisive deal breaker.

Asbestos. This fibrous, durable, and carcinogenic material has been used in many building products. In residences the most serious threat is from asbestos insulation on heating pipes and around parts of furnaces. This was a common use of asbestos in houses approximately 20 to 40 years old. The problem may be acute if the pipe wrapping is ragged around the edges and seams. This allows cancer-causing asbestos fibers to escape. (For more details on asbestos, UFFI, radon, and other health hazards, refer to the ''Indoor Air Quality'' section in Chapter 24.)

Water quality. There are many possible water quality problems ranging from minor inconveniences to serious contamination. For instance, well water with a high mineral content may clog pipes and pose maintenance problems. But these are relatively minor home maintenance concerns.

To uncover serious problems, such an unhealthy traces of leakage from neighboring septic systems, or a high lead level, a lab test of tap water is needed. No home buyer expects to discover a Love Canal in the back yard. But a water test simply makes sure that there are no hidden problems such as elevated lead levels or other contaminants from nearby land fills, factories, or more unlikely sources.

Chronically wet basement. The key word here is ''chronically''. Leaks, floods, dampness, mold, mildew, and other persistent problems can render half the space in many houses with a full cellar useless for living or storage. Also, porous basements are susceptible to foundation cracking, excessive settling, undermined foundation footings, and other serious structural faults.

Some seemingly insignificant problems may indicate more telling trouble that cannot be spotted easily in a walk-through. Stains under a faucet, for instance, may be the only visible signs of ''hard'' water with a high mineral content. Pipes and water heater linings may be encrusted, operating inefficiently, and ready for replacement.

Remedies for basements doubling as swimming pools are possible but expensive. Sometimes the only recourse is to reexcavate the foundation in order to apply new waterproofing and drains below ground level—a major undertaking.

Zoning and other special restraints. Over 98 percent of all cities in the country with a population over 10,000 have comprehensive zoning ordinances and building codes.

Before buying, find out about current zoning, and what many towns refer to as the master plan. The plan may show the next phase of residential or commercial expansion, where new roads will be built or existing roads connected, where a new exit ramp will be added to a nearby highway—all factors that can change a neighborhood. Changes are most likely if the property is near a border between differently zoned areas, particularly if one is nonresidential.

If you plan to buy a house contingent on plans for expansion (adding an extra bedroom and bath, for instance), check regulations that control how much of the plot may be covered by the building, and how close the building can extend toward the property boundaries.

Also investigate any infringements on the property, such as a utility company right-of-way, or an easement, such as a common driveway shared with an adjoining property owner.

Hidden Home Buying Costs
Surprise Charges That Can Empty Your Checkbook

The average price of a new house is close to $100,000—enough to stretch most home buying budgets to their limits. But there is one more major expense, in addition to furnishings and landscaping and turning on the utilities: closing costs.

The closing, also called the settlement, is the official ceremony during which ownership changes hands. Contracts are read, documents are signed, checks are exchanged, and the deal is made. The deal costs a lot of money. You know that going in. But the surprise to many buyers is that executing the deal costs a lot of money, too.

There are approximately 20 different types of closing costs over and above the cost of the property, as well as other "surprise" expenses for items appended to, but technically not part of, the property.

The National Association of Realtors estimates that the mechanical charges of closing the deal, such as loan origination fees and document transfer fees, total 3.7 percent of the house price. This does not include real estate broker fees, which the NAR estimates at an average of 5.6 percent of the house sales price. Both rates vary widely. And in one area the buyer may be expected to pay for a particular settlement charge that the seller commonly pays for in a different region.

The first official notice of closing costs is called the "Good Faith Estimate." It is supplied by your lender when you file a loan application. And "good faith" is an accurate description, since there is no requirement that the estimate be within a specified limit of the actual costs.

A second notification, called the "Settlement Statement" but generally referred to as the "HUD-1," includes the actual charges. It is provided at the closing. And it may contain a few surprises. Both notifications are mandated by the Real Estate Settlement Procedures Act (RESPA), established by the Department of Housing and Urban Development.

Since unexpected costs can break a home buying budget, it's important to have enough lead time to gather the required funds. Prior to the RESPA notification, it is essential to go over the extensive list of potential costs with your attorney. Also, the real estate agent handling the transaction should work with you to estimate closing costs as part of the prequalifying process, in which it must be determined if you can afford to buy the house.

The extras can be large enough to kill the deal, just the way state and city sales tax on a $10,000 car can make the car unaffordable if you have up to, but no more than, $10,000 to spend.

But even the protection of RESPA, the help of your real estate attorney, and the prequalifying estimate of a real estate agent may not prepare you for additional charges encountered at the closing.

For example, the current owner may have 750 gallons of fuel oil (at $1 per gallon), left in the tank. Technically, this is not a closing cost, even though you have to write a check for the amount at the closing when it is too late to do anything about it. Anything that is not physically part of the property or expressly listed in the contract of sale can be considered separately and sold independently as personal property, not real property.

Sometimes the distinction between the two is extremely fuzzy. For instance, if the shelves in the den are screwed into the wall studs, and trimmed with molding like the doors and windows, they would be considered part of the structure—"built-in." But a freestanding bookcase in the same location would be considered a piece of the owner's furniture. Problems may develop when the shelves look built-in, but are held in place only by "temporary" brackets for safety. Some owners even take the light bulbs when they move out.

Attorneys may talk about "what is conveyed" (read, what you get for your money). A safe rule-of-thumb is that anything that could be removed without damaging the basic structure could become an extra at the closing. The trick is to anticipate these hidden costs in time to make a decision about them.

The flip side to this question is that you may not want some of the items that are included in the sale. For example, if the house comes with appliances that are old, inefficient, and ready for replacement, it would be a liability to receive them along with the house. But unless they are excluded from the sale, you will get them with the house. You will then have to pay for new appliances and dispose of the old ones. Disposal also can be a problem when you inherit a garage full of old newspapers and broken window screens.

Generally, the surprise costs over and above true closing costs fall into two categories: stockpile costs and takeover costs.

Takeover costs can include built-in furnishings, major appliances, a wood stove, a surface-wired intercom system, and many other potentially portable items. Stockpile costs can include partial payments remaining for ongoing projects and commitments,

It's a nice bonus: finding that the utility room is equipped with new appliances. But this Speed Queen washer and dryer are considered portable, since they can be disconnected from the plumbing system. The adjacent built-ins are probably part of the house. But sometimes cabinets too, can disappear with the furniture.

for instance, a partially paid snow removal contract, a lawn care contract, fuel oil left in the tank, several cords of wood for the stove.

All of these costs are negotiable. But the best policy is to uncover them early, and make them part of the more general negotiations on the overall sales price of the property. Between homeowner's insurance, title insurance, attorney's fees, real estate tax escrow payments and seemingly endless other charges, it pays to avoid costly, last-minute surprises. Chances are that your bank balance will be low enough without them.

Titles and Title Insurance
The Ins and Outs of Protecting
Your Right of Ownership

Over 90 percent of all new homes are sold with a form of warranty. These policies cover the tangible sign of ownership—the building itself. But it is equally important to establish and protect your right of ownership—of a building, and any other real estate.

Although paying thousands of dollars and signing piles of legal papers may seem like more than enough proof, home ownership can be questioned so many ways that mortgage bankers insist on a different kind of warranty against losing their investment in your property. It's called "title insurance."Lenders insist on it to protect the mortgage amount (not your share of the deal, the down payment), just in case a claim against your right to the property is upheld.

Records of a title, or official recognition of ownership, are open to the public—in the county court house, for example. On new subdivisions, where parcels of land have just been created, the title record may be very new and very short. On older properties the records are more lengthy. Sometimes they are difficult to decipher.

Every link in the chain of ownership is important. For example, even if a seller transfers ownership to you in good faith, a descendant of a previous owner may lay claim to the property based on evidence such as an old will that breaks the chain. Your seller may never have owned the house legally, even though he lived there.

Weak links and outright breaks in the chain of ownership should be uncovered by a title search made prior to sale. Traditionally, this search was conducted by a real estate attorney, and in some areas an attorney's opinion may still be required by a local bank. More often, the search is made by a specialized title firm that verifies the findings in one of three documents: an Abstract or Certificate of Title, a Torrens Certificate (used in only a few areas), or a title insurance policy.

The title company's search is made through public records you could search yourself. But some of the title systems are very confusing. For instance, one system, called the *Grantor-Grantee Index*, lists every seller and every buyer by the year of the transaction. To trace the chain of ownership you must find every sale date, then check the alphabetical buyer or seller listing for that year. But the names are alphabetized only by the first letter. So you must look through all the M's, for example, which are further sorted according to the day of the year the documents were recorded. It's a mind-boggling system.

Dealing with such a convoluted mess of records makes it easier to understand why some mistakes are made in title searches. For instance, one title-searching firm may inherit defects in a previous search made by another firm. Few searches actually trace the chain back to an original owner.

Also, some title defects may escape even a very professional and thorough search. For example, claims against your right of ownership can arise from simple mistakes in legal documents, forgeries, documents executed under a fabricated or expired power of attorney, or defective foreclosure proceedings against a former owner.

Title insurance is designed to protect the bank's investment (and your equity under a separate policy) from these and other defects. Lenders routinely make title insurance a prerequisite for obtaining a mortgage. They generally recommend you do the same to protect your share.

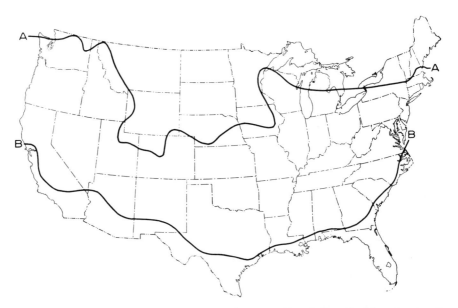

Along with title searches, most lenders require a termite report, although above the A line where termites don't live it shouldn't be necessary. Below the B line the problem is even worse. Along the southern edge of the country dry-wood termites don't have to build mud tunnels up the foundation. They can fly straight for the wood.

Like many other costs associated with buying real estate, the price of title insurance policies, and the extent of coverage, varies. It pays to comparison shop. Typically, policies are priced per $1,000 of coverage. The charge is assessed as a one-time fee, which may be $500 or $600 on a $100,000 house.

A thorough policy should offer protection against defects such as mistakes in documents drawn up for previous transactions that may elude a title searcher. With such a large investment at stake, you should be sure what is and isn't covered. Avoid dealing with firms that gloss over exclusions and underplay the risks from claims excluded by a policy. A firm representing itself as an agency of the bank you're dealing with also should be avoided. That practice is illegal.

While it may be nice to have the peace of mind provided by title insurance, critics of the industry argue that the whole idea of title insurance is redundant. The reasoning is that if you pay once for a title search you shouldn't have to pay again for insurance in case the search was inadequate.

This kind of insurance strikes many consumers as just another form of product service contract. Theoretically, a product warranty, whether for a stove or an acre of land, should provide adequate protection against defects. But in addition to providing peace of mind for homebuyers, title insurance also helps to support the secondary financial markets for pools of mortgages by increasing the security of the loans. As a practical matter title insurance continues to be an unavoidable expense, whether you like the idea or not, particularly since you won't get a mortgage without it.

The American Land Title Association[1] can provide more information on titles, title insurance, and the risks associated with securing clear and undisputed ownership of property.

Real Estate Buying Schemes
"Double Closings"-A New Name for No-Money-Down Deals

"Double closing" is the new term for a money-making technique that may be gradually replacing the overworked and somewhat tarnished phrase "no money down." But this new twist on an old theme appears to be just another bit of salesmanship that manipulates sellers, and, supposedly, unsuspecting bankers, to generate more than the funds needed to buy a house.

Despite extreme skepticism by industry trade groups such as the National Association of Realtors and the Mortgage Bankers Association of America, a flood of television programs, books, articles, newsletters, and other expressions of no-money-down techniques continues to present implausible testimonials and case histories showing how easy it is to accumulate real estate without spending money—not a cent of your own bankroll, some programs boast.

While many real estate professionals say that, technically, it is possible, real estate agents, bankers, and others note that buying without spending, or buying and gaining cash in the process, are risky and highly unusual practices generally not in the financial interest of lending institutions or home sellers. Implied in their statements is the idea that buyers who do pull off no-money-down buys, do so only by conning a seller, and maybe even a banker, into going along with a highly suspect deal.

The fact that risks are glossed over or not mentioned at all in many no-money-down sales pitches, may be at the heart of an investigation of no-money-down programs by the Federal Trade Commission, according to the National Association of Realtors. A recent article in that association's newsletter, *Realtor News*, says, "The NAR is cooperating with the FTC in its investigation of the 'no-money-down' programs."

Normally, homebuyers put down as little as 5 or 10 percent on what are called high-ratio loans, or as much as 25 or 30 percent of the purchase price on more conventional deals, and borrow the difference. Although it may fly in the face of common sense and experience, double-closing techniques supposedly can eliminate the need for any down payment and even generate excess funds.

Faced with the high cost of housing, even in a market favorable to homebuyers, many consumers have been lured by the rosy-sounding alternative of "instantaneous cash" that is typical of the terminology used to advertise no-money-down seminars.

---

[1]American Land Title Association, 1828 L. Street NW, Washington, DC 20036

The idea of buying a house without a down payment gained popularity when mortgage interest rates were high. In 1981, for example, when interest rates averaged over 15 percent nationally, the National Association of Realtors Housing Affordability Index was 69. That means a family earning the median income could afford only 69 percent of the mortgage on a median-priced home. The most recent Index ratings are at, and sometimes over, 100, meaning that a median-income family can more than afford to qualify for enough financing to buy a median-priced home.

Now, in a more favorable real estate market for conventionally financed buying, "no-money-down" techniques have lost some of their allure as an alternative route to home ownership. But these schemes have gained popularity as pure business propositions in which a house is disassociated from its traditional attributes and, like pork belly futures, becomes no more than a vehicle for generating cash.

A recent article in the *Real Estate Advisor*, a newsletter whose editors include several well-known proponents of no-money-down techniques, describes how one man used the double closing on a 160-unit townhouse property. Instead of telling the bank what he was paying for the property, "I told them to go out and appraise it and tell me how much they'd put up," the article stated. Apparently the bank provided $1.3 million in financing, $200,000 over the purchase price of $1.1 million.

Asked about these claims, a spokesman for the Mortgage Bankers Association of America (MBA), a group representing some 2,000 lending institutions, said, "It's hard to imagine that any lender would avoid asking the most basic question: 'How much are you paying for the property?' I don't see any reason for a lender to make what amounts to an unsecured loan for money above the value of the property."

Another pitfall not mentioned in the *Real Estate Advisor* article arises from the disparity between the owner's and the bank's appraisals—in this case $200,000. Even if this difference were not noticed by the lending bank, it would inevitably be seen as the mortgage was examined prior to resale by the bank into larger pools of mortgages held by investors, a common practice today. Because the mortgage would not be properly collateralized by the property, "there's no way you could resell it," says the MBA spokesman.

A case history explaining how to approach the other source of funds prior to closing, the seller, is also offered in the newsletter. In this instance, after settling on a purchase price, the owner agreed to sign over the deed but wait several months for payment. During that time the buyer got a home improvement loan for $5,000, improved the property, rented it, then refinanced for double the purchase price based on increased value from the home improvements, and netted $22,000—all without spending a dime, according to the article.

Asked about such scenarios for generating cash, a spokesman at the National Association of Realtors commented, "It's completely unrealistic for consumers to expect a seller to transfer ownership without receiving funds. There's just no reason for them to do it."

While "leveraging," or making your investment with someone else's money, may be an accepted principle of big business wheeling and dealing, it holds many traps for inexperienced real estate investors—even if they can find bankers and home sellers as incredibly stupid as those supposedly found by no-money-down proponents.

For one thing, some consumers may be tempted to forget that cash generated by taking on larger mortgages from banks or additional loans from sellers is, in fact, still a debt that must be repaid.

Many no-money-down and double-closing programs also minimize risks for sellers who accept no-money-down offers. The Mortgage Bankers Association points out that if "excess" cash, generated by a second mortgage granted by the seller to the buyer, is lost in poor investments, the buyer may not have enough funds to repay the bank or the seller.

In fact, without any equity in the property, the buyer, unlike a typical homeowner, may have nothing to lose from foreclosure. That's reason enough for any sane banker not to make such a loan in the first place.

Consumer enthusiasm for no-money-down seminars and television programs may be dampened by low interest rates and a more realistic picture of the risks associated with these ventures that may result from the Federal Trade Commission's (FTC) investigation.

Although the FTC neither confirms nor denies the existence of an investigation as a matter of policy, sources at the National Association of Realtors report that the investigation was triggered in part by complaints from students who attended seminars and were unable to recreate the kind of money-making deals attested to by lecturers running the programs. Surprise, surprise.

Refinancing Options
Weighing One-Time Costs Against Long-Term Savings

When mortgage rates ease, many mortgage bankers get 3 months or more behind in their paperwork. The backlog is caused by an onslaught of mortgage refinancing applications from homeowners trying to lock in lower interest rates.

Over 2 million refinancing loans could be made in such times. Homeowners jump at the rates because the deals seem almost too good to be true. After all, how often do you get a chance, years after you've bought a product (in this case a mortgage loan), to buy it all over again for less money?

But refinancing is not always a good deal. Sometimes the one-time costs of making a new loan outweigh the long-term gains from a lower interest rate. That's the complex decision facing many homeowners.

There are two main reasons for refinancing: to exchange a high-rate loan for one with a lower rate; and to trade in the insecurity of an adjustable rate mortgage (ARM), even if the rate is moderate, for the security of a fixed rate.

Simple arithmetic seems to indicate that if your interest rate is any higher than current rates, you should refinance. Even a 1-percent change has dramatic consequences.

Here's the effect on a 30-year, $80,000 mortgage: At a 10-percent interest rate, monthly payments for principal and interest are $702.06. At 11 percent, payments are $761.86. The difference, $59.80, may not break the budget in any 1 month. But over 30 years of 12 payments a year, a 1-percent interest rate decrease saves $21,528. If pressed, you probably could think of something to do with this money other than giving it to the bank.

On larger loans, the loans where refinancing nets a greater percentage rate change, long-term savings are much higher. For example, monthly payments on a 10-percent, 30-year, $100,000 mortgage are $877.57. At 15 percent, payments are $1,264.44. The difference, $386.87 every month, over 30 years, is $139,273.20. Large numbers such as these can create waiting lines at lenders.

But refinancing has a price, in the form of settlement costs and "points." (One point equals one percent of the loan amount.) Both are one-time costs charged by the lender for making the loan. In some cases, paying off your existing mortgage before it is due incurs penalties—yet another cost to balance against long-term savings from a new, low-rate loan.

Points are simply a charge for doing business. The bank has something you and a lot of other people want—a big loan at relatively low rates. Points are part of the price tag.

Like other components of mortgage financing, points are negotiable. But they are related to the interest rate. A lender with the lowest rate may charge more points than competitors. Since the two charges are connected, you can't comparison shop for financing on interest rate alone.

You can compare rates and points together as Annual Percentage Rate (APR) figures provided by lenders. In APRs, points are averaged out over the full life of the loan. In banking terminology, averaging out the costs this way is called *amortizing*. (Some lenders allow points to be financed along with the loan amount.)

Normally, points are charged when you make the loan. But they have less impact the longer you hold the loan. For instance, paying three points on a $100,000 mortgage

Between fixed rate loans for different terms, and a basket full of different adjustable rate loans, financing can seem more complex than the house itself. But try explaining this eclectic example to your banker. It's a Japanese-style farmhouse, built by Pole House Kits of California (formerly a Hawaiian company) in Virginia.

($3,000) averages out to $1,000 a year if you stay in the house 3 years. If you stay 30 years, the three points charged to refinance average out to only $100 a year.

You may not know for sure how long you'll live in your house. But to make an informed decision about refinancing, you have to take an educated guess.

If you plan to stay for at least 4 or 5 years or longer, try to negotiate with the lender to increase points up front for a decrease in the long-term interest rate. The longer you stay in the house, the more important it is to have a low rate. But if you plan on moving before then, it will cost less to pay fewer points up front, even if the long-term interest rate is higher.

The approximate rule of thumb for trading points and interest rates is one point for ¼ of a percentage point long term. Since other factors, such as the impact of real estate taxes, may effect your decision, it is wise to consult an accountant before refinancing. Check rates and terms at your present bank, and at least two other lenders.

The other potential roadblock is the cost of closing the deal—called settlement or closing costs. These include a dozen or more separate charges for items such as a termite inspection, a survey, and various transfer taxes.

Sound familiar? They should, because you paid for these services when you bought the house and got the first mortgage. Even though you still own the house, lenders insist that you go through the process again. Many even insist on a second survey and title search, even though they are obviously redundant.

Settlement costs also vary widely; and they are negotiable. Generally, they represent about 4 percent of a typical loan. Some lenders allow you to add them to the loan amount. Of course, this means you are borrowing the money to pay closing costs and will pay interest on the money.

But many settlement costs, unlike percentage "points," are relatively constant. For instance, charges for a survey, say $300, are based on the labor required to do the job, not how much the land is worth. This charge would represent 10 percent of a $3,000 lot, but only 1 percent of a $30,000 lot. Settlement costs may seem exorbitant on a small loan, but more reasonable on a large loan.

If you have been saddled with a high-rate loan, or an adjustable-rate loan that gives you an uneasy feeling, weigh the options carefully before deciding to refinance. Even though some of the cost and charges may seem unreasonable, many homeowners will find the price well worth the long-term savings from a lower interest rate.

Remodeling Home Equity
Remodeling Projects That Make Sense and Money

Home remodelers might take a tip from an unlikely source: Richard Secord, testifying at the Iran-Contra hearings. He said, "Can't I have two purposes?" Of course, he wasn't talking about houses. He was referring to supporting his cause and making a profit, a plan smart remodelers can follow by paying for projects that make their home more comfortable, spacious, and convenient, and, at the same time, a lot more valuable.

A year-long home-remodeling contest conducted by *Better Homes & Gardens* has shown that remodeling, strictly from a financial point of view, is a terrific investment. Comfort, convenience, and extra bedrooms aside, it's a field in which the financial rewards are, on average, a lot greater and the risks are a lot smaller than with other potential money-makers, say, the stock market.

The magazine accepted 1,385 entries from readers, a group with the following characteristics. Ninety percent were married, 27 percent were two-person households, 42 percent had four or more people living at home. The group had a median income (median means half were higher and half were lower) of $44,053. Sixty percent did at least some of the work themselves.

Perhaps the most significant result was that through a full range of projects, from whole-house remodeling to bath do-overs, homeowners reported an average increase in their home's value of 36 percent. The increase was most dramatic in the case of whole-house remodeling projects.

The *Better Homes & Gardens* group reported that whole-house jobs cost an average of $46,100 and increased the median value of the group's homes 108 percent, from about $57,000 to $120,000. Although statistics from a limited, selected group such as the *Better Homes & Garden's* remodelers are not necessarily representative of nationwide trends, the results from whole-house remodeling in this group were nearly identical to results reported in a survey by *Practical Homeowner Magazine* (see Chapter 13, p. 185). That study found that overall "face-lift" projects returned 107 percent of labor and material costs immediately after completion.

Although no other remodeling project of the *Better Homes & Gardens* group created the financial windfall of whole-house jobs (108 percent is a bit better than you're getting on savings or bonds or CDs or anything else), several other projects proved lucrative.

Room additions, for example, cost the group an average of $25,000 and increased the value of homes by 44 percent. General interior remodeling (not including projects limited to kitchens or baths) cost an average of $7,700 and increased home value 30 percent. Structural improvements, including exterior deck additions, cost an average of $6,700 and raised home value 27 percent. Kitchen and bath remodeling projects, which cost an average of $5,200, raised home value 26 and 27 percent, respectively.

But there is a dark side to the financial gains of home remodeling, aside from the capital gains taxes that you may eventually have to pay on your profits. It is the time, with all the attendant dirt, debris, and disruption, that these projects take. Here's the bad news.

ABOVE: Decks continue to be one of the most popular home improvements. And they are profitable, since a deck's cost is often quickly outstripped by an increase in home value. To maintain a uniform finish in the weather this redwood deck was treated with a clear sealer. BELOW: Whirlpool baths are another hot item. This Jacuzzi Vectra is portable, since piping and pumps are built in behind wooden side skirts.

Almost a third of the group's whole-house remodeling jobs took from 6 months to a year to complete. Worse yet, almost half dragged on for over a year. Almost half of the group's room addition projects took 6 months or more to finish. So did about 40 percent of the interior face-lift jobs. The smaller jobs, such as kitchen and bath remodeling, fared better. About a third of each type were finished in less than 3 months.

So your home equity riches from lucrative, "two-purpose" home remodeling won't come so easily after all. Remodeling may be one of the best things to do with your money, but only if you can stand to donate all the time required to make your investment grow. The kicker to remodeling's yellow brick road is simply the time it takes to reach your remodeled castle at road's end.

Time Finding A House

Q. I am familiar with the real estate market in our area and know that we will have no trouble selling our present house. But I don't know how much time to allow for finding a new house in a new area. Is there some rule of thumb?

A. Most rules about buying and selling homes can be bent out of shape by high or low interest rates. For example, when many buyers and owners apply for loans, the rate of applications can overwhelm the rate of loan processing. So even if you find a house immediately, it could take several months to push the red tape out of the doorway and move in.

Also, finding the "right" house is a very personal process with many variables. Obviously, your case could be quite different than the norm. But most buyers search between 2 and 3 months before buying a new house. According to a recent survey of 5,000 homebuyers by the National Association of Realtors, first-time buyers look at an average of 8 homes over 3 months before buying.

Repeat buyers look at 11 homes in 2 months before making a final selection. This group knows the real estate ropes a little better and qualifies for mortgage money with equity built up in their present homes. That helps them get more done in less time.

The NAR survey also asked how buyers found their homes. Sixty-four percent found them through a real estate agent, 15 percent from a "for sale" sign, 8 percent from newspapers, 5 percent through a friend, 3 percent knew the seller directly, and 5 percent through other means including magazine ads.

The NAR survey also found that 99 percent of the home buyers were satisfied with their purchase but only 64 percent were satisfied with their real estate agent.

Buying Based on a Model Home

Q. Is it true that the model homes in developments under construction are built better than the other houses? If so, how can you really judge what your house will be like?

A. I have been on jobs where the best carpenters, for example, were pulled off other projects to do trim work on the model. Since this is the sales sample for other houses, it's only natural for the developer to make the best possible presentation. To put it tactfully, other houses are not likely to be built any better than the model.

Model homes also display all of the optional "upgrades"—the extras such as stone facades, high-tech security systems, and other built-ins that increase the cost of a standard model. Unless the builder's sales representative is very clear about what's standard and what's not, you may lose track and come away with a slightly distorted impression of the house's comfort and convenience.

But some builder's are very low-key. They let you poke around the model on your own. Just remember during your walk through that you are on the receiving end of a sales pitch, no matter how subtle.

For instance, some builders now use audio tapes and other aids to make the most favorable impression. *Builder* magazine has reported on several such sales techniques. At an ocean-front condominium development in Fort Pierce, Florida, heat sensors detecting a potential buyer's presence in a room trigger a tape of breaking waves. Perfume is sprayed in bathrooms twice a day. An apple pie simmers in the oven. As a result, the house seems more like a home: lived in, cozy, and comfortable.

Carefully viewing a model cannot substitute for paying close attention during the construction of your particular house. You should visit the site as often as possible and have regular meetings about job progress.

Builders are not often anxious to devote labor and materials to repairs and changes on a nearly completed house that's already sold. Since the emphasis is on building other homes in the development, you should try to have any required repairs and alterations made while your job is still underway.

Making Repairs Before Sale

Q. Before selling a home does it really pay to make many repairs and improvements? Since I wouldn't be doing it myself, tending to the minor repairs and painting inside and out will cost several thousand dollars.

A. Obviously, making a house look better also makes it easier to sell. What's not obvious is when you reach the point of diminishing returns: when money spent on repairs no longer spurs a sale or raises the offering price.

There is no financial rule of thumb that can identify this point. But a sensible approach would be to fix the problems that would stand out to you (and become bargaining chips in price talks) if *you* were buying the house.

Play the devil's advocate. Make a list of what's wrong, then start repairs in the areas that make the biggest impact. For instance, it's important that the entry into the house—the first room making the first impression—is clean and uncluttered. Paint the walls in that room before the walls in the basement.

Generally, spend on cosmetic improvements before replacements. That means pay the painter before you pay the carpenter to replace a deteriorated sill in the garage, even though that sill is more important to the long-term durability of the house than a new coat of paint.

Some real estate agents suggest that showing the house really should be a show. For example, in a recent edition of Real Estate Today, an industry trade letter, an Illinois broker suggested that home sellers, ''Turn on all the lights; even on a bright day, lamplight is a dramatic enhancement. Select soft music to play on the stereo. A drop of vanilla on a light bulb will create a wonderful aroma''

═══ Thirty Three ═══

PRODUCT AND CONSUMER GUIDANCE

Home Consumer Checklist
Updating Common Home Consumer Concerns

It is probably a mistake to bestow human qualities on inanimate objects. It's one thing to assume from a certain look that your cat is being ''spiteful'' or that your dog is ''sorry.'' It's quite another to assume that your home appliances are counting the days left in their warranties so they can collectively conk out a day after the protection lapses. That's real consumer paranoia.

Even so, it is satisfying and sensible to beat those little devils to the punch. Checking the status of appliance warranties, insurance, home security, phone costs, and many other consumer concerns may help you prevent problems, and save time and money in the long run. Of course most people already know this. But it can't hurt to hit some of the highlights. One or two just could be flaring out of control.

☑ **Warranties.** Many consumer products, including houses, cars, tools, appliances and other items are covered by warranties—covered when they are new and least likely to need repairs. Rarely will a manufacturer who says that his product will last for 10 years, warranty the product for 10 years.

So as your car and dishwasher approach the end of their warranty periods you should take stock. If there are problems—even minor ones that could lead to worse trouble later on—don't put off the repairs, particularly while they still can be made for no- or low-cost under warranty. Put simply, you should take full advantage of free repairs since you paid for your fair share of them in the original purchase price.

☑ **Service contracts.** If service contracts (typically, maintenance and repair contracts above and beyond warranty protection) are about to lapse, let them lapse, unless you own a bona fide lemon. In almost all cases, the costs of service contracts outstrip, by a staggeringly wide margin, predicted life cycle repair costs of all types of appliances.

☑ **Home insurance.** Many agents routinely adjust their clients' home insurance coverage to reflect predictable increases in home value. Some don't. That can have serious consequences when appreciation, which can be dramatic in only a few years of ownership, is not matched by increased insurance coverage.

There is only one level of home insurance that is adequate, enough to cover rebuilding costs if your home burned down tomorrow. If you are not sure whether or not your home insurance is upgraded automatically, and you have not talked to your agent recently, and particularly if you have made substantial home improvements, call.

If you have bought new camera equipment, computers, stereos, antiques, or other high-cost or hard-to-replace items, make sure that the policy you have now covering fire and theft loss covers these items, too. In some cases, particularly if you use special tools or equipment professionally at home, the items may require special coverage.

☞ **Home security**. Since no home security system is burglarproof, having the backup protection of a detailed record of items that might be stolen is important for two reasons. First, a record of ownership may be the basis of a fair insurance settlement. Second, providing police with a serial number on a camera or a photograph of jewelry, for instance, can make the difference between losing the item forever and getting it back.

Put burglars under the glare of a spotlight with intense, high-pressure sodium lighting normally reserved for parking lots and baseball stadiums. General Electric's Miser Deluxe HPS floodlight throws a 125-degree light beam, roughly twice the area of a standard floodlight. The photoelectric cell turns the fixture on at dusk and off at dawn automatically.

After a not very professional burglar took a tape player from my house one weekend, I realized I had not recorded the make, model, and serial number and started searching for the original sales slip. Very late that same night, the policeman who had answered the burglary call initially called back to say that another officer had stopped someone for a traffic violation and was in the process of questioning him about a tape player in the back seat.

He said that it just might be mine from the description but that without a serial number they couldn't make an arrest. By that time I had found the number, which I relayed to the first officer who relayed it to the second. It turned out to be my tape player, which I got back a few days later, complete with a little white dust left over from the fingerprinting kit.

There are some elaborate security services that include videotaping your home and all its contents. But, at the very least, keep a record of models, makes and serial numbers.

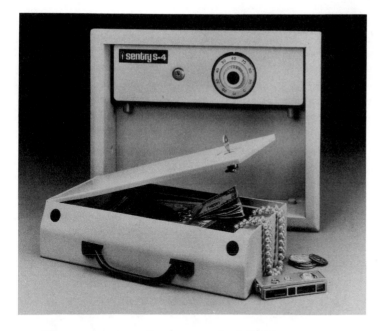

A hidden last line of home security defense is provided by the Sentry S-4 Wall Safe. A combination lock gives access to a removable, key-locked strongbox. The unit fits between 16-inch-on-center wall studs, and sits flush with the wall surface so it can be concealed by a picture or mirror.

There are so many other items to check. But here are two more reminders of areas where you may be able to improve the home consumer status quo. If you make many long-distance calls, look into the competitive rates offered by long-distance firms. The same goes for credit cards, which are available at widely different interest rates. If the one you're carrying around is still charging a rate in the high teens instead of the low teens, switch.

Hints From the Homestead
Traditional, Low-Tech Solutions to Everyday Problems

Practical household hints may not be laboratory-tested and UL listed. But, somehow, the ones that work are passed on from generation to generation. Some are catalogued in strange-sounding publications from the past: tips on splitting wood in an 1873 issue of *The Register of Rural Affairs*; how to ward off mosquitoes in an 1888 publication called *Dr. Chase's Receipt Book*.

Other remedies for household problems are just known, as if by osmosis. For instance, I'm not sure where I heard that one of the best ways to conceal small scratches in hardwood furniture was to rub the blemish with freshly cracked walnuts. But it works.

It is an easy, inexpensive, nontechnical solution—nut oil and walnut meat instead of high-tech chemical concoctions hyped with socko-boffo advertising. Part of the pleasure in using such traditional homestead tips is bypassing expensive products and complicated gadgets that may not even do as good a job as something simple, like a walnut. It's fun to beat the system.

Some tips come from friends, other carpenters, my dusty, 1955, 11-volume set of the *Popular Science Do-It-Yourself Encyclopedia*, and other, even stranger sources. Many can be found in three interesting books.

☐ *Homestead Hints* (Ten Speed Press), is a book that collects many types of household instruction from nineteenth-century publications. The text is somewhat stilted and archaic, which just makes the tips seem even more worthwhile.

A reprint from an 1883 edition of *Practical Housekeeping* advises, ''To clean a papered wall, cut into 8 pieces a large loaf of bread 2 days old, blow dust off wall with a bellows, rub down with a piece of bread in half yard strokes, beginning at the top of the room. If done carefully, so that every spot is touched, the paper will look almost like new.'' No guarantees are made for 3-day old bread.

Other tips from the *Homestead Hints* collection include renewing the stain on dull floors by rubbing with beeswax and turpentine. Another tip for carpenters and do-it-yourselfers is to dip nails in lard or soap before driving them into hardwood. This trick (with an updated material substitute), was passed on to me by a carpenter who carried a small candle in his toolbox. He ran wood screws across the wax before turning them into hardwood furniture and stair treads.

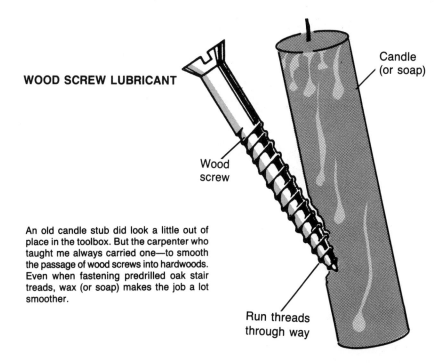

WOOD SCREW LUBRICANT

Candle (or soap)

Wood screw

Run threads through way

An old candle stub did look a little out of place in the toolbox. But the carpenter who taught me always carried one—to smooth the passage of wood screws into hardwoods. Even when fastening predrilled oak stair treads, wax (or soap) makes the job a lot smoother.

☐ *Country Comforts*, by Bruyere and Inwood (Sterling Publishing), was published in 1981. It's one of my favorites, with wonderful how-to action drawings done in the old style with a lot of cross-hatching and shadows that turn detailed construction information into easy-to-understand pictures. The subject matter is appropriate technology (a low-tech, hands-on approach), for rural homestead living.

After pages of illustrations that let you peek inside a fireplace to see exactly how every stone and brick fits together, *Country Comforts* offers several tips on cleaning up. Here's an example:

Clean off exposed mortar joints with a solution of 50 percent muriatic acid and 50 percent water, using a steel brush to take stains off the rock surface. Then wash the surface to remove acid residue. As a finishing touch, soak a sponge in Coca-Cola and wash the rocks with the mixture.

As one of the authors says, "A mason told me this one. I thought the guy was off his rocker, but it really works. It gives the stone a nice clean feeling. I don't know what that says about Coca-Cola in one's stomach though."

☐ *The Do's and Don'ts of Yesterday*, by Eric Sloane (Walker Publishing Company), first published in 1972, is filled with colonial know-how. For instance, a few paragraphs and a simple drawing show how to make a barometer.

Seal a wide-mouthed bottle with a piece of rubber balloon. Then glue one end of a "pointer" (a straw or sliver of wood about twice as long as the bottle opening is wide), at the center of the balloon cover with the other end projecting parallel to the floor past the bottle mouth. Variations in air pressure cause the balloon surface to expand and shrink. So when the "pointer" points up, fair weather is ahead; when it points down rain is on the way—maybe.

By the way, the tip on splitting wood, according to *The Register of Rural Affairs*, is, first hollow out a very large log, then set a smaller log vertically in the hole. This keeps the wood upright through successive blows of an ax; a real time-saver. And the *Dr. Chase's Receipt Book* plan for keeping away mosquitoes during the night is to open a bottle of strong mint oil (called pennyroyal in the original text), and fill the bedroom with its fumes.

Consumer Reports Update
Consumer Reports Has Its 50th Anniversary

In 1936, the first issue of *Consumer Reports* analyzed breakfast cereals, Alka-Seltzer, soap, stockings, milk, toothbrushes, toys, and credit unions. Fifty years later, some of the products, and all of the prices, have changed. But many of the principles adopted by the consumer organization in 1936 are still operative.

Half a century ago, the idea of examining consumer products in depth was innovative. The idea of publishing the results in a magazine without advertising was radical. The general consensus then was that the magazine that has over 3 million subscribers now was doomed to failure.

The idea began with a 1927 best-selling book called *Your Money's Worth*, by Stuart Chase and Frederick Schlink. The muckraking book triggered a barrage of mail, causing Schlink to convert an informal club for consumers where neighbors shared views on products and prices, into a product testing organization named Consumers Research. Two months after the stock market crash in 1929, the organization began publishing a regular bulletin.

Four years later, working with an engineer named Arthur Kallet, Schlink published a second book called *100 Million Guinea Pigs*. Based on the premise that consumers had become "unwitting test animals in a gigantic experiment with poisons conducted by food, drug, and cosmetic manufacturers," this book also became a best seller.

As the organization grew, though, labor problems developed between staff and management. Schlink is described by the organization's own history of events as becoming autocratic, hiring and firing with self-righteous zeal. Employees unionized. More were fired, and a strike ensued. When attempts at settlement failed, Arthur Kallet and 30 other employees left to start a new group, Consumers Union, the organization which now publishes *Consumer Reports*.

The small, idealistic group published the following statement to sum up the magazine's purpose. "To give information and assistance on all matters relating to the expenditure of earnings and the family income; to initiate, to cooperate with and to aid individual and group efforts of whatever nature and description seeking to create and maintain decent living standards for ultimate consumers."

From the first issue, the group adopted standards followed today: to accept no advertising, to prevent use of its findings in advertising, and to buy all tested products at retail. Initially, product testing was not overly technical. For example, to report on stockings staff members wore one pair a day, then passed them on to another "tester." Problems such as "slugs, bad casts, and rings" were quantified, and the "Best Buy" turned out to be S. H. Kress' Siren brand for 50 cents a pair.

The magazine turned to an intern at Mt. Sinai Hospital in New York for a report on Alka-Seltzer. Dr. Harold Aaron, who continued to write for the magazine for 30 years, found, "Its chief appeal is the noisy fizz it produces. When its claims are properly analyzed they vanish like gas bubbles in the air."

Cars were tested by a young college graduate with an educational background in poetry and literature named Laurence Crooks. He laid out a test track behind his garage. In his first report, Crooks wrote that cars were, "deliberately cheapened to promote their obsolescence."

By 1938, subscriptions reached 85,000, despite some strong attacks by prominent organizations. For example, more than 60 newspapers refused to sell advertising space to the magazine. *CR* reports that the refusals were based on pressure from other advertisers, whose products were examined and questioned by *Consumer Reports*. After *CR* called into question the Good Housekeeping Seal of Approval (were magazine advertisers approved more easily than others?), *Good Housekeeping* accused Consumers Union of prolonging the Depression. U.S. Postal inspectors banned a special *CR* publication on contraceptives. The magazine was even banned in some schools.

The idea that consumers should get a close, impartial look at the products they bought ruffled a lot of feathers about 50 years ago. But subscriptions continued to grow until World War II. At that time there was little to analyze since durable consumer goods were scarce. So *Consumer Reports* concentrated on products such as women's factory work clothes, and devoted more space to prolonging product life through maintenance and repair. Articles reflected concerns in the wartime home, and included such titles as "Coffee: How to Get More Cups per Pound."

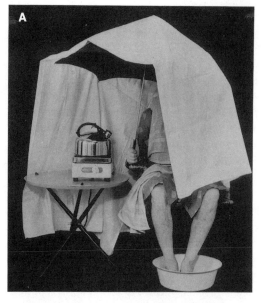

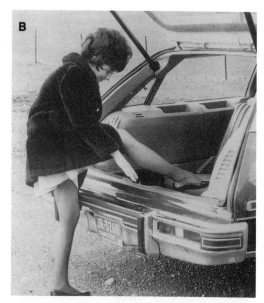

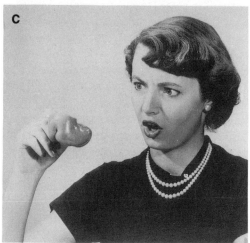

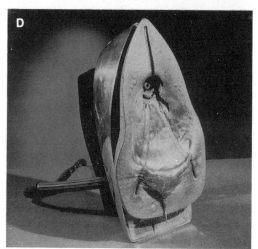

In decades of testing new products, Consumer Reports found that (A) a 1952-vintage vaporizer worked no better than a homemade steam tent; (B) that a 1974 Buick wagon had a rear-facing seat that was tough to reach; (C) that plastic dishes tested in 1951 melted into a blob when filled with boiling water; and (D) that a 1951 automatic steam iron got just a little too hot.

Postwar demand for housing and the related stream of consumer goods, caused the magazine's subscriptions to rise sharply to 100,000 in 1946. In 1956 the rate was 800,000; in 1974 it was 2 million.

Today, *CR*'s operations are more sophisticated and more technical. In fact, some accuse the magazine of ignoring obvious and prominent consumer concerns, such as the styling of a car, and reducing virtually every product to its most mechanical pieces.

Yet *CR* conducts taste tests on ice cream and other foods that are inevitably subjective, despite the fact that testers try brands according to a methodical pattern and are placed in isolation booths so they cannot see or hear reactions of other testers.

Engineers at *CR* have also come up with some Rube Goldberg contraptions to help in product testing. For instance, staffers designed and built a wooden "flute" through which wind and water blow against different brands of tissues covering the holes, a rotating drum to toss luggage, and a derriere-shaped mechanical ram to test mattresses.

Before mass production and efficient transportation systems made it possible for companies to sell products nationally, consumers and producers were closely intermingled. Food, clothing, and furniture were made and sold locally. Consumption was direct. Consumer response was immediate. There was little need to sum up a product or put a particularly favorable cast on it with advertising. Consumers knew the producers personally.

But few products are sold or consumed that way today. Consumers who have a complaint often must wade through a salesperson, a store manager, and others in the lengthy chain of production before reaching the initial producer. The current marketplace is convoluted. Products are complex. While some firms connect with consumers over toll-free information and service telephone lines, many producers seem remote.

The success of *Consumer Reports* seems based in large part on its ability to short-circuit the often circuitous route from producer to consumer. Unbiased product analysis, cut-and-dried or not, helps buyers see what sellers have to offer, unfettered by advertising claims and sales hype.

Trade Names
What Happens When Product Names Become Household Words?

Would you ask the druggist for medicated lip balm and a package of adhesive-backed bandages, or would you say, "Chapstick" and "Band-aids"? Would you ask the home center to deliver plastic laminate panels and paper-covered gypsum drywall board, or would you say, "Formica" and "Sheetrock"?

Those well-known brands are in a select group. Of over 600,000 names, phrases, and images registered by the U.S. Patent and Trademark Office, only a few dozen have become synonymous with, or even replaced, a generic product description.

You might think that kind of recognition would be welcomed by companies. After all, every time someone asks for Kleenex instead of facial tissue, it's free advertising.

But trademark and brand name recognition is a two-edged sword. When consumers start to use a brand name such as Scotch tape to describe adhesive-backed tape made by several firms, it helps fledgling companies to increase sales and gain a share of the market. You say "Scotch," but you probably don't care who makes it. That's good for Scotch brand's competitors, but it's bad for 3M, the manufacturer.

Also, widespread, continued, unchallenged use of a trademark can lead to litigation that makes the name, phrase, or image part of the public domain. Then, anyone can use it.

That's what happened to E. I. DuPont de Nemours & Company in 1936 when the firm lost ownership of the word "cellophane." DuPont's trade name became a

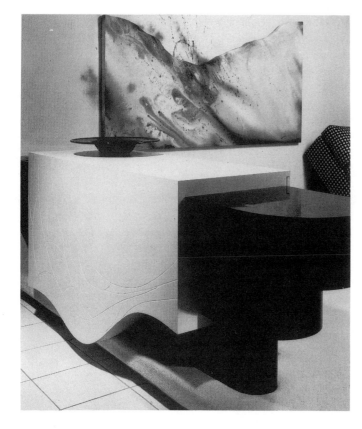

Like most consumers, you probably ask for "Formica," even when the lumberyard stocks plastic laminates from another major manufacturer, Wilsonart. Their new Solicor panels feature laminate sheets with color throughout the material, allowing built-up, layered applications, while reducing the visibility of nicks and scratches.

generic term for cellulose plastic wrapping that could be printed on any company's package.

In the landmark cellophane case, court rulings established a precedent. To protect a trademark, firms must actively challenge misuse of the name. Companies need not always prevent the misuse. But if they can produce evidence that they have tried to curtail it, they keep the exclusive legal right to use the trademark.

Fifty years after DuPont lost the rights to "cellophane," the company faced a challenge to another of its trademarks; Teflon. As the *Washington Journalism Review* reported in a recent issue, this trademark infringement started not with a competing firm but with Representative Patricia Schroeder (Democrat-Colorado).

She is credited with labeling Ronald Reagan the "Teflon President." The phrase imaginatively transposed the nonstick quality of Dupont's cooking surface to a perception that the President's public image often remained untainted by potentially damaging events. The phrase was widely used since coined in 1983.

Even though this trademark infringement was unusual, and did not represent competition from another company or a threat to cookware sales, DuPont's attorneys had to respond. They sent letters to newspaper and magazine editors and even bought advertisements to establish a public record of their trademark defense. Yes, sometimes legal technicalities are a little bizarre.

Even occasional infringements for little-known products may trigger a warning letter from a manufacturer. The public, and even those in retail sales and the media who know the trade name from the generic name, are not always cooperative.

One reason is that brand names are convenient communication shortcuts. Both do-it-yourselfers and home center dealers, for instance, are likely to say "Formica" even if they are handling Wilsonart laminates, made by Ralph Wilson Plastics Company, "Durabeauty" panels, made by Sterling Engineered Products, or some other brand of decorative plastic laminate.

Generic product descriptions can be lengthy and confusing. For instance, the long-winded, generic description of a hypothetical home improvement project could read as follows:

You repair the photo-duplicating machine copy of the contract with transparent adhesive-backed tape; order plastic laminate and a new garbage disposal appliance for the kitchen; tighten a threaded, hand-turned bolt fastener on a rigid clear plastic shelf with an adjustable, spring-loaded pliers; and take a break with a cola-flavored carbonated soda from the cellular extruded polystyrene cooler.

The trademark version of the same scenario is a lot more economical and understandable. You repair the Xerox copy of the contract with Scotch tape; order Formica and a new Disposall for the kitchen; tighten a loose Wing Nut on a Plexiglas shelf with your Vise-Grip; and have a Coke from the Styrofoam cooler.

According to Calvin MacCracken, author of *A Handbook for Inventors* and holder of over 300 patents and trademarks, some companies contribute to this problem by choosing nouns for brand names instead of adjectives. He cites noun brand names such as "aspirin" and "escalator" as bad choices. (Both of those trademarks have become generic product terms that anyone has a legal right to use.)

MacCracken says choosing adjective trade names makes it more difficult for consumers to use the terms generically. He also says brand names should not be too descriptive of the product. MacCracken cites "Kodak" as a good example. It is unique and highly recognizable, but modifies, rather than replaces, the generic words "camera" and "film."

But public response to a trade name can be so overwhelming that even a good choice, such as "Thermos" (originally used as an adjective describing "bottle"), becomes a generic term.

Trademark misuse is not a problem with "no-name" brands, which now have a small niche in many supermarkets. They carry such memorable product names as "Tomato Soup" for tomato soup, and "Chopped Walnuts" for chopped walnuts.

But misuse is a problem for many types of building and decorating products with famous trade names, including Fiberglas (the generic version ends with two esses), Jacuzzi (one brand of bubbling baths and spas made by Roy Jacuzzi), Naugahyde (the imitation leather), Plexiglas, Lucite, and more. You also will be making life difficult for trademark watchers by putting Tabasco on your Jell-O, and playing Ping-Pong without taking off your Stetson.

Perhaps in the dreams of trademark and patent attorneys, children stop the ice cream truck to order a flavored frozen ice bar on a stick. But in real life, kids still ask for Popsicles.

Mail-Order Shopping
The Best Selection Is at the End of Your Phone

Ordering products through the mail instead of buying in person does require a leap of faith since catalog pictures and brief descriptions must substitute for the real thing. But consumers' faith can be rewarded with several benefits, including convenient and nearly instant access to a vast selection of goods—more than any store or shopping mall could possibly stock—offered by firms that publish approximately 6,500 different mail-order catalogs every year.

Mail order, the process of selecting goods from a catalog and mailing in your order, has grown to a $50 billion a year business due in large part to the success of its most convenient application, which might better be called tele-mail ordering—ordering by phone and receiving goods by mail.

The growth has been spurred by the use of credit cards, which account for almost 80 percent of mail-order catalog sales, and 800 telephone numbers, introduced in 1969. Together, they make ordering by phone very easy.

Anyone with a credit card can buy food, furniture, fur coats, and so on, specify color and size, arrange shipping, payment, and delivery at their convenience—all in a minute or two. It is a most painless way to part with your money.

Many retailers, from large chain stores to smaller specialty shops, provide toll-free telephone lines to take customer orders 24 hours a day. When the urge to buy strikes, they're ready. But mail order does have some disadvantages. L. L. Bean, the outdoor outfitter, is a noteworthy example because shopping there in person is a memorable experience that cannot be duplicated over the phone.

Even Bean's most efficient and solicitous phone operators cannot replace the personal attention of a knowledgeable salesperson who is a bit of a character—bright, bushy-tailed, and ready to help at 3 in the morning—when almost all the vacationing shoppers have gone to bed and you have the store and the salesperson's attention to yourself. Bean's (and its mail-order phone operation) is open 24 hours a day, every day. On the other hand, shopping by phone gives you access to all sorts of specialty stores all across the country.

Mail order also is economical. Even the expense of mail-order shipping will pale next to the transportation costs of local shopping. And, of course, while many consumers do not own a car or live near a bus line or a subway convenient to local stores, almost everyone has a phone. This makes tele-mail-order shopping invaluable to millions of consumers who are, for a variety of reasons, housebound.

Tele-mail-order shopping evolved from a service provided by traveling salesmen to many American consumers well before Bell invented the telephone. These early entrepreneurs brought a wagon's worth of goods to rural, isolated consumers, even into the 20th century. They carried new household appliances, tools, and other goods like a portable general store.

This practice evolved into mail order—carrying a catalog of goods to consumers instead of the goods themselves. It was first synthesized on a large scale by Aaron

Montgomery Ward in 1872. The Direct Marketing Association, a New York-based mail-order trade group, reports that Ward's catalog had grown to 240 pages and thousands of items sold direct to consumers by 1884.

Most home furnishings now are available through the mail. Some, like this elegant Shaker dining chair, is sold finished, and in kit form (for about half the money), by Shaker Workshops of Concord, MA. This reproduction uses authentic Shaker chair tapes woven over seat and back.

Ward's success prompted another businessman with a now recognizable surname, Richard W. Sears, to start selling watches by mail in 1886. Seven years later Sears, Roebuck & Co. was formed. And by 1897 the Sears catalog had grown to nearly 700 pages containing over 6,000 items. These mail-order pioneers were followed by many others, such as Spiegel in 1905. A year later, Sears distributed 500,000 spring catalogs and became one of the country's largest retailers, with annual sales exceeding $50 million.

Fortunately, even the ultimate mail-order item—a house—can be checked out in catalogs and bought over the phone. Unfortunately, they are no longer available at the nice price ($5,140, including all precut materials), when Sears sold this house by mail in 1918.

Almost every type of product, including complete houses, have been sold by mail. Easy access to a vast selection of products has made mail order increasingly popular with consumers, so much so that the Direct Marketing Association estimates that by 1990 one of every four retail sales will be what the association calls a direct sale, made through the mail or over the telephone.

Here are some mail-order shopping tips.

From the Federal Trade Commission. Allow adequate shipping time. Check the company's return policy prior to ordering. Read product descriptions carefully and do not rely only on pictures. Check the firm's reputation with the local Better Business Bureau or consumer protection agency. Keep a record of the transaction, including a canceled check, charge account record, and details of the original order form.

From the Direct Marketing Association. If you must return merchandise for any reason send it back "return receipt requested," a postal form that eventually provides you with a record that the firm received the goods you returned. If you cancel a mail-order purchase charged on a credit card, the seller must credit your account within one billing cycle after the cancellation.

Mail-order catalog sources. The Direct Marketing Association offers, for $2, the "Great Catalog Guide," which lists hundreds of mail-order firms selling hardware, tools, housewares, home furnishings, craft supplies, computers, books, sporting goods, toys, and other types of products. Order from the Direct Marketing Association.[1]

A unique book, called *Shop By Mail Worldwide*, by Anne Flato and Marilyn Schiff (Vintage Books), lists hundreds of catalogs from specialty shops, department stores, and other sources from over 25 countries, including home furnishings, cookware, cameras, furniture, rugs, and other items.

---

[1] Consumer Services, Direct Marketing Assoc., 6 East 43 Street, New York, NY 10017

Index